COUNTDOWN
to a New Library

Managing the Building Project

JEANNETTE WOODWARD

COUNTDOWN
to a New Library
Managing the Building Project

Jeannette Woodward

AMERICAN LIBRARY ASSOCIATION
Chicago and London
2000

While extensive effort has gone into ensuring the reliability of information appearing in this book, the publisher makes no warranty, express or implied, as to the accuracy or reliability of the information, and does not assume and hereby disclaims any liability to any person for any loss or damage caused by errors or omissions in this publication.

Project editor: Joan A. Grygel

Cover : Tessing Design

Text design: Dianne M. Rooney

Composition in Minion and Helvetica using QuarkXpress 4.04 on a Macintosh platform by the dotted i

Printed on 50-pound white offset, a pH-neutral stock, and bound in 10-point coated cover stock by McNaughton & Gunn

The paper used in this publication meets the minimum requirements of American National Standard for Information Sciences—Permanence of Paper for Printed Library Materials, ANSI Z39.48-1992. ∞

Library of Congress Cataloging-in-Publication Data

Woodward, Jeannette A.
    Countdown to a new library : managing the building project / Jeannette Woodward.
       p.   cm.
    Includes bibliographical references and index.
    ISBN 0-8389-0767-9
    1. Library buildings—United States—Design and construction.   I. Title.
  Z679.2.U54 W66   2000
  022'.3—dc21   99-086661

Printed in the United States of America.

04 03 02 01 00   5 4 3 2 1

———————◆————————————————————◆

To my children
    Laura and Chris
and to
    Betty Budell,
        the best role model
        any new librarian
        could possibly have

Contents

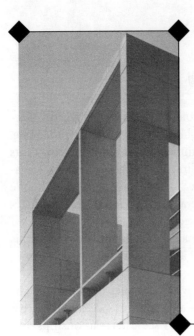

Introduction

All librarians, deep down, loathe their buildings. Something is always wrong—the counter is too high, the shelves too narrow, the delivery entrance too far from the offices. In short, libraries are constructed by architects, not librarians. Do not trust an architect: he will always try to talk you into an atrium.

—Elizabeth McCracken
The Giant's House

I don't know whether I'd go so far as to say we loathe our buildings. In fact, on cold winter days, I really enjoy my own library atrium, but buildings certainly generate far more than their share of angst among librarians and archivists. Again and again, brand new buildings costing the moon turn out to be terminally flawed. Before continuing, perhaps it's only fair that I bring my own prejudices out into the open and hazard some guesses as to how those flaws occurred.

For the most part, the fault does not lie with librarians. As researchers, we seek out information before launching into a building or remodeling project, and a substantial body of well-written, informative literature is available to help us. Most of this literature is concerned with those functions that are clearly the responsibility of librarians. For example, sources provide excellent guidance for determining how many seats are needed or how much space should be allocated to book stacks. To a greater or lesser extent, the literature assumes that building professionals involved in the project (such as architects, contractors, engineers, and designers) will translate the library's needs, as communicated to them by librarians, into a successful, functional building. Such is not always the case.

THE LIBRARIAN'S BIRD'S-EYE VIEW

The basic assumption that underlies this book is that the traditional division of responsibility between building professionals and librarians is no longer adequate. The modern library building has become so complex that it tends to grow of its own accord, figuratively reaching out in every direction without clear or consistent guidance from any single individual. If the library building is to serve the needs for which it was designed, there must be a key individual who monitors progress at every stage to be certain that the project has not taken an unexpected turn. Although one (or more) building professional is officially entrusted with this responsibility, most of your fellow librarians and archivists will testify that something always seems to go wrong.

We librarians are, of course, rank amateurs when it comes to building technologies, but we *do* know about libraries. With a little effort, we can acquire a bird's-eye view of the entire project, allowing us to see interrelationships and areas of potential misunderstanding. As you will discover from the comments of librarians included in the Tips and Tales sections, some vital piece of information may not be communicated. For example, the floor in the stack area is not built to withstand the weight of book stacks; the integrity of the vault is violated by punctures and cutouts; the complex security system allows thieves to leave the building unobserved; or the roof leaks on the library's most valuable collection. Such problems may require a degree in engineering to solve, but if someone had established effective channels of communication in the very beginning, such problems might never have occurred at all.

Naturally, it is impossible for the information professional to acquire the expertise of an architect or engineer, a plumber, or an electrician. It is possible, however, to understand how the components of a construction project knit together to create a completed building. No one knows better than members of our profession that the absence of information is at the root of many problems. Therefore, this book will outline the kinds of information needed to embark upon a building project. Reading *Countdown to a New Library* will not magically transform you into a building professional, but it will serve as an overview of the entire process, not merely of the librarian's traditional role. Just as a classification schedule helps you see where a particular volume fits into the bibliographic universe, this book is intended to help you see how components fit into the building project, where people are not making contact with each other, and where gaps in communication can be most damaging.

TIPS AND TALES FROM THE TRENCHES

Throughout the book you'll find Tips and Tales sections, that is, advice and stories from many of your fellow librarians and archivists who are veterans of a variety of building projects. In the past, an author could hope for input from only a relatively small number of colleagues; today's electronic discussion lists have made it possible to get input from many more. These tips or tales are a vital part of this book. Veterans of library building projects were extremely frank in their comments; therefore, I have tried to protect their privacy by changing small details in their stories if that seemed wise. However, I have not changed the tone of the comments. You'll discover that some librarians remain battle-scarred from their experiences, and it would be less than truthful to pretend that all stories have happy endings.

As I received each tale of triumph, woe, or something in between, I mentally applauded. Building a library is one of the most difficult construction projects. Its extraordinary demands that range from ultrasophisticated network access to environmental controls for archival materials would challenge any builder or architect. Yet the information professionals, whose expertise lies in entirely different directions, put on their hard hats and taught themselves the basics of architecture, electrical engineering, disaster preparedness, and a dozen arcane specialties. Please think of them as members of your project team, and take their advice to heart.

Throughout the book, you will encounter seeming conflicts of opinion. One of the librarians in the Tips section may make a recommendation that another librarian contradicts. This is because today's library is expected to fill so many roles, some of them at odds with one another. Today's library is the community meeting place, the computer center, the book repository, the video store, the copy center, and/or even the theater and children's day camp.

In addition, libraries have a historic tradition much cherished by librarians, older faculty members, and many community users. For example, my own mental image of the perfect library is the old Free Public Library of Madison, New Jersey, where I held my very first professional position. Though small, it was one of the oldest and most beautiful buildings in the area. Visitors first thought it was a miniature cathedral until they discovered that the subject matter of the Tiffany windows was the love of books and learning. Those gorgeous windows shed a soft many-hued light that is impossible to describe. One really couldn't read by their mysterious glow and the lovely chandeliers cast an equally misty light that was effective mainly in catching the gleam of the hand-stenciled, gold-leaf fleurs de lis covering the walls. It was, therefore, necessary to illuminate the long trestle tables with hand-tooled brass lamps. The memory of the treacherous metal stairs winding through glass-floored stacks has faded, but the glow of the Tiffany windows remains. There will always be a part of me that believes this is what a real library looks like.

The cost of renovating such libraries is often prohibitive. Few communities can afford to restore their historic jewel boxes while providing for the vastly expanded needs of a modern library. Invariably, something has to go. Adequate funding to support the library depends on the support of a large segment of the tax-paying public or university community. Historic libraries may be too small and too limited in the services they can provide to attract this support, and no one understands this better than a librarian. In general, we library building planners usually come down on the side of common sense, but that does not mean that we have souls of Formica and polyurethane.

BEYOND THIS BOOK

A book of this length cannot cover everything you will need to know before embarking upon a building project. Neither can it anticipate the needs of every type of library, the disaster potential of every working relationship, or the unique constraints of every situation. Therefore, you may want to refer to the lists of professional associations and organizations and supplemental reading at the end of the chapters for helpful sources of additional information.

In general, *Countdown to a New Library* is more of a "hard hat" book than some others, occasionally emphasizing building technologies over library functions. This emphasis was chosen because of the numerous difficulties librarians in every type of library are currently experiencing with their new, high-tech buildings. Of course, in a book of this length, it is not possible to cover every aspect of construction from foundation to rooftop, so the emphasis is on those areas in which a library may differ from other building projects. For example, plumbing is given short shrift because it is not unique to a library setting, and telecommunications is emphasized because it is so integral to modern libraries. Roofs have been allotted a generous section because library horror stories about leaky ones destroying valuable collections are legion. Furthermore, depending on the library, climate control can be much more than simply a matter of heating and cooling, and security means more than a burglar alarm and a good book detection system.

Libraries are changing rapidly, and designing spaces to meet the needs of tomorrow's library users can be quite a challenge. For excellent, right-on-target advice on specific library functions, I strongly recommend that you obtain a copy of *Checklist of Library Building Design Considerations.*[1] You may find that by the end of your project, you've memorized substantial sections of it.

In fact, you will discover that educating yourself for the work ahead is really a full-time job and will mean consuming a library of literature before your building is complete. I often wonder how those poor underprivileged souls in other professions, who don't have the resources of a library at their fingertips, can possibly survive a building ordeal.

WHO NEEDS THIS BOOK?

Although this book will be useful for many types of projects, it will be of greatest assistance to those of you who are designing a building from scratch or who are adding a wing or two to an existing structure. Renovation projects that involve no new construction are also covered. In addition, the book will be helpful for archivists and rare-book librarians who manage collections housed within library buildings. However, although some special consideration has been given to archival collections, this book will be inadequate to meet the needs of those who are designing buildings intended specifically to house special collections.

WHEN YOU GET THE GREEN LIGHT

No two institutions share precisely the same set of priorities, personalities, and extenuating circumstances. The length of time from the first glimmerings of interest in a new library until its dedication varies from a year or two to as long as twenty years. A new building or addition is sometimes planned amid furious activity, and then the plans are put aside after a negative vote by the legislature or city council. Years later, when the political climate is more favorable, the project may be resuscitated or shelved a second time. Just to have a starting point, we'll suppose that the first semiserious discussion of the new building, addition, or major renovation occurs about five years before the dedication ceremony. Your central administration, governing body, architects, and contractors will all have their own ideas about the order in which decisions and commitments are made, so the sequence is also somewhat arbitrary. Although this book is structured around the sequence of a library-building project, in the real world, you may want to jump ahead, say, to chapter 5 and come back later to chapter 3. However, every step is essential to the planning and construction of a new building, and most are necessary for an addition or renovation.

Countdown begins by discussing ways you can prepare yourself and your library staff to function effectively in the midst of a building project. In chapter 2 you will become familiar with the dramatis personae of a project: the architects, contractors, and engineers who will soon be your constant companions. The chapter also explains various project delivery systems and delves into contract and liability considerations.

Discussions of recent library developments and future prospects introduce chapter 3. The chapter also covers the important tasks of identifying a site and determining space needs. In addition, it examines the unique planning considerations of a renovation or remodeling project.

Chapter 4 gets into the "nuts and bolts" of a major construction project by focusing on the building shell: roof, atrium, and entrance. Requirements of stand-alone libraries as well as those for multiuse facilities are presented.

Environmental and human needs are the subject of chapter 5. Topics include the ways humans interact with their buildings and the conditions under which they are most comfortable and most productive. In this chapter you will find information about design considerations for lighting—both natural and artificial—energy efficiency for new and older buildings, and compliance with the Americans with Disabilities Act.

Chapter 6 is devoted to planning for information technology, possibly the most crucial and problem-riddled task involved in designing a twenty-first-century library. The chapter also discusses building infrastructures, including electrical service and the equally high-tech system of climate control.

In chapter 7 we consider all those ominous "what if's" that could threaten the building as well as library users and staff. Such threats could come from a variety of sources such as vandals, fires, floods and other natural disasters, and toxic fumes.

Next, chapter 8 looks at considerations involved in selecting the floor materials, wall coverings, and furnishings. Cleaning and maintenance, custom furniture, ergonomics, computer workstations, and shelving issues are all considered here.

The chief task that remains is perhaps the hardest: that all-important job of surviving and even prospering while everything around you is in chaos. Chapter 9 addresses these concerns and some issues that are unique to library services during a building renovation. In this "betwixt and between" period, you will be planning your signage system, using your old library as a laboratory to determine what information users need and where, and scheduling walk-throughs of the new building.

Finally, in chapter 10, you're ready to bring order to the logistical nightmare of moving the collection. Is that all? No, 'fraid not. You will be spending most of your first year on a crisis-a-day shakedown cruise.

NOTE

1. William Sannwald, ed., *Checklist of Library Building Design Considerations* (Chicago: American Library Assn., 1996).

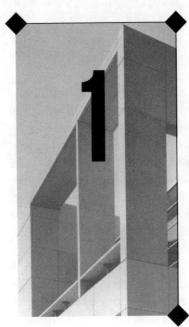

Getting Off to a Good Start

Many librarians, describing their first experience with "begetting" a new building, complain bitterly about their naiveté at the start of the project. If only they had known. . . . If only they had been prepared. . . . This book will provide some of that advance preparation. In a sense, however, you will always be playing the role of Columbus or Balboa, exploring uncharted seas. There is no way to anticipate all the crises that may await you. Nevertheless, you can have a game plan that will prepare you for most eventualities. If you have a good, clear idea of your goals and how other librarians have achieved similar goals, you're infinitely better off than if you approach the project unprepared.

PREPARING YOURSELF FOR WHAT'S AHEAD

At last, it's finally happened! You've received a tentative go-ahead to begin planning a new library or addition. You've been given permission to dream and to work harder than perhaps you've ever worked before. The wheels will soon be set in motion, but suddenly you're getting cold feet. Where do you begin? What do you do first? What do you, a librarian, know about bricks and concrete and load-bearing walls?

It may sound a bit simplistic, but you begin with yourself. Assuming that you're the library director or a member of the team that will be shepherding the project to completion, you've got an awesome job ahead. It will require all your intelligence, patience, humor, flexibility, interpersonal skills, strength of character, and intestinal fortitude to emerge triumphant from the experience with a functional building and most of your nerves intact.

TALE

Building a library is exciting, enervating, nerve-racking, and the best and the worst of everything.

You're the Expert

You will be spending the next few years with dozens of specialists in the building trades and related professions. At times you will feel overwhelmed, even "cowed," by their technical knowledge, and you will cringe at your own inexperience. No matter what their specialty or however varied their skills and experience, you will find one subject on which most building professionals are universally ignorant: They will be as newborn babes when it comes to the nature and function of a library. Here, you alone are the expert. Perhaps you never thought of yourself that way, but now is the time to start. Without your expert guidance, the building that emerges from the rubble might be suitable for a factory, an office building, or a department store, but it won't work as a library.

Over the years, you've acquired an extraordinary amount of information about libraries from your library school classes and your work experiences. For example, you know roughly the number of staff members who will be working in the new building and the areas to which they will be assigned. One librarian in the Midwest could not convince her architect that a building of 100,000 square feet would be staffed by just a dozen people. Additional offices and service desks kept appearing mysteriously on floor plans because the architect was convinced the librarian must be mistaken about staff size. Libraries are indeed very different from other large buildings, and only you know precisely how they differ.

Libraries are unique in the building trades. Only infrequently does a contractor or architect arrive on the scene equipped with an intimate understanding of book stacks, OPACs, or library traffic patterns. Look around. How many libraries do you see? Over the course of their careers, architects may design hundreds of apartment buildings, office complexes, and strip malls, but only a few architects ever plan a library. You're the one who must take responsibility for this part of their education. Don't allow an architect or contractor to make unilateral decisions that will determine how the library functions.

Your Sphere of Authority

You must strenuously oppose design features that interfere with the library's effectiveness. This means clearly delineating the architect's and contractor's sphere of authority and yours: the details best left to the judgment of a building professional, those that you should at least be consulted on, and those that you *must* approve. The items in the latter two categories are far more numerous than most building professionals believe, and you may have some heavy weather ahead until everyone settles down to a comfortable working relationship. (See chapter 2.) Just remember that library considerations affect diverse considerations such as hardware on the panic doors, wiring details, lighting requirements, and the desirability of design elements like balconies and atria.

TIPS AND TALES

I would emphasize knowing what you want, being able to articulate it, paying attention to all the details, and not assuming someone else (like the professionals) will take care of something,

I found that my suggestions were often pooh-poohed. I wish I had stood my ground more often, though it might not have done any good—my position wasn't viewed as particularly authoritative or important.

Stick to your guns when you're told things like "you really don't need all those outlets." The few times that I had a chance to talk to anybody, I was treated like an eejit (as my Irish friends would say).

I recommend Prozac, lots of it.

Get into a frame of mind that lets you enjoy the project, and most importantly—have a generous budget for chocolate.

DONNING YOUR LIBRARY HARD HAT

It won't be long before you discover that you have two full-time jobs. Unless you're starting a new library from scratch, you still have the job of taking care of the day-to-day needs of an existing library. In addition, you have the second and equally time-consuming full-time job of planning a new library building or addition. As the song puts it, "Something's gotta give!"

If your library is large enough to enjoy the luxury of an assistant director, consider delegating one job or the other. It is usually best for the director to use whatever clout he or she has for dealing with trustees, deans, and other decision makers. This means that it is more usual for the assistant director to take on responsibility for the existing library while the director plans the new one. It may be, however, that the skills and interests of the people involved make it preferable to assign the planning role to the assistant. Even if yours is a small library with a limited staff, delegate as many responsibilities as possible.

If you've always been the kind of supervisor who micromanages, break yourself of the habit now before you drive yourself bonkers. Nothing is more important now than prioritizing your time. It's all a matter of deciding what comes first, what will eventually glare, and what can safely be swept under the carpet. Lots of good and worthy projects can be swept under the carpet, and no one will be the wiser. When you delegate routine matters, don't insist on approving every little decision. You will send the message that you distrust the person to whom you delegated the responsibility, and you will still be doing two jobs.

IDENTIFYING AND COMMUNICATING WITH KEY PLAYERS

You, of course, are not the only participant in the project. If you are working in a public library environment, your library board and numerous municipal or county administrators will be active participants in the building process, as will philanthropical individuals and foundations making financial contributions. In a university environment, the stakeholders include the board of trustees, benefactors, university president or provost, and an assortment of administrative staff members. Identifying these participants and determining how they will share in the decision-making process should be on your "to do" list as early as possible.

Occasionally, a city council member, university president, or board chairperson views the new building as his or her own monument. Since these people have only a limited understanding of how the library functions, they are especially vulnerable to the extravagant enthusiasms of architects. Before your boss

TALES

Reality is different from theory. The architects made the plans. The treasurer approved them. The library director had limited input.

I was involved in a library building project several years ago in a New England state. I was hired about a month before bids were opened for a long-awaited addition to a 1905 building. The director whose vision this was had such a hard time with the trustees that she quit six months later. The trustees (who knew everything) micromanaged the building project, drove the architect crazy, asked the staff for input on colors and then ignored it (making them furious), and refused to hire an engineer or clerk of the works who could look out for the library's best interest.

or your board ever gets near an architect, they need a crash course in libraries too. Don't assume that because they've approved or disapproved your annual budget requests and listened to your tales of woe they know what happens in a library. Their impressions of day-to-day library activities may be as vague as those of your users. In fact, they probably view the library from the standpoint of users. That is, public services are all they see, and the only important materials are the ones they need.

Who decides what? When can you resolve an issue without additional input, and when must you seek approval from someone at a higher level? Work together to agree upon procedures for communicating information, obtaining input, and making decisions. Reduce the number of people who must be regularly consulted to a manageable number. If you are in a public library, ask that your board appoint a subcommittee of no more than four or five people who will work directly with you. Encourage the board to choose people with the time, knowledge, and experience to contribute significantly to the process. What you don't need is deadwood, people whose egos demand that they be consulted but who have little or nothing to offer.

TIP

Come to agreements with trustees and whomever else (city, county, state officials) has the final say on what decisions.

Once the major players have been identified, spend time together. You can safely assume that they know little about libraries, but if they've been well-chosen, they can bring a variety of other expertise to the planning process. Get to know each member's special strengths. Be sure you understand how much personal involvement your boss or your boss's boss is anticipating.

TIPS AND TALES

After we did considerable work in developing the program statement for the expansion, all justification and explication of the project to state university central administrative offices and state building commission was done by nonlibrary personnel from our campus.

As construction reached its final phases, the director learned that the campus chancellor planned to come view the nearly completed and remodeled facility. As the director was waiting for word of this expected visit, suddenly one day the chancellor strolled by the director's office on this tour in the company of his special assistant, the assistant chancellor for administrative services, and the building project manager, none of whom stopped in to say hello to the director, much less include him on the tour.

During the construction, the library director was advised that he need not attend the weekly construction progress meetings, unless invited. This led to many small surprises.

If you aren't included in planning meetings, be bold and ask to be included and say why.

Counter the "Libraries Are Facing Extinction" Argument

As your construction project ascends from one approval body to the next, you will inevitably encounter a board member or bureaucrat who is convinced that there is no point in spending money to build or renovate a library since it will be obsolete in five to ten years. Naturally, academic and public officials prefer to save money wherever they can. The media's current fascination with the electronic library provides an excellent excuse.

You will be tempted to become angry and defensive after you've heard the same argument for the twenty-third time. Anticipate your reaction and have a canned speech and written handout ready whenever the subject might come up. Of course, it's true that librarians are worried about the future. No, we don't know exactly what the future holds in store, but we do know that the simplistic argument about the death of the book and universal delivery of electronic information is a smoke screen. Libraries are complex social institutions that provide a wide variety of services. You need not feel guilty or defensive; you are simply dealing with people who have a very limited picture of a library.

On some relatively calm and restful day when a new library is little more than a gleam in the library staff's collective eye, write a brief statement that speaks to the library doom and gloom argument. Limit your literary effort to a page or two, and address the issue as simply and clearly as possible. Such esoteric points as the global information economy will not go down as well as local arguments illustrating how important the library is to your community. Make it clear that the book will not disappear anytime soon and that the library will be delivering both print and electronic information for the foreseeable future. Dial-up access to the virtual library is all well and good, but the library is far more than a Web page. Steer clear of arguments about whether books or electronic equipment are more important. Make it clear that hard-copy collections are still growing and enjoying heavy usage. Collect statistics on library use including civic groups using meeting spaces, educational programs, services for the unemployed, and other functions that bureaucrats tend to forget when they see the library going the way of the dinosaur.

Learn to Cope with the "Hurry Up and Wait" Syndrome

Most librarians report that their building projects progressed not steadily but in a series of lurches. Long delays were followed by sudden bursts of activity when everything became due yesterday. Projects that simmered on the back burner awaiting approval from a dozen different officials, government agencies, or advisory boards suddenly were given the full-steam-ahead, and everyone was caught unprepared. Frequently, librarians found out about deadlines by accident or were forced to work round the clock to have their input ready for spur-of-the-moment meetings.

From the very first moment when your building project acquires some sort of tentative official status, start spending time on your own preparations. Many of the tasks described in the rest of this chapter can be done long before they are needed. Having a recommendation or request ready at the strategic moment can make all the difference between success and failure. It is also important to spend these quiet intervals bringing your building expertise up to speed. Use the time to take courses, read books and articles, and take frequent busman's holidays.

Create an Information Blitz

Many crises are avoidable if everyone is kept fully informed. Making use of her extensive experience with pathfinders and "quick bibs," one librarian got into the habit of creating one-page information sheets on every aspect of the planning and construction process. When the board and the architect were considering the best site, she gave all participants copies of her one-page bulleted list of the ten most important location considerations. Then she explained her points quickly and clearly and relinquished the floor before she'd lost the attention of her listeners.

All through the design and construction phases, that librarian had small stacks of one-page handouts ready. One briefly and succinctly explained preservation issues; another dealt with library security requirements. She never distributed more than one handout at a time and never included more than the barest essentials on a sheet. Large type, lots of white space, and important points emphasized with bold print and bullets distinguished all her masterpieces. Best of all, the handouts were always ready ahead of time, so when the conversation turned unexpectedly to a new subject, the librarian was ready. When new team members arrived on the scene, she began the process all over again. Although I don't know it for a fact and she never talked down to anyone, I wouldn't be surprised if this librarian began her work life teaching third graders. She never argued, never became hysterical or irrational; she just kept plugging along distributing and interpreting her information sheets. The success of her new building speaks volumes for the efficacy of her method.

FUNCTIONING EFFECTIVELY IN A HIGHLY CHARGED POLITICAL ENVIRONMENT

Every library is enmeshed in some sort of political environment. Of course political considerations are a part of any human endeavor that involves large sums of money, but in some libraries they may become such an overriding concern that they jeopardize the success of the project. How can you cope? Well, first of all, take a good look at your community. Think back on the role of politics in past library decisions. You will know the extent to which library issues have been seized upon by competing political factions. You can probably predict many of the challenges that lie ahead even without the help of a crystal ball.

Effectively using the skills and resources of your board and library users is always necessary, even in the calmest of times. If the library is going to be at the center of a political firestorm, these supporters will be absolutely essential to the success of the project. As soon as you see the new library or addition looming on your horizon—in fact, long before any official approval is obtained—begin mustering your library's political strength. If you have some influence over the appointment of your board, seek out good politicians who have connections with decision makers in your community. Look for articulate people who will speak out and help communicate the library's needs to local government representatives and other citizens. Make them stakeholders in the project by keeping them informed and going to them for advice. Even if you have little or no influence on the election or appointment of the board, *never* see your board as the enemy. Though you might willingly wring a few necks, you have far more influence over this group than you do over the other powers that be. Make allies on the board; work with them, inform them, and finally, make them participants rather than spectators.

Academic libraries also operate in highly charged political environments. Of course, you're familiar with your usual chain of command, but you may find that the real decision makers are people you've never worked with before. Set yourself the task of trying to identify these unknown players. Consider how your needs and insights can be communicated to them without appearing to go over your boss's head.

Get Your "Friends" Involved

In addition to developing support on your board or among your administration, you should foster the same kind of "people resources" in your Friends group. Most libraries already have a Friends of the Library group of some kind. Take a good look at yours. If it's been inactive, what can you do to bring it back to life? Begin identifying regular library users who have the kind of political skills you are seeking. Personally invite them to participate. Use some of your precious staff time to plan activities that will reinvigorate Friends' meetings. Then, as the building project begins in earnest, make regular reports to the group, encouraging them to attend hearings and lobby for the new library.

Start New Library Groups

Occasionally a library has a Friends group that is, you might say, "on its last legs." Most of the members joined in 1956, and it has gradually become stagnant and fusty. You know deep down that the articulate, politically savvy newcomers you're looking for would never want to join, and anyway the old guard would discourage their advances. If this is a good description of your Friends, all is not lost. Start one or more new groups that can coexist peacefully, side-by-side with the existing one. Book discussion groups work well for this purpose, or you could develop a special fund-raising group for the new library. The point is that you will want to hand-select as many of the members as possible. Once they're hooked, you must keep them involved with activities and responsibilities. One way or another, nurture a sizable group of people who are both involved in the community and possess the kind of political skills the library so badly needs.

Steer Clear of Dissension

Remember that building projects cause tempers to flare and nerves to fray. It is not even unusual for heads to roll in such a highly charged environment, and you certainly do not want to place your own head in danger. You will have to balance your determination to build the perfect library with your instincts for self-preservation. When the last carpenter has left, you can bid adieu to the architect and contractor. If your superior diplomatic skills failed you and you nearly came to blows, you need never speak to them again. Your job, however, should be just as secure as the day you took on the project. In fact, you should have established such a good working relationship with your superiors that they now understand far more about the library and its needs.

TALES

The building was designed by committee—we had a community group of thirty-five people involved in the planning stages and still ended up with a beautiful, functional building.

As the saying goes, "For God so loved the world he did not form a committee." That goes double for construction projects.

The president decreed that the campus store will be in the new learning center building. No one has been able to overturn that directive to this point. Why not bring in Kinko's? Cool if it were a big building, but it's only 22,000 square feet.

Get Support

It is an unfortunate fact of human nature that we all prefer that someone else take the blame when things go wrong. Depend upon it: Many things will go wrong during a building project. Hours will be spent arguing over who is at fault. Even when you are working with the nicest and best-intentioned people, you will want to protect yourself from such recriminations. It happens all too frequently that the individual who has done the least is the most critical of the work of others. The best way to avoid problems is to provide ample opportunity for input from all the important stakeholders.

Be sure you have plenty of support before going out on a potentially controversial "limb." If you don't have support and believe strongly that you are in the right and your colleagues in the wrong, tread carefully. If it's important enough, launch an educational campaign to clarify the situation. Assemble and present factual information to support your point of view. If, however, you begin to see yourself as a St. Joan who alone understands what's really needed or you feel like a suffering martyr, buffeted on all sides by ignorance, stop! Pull yourself together. You're not going to survive this project unless you can calm down, back off, and acquire a more detached attitude.

ESTABLISHING LINES OF COMMUNICATION

Several years ago, I worked in a library that had a gaping hole in the floor in front of the circulation desk. Patrons joked that anyone not returning books on time would be hurled into the chasm. It seems that a special (and very expensive) type of flooring material had been used. It was intended for easy removal when, at some time in the future, the library would expand to the floor below and a staircase would be erected. Unfortunately, the floor chose to remove itself much earlier than planned. The architect had passed on an instruction booklet to the builder describing how the flooring material was to be installed. Unfortunately, one vital page was missing.

TIP

Our project supervisor (hired by us to oversee the work of the contractors) advised me to leave the decision on shingle, exterior trim, and brick color entirely to the board. I think he was wise. It is a very big decision. If it is a wrong decision it is very obvious, and we will have to live with it for a long time. It is better if the board has no one to point a finger at!

There was probably nothing the librarian could have done about this particular instance of miscommunication, but many other tragedies are easily avoided if the efficient flow of information becomes a priority for all concerned. The basic problem is that information often gets lost or buried before it gets to the right person. Changes requested by the librarian may have to go through so many different intermediaries that when they finally reach the contractor or subcontractor who can execute them, it is too late to make the alterations. Changes that once might have cost nothing to implement may later require extensive retrofitting at a cost of many thousands of dollars.

In many situations, librarians are prevented from communicating directly with building professionals by administrators who fear their "add-ons" will drive up the cost of the project. This understandable concern can be alleviated if a clear procedure is established for approving financial commitments. Work out a system whereby key players involved in the building project routinely "copy" one another on important memos, making it clear that this is for information only.

Help Building Professionals Communicate

TALE

I met on-site with the county engineer, the construction foreman, and the architect every other week. It was tremendously helpful to know the building from the ground up.

Although you don't have a lot of say in the matter, it's vitally important for your contractor, architect, and other building professionals to communicate well with one another. Any time you can bring them together, do so. They are all extremely busy, and unless they work together frequently, they may not take the extra time to make sure they really understand the other's perspective. Based on personal experience and the comments of other librarians, it seems as if far more time is spent passing around the blame for a mistake than is spent fixing it. When problems are identified at an early phase, they are usually easy to fix. Simple, inexpensive solutions are often the best ones. This means success depends on a librarian who stays abreast of what's happening and on a contractor who checks back with the architect when something just doesn't feel right.

Write It Down

Get used to putting things in writing. In the classic Japanese film *Rashomon*, several people describe their memories of the same incident. Each is perfectly honest, but each appears to have witnessed an entirely different event. This is often true of meetings with the various participants in a building project. Each will take away a different understanding of what occurs.

Follow up on meetings with memos outlining the decisions and commitments made. If a decision could not be made without more information, identify the person responsible for providing that information and the time frame in which the decision must be made. Mention anyone who has volunteered to perform a task or who has been asked to take on a responsibility. Although no one enjoys taking minutes, appoint yourself as official or unofficial reporter of the discussions in which you participate. Distribute photocopies of the minutes to everyone involved. If other members of the group understood matters differently, now is the time to present their differing interpretations while the meeting is fresh in their memories. Some people, of course, will consign your minutes and memos to the trash can, but at least you've provided an opportunity for them to express their views. When an argument arises months later, you will be able to produce written evidence to support your position.

At this point, it is important to include a few additional words about the whole business of taking minutes. How many meetings have you attended at which a full five minutes were spent arguing about who will be responsible for minutes? Few chores are so unpopular. Nevertheless, the page or two of notes you take during a meeting or discussion can pay astounding dividends. First, you are establishing your interpretation of what happened as the official one. If minutes are distributed and group members are asked to submit corrections, you have provided an opportunity for the expression of other interpretations. Even though people rarely avail themselves of this opportunity, your minutes will usually be taken as the official version of an event in a court of law or in an arbitration hearing.

Make it a point to present participants in their best light. Of course, you must not distort what actually happened, but the difference of just a few words can make a comment sound wise or foolish. Be sure everyone sounds wise because they will be more likely to actually read what you have to say. We all enjoy nothing more than to read complimentary things about ourselves. It's all very well to have the minutes available for ammunition in some future dispute, but it's much better for project participants to understand one another right now.

Never use your minutes to make yourself look like the only intelligent member of the discussion. Never use them to give voice to all your grievances or get revenge on an adversary. You'll simply initiate a spate of angry memos accompanied by hurt feelings and embittered reprisals. Focus your efforts on the building, not on the personalities. If you don't, by the end of the project, you may be seething with hostility, and others may be feeling exactly the same way. The last thing you want to do at this point is to set off a tinder box of explosive feelings.

REALIZING THAT YOU CAN'T DO IT ALL ALONE

If you are imagining that the entire library staff is going to be doing their usual jobs while you drive yourself to a nervous breakdown with added responsibilities, better think again. Take off that halo. You're all in this together. Your staff's library lives are going to have to change almost as much as yours. Review the library's priorities. What functions can be compressed or postponed? How can you free staff time for the many tasks that a construction project involves? You're going to need someone who is in charge of public relations, whether this is an official position or is incorporated into an existing job description. Look around your staff. Don't stop at the professional staff. It doesn't take an MLS to be a charming and effective organizer. Your library probably has some highly competent staff members who are active in the community and would make excellent library publicists.

Get Staff Involved

In most cases, you are enlarging your present library or designing a new building to replace an existing structure. This means that you already have a laboratory in which to experiment with new ideas and a staff of experienced professionals and paraprofessionals who together possess many years of library experience. Bring everyone in the library into the planning process. Not only will working together as a team improve their morale and job performance but it will improve the quality of your own library work life as well. Involve them in creating the checklist. Work together to weigh the importance of individual items. They can help you separate the "absolutely essential" from the merely desirable.

Don't forget that there are other employees who should be involved in the project as well. Custodians can provide expert suggestions on which materials wear well and which are especially difficult to clean. Engineers, electricians, and all-purpose handy people on staff can also troubleshoot plans, identifying problems in their particular areas of expertise.

Library directors who have suffered through a building project often relate that they felt like martyrs, abandoned by people who didn't understand how hard they'd worked and how much frustration they'd experienced. It is sometimes hard to avoid such a neurotic outlook when board members demand the sacrifice of stack space for a reception area or the president cuts the construction budget by another million dollars. We do sometimes feel that we alone are holding up the bloodstained banner, and such an attitude can seriously interfere with our judgment. Involving the library staff provides a support group on which you can depend for informed advice and encouragement. These are people who understand both the mission and the practical reality of a library. Although opinions will differ sharply, they will tend to see the project in much the same way you do.

Nevertheless, be careful that you do not unload all your frustrations on the library staff. Naturally, you will feel the need for a sounding board when the board chairman has done something really dastardly, but your staff should not be used as confidantes. It is especially unwise, in a moment of anger, to utter insults or make wild accusations that you will long regret. You might instead develop a network of librarians outside your own library with whom you can let down your hair—professionals who will understand what you're going through but who will regard your verbal torrents as confidential.

TIPS

Insist on staff involvement; they have to work there every day!

The staff is heavily stressed during a building project. If they are also heavily involved and have bought into it, they take the added stress with courage and good humor. At least ours did.

We had an incredible battle rearranging the interior to make sense, but the staff finally won that one. The staff and I kept each other going.

Tap Staff's Institutional Memory

Pooling the experience of staff members can result in some unexpected bonuses. One staff member may remember a crisis that occurred because of a badly designed media viewing area; another will recall an error that made it impossible to use a service elevator or work space as had originally been envisioned. Such memories can keep you from making many costly mistakes. Invite staff members to walk through a typical work day using the preliminary floor plans. Looking through their eyes, you will discover a gaggle of traffic problems, unsupervised niches, poorly organized work spaces, and noisy reading areas. You will wonder how you could possibly have missed such obvious problems, but you are in no way at fault. We each view the world from our own unique perspective. Your role is not to be omniscient but to integrate the many views into one coherent whole. Staff are probably the ones who will catch the details while you are focusing on the big picture. Although some initial brainstorming sessions will be useful, staff must also be attuned to the project schedule so they don't identify problems after it's too late to do anything about them.

DEVELOPING YOUR SKILLS

Although you are an expert on libraries, you still have a lot of homework to do before you're ready to launch a building project. For example, you have a new vocabulary to learn. Although you certainly have every right to insist that the architect and other building specialists speak English and avoid jargon, you must meet them half way. Describing the fittings for a large, complex building requires an understanding of hundreds of new terms. (They are not gizmos or thing-a-ma-jigs.) Small details like locking mechanisms that you may never have noticed come in endless varieties. A certain minimal understanding is needed to reinterpret technical details in terms of the library's needs.

Your local technical college offers a wide assortment of courses designed to introduce students to the building trades. You might audit a course in architectural drawing and learn to read a blueprint. Electrical connections, data lines, load-bearing walls, and plumbing fixtures are clearly indicated on a floor plan and obvious to a building professional. They are easily overlooked, however, unless you acquaint yourself with the symbols in standard use.

Branch out, if you have time, to other introductory classes dealing with electricity or heating, ventilation, and air-conditioning (HVAC) systems. The point is simply to acquire enough vocabulary and basic information to communicate effectively. If you haven't the time for a course, take a look at your own library shelves. Public library collections are especially rich in basic architecture and construction texts. Even "do-it-yourself" homeowner books can be helpful.

TIPS

Read all you can. You can't learn too much!

When it was evident that we would add on to our building, I was sent to participate in a very good workshop. It covered everything from planning and blueprints to how to deal with the architects. I can't recommend workshops and focused conference sessions enough!

Know how to read a blueprint. There will be construction mistakes, and only by knowing what the blueprints include will you be able to have change orders written at no cost to you. (This is very important as change orders add up quickly.)

Architects, project managers, contractors, etc., were all surprised to learn that I knew how to read a blueprint. They're much more careful when they know you can keep tabs on them.

We had 30-inch shelves installed as 18-inch shelves and outlets installed 6 feet apart when they were supposed to be 4 feet apart. These are examples of mistakes that were corrected at no cost to my project since I could go through the blueprints and point out the mistakes. I really recommend staying on top of these details.

Fixing mistakes will cost money, but it's better than living with a gross error for years afterward.

Understand Where the Money Comes From

How much do you know about your library building budget? How is it divided? Will you have any freedom to move funds around if some bids come in lower and others higher than expected? Plan to meet individually with key staff members in your business office or purchasing department. Become familiar with their procedures. Ask about other building projects in which they've been involved, and find out how they expect your project to proceed (based on their past experiences). It is extremely important to develop a good working relationship with individuals in these offices. It is not usually difficult to follow their rules and submit the right paperwork at the right time. In exchange, they will be your friends for life.

The people who pay the bills often have an undeservedly negative reputation. They're the ones who must satisfy the auditors and whose jobs are on the line if any financial irregularities should be discovered. It is only natural that they lose their cool when their procedures are ignored. If you spend the time to get to know these people as human beings, you will be amazed at how they can expedite your requests and keep you informed of progress on bids and contracts.

Become a Building Connoisseur

As soon as a building project appears on the horizon, start looking at other buildings. When vacation time rolls around, take a busman's holiday. Learn what it feels like to enter a new building, to look for a particular office, to ride the elevator, or to find the restrooms. Watch what other visitors do. Although you'll want to take care that security officers don't identify you as a stalker, take notes on what tends to confuse people and where visitors look for assistance. Become a connoisseur of buildings. (See also Fact-Finding Missions in chapter 6 for technology-related observations in other buildings.)

MAKE A SCRAPBOOK   When you visit these buildings, take your camera along. Start a scrapbook illustrating the features you like and want to incorporate into the new library. Just describing these features to the architect isn't enough; there is simply no way to transmit the picture in your mind to someone who doesn't have the same frame of reference. When trying to communicate your vision of the library, you may be tempted to couch your specifications in vague terms such as "public image," "library philosophy," or other subjective phrases. This is a sure way to derail your project. You will believe that you and your architects are in perfect agreement until that fateful day when you look with horror at the way they have interpreted your suggestions.

LOOK AT ALL TYPES OF BUILDINGS   Don't just look at libraries. In fact, it is sometimes better to look at other kinds of buildings because you won't be distracted by library functions, and you will be more likely to focus on architectural details and building materials. Visit museums, hotels, office buildings, and theaters. Take pictures of flooring materials, stairways, doors, windows, signage, counters, and all the other details that go into a modern building.

For example, during a summer vacation, I visited a friend in Reno, Nevada. Not being much of a gambler, I found the casinos rather boring until I began looking at them as if they were libraries. In that tawdry world of excess, I discovered samples of almost every conceivable building material. Some casinos had opened only recently while others were showing their age, so I could see how wall treatments, carpeting, and restroom fixtures held up over time. In addition, I discovered that designers rarely think about the people who will be cleaning the new building, especially its complicated surfaces that get dirtier as the years go by. Designers may not notice that light fixtures are positioned in such a way as to make them unreachable when bulbs inevitably burn out. It was interesting to compare older casinos with older libraries. Because the profits for some older casinos had declined, they no longer had the money to spend on expensive equipment like lifts and "cherry pickers" to reach those hard-to-get-to places, and so those places got grimier and more tattered. It was clear that the more elaborate the decoration, the more rapidly the casino aged.

Become a Catalog Junkie

It's helpful to put your name on the mailing list for as many building-supply catalogs as possible. Don't stop at library catalogs. There are hundreds of construction-trade catalogs that are free for the asking. Of course, you should begin with the buyers' guide issue of *Library Journal*, but go on to explore the world of restroom equipment, door and window manufacturers, and lighting fixture distributors; the list goes on and on. ConstructionNet on the World Wide Web is a good port of entry into this unfamiliar world. In fact, the Web in general is full of good ideas. However, you will want to obtain printed catalogs so that you can cut them up, adding pictures of desirable features to your scrapbook.

Take care, however, that the materials and equipment you find in catalogs are in the moderate price range. A friend found herself accused of driving up building costs with her demands when the real reason for cost overruns was the architect's patrician taste. Architects may not mean to be extravagant, but they do not share your priorities. As a catalog junkie, you'll gradually come to know what things cost and will be alert to wasteful spending. If you can buy an item "off the shelf"—in other words, if it is made in huge quantities on an assembly line—it will be much cheaper than one made in small, buyer-initiated production runs. It is amazing how "plain vanilla" materials in the hands of an accomplished architect can be used to create a unique and imaginative structure.

UNDERSTANDING THE COMPLEXITY OF A MODERN BUILDING

Libraries are very big buildings. Not big enough, maybe, when you're trying to squeeze in a few thousand more books and the new addition is several years overdue. Nevertheless, think of the number of fluorescent tubes that burn out at the exact hour and minute the custodian announces he's run out of replacements. Remember how many yards of carpet you found would be needed the last time you decided you couldn't stand shag avocado another minute? In addition, think about the thousands of bits and pieces of shelving hardware, and the panes of glass whose life expectancy is directly proportional to the number of skateboards and softballs in the immediate area. The complexity of a building gets overwhelming, to say the least. Occasionally the library seems even larger, as when the climate ranges from arctic levels in the basement through a somewhat temperate zone on the street floor to equatorial heat at the top.

There's no getting around it. Library buildings are fraught with endless peril; ultimately, you're the one who must get the roof patched. (I know you told them flat roofs leak, and they said you didn't understand architecture.) As you begin a building project, bear in mind the many experiences you've had as a librarian.

Some problems are inevitable, and no architect and no builder can save you or your staff from grim reality. On the other hand, some problems were caused by building professionals who failed to understand how libraries really work.

The World of Smart Buildings

Soon after you begin your research, you'll come across the term *smart building*. Although it seems to mean different things to different people (especially in the advertising industry), it usually refers to a coming together of new technologies including computer automation, space-age materials, and energy management. Combined in a modern building, all this technology provides the ability to adjust and adapt systems to the needs of building occupants. In addition, the term usually refers to the increased energy efficiency made possible by more-responsive systems. The often less than satisfactory results of today's fledgling experiments with smart buildings are a major reason why librarians should become more involved in their construction projects.

The literature you pore over will herald the arrival of thousands of new materials. Many, like superconductors and composites, promise to have enormous impact on the building industry. For example, a new composite tile flooring is expected to outlast traditional materials, surviving daily use indefinitely and eliminating the need for routine replacement. Another space-age innovation is shape-memory alloys. These are metal alloys that when stimulated by either heat or electricity change their shape and other physical properties. Although they are still under development, they appear to be especially useful in preventing major earthquake damage. Piezoelectric cells are yet another exciting new wrinkle. Tiny electric devices that vibrate very rapidly, they can dampen vibrations, which are a major cause of wear and tear on a building's structural components. Piezoelectric cells may, therefore, mean fewer repairs and a longer useful life for modern buildings.

Environmental controls are additional aspects of "smart" buildings. Experts have concluded that although 36 percent of the nation's energy is gobbled up by its buildings, this figure can be cut in half by the year 2010 if the technologies associated with smart buildings are implemented. For example, in a hyperintelligent building of the future, workers might be given special ID cards recognized by a central computer system as they arrive. Once the workers are in the building, the system would automatically open doors, serve refreshments, and control the systems in the immediate vicinity, including lighting and temperature control. When no one is in an area, the systems would be powered down to reduce energy costs.

Has the Future Arrived?

Not only can we expect these wonders to revolutionize the "smart" building of the future but the term is also being applied to the present-day automation of nearly every aspect of a building's infrastructure including lighting and communications. By controlling these systems with a main computer, a building can be not only more functional but also more energy efficient. The smart or intelligent building of today contains an abundance of microprocessors that operate internal systems—lighting, ventilation and air-conditioning, power, elevators, fire safety equipment, and security equipment. In addition, they support sophisticated telecommunications systems for voice, data, and video transmission. An inexpensive semiconductor device, a neuron chip now in production, is expected to make it possible to automate hundreds of functions that have in the past been manually controlled.

Soon, you will find yourself surrounded by building professionals who are bubbling over with enthusiasm for these innovations, and, certainly, your new building should be technically sophisticated. So what's wrong with this picture? The problem is that apostles of modern technology work in a world that is entirely divorced from the realities of library management. They are always planning and constructing buildings, never maintaining existing structures. Before you allow yourself to be carried away by their rosy visions of the future, take a moment to think about your own library environment.

The last time the temperature rose or plummeted to unacceptable levels, how difficult was it to have the problem remedied?

How computer literate are your maintenance supervisor and staff?

How responsive is your central administration when it comes to calling in outside technical expertise?

How generous has funding been for library preventive maintenance? Is "deferred maintenance" the option of choice when budgets are tight?

Have new electrical circuits been installed when you needed them, or are electrical wires strung haphazardly around the library?

Has your roof been repaired and replaced on schedule, or must you cope with leaks and buckets for months before something is finally done?

Next, look beyond your own library building. If you are in an academic library, how well maintained are the other buildings on your campus? Public librarians might select other county or municipal buildings for comparison. Ask the facilities manager or staff members whose offices are located there about climate control, maintenance, and repairs.

Money spent on new building materials that reduce the need for routine maintenance is usually well spent—as long as the materials have been thoroughly tested. You don't want to incorporate them into your building and then discover unanticipated problems. What might work fine in a laboratory can be a disaster in real day-to-day situations.

New automated HVAC and other systems can also be good choices, but they require regular monitoring. Such systems depend upon computer software and hardware that is subject to all the same tragedies you encounter daily with your desktop PC. Therefore, the maintenance and repair personnel who work on the system must not only be able to cope with mechanical problems but they must possess computer skills as well. If your library is located far from a large metropolitan area, your local servicepeople may not be up to the job. Will the library budget stretch to fly in an expert technician?

How Much "Smartness" Can You Handle?

Later chapters discuss these systems in greater depth, but early in the project you should consider just how much "smartness" your library can handle. Be prepared to ask architects and engineers about the kind of monitoring that must be done to maintain any recommended system. Be sure you've given some thought to who will be taking care of your building and what kind of training they will be getting. Consider that even if extensive training is provided by the vendor as part of the purchase price, turnover among building engineers and maintenance staff is extraordinarily high. Consider how the system will be maintained five or ten years from now when the current staff have gone their separate ways.

No matter what you discover in library literature about a new building in Denver or San Francisco or Oshkosh, remember that your situation is not quite like any other. What may work in one environment may be a disaster in another. It may be your grasp on the realities of everyday library existence that best qualifies you for the work ahead. Don't let your unique perspective be eclipsed by what can sometimes be the uninformed enthusiasms of those around you. Continually draw from your past experience to inform your decisions, but make sure you're not stuck in a rut. New technologies can greatly enhance the library; they just can't alter or transform the environment in which the library operates.

2

The World of Architects and Contractors

As you will discover from the Tips and Tales sections, building or renovating a library is a lot of fun, but there's no denying there will be days when you want to tear your hair out. If there is such a thing as a key to success, it may be found in establishing productive working relationships with the building professionals who will be involved in your project. A good place to begin, therefore, is with a basic understanding of who these people are and how they are selected.

HOW NEW BUILDINGS HAPPEN

Unless you've recently contracted to have your own house built, you may feel that you're totally in the dark about the way buildings come into being. Even if you've worked with an architect or contractor on your own home, you may still find the sort of wheeling and dealing that goes into a large building project rather overwhelming. So how does it all happen? The following is a brief description of the basic project delivery systems currently in use in the United States.

Design-bid-build is the traditional project delivery system in the U.S. construction industry. As owner, your library or parent organization contracts separately with a design firm and with a builder. Your organization as owner contracts with a design firm to provide complete design documents that will then allow the library to solicit fixed-price bids from builders (contractors) for the performance of the work. The contractors enter into an agreement with your library to construct a building in accordance with the plans and specifications. This system ensures, for better or worse, that design and construction functions are totally separate. Thus, the contractor is only chosen after the design has been completed.

In some areas the library works with a general contractor who in turn hires sub-contractors; in other places libraries must contract directly with several prime contractors like those providing general, mechanical, and electrical services.

The *construction management at risk* project delivery system also involves the owner's contracting with the design firm and contractor separately, but the contractor is selected early in the project before plans are completed. The contractor performs construction management services and construction work, in accordance with the plans and specifications, for an agreed-upon fee. Because contractors enter the picture much earlier, they are able to have considerably more input into the design process. In fact, this is essential because the cost of the building has already been agreed upon, so it must be possible to construct the structure designed by the architect for the agreed-upon price. Since both building professionals are on board earlier, this method allows the project to progress at a much faster pace than with the design-bid-build project delivery system.

In the case of the *design-build* project delivery system, the library or its parent organization contracts with just one entity that performs both design and construction as part of a single design-build contract. With this system there is a single point of responsibility for both design and construction services. Specific work may be contracted out to other companies, but only the design-build firm is responsible directly to the owner. The discussion in this book will devote considerably more attention to this option than to the other two since the design-build delivery system is a recent innovation that is sweeping the world of publicly funded construction. It is important that you be prepared if your parent organization is moving in this direction.

THE WORLD OF ARCHITECTS

As the building planning process of libraries becomes increasingly stressful, take comfort that librarians have been coping with building crises for hundreds, even thousands of years. Assurbanipal's librarian in ancient Babylonia endured many of the same headaches. Leaky roofs are nothing new; think how much more vulnerable (as well as heavy and breakable) those clay tablets must have been. In theory at least, we should have an easier time of it with all our modern conveniences, but sometimes I wonder. For instance: Did those ancient Babylonian librarians have to contend with architects?

Probably the ancients had someone comparable, but I doubt that any ancient architect ever designed a balcony on an upper level overlooking a fountain in the foyer. Few modern architects have ever paused to think of how a ten-year-old child will use such a golden opportunity. The splashing you hear represents a sizable portion of the book collection being hurled joyously into the fountain. The graciously curving central stairway with which I was once burdened served a similar function, but the books were aimed at the crania of friends below (by college students who also enjoyed sliding down the spiraling banister).

Such errors in judgment are the result of the delight architects experience when commissioned to plan a library building. Rarely do they have so much scope for their imagination. Think of all that open space! What an impressive monument to their genius! Office buildings are too boring with their endless halls and small cubbyholes. Classroom buildings offer few opportunities to really create.

Vanderbilt University Medical Library, Nashville, Tennessee

TALES

From the start, everything suggested a good working relationship with the architects. We spent a lot of time poring over blueprints, pinpointing the location of every outlet and window, but somewhere along the line we neglected to make sure the architects knew what they were doing.

The stairs only go to the third of five floors. We also have another staircase that doesn't go anywhere but can be clearly seen from the outside of the building.

The marble counters retain the cold, which means you can freeze meat most of the year.

The clocks are so high that it requires maintenance to change them with the tallest ladders they have.

But a library! Think of all those imposing edifices from the old Carnegies to modern chrome-and-glass extravaganzas. Each looks magnificent until you have a chat with the librarian.

As you enter one of the newer libraries, you may encounter a mystic maze of electric cords strung from wall to wall dipping precariously between computer workstations and book stacks. Apparently, the architects were picturing a medieval library. Despite the librarian's input, the architects somehow failed to comprehend the plethora of personal computers, photocopy machines, printer stations, microfilm readers, and VCRs that have become standard in a modern library.

If you were to continue your progress through the building, you might encounter temperatures ranging from arctic to tropical. That might be due to the charming atrium at the center of the building. The architects apparently failed to consider the resulting heat gain in summer and heat loss in winter when designing the climate control system. The smell of decaying vegetation rises from the atrium's tropical jungle that overburdened staff members are too busy to care for properly.

As stated previously, make arrangements to visit as many libraries as possible. As the quotation that begins this book so vividly illustrates, librarians spend a great deal of time finding fault with their buildings. Sometimes they ascribe the fault to their predecessors or to changes in technology. More often, they lay the blame at the feet of their architects. Regard such ravings with caution, but do listen.

Some architects are flexible enough to respond to the library's requirements; others are not. It is not possible to know what really transpired during the planning and construction phases of any given library, but patterns do emerge. Look at the architect's work as a whole rather than judging him or her by any one building.

Choosing the Architects

Considering how important the architects are to your building project, how do you choose the best ones available? Of course, you will not have a free hand in the choice, but you can at least make sure the decision makers are prepared with the right information. Begin with a list of architectural firms that have demonstrated experience in projects similar to yours. Since library commissions are few, also look at firms that have designed other public and commercial buildings in your area. Analyze the buildings' good and bad qualities as you might a library. Does form follow function, or does it seem to be the other way around? Try to identify and interview the individuals who were involved in the projects. Ask how receptive the architects were to their suggestions. Did the architects appear to have a separate agenda, or did plans emerge from the expressed needs of the owners and users? (See also chapter 6, Fact-Finding Missions, for technology design considerations.)

The American Institute of Architects can provide project-specific lists for your area. Begin with as long a list as possible, and compare the architects' past work with your own project. Compare project size, project scope, time line, experience with nonprofit organizations, and reported interactions with clients. Invite the architects under consideration to make a presentation so you can discover how they perceive a library's role. Do the architects do most of the talking, or do they listen more than they talk? Do they ask the right questions? Did they come to the presentation prepared with knowledge about libraries in general and your project in particular? Do the architects communicate in jargon or in understandable terms? Are they accustomed to working with groups of people such as committees and boards? Do they understand and accept your budget limitations and the tight budget constraints that libraries must work under?

You and your associates will want to be wary of free services or the offer of a substantially reduced fee structure. No matter how large or small, your library will require many hours of highly individualized and highly professional labor. It is usually not possible to adapt the design of another building to the library's needs. Neither should you take a chance on a fledgling architectural firm that is looking for a large project to make a name for itself. The money saved in architectural services will not outweigh the problems that will ensue if the building is not properly designed.

Why are the architects under consideration interested in your particular project? Can you detect any particular enthusiasm or commitment, or are they simply casting their nets for any business that presents itself? Ask them about the specific expertise that makes them the best choice for your project. Inevitably, the discussion will generate ideas, and it is important to note whether those ideas are focused on form or function. Are the architects describing what the building will look like, or are they focusing on what activities will be taking place within it? During these first contacts they will, of course, know little about libraries, but beware the architect who enthusiastically discusses the granite exterior or the dramatic staircase.

Seek out architects who are willing to participate fully in fund-raising. This means that they are willing to include deliverables in the contract such as presentation-quality visual materials, floor plans, material boards, renderings, and even computer model walk-through imaging. Ask about a presentation-quality site plan as well as exterior and interior perspectives and models. These can be extremely useful tools for increasing enthusiasm among your patrons and donors.

It is not uncommon for the library capital campaign to be offered in-kind gifts from local businesses. These are sometimes welcomed with open arms, but they may also create problems. Deciding not only what is acceptable but what gifts will be sought out should be part of the contract. Since the architects' fees may be tied to the total cost of the project, it is especially important that they not artificially inflate costs by discouraging gifts.

TIPS AND TALES

Be sure the architect you select is willing to work with you, listening to your needs and your suggestions.

We had generally good experiences, and the libraries we wound up with were probably more than 90 percent satisfactory. (I challenge anyone to show me a library that is 100 percent satisfactory to everyone!) So I guess the moral is: choose your architect and your contractor very carefully.

Take some time and find a design firm you can trust and that has experience in designing a library, a museum, or an archive. We spent over six months looking for our architect, and the result has been well worth the effort. Be sure you're comfortable working with the firm you select because things get pretty intense in the latter stages of the project.

I'd say that one of the requirements for a good architect, apart from experience and ability in designing libraries, is flexibility and a willingness to present alternatives.

The architect should have the diplomatic skills to deal with college presidents, librarians, donors, and others and in some cases to negotiate compromises among them.

Try to make your building a community showplace without being the architect's monument to himself/herself.

Lessons Learned from a Real Project

Although it is a great deal larger than most library projects, Chicago's Harold Washington Library Center is a good example of what happens when a lot of people set out to build a library. In some ways, the end result was extremely successful. For example, Chicago was one of the first to select a design-build firm for a large library project. In general, that decision saved money and avoided numerous complications. Architecturally, the building is of great interest, an adaptation of the first modern library, the Bibliotheque Sainte-Genevieve, to modern requirements.

In many functional respects, the design was successful, but in others, it left librarians feeling dissatisfied. Thomas Fisher, writing in *Progressive Architecture*, discovered that dangerous icicles were falling from the building's metal cornice 130 feet up and that visitors could not find the library since the entrance was on the third floor with few signs or architectural cues to direct new arrivals. The fact that official signs—gold on light wood—were few and were hard to read made it even more difficult to find one's way. At the time the article was written (some two years after the grand opening), the building was cluttered with hundreds of much-needed makeshift signs directing users through the facility. Fisher quotes his design professor, who once said that if a building needs a lot of signage, there is something wrong with its plan. Following are some of the other problems Fisher identifies in the article:

The narrow "single-file" escalator is hidden behind the projecting wall of the front vestibule.

On the mezzanine level, visitors imagine they have found the library only to discover that what they're entering is the separate children's library.

Work areas for the children's library on the second floor mezzanine are located on the sixth floor.

Librarians leaving the building or visiting the break room on the ninth floor must take an inconveniently located single-file escalator or one of only two staff elevators that double as freight elevators and have no lights to show what floors they are on. Fisher quotes a librarian as saying that "You can blow most of your break time getting there and back. It takes me 10 to 15 minutes just to get from the staff entrance to my desk in the mornings."

Skylights on the second floor block the librarians' view of reading spaces and stack areas from the central desk.

High partitions around study carrels and freestanding bulletin boards further block the view from the central circulation desk.

Important areas, such as the children's library, are wedged into the leftover space around the lobby and among the skylights.[1]

In support of the architects, one must admit that the Washington Library is a gorgeous building and many of these problems are solvable. The dramatic design gives the library a sense of importance that is a key ingredient in any recipe for the future survival of public libraries.

The Architects' Point of View

If you have a chance, take a look at the San Francisco, Denver, or Chicago main libraries. All three are amazing buildings, and all three say loudly and clearly that libraries are cool, trendy, and ready for the twenty-first century. After early encounters with architects, I thought that all I wanted was a vast warehouse or supermarket that tempted no architect's creativity. Now, after years of ranting, I have come to realize that the public's image of the library depends to a considerable extent on its architecture. We do, indeed, want a building that shouts "I'm an important place; I'm the focus of my community." I no longer begrudge the architects their awards as long as they do not turn a deaf ear to my service-oriented pleas and those of my colleagues.

Meeting Your Architects

At some point after the "go" decision has been made, you will be asked to meet the architects. Ideally, your involvement should begin even earlier when you are invited to meet any architects being considered for your project. One way or another, however, a first encounter is looming on your horizon. How should you handle it?

This first meeting is a momentous one because it will set a pattern for future encounters. Most architects begin a project with enthusiasm and with a sincere desire to design a building that will please the people who will be using it. They also, however, begin with a picture in their minds of what a library should look like. It will be up to you to gradually change and fashion that picture until it reflects the realities of a modern library operation. Not only do the architects have a picture of a library embedded in their subconscious but they have a picture of librarians as well. Unless they have been involved in other library building projects, that librarian picture is probably of a fluffy older woman in orthopedic oxfords, immersed in her books, who knows nothing of architecture or construction. This image must be dispelled immediately if you are to exert any influence on the project. Therefore, careful preparation for this first meeting is essential. Following is an action plan to prepare you for the first meeting:

1. Go first to your library shelves and find a glossary of architectural terms. Although you will find a number of these terms sprinkled throughout this book, you will need many more to describe the library that is taking shape in your mind. It is wise to get the vocabulary under control before

you begin the project. If you are familiar with widely used terminology, you will be able to conduct this first meeting on a much more professional plane. This should be a conference between colleagues, not the more typical "doctor-patient" consultation.

2. Make a very short list of the things the architects should know about the library before proceeding further. (See the section on this topic later in this chapter.) Go over this list again and again, whittling it down to the items you are absolutely sure you can cover in the time available. Remove or explain any library jargon. Be sure that you are not assuming knowledge that the architects may not possess. In other words, begin at a very basic level and don't digress. You want to be certain that they leave the meeting knowing more about your vision of a library than they did when they arrived.

3. Try to arrange the meeting so that you are alone with the architects. This is not always possible, and you may be one of a group meeting together. The more people present, the less control you have over the meeting. You probably can't dislodge the principal, president, board chairperson, or county commissioner, but you may be able to schedule another occasion when you can meet with the architects more privately.

4. Have your first round of written information about the library ready to hand the architects. This first offering should be no more than two or three pages with wide margins and lots of white space. The point is that you are beginning their library education. The next time you meet, refer to the information you provided. Make the architects feel just a little guilty if they have not read their homework. If necessary, provide another copy, and make it clear that you will be discussing it later.

5. Be sure the architects take away an image of you that is friendly and competent. Welcome them enthusiastically to the team, but keep the ball in your own court.

At one time, I thought it was a very good idea for the architects to meet with the library staff to better understand their needs; now I am not so sure. In an article written by an architect for a professional architecture journal, the architect discussed a major public library project in which he had been involved and emphasized how sensitive he had been to the needs of the library staff. It was immediately clear that he had missed the boat entirely. He had listened while several dozen people expressed their frustrations with the old building and their hopes and dreams for the new library. Out of this mish-mash, he seemed to pull the most irrelevant points and miss the really important ones. This was probably not entirely his fault because he lacked the body of knowledge needed to evaluate the relative importance of the diverse contributions.

The library staff will naturally want to be involved as much as possible, but their contributions should be honed and shaped in just the way you prepared for your first meeting with the architects. Work with the staff to prepare for any meetings. Make a list of priorities, and help staff understand the importance of hammering away at important points. When they do meet with the architects, staff should have their agenda and talking points prepared and be ready to redirect discussion if it veers away from these key issues.

WHAT ARCHITECTS NEED TO KNOW

Because libraries are such an integral part of your life, you may forget to communicate simple, basic information. Before any architects begin sketching floor plans, they will need a crash course in libraries. By this I do not mean anything remotely resembling the introduction to library science you remember from library school. Although it may be obvious to you, the architect must be told who will use the library. How will they use it? Children have very different needs from elderly adults, and college students use a facility in still different ways. What do staff do when they're working in the cataloging or processing area? How many patrons will need to use the public computers or VCRs or rest rooms at one time?

Architects need to know, for example, that your patrons will enter through only one door and that all other doors will be emergency exits. They need to know that there will be a book security system at this door and a service desk nearby so that patrons setting off the alarm can be asked to return. They need to know how much space should be devoted to book stacks and how much to computer use. One would also think that with all the stereotypes of the dowdy librarian shushing noisy patrons, they would know that a library should be a relatively quiet place, but this is often not the case.

Your Present and Possible Future Needs

I sometimes think that architects fall victim to a sort of "Sleeping Beauty" complex. Since you entered the library profession, you've seen constant change. Almost every year of your professional career, you or your colleagues have made substantial alterations to the library. You've knocked down stacks and moved them to areas experiencing rapid collection growth; you've added phone lines; you've wired study carrels to provide computer access and upgraded the electrical system to accommodate all the new equipment. An architect works with a snapshot of a building frozen in time.

Wendell Wickerham of the architectural firm of Shepley Bulfinch Richardson and Abbott expressed frustration that architects work very closely with a building until it opens, but then they lose contact with both the staff and the activities that take place in the building. It is, therefore, difficult for the architect to determine exactly which ideas function well and which should not be repeated. One of his firm's major projects was the Leavey Undergraduate Library at the University of California. Overall, Leavey was an extremely successful library project, but Wickerham, not fully understanding library security problems, was disappointed that the patio he designed, complete with pleasantly situated tables and chairs, went unused.[2]

An architect soon moves on to another project and fails to see how the building changes over the years. Once our architect tried to cut the carpet around the stacks so that they would rest more securely on the cement floor. It did not occur to him that those very stacks would be moved twice in the next ten years. This is information that only you can communicate.

If you are going to have a successful relationship with your architects, begin by clarifying which decisions you must make (or at least exert considerable influence over) and which offer more opportunity for the architects' imaginative design features. I don't know how you feel about working in an enchilada-red building like the San Antonio Public Library, but it's not your issue. Of course, you're free to express an opinion, but make it clear that it is not the same as your opinion on the load-bearing capacity of the floors. Let the trustees, the general public, the media, and anybody else so inclined debate these peripheral issues. Just be sure you don't get caught in the crossfire.

Begin making a very precise list of just what your issues are. Let it evolve gradually over time as you delve into library literature, visit other libraries, talk with your staff, and analyze concerns about your present library building. (Chapter 3 provides guidance on issues that will affect the future of your library.) It will soon become quite a long list, so be careful to stick to the basics. Just because you happen to come across an attractive design feature or hate the color green, don't include such minor points. Your list should be focused on *function,* and peripheral issues will serve only to confuse your architects. Of course, you can't possibly cover everything. The point is to train your architects on the kind of issues you consider important. At the same time, understand that the architects' values are important too. Try hard to be encouraging and supportive of their creative input when it does not have a negative impact on function.

Use of Different Spaces

In addition to basic information about library functions, begin describing specific library spaces. Will you need classrooms for bibliographic instruction? Meeting rooms that can be used when the library is closed? What about a twenty-four-hour study area in an academic library? This may be the appropriate time for an impassioned plea for adequate restrooms if your library's only conveniences are located off a dark hall or in the basement.

Consult published standards to estimate space requirements for collections and reading areas. Be sure that you make it clear that a space or area does not necessarily mean a room. Walls in a library should be kept to a minimum since they reduce flexibility and make supervision difficult. They also impede traffic and cause both patrons and staff to waste time and energy taking the long way around.

Once you have a general description of the spaces you'll be using, the architect will need to understand the relationships among them. Which ones should adjoin one another? Which can be widely separated? Make it clear that libraries, though spacious, are short-staffed and that staff time is valuable. Staff need to be able to do their work efficiently with the fewest number of steps. Patrons also resent having to walk a great distance unnecessarily. Don't attempt to draw a floor plan. Architects are far more knowledgeable about the technical and aesthetic considerations that go into such a plan. Be clear from the start about your roles, respecting their professional expertise but also demanding respect in your own professional sphere.

Other useful additions to your "magnum opus" are statistical summaries showing the way space has been used in other libraries similar to your own. Information included might cover collection and staff size; numbers of study carrels, tables, and computer workstations; and floor space allotted to circulation, periodicals, acquisitions, and cataloging functions. Although you don't want to tell your architects how to do their job, see if you can get hold of other library floor plans so you can point out both the positives and the negatives. (See chapter 3 for help in identifying space needs.)

Libraries Are Not Affluent Institutions

Since long before Andrew Carnegie financed the building of thousands of libraries, new library construction has depended upon outside funding. The result may be generous or meager, but it bears little relation to the library's operating budget. Your university development office may solicit foundation grants or the voters in your municipality may approve a bond issue, but any funds obtained are earmarked specifically for the building project. None can be expected to support your everyday operations. It is a sad fact of library life that a new library will further tax your resources, forcing you to do even more with less. Any increases in your operating budget will inevitably be swallowed up by the increased workload of a larger, more popular library.

If your institution chooses a traditional project delivery system, a universal law of nature states that the building that the architects initially design will cost far more money than has been budgeted. Of course, everyone concerned had a wish list, and the architects brought their own visions of grandeur that substantially inflated the cost. Now it is clear that the proposed building must be trimmed down to an affordable package, and a group or consulting firm is given the task of cutting enough fluff to allow the project to come in under budget. Unfortunately, what you consider necessities and what others, especially architects, consider necessities are poles apart.

Another law of nature states that early in the process, it will be suggested that the library can do without a central light switch panel, half the planned temperature zones, and windows that open. Well, it can't! Neither your staff nor your patrons should be asked to make such sacrifices to preserve the cherished atrium or spiral staircase that your design professionals hope will win architectural awards. The library is not just a showcase for their talents.

There are many ways that features incorporated into the plans now will mean lower utility bills and fewer maintenance expenses later. On the other hand, design features can considerably increase the cost of operating a library. For example, in buildings with atria, it is very difficult to balance air flow; therefore, service calls to repair malfunctioning circulators, pumps, blowers, and other HVAC components are more frequent. You needn't overdo your impassioned speeches about library poverty, but be sure your architect understands that your operating budget is not generous.

Staff Resources Must Be Used Effectively

As mentioned earlier, library staff size inevitably surprises architects. That such a large and expensive building can be staffed by such a small number of people continually confounds them. Stress with your architects the fact that libraries are unlike many other buildings in that funding is far more readily available for capital outlay than for ongoing expenses. In contrast, when a corporation decides to construct a new office building, expenditures for the building are part of the overall corporate budget. If the corporation is doing well, one might expect more generous funding for construction, staffing, and other corporate needs. Hard times would result in across-the-board cuts. What all this means is that careful architects should design the most efficient library possible, one that requires the smallest staff to operate and one that uses staff time most efficiently. For example, a single, centrally located light-switch panel that allows one staff member to turn off all the lights in the building is not the luxury it might be in an office building where staff are assigned to all floors. Security cameras are far less expensive than having staff members physically monitor the same spaces. Be sure that the architect understands that you want to operate your new building efficiently with the number of staff currently employed. Considering the present uncertain state of libraries, it might even be desirable to plan for a reduced staff.

WHAT TO EXPECT FROM YOUR ARCHITECT

Before entering into an agreement with a firm of architects, you should obtain the American Institute of Architects (AIA) publication *You and Your Architect*.[3] This sixteen-page booklet was developed by a group of architects, owners, lawyers, and insurance risk managers. It presents AIA's interpretation of the architect's role and responsibilities, and it is important that you be acquainted with this perspective. Since it is brief and simply written, you can provide it as suggested reading for other members of your project team. Included is a four-page removable instruction sheet addressed to the architect. It provides an opportunity to go over basic information so you can be sure you and your architect are both literally "reading from the same page." Becoming familiar with this preagreement checklist can alert you to issues and problem areas that may come up in your relationship. Discussing these items with any potential architects can help you make a final decision about whether this is the firm you want to design your building.

AIA forms have regulated transactions within the construction industry since 1888 and have provided an important service by establishing standards to guide business transactions. The institute's publications constitute a coordinated system that spells out the legal relationships among owners, architects, contractors, subcontractors, and others. Since AIA documents have been around for so long, they have usually been tested in the courts, and legal interpretations have been amassed.[4] If your parent institution or its lawyers have a question about a provision, there is a whole body of literature available for review. Because the AIA documents will serve to clarify the roles and relationships of all of the parties involved in your construction project, they should be part of your professional reading (even though most are far less lucid than the pamphlet previously cited).

Other organizations in the construction industry like the Engineers' Joint Contract Documents Committee also publish contract forms, and some of them are more likely to be protective of the owner. It may be in your library's interest for you to familiarize yourself with the different available forms because the competition among industry associations may work in your favor. The Associated General Contractors and the Construction Management Association of America are yet additional sources of standard documents.[5] You will quickly find yourself overwhelmed by unfamiliar terminology, but you will at least be able to talk intelligently with your library's legal counsel about expectations of your architects. If you believe that your library has insufficient access to legal assistance, be wary of highly customized contracts since they must be scrutinized very carefully.

Cyburbia, an interesting Web site sponsored by the State University of New York at Buffalo School of Architecture and Planning, is a directory of about 7,000 links to sites about planning, architecture, and related professions. In addition, it includes information about 130 architecture and planning-related mailing lists. Checking this site from time to time will familiarize you with many architectural issues and, in some ways even more important, with the perspectives of architects themselves.[6]

Architect Contract

Before much more time passes, find out about B141, the Owner-Architect Agreement, otherwise known as the architect's contract recommended by AIA. You should at least browse through *The Architect's Handbook of Professional Practice,* which contains very useful explanatory material entitled "B141 Commentary."[7]

You might also take a look at the *Annotated B141,* which is a provision-by-provision discussion of the Owner-Architect Agreement.[8] It explains the purpose of key provisions and provides a series of "practice pointers" intended to guide architects. In addition, it includes a number of liability alerts regarding the dangers that can arise from making changes in the standard document.

Another AIA publication, *Compromise Contract Language Alternatives,* illustrates a series of hypothetical owner-suggested modifications to the document and comments on the problems these create for both the architect and the owner.[9] Possible alternative compromise language is suggested. Of course, you will discover that many of these modifications in the contract serve to protect the owner and increase the architect's responsibility. If being forewarned is forearmed, then this is the publication for you.

Does it really matter, you may ask, what is included in the architect's contract? Most emphatically yes, and the most important part may not be what you actually read in the contract. Since much of it consists of references to other sources, documents outside the body of the written contract may make all the difference in holding architects responsible for their mistakes. The phrase "attached hereto and made a part hereof" can mean much to the success or failure of your project. The terms of whatever documents are referenced are just as binding as the terms and conditions in the body of the contract. Even if the document referenced is not physically attached, it is probably a binding part of the agreement. Not only inexperienced owners but professional contractors with many years experience may overlook these potential land mines. The specifics relating to a particular project are often quite brief, simply naming the parties; the name and location of the project; and the terms of the price, payment, and schedule. Referenced items, on the other hand, are often so numerous that few people are willing to spend the time looking each up separately to be sure the references mean what readers think those items mean.

TALE

Due to a budget freeze on travel, my enrollment in an excellent seminar on building project planning was delayed by a year. When I finally got to take it, I learned about the elements of a standard architect's contract on such projects as mine. My own campus folks, despite having several other projects under their belts, never bothered to share with me just what I did and did not have a right to expect from the architect under terms of his contract with the campus. That might have saved some confusion and misunderstanding and also might have given me more info and confidence as the project got underway. Taking the seminar in time might also have schooled me in what kinds of questions to ask to save me some time and effort. . . . We saved the taxpayers several hundred dollars by not sending me that first year. But then . . . we spent the same amount next year—a year too late.

Architect Liability

Let us assume that due to the architects' error some dreadful problem arises, jeopardizing the success of your building project. Are your architects responsible? Can you sue them? Though it pains a librarian to be as equivocal as a lawyer, the answer is unfortunately "maybe yes and maybe no." If architects fail to exercise reasonable care in the performance of their duties, they can be held liable to persons who are injured as a result of their failure. These persons can include the contractor, the owner, and any others involved in the project who as a result of the architects' acts or omissions on a project have incurred financial losses.

This does not mean, however, that architects are automatically liable if something goes wrong. As long as they can demonstrate that they have exercised reasonable care, it is extremely difficult to hold architects responsible for many problems. The courts have interpreted this obligation as nothing more than exercising the ordinary skill and competence expected of members of the profession. The owner is merely purchasing the architects' services, not insurance that everything will be done correctly. Nevertheless, architects have usually been held liable for obvious carelessness or other situations in which it is fairly clear that they "should have known better."

In complicated legal battles, architects sometimes succeed in avoiding liability by providing experts who will testify that they did, in fact, exercise reasonable care under the circumstances. In such cases, the owner or contractor will have to prove by a preponderance of evidence provided by their own expert-witness testimony that the architect did not exercise reasonable care. With more traditional project delivery systems, much time and energy is often spent passing blame back and forth between architect and contractor. One of the reasons many people feel positively toward the recent growth of the design-build industry (discussed later in this chapter) is that it brings the architect and contractor under one umbrella. Although this is a new development and case law is inconclusive, there has been a tendency to hold the architect to the higher standard required of the contractor.

TIP

Measure, remeasure, and remeasure! Don't take an architect's word on anything.

THE WORLD OF CONTRACTORS

As you've probably already noticed in the Tips and Tales sections, librarians often spend their work lives at war with architects. Rarely does the atmosphere become any cozier than that of an armed cease-fire. Contractors, however, seem to escape much of our venom. I used to think the basis of the conflict with architects was sexism since librarianship is a female-dominated profession and architects were usually men. However, in recent years, more and more women are becoming architects, and yet I see no movement toward reconciliation.

Recently, however, I have adopted a new hypothesis (probably no sounder than the old one). We usually begin our relationship with our architects when we are filled with excitement and enthusiasm. The architects appear to share that enthusiasm and weave verbal visions of the ideal library. It is probably inevitable that we blame the architects when the fluffy pink clouds part and we behold our less-than-perfect library building. On the other hand, we usually begin our relationship with the contractor at a low point. He or she probably does not want us to set foot on site and throws a first-class temper tantrum if we forget our hard hat or step in the wrong spot. The contractor makes us feel like naughty children, and we complain that this is *our* building.

As the project progresses, we gradually get used to one another. We discover that we're more welcome if we heap praise on the contractor's latest efforts. Since we really are delighted to see the building take shape before our eyes, the atmosphere starts to thaw. At about the same time, however, we begin noticing little problems. The cabinets we were promised in the processing area have disappeared from the plans. The contractor has a more recent set of blueprints, and somehow the conference room has shrunk by four feet. This means the custom-built conference table that's already been ordered no longer fits. "That's just like an architect," the sympathetic contractor assures you. Contractors have had years to hone their resentment of architects (in fact, the two professions have probably been at odds with one another since the building of the pyramids), and you're more than willing to join the lynch mob. As the project progresses, you encounter more and more unpleasant surprises, most of which have to do with the design of the building, and your most understanding confidante is inevitably your contractor. Of course, the contractor is creating his or her share of problems, but it will probably be months or even years before you discover them.

Choosing a Contractor

Depending on your own unique library environment and the individuals involved in the building project, you may or may not be consulted in the selection of a general contractor. In some organizations, it may be considered none of your business and will be handled entirely through a purchasing or facilities department that sends out requests for proposals (RFPs) and selects the low bidder. Nevertheless, a few words of caution are in order in hopes that you can use your influence to avoid potential catastrophes.

Large institutions and governmental units have usually had experience with other building projects and know the ropes. Small public and college libraries, however, may not have access to this kind of expertise. Board members may imagine that they can select a library contractor in much the way they chose one when they built their own homes. This is not the case. To begin with, libraries are large, sophisticated, and expensive buildings. Any contractor under consideration must have had experience constructing other buildings at least as large and expensive as yours—preferably larger and more complicated. Of course, every building project is different and requires a new approach, but you do not want to be an experiment or a practice exercise for your contractor. You want someone who's already a pro.

Be sure that you consider only large, stable firms. Although Board Member Smith's brother-in-law may be in construction, this is not the place for a small businessperson. Be sure that decision makers have extensive bank references before signing any contract. One of the worst things that could possibly happen is to have your contractor go bankrupt before the project is completed.

In addition to these words of warning, be sure that your project team is considering only contractors who are licensed in your state. Insist on documentary evidence of this status. Find out how long the contractor has been in business, and avoid any contractor who moves often or who hasn't been in the area long enough to provide local references. It is a good idea to call previous customers and request references, but request a list of *all* recent projects (not just the ones the contractor is most proud of). You can also request references from material suppliers and subcontractors. Check into the other types of buildings the contractor has experience with (residential, commercial, etc.) and visit former customers at their building locations. While you're there, find out whether the contractor has kept to the schedule and the contract terms. Ask how problems were resolved on previous jobs and how willing the contractor was to make any necessary corrections.

Then, obtain bids from a number of qualified contractors using an RFP or identical specifications so that you can compare prices accurately. Ask the contractors for recommendations and references from banks and insurance companies, and review those responses carefully. Be suspicious of estimates that are not accompanied by "back-up detail" including the names of sources for materials and subcontractors. You should also be suspicious of estimates based on a printout from a computer program or a boilerplate estimate that was really prepared for someone else's project. Then make sure you have read and understood all terms and conditions. Remember that this is a language unfamiliar to you, so obtain legal advice when necessary.

In addition, here are some other important ways to protect yourself and your project:

Ask for a bid bond that guarantees that the party bidding for the contract will, if the bid is accepted, enter into the contract and furnish performance and payment bonds for carrying out the work. Be sure that the cost of bonds is paid by the contractor and included in the bid.

Check that the contractor is a member of recognized local and preferably national professional organizations.

Insist that the contractor carry worker's compensation and liability insurance coverage. Insurance companies can provide evidence of coverage by issuing a certificate of insurance. They can also notify you in case of policy cancellation.

The Contract for Construction

Contracts and warranties, especially their sticky, tricky little clauses, define the legal obligations of all the participants in a building project. These documents are vitally important when it comes to clarifying who does what and who is responsible to whom. Conflict is an inevitable part of most building projects, and it's best to be fully prepared.

The most important document in any legal dispute, the Contract for Construction, is an agreement between the owner and the general contractor. Often referred to as the general contract, it establishes the rights and obligations of each party. In addition, it provides the framework of the whole project as well as the basis for most courtroom litigation. Insist that the contractor provide a contract bond for the project. This will guarantee the fulfillment of contract obligations. Contracts covered can include both construction and other types of work or services.

GENERAL CONDITIONS   Incorporated within the Contract for Construction are a number of "general conditions." For example, you might insist on a maintenance bond that requires that the contractor redo any unsatisfactory work or replace any materials at his or her own cost within a specified time after completion of the work. Also be sure that any contracts include the time frame in which the work must be completed. Check that contracts include a description of what constitutes substantial commencement of work and a notice that failure to substantially commence work within twenty days from the specified date without lawful excuse constitutes a violation of the contract. Be certain that the schedule of payments showing the amount of each payment is included and that any down payment does not exceed 10 percent of the contract price. To help keep track of payments, consider engaging a funding-control service (also called builder's construction-control, fund-disbursement, or cost-disbursement service).

Although some of these conditions and bonds will be explained in full, most will simply make reference to American Institute of Architects *Document A201*.[10] It is extremely important to have a copy of this publication handy and since you work in a library, it should not pose a problem. *A201* includes many of the specific requirements that define the obligations of the owner and the contractor. If you are in a law library or have relatively easy access to one, investigate the *AIA Citator Service*. At least you should know that it exists because if and when a conflict arises, it is the best source of information on the ways in which specific clauses found in AIA documents have been construed by the courts.

SPECIAL CONDITIONS   In addition to "general conditions," the Contract for Construction contains several "special conditions." These may address any topic related to the project. For the most part, they concern technical requirements, and naturally they tend to be the most difficult to understand and the most important. Most of the plans and specifications pertaining to the project are not actually physically included within the contract. (They're too big and bulky.) However, they are referred to throughout the document. Of course, this means they are very easy to miss because you probably don't have all these materials on hand. Check the general contract's "incorporation clause" carefully to clarify which additional documents may affect your rights and obligations.

WARRANTY CLAUSE   This is one of the sections that should be read very, very carefully. When most of us see the word *warranty* we tend to relax, believing that it guarantees all the work done on the project for a specified period of time. Unfortunately, this is not really true. What it usually says is that the owner must notify the contractor of any nonconforming work within one year of substantial completion to trigger the contractor's obligation to make repairs without additional cost to the owner. The contractor is legally liable, in most instances, at any time within the applicable statute of limitations for negligent, nonconforming, or defective construction or for cost overruns. Some librarians believe that the warranty clause is nothing more than a wordy attempt to weasel out of this obligation.

As is clear from the section on hiring a contractor, bonds and warranties are usually quite narrowly defined. If the basement leaks six months after you move into the new building, you need to know who will pay for it. How long is the contractor obligated to fix things? Most contractors provide a warranty or guarantee, but what's included varies with the individual contractor. In most cases, the fine print will have you tearing your hair out. It is inevitable that there will be situations that are not covered, but try to get the most inclusive language possible. Request specific wording that lists only what is *not* covered and includes a clear statement that everything else comes under the warranty. Discuss these issues as early as possible, preferably before the construction contract has been awarded.

PERFORMANCE AND PAYMENT BONDS　The contractor is usually required to provide performance and payment bonds as part of the Contract for Construction. A performance bond is a separate contract that promises the owner that the work will be performed either by the original contractor or a substitute contractor. Also require a payment bond if it is not included in the performance bond. Often referred to as a labor-and-materials bond, it guarantees that bills for subcontractors' labor and vendors' materials used in the work project will be paid. A surety company issues the bonds, and it is in that company's interests that the contractor meet its obligations. The contractor may be more likely to listen to the surety company than to the owner or the architect. Insist that an insurance or surety company stand behind the bond if the contractor fails to perform.

ARBITRATION　In case of a dispute between owner and contractor, arbitration is the usual method of resolving conflict. Therefore, most construction contracts contain an arbitration clause. Either the actual clause will be included within the contract or it will be incorporated by a reference such as "Paragraph 4.5 of A201." References to standard AIA documents have the advantage of being widely accepted and therefore reasonably open and aboveboard. However, you should know what you are getting into, so at least make sure you have A201 on hand. If it is incorporated by reference into the arbitration clause, you are usually agreeing to arbitrate any dispute arising out of the contract by submitting the dispute to binding arbitration conducted in conformity with the Construction Industry Rules of the American Arbitration Association.

The American Arbitration Association (AAA) sets the rules for the arbitration process. You can obtain a copy of the rules from an AAA office, which can be found in most major cities. Cases are categorized by the amount of money in dispute. If the amount is under $50,000, your case qualifies for fast track procedures. Next comes the regular track, and for very large amounts there is a large complex track. A fee ranging from $500 to $7,000 is paid to the AAA at the time the demand for arbitration is filed.

THE DESIGN-BUILD DELIVERY SYSTEM

One of the big changes in the building industry in recent years is the emergence of the design-build project delivery option. Although it is currently the subject of many books and articles in the building trade, the term "design-build" is only gradually appearing in library literature. If you will have a role in contracting for the design and construction of your building, you should be aware of the advantages and disadvantages of design-build. It is also important to have a grasp of the basics if you will be working with a design-build firm on a day-to-day basis.

Traditionally the owner hires an architect or engineer to design the facility and produce plans to send to several contractors for competitive bidding. When an owner chooses the design-build option, the same corporate entity both designs and constructs the facility. The designer and contractor are, in a sense, partners representing the same firm. They may both actually work for the same firm or they may be from two or more companies working together as a joint venture. Still another configuration involves one of the firms serving as the prime contractor and the others as subcontractors. No matter what the specific arrangement, the owner contracts with only one entity that will be responsible for both designing and constructing the facility. This provides the library with greater fiscal control of the project—an important point when safeguarding taxpayers' money.

An excellent example of the design-build approach is the experience of the Harold Washington Library Center in Chicago. The dramatic new building was the creation of the SEBUS group, an acronym taken from the names of the four major team members involved in the project. (Schal Associates was the construction services firm involved. A. Epstein and Sons International was an engineering/architecture firm that provided the engineering expertise, but another group of architects, Hammond Beeby and Babka, was primarily responsible for the design of the building. The final team member was the developer U.S. Equities Realty, Inc.) Working together in a joint venture, they guaranteed to provide the 765,000-square-foot building for $144 million. The group was chosen from a field of five contenders in a hotly contested design-build competition.

It was unusual at the time for a large public building project to use a design-build process in conjunction with a developer. Public controversy had for years surrounded the project, largely because the state of Illinois had built two major buildings that came in far over budget and way behind schedule. The city of Chicago had a credibility problem in convincing the public that it could deliver the library on time and within budget. The competition enabled the city to require that the library be completed within the $144 million budget. Only the design-build option could provide this kind of certainty because the city would be dealing with one vendor and one price. In addition, Chicago needed a mechanism to allow public input and remove the potential for political influence from the decision-making process. During the competition 30,000 people visited a display of the five proposals, and 8,000 of them provided written comments to the jury. The competition process also finalized major design decisions at the beginning of the project.

Although the 10-story building (with its 9,200-square-foot skylighted Winter Garden, its circulating collection of more than 2 million books, and its seating capacity of 2,337, not including the 400-seat auditorium and classrooms) is not your average library, it incorporates a lot of the issues involved in choosing the design-build approach. The design-build process is also a frequent choice with small homeowners, so size really should not be a factor in your decision. Since design-build is the fastest growing method of delivering a building in both the United States and in Europe, you probably have design-builders in your area.

Advantages of Design-Build

It is becoming obvious that a great many owners believe there are significant advantages to choosing this option compared with more traditional project delivery methods. Among these advantages is a normally shortened project delivery time. Furthermore, the planning phase need not be complete before construction begins, and there is no waiting for contractor bids to be submitted. In addition, the last months of the design phase can overlap the first months of the construction phase, saving both time and money.

Fixing Responsibility with a Single Vendor

Another big advantage of the design-build system is a single point of responsibility. In traditional construction, architect and contractor spend a great deal of time pointing fingers at one another, blaming each other for every problem that arises. Warranties may not be honored and protracted litigation may become necessary to fix responsibility. The design-builder, on the other hand, takes full responsibility for the outcome of the project.

In chapter 1 you read about the defective floor installation that resulted in a large hole in front of the circulation desk. Litigation went on for years while architect and contractor argued the seemingly arcane question of whether the architect had provided every page of an instruction booklet needed to install the flooring material properly. When the designer and builder are the same entity, that entity is responsible for everything. As a rule, architects do not guarantee the outcome of their work but agree only to exercise reasonable care. In other words, they promise not to make any really stupid mistakes. With the combined system, the design of the building is usually subsumed within the designer-builder's warranty. This is usually a big advantage, although as will become evident later, the owner must be ever vigilant.

In traditional construction projects, the contractor is ordinarily entitled to additional compensation if he or she must deal with errors, omissions, or ambiguities in the architect's plans. In other words, with traditional construction models, the contractor stands to make money when the architect makes mistakes. Since the design-build model unites designer and builder into the same entity, that entity must assume full responsibility for its work. However, change orders that arise from the owner's wishes still cost money, unless it can be established that the change is needed to rectify an error.

Design-build agreements allow performance warranties to be much more comprehensive. Again, this is possible because it is so much easier to fix responsibility for problems. However, even in design-build projects, the performance warranty will generally have exclusions in areas for which the owner is responsible. Designer-builders often take on more responsibilities than traditional contractors, sometimes providing turnkey services. This means that certain responsibilities that the owner normally assumes may be included within the design-build contract.

Improved Communication between Architects and Contractors

When architect and contractor work for different companies, they have few opportunities to meet with one another. If your building is being planned and built by two or more traditional firms, you are going to have to assume some responsibility for communication or risk major misunderstandings. Of course, the whole point of plans and specifications is to communicate the design concepts, but specifications can't transfer expertise from one professional to another. With design-build projects, expertise can be better shared. A single organization allows for improved communication and continuity between designer and builder. The adversarial approach to the project, frequently encountered among building professionals, can also result in mistakes and added expense. In theory, at least, everyone on a design-build project is working toward the same goals and is part of the team.

Of course, you know very well that communication, even among your library staff, is not necessarily improved by working under the same roof, so a unified organizational structure does not guarantee good communication. With all the new technologies involved in a library, architect, engineer, and contractor should all be knowledgeable about the entire range of materials, equipment, and systems processes that will be incorporated into the new building.

Disadvantages of the Design-Build Model

Unfortunately, attractive as it may be, there is a downside to the design-build option. Although many libraries have good experiences to recount, you do lose some of the safeguards associated with multiple vendors. For example, you lose the system of checks and balances that is characteristic of traditional construction. In the past, the architect or engineer, to some extent, played the role of watchdog, helping to ensure that the facility was built as designed. Designers, at least in theory, owed their loyalties to the owner. Since designer and contractor were not members of the same team, they were to some extent adversaries and might be willing to blow the whistle on one another when they discovered irregularities.

Because the architect and contractor are part of the same corporate organization in design-build agreements, the old assumptions may no longer be valid. For example, the design professionals or architects are not *your* consultants; they are on the contractor's team. Considering the strong negative feelings librarians often have about architects, this may not seem important, but usually the owner has a right to see the architect as an advocate or a partner when it comes to conflict with the contractor. Association with the contractor may cause architects to place such factors as cost and ease of construction over other criteria that you consider important. Although it is always a good idea to hire someone specifically assigned to the job of watchdog, this becomes absolutely essential when dealing with a design-build firm. (See the section on watchdogs later in this chapter.)

You and the others on the project team may also be provided with less information than would otherwise be the case. You will no longer have access to the sort of candid appraisals that an independent architect can provide. Problems may be glossed over or hidden. (However, the outside consultant or watchdog is really a better solution anyway since even in traditional construction, architects may have their own agendas.) Less information can result in less control, but it is possible to specify the kinds of information and the degree of detail that the designer-builder must provide to the owner.

Another disadvantage of this system is that it is difficult to select a design-build firm through competitive bidding. A company must be chosen at the beginning of the project when little information is available about cost. With traditional projects, the architect's fee is firm, and construction RFPs do not go out until the building has been designed. That way, contractors know what they

TIP

People who get into the facilities and construction business do not do so because they have great communications skills.

are bidding on. When the services of architect and contractor are lumped together, separate bids are no longer possible. (It is possible, however, to specify that subcontractors be chosen through competitive bidding.)

Because the usual bidding process may be eliminated, the library must be extremely clear about its requirements. You will need to work with facilities experts to determine how large a building can reasonably be built with the funds available. Be specific about your most important technical requirements, such as electrical load and data capability or sophisticated environmental controls for a special collection, but leave some room for negotiation. You don't want to find yourself burdened with a designer-builder who, after having been selected for the project, tells you that the proposed building does not provide for the library's most important needs.

Contract Considerations

Using the design-build system may have legal repercussions. It may be that your state or municipality has laws that severely restrict the use of designer-builders. Furthermore, licensing restrictions for design professionals and contractors may limit the permissible types of design-build structures. Insurance and bonding may also be more complicated to arrange. This situation is changing rapidly, however, as the delivery system becomes ever more popular.

Special care must be taken with the design-build contract so that the owner gets more protection rather than less. Standard contracts favor the designer-builder, and many provisions may be intended to transfer liability from the designer-builder to the owner when construction in accordance with the plans does not achieve the results intended.

You will want contract provisions to resemble the standard AIA Contract for Construction. Architects are usually held responsible only for exercising a reasonable degree of skill or care, and they do not normally warrant or guarantee a successful outcome for services. The case is totally different for the contractor, who *does* warrant that the result of his or her services will be a successful project. In other words, the designer-builder should assume the traditional obligations of the contractor, not those of the architect.

If you are entering into a design-build agreement, be extra careful, in reading over the provisions, that the standard of care is not changed by contractual agreement. The phrase "appropriate levels of skill and care" should set off alarm bells because it is an attempt to hold both architect and contractor to the standard that normally applies to architects only. Instead of gaining greater accountability from the architect, you would be losing the level of accountability that has come to be expected of the contractor. Tread carefully. This is certainly a matter that should be discussed with a lawyer, but it might also be helpful to add a reference to the A201 warranty clause when negotiating the contract.

Your lawyer should go over the contract carefully and probably propose substitutes for a number of its provisions. If at all possible, use the services of a lawyer who is familiar with the design-build system and who can craft sections clarifying the parties' rights and remedies to reflect your institution's assumptions and understandings about the project. Boilerplate provisions might work with traditional construction, but they are not adequate for this new environment. Although the design-build option may provide additional protection for the owner, it is quite a new development, and the courts have not really established clear guidelines.

Who's the Boss?

Another potential disadvantage of the design-build system is the possible confusion about who is in charge of the work. Who is the prime contact with the owner, and who is serving in the role of subcontractor? This may not be an issue if the two are really one entity. However, all sorts of business arrangements such as joint ventures and limited liability companies complicate the problem. If you've ever felt like a Ping Pong ball being batted back and forth between an architect and a contractor who are blaming each other for a problem, you'll see that working with them as one entity has some real advantages. The majority of court cases have held that a designer-builder is more nearly like a contractor than like an architect or other design professional. Thus the same warranty standards may apply to the architect's work as to contractors. It definitely appears that the architect can be held to a stricter standard in a design-build agreement than when there is a separate contract for architectural services.

Additional Snags

There are also potential licensing, insurance, and bonding problems when dealing with design-build firms. The insurance carried by architects and other design professionals ordinarily excludes construction services, and contractors' general liability policies exclude professional services. This could create a sticky wicket if it becomes necessary to make any claims. General liability policies also have little or no deductible, whereas professional liability policies have large deductibles. Surety bonds create similar problems. Be sure that someone in your organization checks into the matter of adequate and appropriate insurance and bonding if you are considering a design-build firm. These are problems that can be fairly easily solved, but the time to solve such issues is before you're irrevocably committed.

CHOOSING A BUILDING TEAM FOR RENOVATION OR REMODELING

If you are about to embark upon a renovation project, the decision was probably made for any or all of the following reasons:

- inadequate space
- inflexible interior design
- outdated electrical and phone systems
- inadequate accessibility for people with special needs
- inability to develop the collections and services you need

In addition, you may be forced to renovate instead of building because of political, fiscal, or historical reasons. You may have hoped to start fresh with a whole new building, but funds were not available. Possibly, your county or city presently lacks the tax base to fund major new construction. Because of its historical or architectural importance, your institution or local government may also have a commitment to your existing library building. You will be seeking ways to improve access, create additional space, and accommodate new technology while at the same time preserving what is most valuable in the old building. How will you bring the library into the twenty-first century and still preserve the flavor of the past?

If your project is a renovation rather than all new construction, be sure the builder has experience in this area. A contractor should be accustomed to working when there are other people such as staff and visitors on the premises. Keeping the two operations—renovation and the library's ongoing services—separate and on track requires a great deal of planning and organization. Such skills are not learned easily. If the contractor has never had to consider how routine activities will continue side by side with construction, you probably don't want to be the one to educate him or her.

When you ask for a contractor's references, be sure that other projects similar to your own are included. Talk to the references who had to work while their building was being renovated or remodeled. Ask how cooperative the contractor was and how much advance warning staff were given when an area had to be vacated. You might even ask for specific examples of how disruption was avoided. If you have the opportunity to interview contractors who are being considered, ask what techniques they have developed for minimizing noise and debris.

In many ways, planning for renovation and remodeling is not so very different from planning a new building, so most of the recommendations contained in this book will be relevant. You will be defining future needs, anticipating growth, and considering how technology will affect library services in the future. However, working with an existing structure adds new challenges. For example, modifications of a historic building may be subject to review and oversight by federal or local historical commissions.

You may find that you will need a more diverse team of building professionals if historic preservation is an issue with your building. For example, you may need an architect who understands how older buildings were constructed and what should be preserved. The National Park Service publishes an extensive collection of guidelines and documents on preservation, rehabilitation, and restoration of historic buildings. If you are contemplating rehabilitation and expansion of a historic building, you should become familiar with what's happening in the field. In a guide to library restoration and expansion published by the Illinois Historic Preservation Agency, Lonn Frye writes: "With each project, architects learn new techniques and easier ways of integrating historic preservation and contemporary design." [11]

HIRING A WATCHDOG

One of the best ways to ensure that you get what you pay for is to hire a watchdog or construction inspector to keep an eye on your project. Larger academic institutions and governmental units usually have some office or department for overseeing building projects. However, such departments frequently lack the time and expertise to effectively look after your building while it is under construction. Although this can be a very sensitive subject, use your persuasive skill (and tact) to obtain the services of a qualified building inspector. The inspector can

- ensure that the building is in compliance with regulations
- prevent unnecessary and expensive change orders

- ensure that the building is safe from hazards
- ensure that the building can pass state and federal inspections
- prepare samples for laboratory testing
- interpret blueprints and specifications
- maintain a construction and inspection log
- measure distances and verify accuracy of structural layouts

Watchdogs come in a variety of shapes and sizes. In some areas they're known as quantity surveyors or building/construction economists. Among their many roles, they estimate and monitor construction costs and serve as consultants to the property owner. Some of them are faculty members who teach in the building and construction disciplines. In addition, some work for financial institutions, with developers, or as project managers. Watchdogs, whatever their name, use their knowledge of construction methods and costs to advise the owner on the most economical way of achieving the construction requirements. Some of them are trained in cost planning, estimating, and cost analysis.

In recent years, the concept of a commissioning agent has taken hold, especially in professional real estate. *Commissioning* may be defined as "a process that ensures that a building conforms to the original intent of the owner." The commissioning agent can be involved in the early design phases; through installation and start-up; and during the installation of lighting systems, HVAC systems and controls, elevators, and structural elements. The commissioning agent represents the owner throughout the planning and construction period, seeking to ensure that design objectives are met, that all systems are functional, and that all equipment is installed properly. Seeing that all needed support documentation is available is another important role.

Buildings have become so much more complicated in recent years that most building professionals may lack the breadth to understand the project as a whole. For example, advancements in technology, improved materials, new methods, and other factors have meant that integration and coordination of the project may be lacking. This integration is an important role of the watchdog, quantity surveyor, or commissioning agent. New materials, such as extra-strong concrete and superplasticizers, make it possible to build flatter floors and smaller columns for greater available floor space. In steel construction, the old standard of 36,000 pounds per square inch (psi) has now been replaced with 50,000 psi, meaning that buildings require less steel. This can mean a savings of thousands of dollars in construction materials and labor costs if your building professionals are well-informed. If they're not, it's up to your own expert to bring such matters to their attention.

TIPS AND TALES

For any building project, you need to have what we call a quantity surveyor on site all the time. A quantity surveyor is usually someone trained as an architect and/or engineer who acts as a building inspector for the client and checks to make sure everything is built as designed, according to the plans, before the work is signed off. This can result in saving several thousands of dollars of work.

The first recommendation I have is to find a project manager who is able and willing to do the work and give him/her the authority to get the job done. Many a project has run into problems when folks decide to manage it with a committee.

Another issue is construction management. If you are talking a project over $15–20 million, which most libraries would be, then you're going to have a mob at the door wanting to manage the project and save money.

If you have a fast-track project or multiple prime contractors, then you need a firm specializing in construction management to help you out. Get them in place early. These folks do as much or more in the design process as they do in managing the contractor.

We contracted with our architect to place someone on site for the entire construction phase. This allows me to have expert technical advice immediately while getting much faster response on submittals, RFPs, and other questions.

Choose one person as the main contact with contractors and subcontractors. Our contact would call me to answer a question someone else had asked. I had no idea what he was talking about, and he would tell me one thing and give someone the exact opposite answer. It got very confusing.

KEEPING YOUR PROJECT ON TRACK

As plans change from day to day, you may lose track of how the new design will affect the library's function. As you solve one problem, you may be creating another. Thus, you will need some way of measuring each round of changes against a set of basic requirements. As the building evolves, it becomes increasingly complex. You will need a procedure for regularly reviewing plans to be sure that the features you've requested are still present and located in appropriate places.

Checklist of Basic Requirements

At the end of the preliminary information you provide to the architect, add a checklist of basic requirements. Although the items on the checklist will be more specific and concrete than the other information, they should, as much as possible, proceed from the information you have already provided. If the architect understands why you want data cabling in the stack areas or a sight line to the video equipment, such considerations are much more likely to appear in the floor plans.

Over time, the checklist may become very long, but it is essential that you continue to check it again and again. New players appear on stage almost daily, and your concerns may not be communicated to later arrivals such as subcontractors. Eventually, however, your checklist will probably not be adequate to meet your burgeoning needs.

The Contractor's Schedule

If this is your first building project, you will discover that it is all unbelievably complicated. There are literally thousands of tasks that must be accomplished, thousands of items to be ordered, and thousands of decisions to be made. All these elements must be integrated into a very structured, rigid schedule. In many instances one subcontractor cannot begin work until another has finished. The electrical contractor, for example, cannot install wiring until after the framing for the partitions is in place but must complete most of the work before the plasterboard installers arrive.

Your contractor's project schedule may be the most essential element in your project plan. Not only is it important for scheduling your actual move but it will give you an idea of which decisions must be made first. The project schedule allows you to plan ahead and avoid those high-stress moments such as when the contractor tells you he needs a decision on locks for all the doors in the building immediately.

Be sure you get a copy every time the schedule is revised. The final schedule may be very different from the one initially proposed. Such a schedule is long and elaborate. Occasionally, you may encounter a contractor who has only a vague idea of what will be happening when. The resulting project schedule is incomplete, and it is clear that the contractor has not thought through the sequence of events very carefully. This is an indication that you are dealing with the type who "flies by the seat of his pants" or who is not accustomed to working on large projects. By the time you discover this, the papers have been signed, and there is little you can do. It will probably be difficult to pin the contractor down without alienating him or her, but do your best. Remain enthusiastic and supportive, but ask lots of questions. Then create your own schedule based on your contractor's responses, and go over it with him or her. It may serve to jog your contractor's memory to check that the plumbers are planning to arrive at the right time or that the electricians will be free when needed.

The Library's Project Schedule

In addition, you'll need to make yourself a separate internal library-project schedule. Such a project schedule is a list of the tasks that must be accomplished, the length of time each task will take, and the order in which they must be completed. You will need to break down your preparations into small definable units that can be given probable beginning and end dates as well as absolute deadlines so you and the staff will know where you are on your project—what activities are on track, what is running behind, and what lies ahead.

The business world has given us some excellent ways of dealing with such complexity, but you don't have to become an expert in any of these systems. Lots of excellent computer software is available to create the most complex plans, and most are quite easy to use. The best known is probably Microsoft Project. Most of the larger construction companies use project software to stay on schedule. If this is the case with your contractor, you might ask for periodic printouts of the project schedule. If your library and your general contractor use compatible software, you might ask instead for a disk containing a copy of the project file.

Preserving the Paper Trail

Yours may be one of those lucky projects that moves along steadily to completion with few detours along the way. Just because there is a flurry of interest in a building project, however, your new building or addition may not be just around the corner. Legislators and board members change. Fiscal conservatives may gain the upper hand. Even after plans are drawn and land is purchased, your new building can be put on hold indefinitely.

Multiyear delays can mean a succession of library directors and architects who know little about the planning that took place before their arrival. Gradually, information can disappear, and changes can get lost or not be recorded.

Plumbers may end up working with outdated blueprints that show incorrect restroom locations, and the millwork subcontractor may be sizing a circulation desk for a space that's been cut in half.

Begin collecting information about the project, whether it's your own research, minutes of meetings you attend, consultants' reports, or notes taken during conferences with the architects. Label materials as carefully as possible, and file everything away. Imagine the years passing. A new architect is hired; your own memory dims. You've put a lot of hard work into the project, and it could all go down the drain unless you can bring the new team members up to speed.

Once the project is back online, continue to collect materials. Libraries are repositories of information. You as a librarian are an information specialist, an expert on collecting and organizing resources. While your building is under construction, vast quantities of written instructions, wiring diagrams, blueprints, service manuals, and installation guides are floating about. Copy *every* single one of them, and file the copies in a safe place. Obviously, this is a lot easier when you're on the premises, as is the case with a remodeling project or a new addition.

Ask to photocopy any brochures or installation instructions that accompany construction materials. Copy guarantees and warranty information. This is especially important with heating and cooling machinery and other high-tech equipment that changes often and will soon be out of production. When systems break down, as they inevitably will, information about model numbers, replacement parts, and liability will all be vital. If such materials tend to get lost at the job site, you may want to routinely request them from manufacturers.

Implementing these procedures may be a true test of your relationship with your architects and contractors. However difficult it may be, be sure you make it clear that you simply want to do what librarians do best—preserve vital information. Explain that you are not trying to check up on your building professionals, and you have no plans to do anything with the materials you collect except to file them away. They will object loudly the first time you remove a sheaf of papers from their office or the construction site, but if you're back in ten minutes, they will come to accept you as a harmless lunatic. The first time they themselves lose a manual or booklet and discover they can come to you for a copy, your relationship will improve considerably.

Don't depend on some other department in your organization to retain this kind of information or to pass it down through the years. Whether you rely on the maintenance staff of your city, county, or academic institution to monitor and service the equipment, you're talking about positions that have an extraordinarily high turnover rate. The physical plant supervisors will take their expertise with them when they move on to other jobs.

One of the most helpful things you can do is see to it that each new generation of workers involved with maintaining equipment is provided with copies of the printed instructions. Never, however, lend your only copy—within hours the information may be trodden underfoot or smeared with a gooey black lubricant.

This chapter has emphasized the preparations that will be needed for the journey ahead. You have a long way to travel, so your preparations must be extensive. A building project should never be begun casually. It will take up most of your time for several years and may have a profound impact upon your career. You now know whom you will be dealing with and the sort of interactions you can expect. Even more important, you now have an idea where you fit into the process and the kind of unique expertise you can provide. Recognizing the contributions that only you can make to the project will give you confidence to express your ideas freely. It should not, however, encourage you to be bossy or opinionated, telling other professionals how to do their jobs.

NOTES

1. Thomas Fisher, "Lost in Chicago," *Progressive Architecture* 75, no. 6 (June 1994): 92.

2. Wendell Wickerham, "Designing and Building Leading Edge Libraries" (paper presented at the 9th annual conference of the Association of College and Research Libraries, Detroit, 8–11 April 1999). Available online at www.ala.org.acrl/pdfpapers99.html.

3. American Institute of Architects, *You and Your Architect* (New York: The Institute.) Available online at http://www.e-architect.com/consumer/yarch.asp and at http:// www.aiapvc.org/yourarch.htm.

4. Werner Sabo, *A Legal Guide to AIA Documents: A101 Owner-General Contractor Agreement, A201 General Conditions, B141 Owner-Architect Agreement, C141 Architect-Consultant Agreement* (New York: Wiley, 1988). With annual supplements.

5. See resources for addresses and telephone numbers.

6. State University of New York at Buffalo School of Architecture and Planning Cyburbia Website available at http://cyburbia.ap.buffalo.edu/pairc/.

7. David Haviland, ed., *The Architects' Handbook of Professional Practice* (Washington, D.C.: American Institute of Architects, 1995).

8. American Institute of Architects, *Annotated B141: Standard Form of Agreement between Owner and Architect with Standard Form of Architects' Services* (Washington, D.C.: The Institute, 1997).

9. American Institute of Architects, *Compromise Contract Language Alternatives* (Washington, D.C.: The Institute, 1997).

10. American Institute of Architects, *Document A201-1997* (Washington, D.C.: The Institute, 1997).

11. Lonn Frye, *Older Library Buildings: Special Building and Design Problems* (Springfield, Ill.: Illinois Historical Preservation Agency, Oct. 1999). Available online at http://www.uic.edu/~build1.htm.

Resources

American Institute of Architects
1735 New York Ave. NW
Washington, DC 20006
(202) 626-7300

Associated General Contractors
333 John Carlyle St., Ste. 200
Alexandria, VA 22314
(703) 548-3118
fax: (703) 548-3119
e-mail: info@agc.org

Construction Management Association of America
7918 Jones Branch Dr., #540
McLean, VA 22102-3307
(703) 356-2622
fax: (703) 356-6388

Engineers' Joint Contract Documents Committee
The American Institute of Architects
1735 New York Ave. NW
Washington, DC 20006-5292

3 Before Design Begins

By now you've established the procedures, working relationships, and lines of communication that will see you through the project; therefore, it's time to begin planning your new or renovated building. If all is going well, you're beginning to have an idea of what lies ahead. You've been introduced to your architects and, hopefully, you've had time for a few heart-to-heart chats. You now have some idea of how much money buys how many square feet of library space, but those numbers will change as plans evolve. The new library will probably expand and contract in concept several times before the first brick is laid. Whatever its eventual size and shape, the completed building must be able to function as a well-designed, technically sophisticated library that meets the needs of its users.

This will be a very busy time for you, and you're going to feel as if you're juggling dozens of decisions with too little information and too many conflicting opinions. You'll need plenty of information on recent library trends and a clear idea of how far you can stretch the definition of a library. The new building must serve future needs as well, so you'll also have to become a fortune teller or at least an informed amateur who can predict probable future directions. You can anticipate both good and bad times ahead, so the new building must be designed to weather years of low budgets and even civic neglect.

Once you have a clear idea of how the new library will function under these diverse conditions, you're *almost* ready to begin thinking about bricks and mortar—the physical details of your particular building. Little can be done, however, until a site is chosen. The site will affect the size of the building, the location of the windows, and many equally vital considerations. If, on the other hand, your library will be sharing facilities with other units, such as with a recreation center or county offices, the site must accommodate other functions and other priorities. In that case, you'll have to adjust your plans to include a number of new considerations. No matter how extensive the project, space needs must always be determined early in any planning process.

However, not all projects begin with a new site and a new building. If you're renovating or remodeling an existing structure, you'll need to add still more complex matters to your list, for example, asbestos removal or coping with a structure that was not designed for use as a library. If all this sounds daunting, take comfort that your new or renovated building is on its way to becoming a reality. It's all starting to happen, and you have a front row seat.

FOCUSING ON RECENT LIBRARY TRENDS

Have you seen any vaulted reading rooms lately? Probably not, unless you're still coping with an old Carnegie building. Today's patrons seek out private places to read and study. If you watch your patrons selecting a study carrel or table, notice how they try to keep their distance from one another. We need not be antisocial to want a little privacy in the library. Most of us try to avoid directly facing another patron, and we seek out nooks where we can feel we have a space to ourselves. This, of course, presents a conundrum for librarians who worry about the safety of their patrons and of their materials. However, we are not about to return to the Carnegies or the big open boxes of the '60s and '70s, so we must find ways of creating individual areas that are both safe and enticing. Security considerations may make real privacy undesirable, but it is possible to give the appearance of quiet nooks even when they are readily visible. As you plan different spaces for different functions, give some consideration to the way patrons use libraries. For example, with computers working their way into so many library spaces, consider whether you need some "click-free" zones far from the clatter of computer keyboards.

Collaborative Study

If you're like most librarians, you're so aware of changes linked to automation that you may have overlooked other recent developments. Have you thought about collaborative learning, for instance? Whether you are building a public, academic, or other type of library building, recent educational and management theory stresses working together in teams, and naturally, teams need spaces where they can get together. Have you planned group spaces in which five to ten people can get together to discuss a project? Have you planned spaces for one-on-one literacy training or GED tutoring?

Be sure that you provide informal spaces for people to meet and talk with one another as well. This social function of a library is one we rarely consider, but it is an important one nonetheless. No matter whether you're talking about a public, school, or academic library, each is a community center. Students profit from studying together, and community groups can combine their research and their deliberations. Computers, too, encourage collaboration and so should be included in the planning of group spaces. A modern library should

accommodate an increase in collaboration between individuals

support learning as a social enterprise

be a primary meeting ground for a campus with a large nonresident population

Media Integration

Another recent development has been the gradual disappearance of the lines separating different media. This merging of media makes separate, specialized areas where one can listen to audiotapes or watch a video all but obsolete. Even media equipment tends to be multifunctional. This means that service points should also be multifunctional for "one-stop shopping." This increasingly tiresome phrase when applied to a library means that patrons should never be sent from desk to desk. There's little reason to locate the microform desk and collection on the second floor when the audiovisual department is housed in the basement. Combining service desks is also a cost-cutting measure that for many libraries is becoming a necessity. Can you integrate different types of media in the same area so that patrons are able to access them without running from floor to floor?

Service Consolidation

If the old model of separate and specialized departments is firmly entrenched in your present library, consider how you can make the transition to the new model as painless as possible. Not only do patrons profit from consolidating or clustering services but you may be able to keep more services available during evening and weekend hours when staffing is at low ebb. Such integration may create problems if staff, who must serve as trainers, are unfamiliar with different types of equipment. Increasingly, librarians are becoming jacks of all trades, and your new library may hasten the trend toward consolidating services. Be sure your staff is ready for it.

As you've already discovered, your staff is doing a lot of computer training as well. It's no longer possible to teach patrons to use reference sources without assisting them to use the computer equipment needed to access those sources. How can you organize and position your staff in such a way that they can provide needed help wherever computers are available?

Planning for Change

Libraries are changing rapidly, so leave your options open. Build as much flexibility as possible into your floor plan. For example, stay away from built-in desks that may have to be relocated in the future. Small rooms with load-bearing walls will also stand in the way of change, as will walls shaped to fit around a piece of furniture. Think of all those card catalogs that were recessed into a wall. Task lighting also inhibits change. Lighting installed for one purpose will be useless when you begin moving things around. Also avoid permanent partitions since it will be important to be able to reconfigure spaces as the need arises.

Changes in the delivery of information in modern libraries affect every aspect of the planning process. For example, how much use are you getting out of your expensive, specially designed index tables? With the advent of computerized indexing and abstracting services, the use of printed indexes is dropping rapidly. Depending on the library and the particular indexes, many can probably be shelved in the reference stacks. The money you might have spent on index tables will buy some nice, standard (hence, less expensive) computer furniture and equipment.

Study carrels should also be chosen with future computer purchases in mind. The type of carrel with a shelf above the work surface may not accommodate tomorrow's computer equipment or even today's large monitors. In fact, you might compare product catalogs to find out whether you pay a premium for units designated as library study carrels as opposed to office workstations. Analyze differences both in cost and in functionality before making your selections.

Avoid low ceilings if you can. Some day you may need to use ceiling space for electrical and data lines. Low ceilings also make it difficult to light an area effectively or to install hanging signs. Make sure your architect understands that there must be room to expand electrical and telecommunications conduits. It's often impossible to tell where you are going to want to hook up a computer or some other piece of equipment. If the past few years are any indicator, some of your stack areas will probably be redesigned to accommodate computer workstations. Be sure data cabling and power outlets are sufficient for this purpose. And speaking of equipment, stay away from the bleeding edge. Make sure anything you purchase has been proven reliable in a library setting.

TIPS AND TALES

Every library needs a well-defined delivery area with a door wide enough to move large pieces of furniture through it.

Halls and doorways, all types of passageways, need to be wide enough. No bad corners. All sorts of book trucks and other "hauling mechanisms" must be used to get books, furniture, and other equipment from place to place.

Our biggest problem is not enough space (we think) to do all we wish. Size is driven by a strict budget.

Round buildings don't use square footage wisely. They also make for lots of funny-shaped rooms that don't work well.

PLANNING FOR THE FUTURE

What does the future hold for your library? All kinds of social institutions are changing rapidly, but libraries are going through an especially rapid metamorphosis. Since we don't really know what next year will bring, how can we possibly plan a library that will continue to serve our public's needs for the next fifty years?

As you work with your board, boss, or committee, you will discover that the media has convinced some of these people that the book is dead. Will Manley, in his article "Clean, Well-lighted Stacks," writes that several years ago he interviewed a famous architect about a library building project. The architect challenged Manley to be innovative and daring. It turned out that the architect's view of the "millennium-three library" had no books at all. Instead, the architect exclaimed, "We can create an ambiance of reflection and research by stressing the concept of books rather than the books themselves."[1] Of course this view is a bit extreme, but you are bound to encounter some who believe that libraries no longer need to spend money housing books since all information of importance will soon be converted to an electronic format. In fact, some believe that the library need not accommodate large numbers of users because most will soon be able to access the library electronically.

On the other hand, you may be working with a computer-phobic administrator or board member who thinks money spent on technology is wasted: "All this computer stuff is just a flash in the pan and takes precious dollars away from the book budget." Unfortunately, there's rarely enough money available to satisfy everyone, and arguments can become heated. Ideally, yours should be the sweet voice of reason advocating compromise, but you will probably find this to be one of the most treacherous shoals of dissension you are forced to navigate.

We have a task ahead of us that's fraught with peril, but a little crystal-ball gazing is possible. Will the digital library totally eliminate the need for printed materials? Most authorities believe it's best to assume that the book collection will continue to grow, though possibly at a slower rate. The book is a wonderfully successful technology in and of itself, and although futurists may predict its demise, there is nothing currently on the technological horizon to replace it.

Printed journals are another matter altogether. The brief length of most journal articles coupled with the computer's aptitude for searching vast quantities of text give electronic formats a very definite edge over their print counterparts. Full-text services like ProQuest and IAC Searchbank are proving to be enormously successful in libraries, and the time will come when infrequently used print subscriptions are routinely canceled in favor of online access. Legal materials are also appearing in electronic formats, and users applaud the powerful search engines that can pinpoint relevant information where they once searched weighty volume after weighty volume.

How will all this affect the design of a new library? No one can be sure of the future, but here are some suggestions. Don't assume major changes in print production in the near future, but take some intelligent precautions. Be sure your building can handle a much higher power load than is presently needed. Install electrical outlets and data connections at frequent intervals throughout the stacks. Imagine what would happen if you took down the stacks in an area and substituted computer-equipped carrels. When you begin economizing, try not to make power and data-line cuts until the bitter end.

One maxim upon which everyone agrees is that you will need more computers more quickly than you anticipate. One new library after another has found that it underestimated the speed of change and the demand for computers. For example, the new Scholarly Communication Center at Rutgers, which is a part of the Alexander Library, included one unfinished area that was eventually intended to be used for additional stacks and offices. Instead, it quickly became necessary to spend $3 million to convert the area into a computer and media center including a one hundred-seat auditorium, a hands-on classroom, and the Humanities and Social Science Data Center. Both the auditorium and the hands-on room were designed for video conferencing and distance learning. As another example, Emory University's Center for Library and Information Resources has been designed to include a Computing Resource Services Center, the Beck Center for Electronic Collections and Services, the Faculty Information Technology Center, Multimedia Communications, electronic classrooms, and group study rooms.

TALE

After running over budget and time, we ended up with a building with no capacity for further expansion, no way of ever rearranging any electronic or electric component.

Harold Hawkins, in his article on "The Uncertain Future of High School Library Design," cautions that "there appears to be less need for expansion of square footage within the library" since, increasingly, the library is no longer the only repository of academic resources. He also concludes that

there will be a continued need for print collections

the humanities will continue to need print materials

science and technology are more dependent upon electronic resources

high school libraries will become more decentralized since electronic libraries can be accessible throughout the building from individual workstations

the learning process is becoming increasingly based on collaborative experiences, thus requiring spaces for group discussion

libraries can expect continued funding for technology

the look of the library will not change radically, but librarians should plan for a gradual decrease in table seating space and an increase in computer workstations[2]

Listen to Users

Libraries are what our users want us to be. Amid the uncertainty and confusion we're feeling about the future, we are gradually coming to realize that we must listen to our users when they tell us what they want. Of course, there must be limits, and we cannot be all things to all people, but be sure you listen with a receptive ear. When you find yourself defensively muttering something like "This is a library, not a computer lab" or "This is a library, not a community center," think a moment. Your users probably already see you in that role or the issue wouldn't have come up. One of the librarians quoted in several Tips sections was asked to accommodate a Kinko's copy service. In the 22,000-square-foot building he was planning, it would have taken precious space from more important library functions. However, in my present 300,000-square-foot library, there's plenty of room for a copy center, and we love having one close at hand.

This brings up the whole issue of balancing practical needs with patron preferences. Patrons like a comfortable, relaxed environment, and food in the library poses a problem. Older, more traditional libraries are steadily losing support, and we are all actively seeking ways of making our libraries more relevant to the public of the twenty-first century. We can readily see from the enormous popularity of bookstores with coffee bars that people enjoy sipping a latte, drinking a Coke, or even munching on a sandwich as they read. In fact, new libraries around the country are being built to accommodate some sort of eating facility. We all know perfectly well that patrons will want to take their coffee with them to the stacks or OPAC computers, and then what do we do? It's a puzzlement that we're all facing.

Look Beyond Traditional Service

Conference and meeting room facilities are also important. You may ask, "Why should we be the one to provide them?" When you're short on space, there may be some justification for a negative response. However, meeting spaces make the library an integral part of your community, even if the people they attract do not normally use the library for other reasons. As Anya Breitenbach, Public Relations Manager for the Denver Public Library, says: "You build this beautiful public landmark and you expect people to be excited about it and drawn to it, but you don't necessarily realize all the ways in which they will want to use it."[3]

There is a lot of evidence to the effect that the "real" users—the ones who check out library materials and spend time in the reading rooms—are a fairly small percentage of the taxpaying public or student body. If, however, you add the people who come in just to use your copy machine, check their e-mail, or type a letter on the library computers, you may be serving far more people than your funding agency realizes.

As I write these words, I feel rebellion growing in the back of my brain. Don't we librarians think of ourselves as being above the role of social director or computer technician? We also think of our book-toting users as very special people— the intellectual elite. Isn't it those people we're there to serve, not the hoi polloi who use our meeting rooms? If the little voice in the back of your brain is uttering similar complaints, you'd better remind it that this "elite" segment of the population or college community is shrinking. It is no longer large enough to win a referendum unaided or create a sufficiently large groundswell of enthusiasm among your faculty and administrators. The library of the future needs friends! Although you cannot possibly have something for everyone, you had best expand your definition of users to include these Philistines at your gates.

Make Peace with the Monumental Majority

Somewhere along the way, you will discover that you must find a way for your proposed library to coexist peacefully with its alter ego, the symbolic library. We live in a world in which most respected institutions have revealed feet of clay. The Presidency, the Congress, the medical establishment, and many other once-revered symbols of rectitude and respectability have fallen from their pedestals. For better or worse, the library has not succumbed to this fate.

Even though many people have not read a book in years, they revere the principles on which libraries are built—or at least the principles on which they think libraries are built. The library, they vaguely believe, is a noble institution glowing with the light of learning. The library represents lofty, learned ideals for many, and such ideals should be enshrined in an equally noble edifice. City council members think that a stately library improves the tone of their municipality. Theirs is no hick town; it's a classy community because it boasts a magnificent monument to learning. River City and Hemlock Falls can hold up their figurative heads proudly, and residents who've never seen the inside of the library can burst with civic self-importance when they view its exterior.

Naturally, architects have a field day with such attitudes. They compete with one another to design the most pretentious, dysfunctional structures imaginable. University presidents are afflicted with a similar malady that I call the "hallowed halls of learning" syndrome. They lean toward oak paneled board rooms in which their portraits can most effectively be displayed. But enough already! Enough snobbish sarcasm! These are our publics, and we must find a way to work with them. It may even be in our own interest to create an eye-catching library that says to the world "Libraries are important, and they're not going away anytime soon."

PLANNING FOR HARD TIMES

Amid the hubbub of enthusiasm that accompanies the planning of a new library, it is hard to remember that libraries are experiencing difficult times. If you've been in the profession for any length of time, you can probably remember grim periods when you held your breath through a series of staff cuts, when you endured a moratorium on book purchases, or when you were forced to cancel periodicals subscriptions. Even though there are always financial constraints, a building project induces an artificial atmosphere of plenty. You find yourself dealing daily with staggering sums of money, hardware and furniture selections that cost the moon. Discussions with professionals may lead you to look on these expenses as mere trifles.

Even library giants have inadequate budgets. A look at the much-hyped San Francisco Public Library will serve as a reminder of what the real world holds for libraries. During the planning and construction phases, Director Ken Dowlin was the envy of librarians throughout the country. Corporate sponsors gave generously to the project, and the building that emerged was a masterpiece of design. Rich materials adorned every surface, and both library and architectural journals were enraptured by the opulence.

The problem was that the near-astronomical construction budget was not reflected in the library's operating budget. When the new library opened its doors, the public flocked to enjoy its many attractions, but there was no budget to support the many new or expanded services required. Staffing had been based on a projected 5,000 visitors daily, but the day after opening, the number jumped to 9,000. Moving the existing collection also required many additional staff hours, as did setting up and configuring the mountains of state-of-the-art equipment. Long lines became common at the checkout desk, and for a period of time it took more than a month for books to be returned to the shelves.

As you may recall, the ultimate firing of Ken Dowlin was a cause célèbre in the library world for quite some time. While the issues were far more complicated than the ones outlined here, it is not unusual for a library director to come down to earth with a bang after a construction project. Once the fairy godmother has waved her magic wand and sent Cinderella to the ball, she tends to disappear, leaving Cinder-librarian to cope with the everyday world of budget cuts and unexpected crises.

San Francisco is not the only new library building that has experienced unexpected and unprecedented public acceptance. San Antonio found that its bright red building was so popular that it had to schedule daily docent tours. In Denver during the first nine months after the new library was opened, 45,000 people signed up to use its meeting rooms. Of course, initial activity eventually levels off, but the moral of the story is that you will never return to the kind of usage you are now experiencing in your older building.

When planning for hard times it is critical that you plan for efficient staffing. As mentioned earlier in the section on educating the architect, library staffs are small and getting smaller, while new electronic resources take an ever larger bite out of the budget. It is important to design a library that can be staffed safely and efficiently by the smallest possible number of people. For example, arrange stacks and work areas so that staff can use their time more efficiently, and centralize light panels, security monitors, and other equipment so that the building can be opened, closed, and monitored by the fewest people. If times change and your budget zooms skyward, bask in your affluence and enjoy! However, it's still best to be prepared for more than one episode of belt-tightening.

Wherever possible, spend money now to save money later. Planning to get the most for your money at this early stage will reap rewards down the line. For example, choose

> workhorse equipment known for low maintenance
>
> the best carpeting you can afford with the longest wear guarantee
>
> energy-efficient systems that reduce the cost of heating, cooling, and lighting

(Each of these considerations is discussed in detail later in this book.)

Although it may sound contradictory, it's important to think big. Generous funding comes only to those who ask for it. Go ahead and design a library that will support exciting new programs and services. You might even plan for luxuries, but be sure you can do without them. Don't leave yourself out on a limb with higher public expectations than you can satisfy.

TIPS AND TALES

Going into the process, make sure you have established priorities that will guide the design and construction. Decide where you will put the emphasis if money runs short. In our case, the priorities I established were collections, staff safety and comfort, and education and event space, then everything else. As our funding has been cut a couple of times since we started, this prioritization has helped keep things on track and helped me make consistent decisions that allowed us to stay on time and within budget.

Build it and patrons will come! We have seen an incredible surge in circulation stats, reference stats, and new patron registrations. My staff feels overwhelmed right now.

Plan far ahead and begin building increased staff expenditures into your budget.

As for ongoing expenses, a new, expanded library will probably cost more than you estimated. Just small expenses such as snow removal and lawn mowing become (in comparison) gigantic.

SELECTING A SITE

Before blueprints can be developed the site must be selected for the proposed library. If you have the opportunity to participate in the selection of a site for the new library, you should feel blessed. Site selection is often a foregone conclusion determined by the availability of a lot that the county doesn't know what to do with or a piece of useless land a citizen or an alumnus has contributed in exchange for a hefty tax deduction. If, however, you are consulted in the matter of site selection, here are some basic considerations:

- size of lot
- real estate costs
- quality of site and configuration

Main Street façade, Queens Borough Public Library, Flushing, New York

- security (see the following section)
- traffic flow (ingress and egress) and traffic controls
- visibility
- proximity to automobile pollution
- accessibility
- population demographics
- environmental consequences
- utilities
- zoning
- site conditions such as buried gas tanks or environmental hazards
- adjacent land and the possibility of future expansion

You might want to assign a point value to each site, depending on the criteria. If one or more criteria are more important than others, the points can be adjusted accordingly. For example, site size can be an important decision factor because larger sites allow more design flexibility including a buffer around the perimeter of the building.

Security Issues

Depending upon your library type and your neighborhood, security may or may not be an important factor in selecting a site. If it does rank high in your priorities, you may wish to break down the elements that contribute to a safe environment. Take a walk around the immediate neighborhoods of sites under consideration. Consider topography, vegetation, adjacent land uses, sight lines, and potential areas for refuge or concealment. Give some consideration to the types and locations of utilities, including their vulnerability to tampering or sabotage. How much emphasis and therefore funding will need to be allocated for security at any given site? What areas will need special attention? What items of equipment and what personnel will be needed to protect vulnerable areas? After a site is selected these observations should be integrated into the design of the building and building site as early as possible. Security planning is much more effective when it is an integral part of the planning exercise rather than tacked on at the end. (See chapter 7 for more information on security and safety.)

A good architect spends almost as much time thinking about what goes on outside the library building as what happens inside. How will automobiles approach the site? How can library pedestrian and vehicle traffic be separated from off-site vehicle areas and pedestrian zones? How can planting beds, berms, fences, and walls best be used as barriers to control access? How can motor vehicle speeds be reduced around the perimeter of the site by the creative use of curves and turns, speed bumps, changes in pavement, narrowing of lanes, and medians?

As security becomes an ever more important issue, keeping track of library visitors becomes essential. The architect must consider how patrons can be confined to designated areas through the installation of high curbs, median strips, planters, fencing, or walls. How can pedestrians, especially children, be kept out of the way of traffic? Crime has become so prevalent that it is not paranoid to consider drive-by attacks, which might necessitate obscuring sightlines from surrounding roadways.

Will the site include a parking lot? If the answer is yes, will the library be located in an area where parking is at a premium and your lot will attract people working in nearby offices and shops? Will there be a separate area reserved for staff parking? Creating and maintaining a parking facility may require the use of static barriers like bollards, planters, and walls as well as operable barriers like sliding gates, pop-up bollards, crash beams, booms, and even those nefarious tire shredders.

Will you require a safe enclosed place to park bookmobiles and other library vehicles? Will you need a separate staff entrance? Is deterring vandalism an important consideration? If so, you may need a wall or fence that discourages climbing. Such a wall may require a special coating that facilitates the removal of paint and graffiti.

Will you need to screen an especially expensive computer lab or multimedia facility from view from the outside? A wall, fence, or plant screen may be needed. Other security barriers can include berms, plantings, ditches, bollards, or natural topographic separations.

Underground Sites

In an effort to find space for a new library or addition where none exists, architects occasionally go underground. For example, they may excavate half a dozen subterranean levels under an existing library. Another strategy is to dig into a hillside so that part of the library is above ground and part surrounded by earth. Occasionally, an all-new library is built from scratch below ground. One example of such a library is the Carl A. Kroch Library at Cornell University in Ithaca, New York. It was constructed underground so that it could be located near the university's graduate library without ruining the looks of the historic quadrangle where it is located. Of special concern in planning was the fact that the new building would house a large collection of rare books.

Construction of the Kroch Library involved waterproofing the concrete structure in a location with a high water table. Another difficulty that had to be overcome was designing a roof that would support soil and plantings but not cause drainage problems on the steeply sloped site. The above-ground entrance or gateway is the adjacent Stimson Hall, a structure that may be converted to library use in the future. A three-story atrium, with mirror-lined skylights, ringed by glazed doors brings sunlight into the structure. A factor that greatly increased construction problems was the existence of bedrock 25 feet below ground level that required blasting.

The Cornell project illustrates many of the difficulties associated with underground construction, although it dealt with them much more successfully than many similar projects. Because underground construction is usually approved due to other traditional buildings occupying the above-ground space, those above-ground buildings will inevitably be affected by the new construction. For example, blasting can and often does endanger nearby foundations.

Water damage poses the greatest danger in an underground building, and for a library, it can mean a major disaster. In the Kroch Library, the drainage system, located under the concrete structure's slab, consists of crushed rock and perforated drainpipe channeled to sump pumps that send water to the sewer system. The library's concrete walls were waterproofed with a heat-weldable reinforced PVC membrane.

In general, underground construction requires the most sophisticated construction techniques available and the most advanced materials to overcome its many inherent problems. Many recent underground structures are widely criticized by their occupants. Special care must be given to lighting, both natural and artificial, or people will feel as if they are in a cave. Roofs that serve the function of a plaza or walkway above ground rapidly deteriorate; therefore, they should be avoided. Imagine a sidewalk with the constant scuffling and crunching of thousands of feet, the weight of service vehicles, or the freezing and thawing that occurs inevitably with the seasons in many areas of the country. No roof is really intended for such abuse, and materials that work equally well underfoot and as components of a roofing system are rare indeed.

It is obvious that the Cornell architects and engineers have carefully considered the problems in waterproofing this subterranean building and have devised a creative and highly functional solution. One wonders, however, what the future will hold for this library. All construction materials break down over time. How will the PVC membrane be repaired? Will the sump pumps be reliable? (A recent disaster in the basement of my own library makes me skeptical.) Cornell is a prestigious and relatively affluent university. Suppose this were a small private college or public library where budget cuts are frequent and deferred maintenance is common in hard times—would an underground building fare as well under these circumstances?

Weigh carefully the pros and cons of underground construction before taking that approach. Such a building poses a much greater architectural and engineering challenge than a traditional structure. Can your project afford the nationally known engineers Cornell employed? Do the decision makers on your project really understand the danger to the foundations of nearby buildings?

If you were to survey a large group of librarians, most would complain of damp basements, and most would be reluctant to shelve valuable materials below ground. While it is true that modern, sophisticated engineering practices can eliminate such problems, consider carefully the realities of your own local situation. Given what you know about other construction projects on your campus or in your city, can you afford to take a chance on such sophisticated, cutting-edge construction?

Differing Site Conditions

It is important that contracts with design professionals and contractors make it clear that they are responsible for performing preconstruction site investigations and for disclosing information about existing site conditions. The term "differing site conditions" covers occurrences or events that would not reasonably be anticipated by the parties involved in the construction process. These are frequently subsurface physical conditions, such as a ledge, unsuitable soil materials, or flowing water. Such unexpected conditions can considerably increase the labor and materials costs of construction without adding to the value of the project. A serious problem with the site could bring about major cost overruns and result in cuts in budgets for furniture, equipment, and other necessities.

If the worst happens, someone must be responsible for the added expense. Common law has tended to hold the contractor to his or her obligations when a job is more time consuming or costly than had been anticipated—except in the case of differing site conditions. Such problems are more often the responsibility of the architect or engineer, but their contracts frequently protect them from liability. If you are using a design-build firm, the joint organization can be held responsible. Otherwise, be sure that design professionals are clearly held responsible in your contracts and that they are sufficiently financially stable to absorb these costs. Be certain that the language in your contracts makes it clear who is responsible in the event that any of the following errors or omissions occur:

- failure to undertake adequate preconstruction investigations or surveys of existing site conditions
- failure to describe existing site conditions accurately or completely in bid and contract documents
- negligence in the drafting of bid or contract documents with regard to the circumstances under which a contractor will be entitled to relief because of differing site conditions
- failure to resolve contractor and design professionals' differing site conditions claims

If you have any particular reason to anticipate a problem, you might recommend that a geotechnical engineer be brought in for expert advice. In fact, negotiations should clarify responsibility for furnishing any required geotechnical engineering or survey services. Prior to signing contracts, all of the building professionals should be encouraged to visit the site to become familiar with the site conditions.

SHARING A FACILITY

The idea of a building complex designed to meet a variety of community needs has become popular in many areas. Although academic libraries may be required to share their facilities with academic departments or classrooms, the demands on those areas are not markedly different from those on the library. For public libraries, the issue of shared facilities may be more complicated. For example, the West Des Moines Civic Campus was built after the "great flood" of 1993 left the city administration homeless. An older plan was resurrected that called for a joint civic campus that would include a police station, elementary and high schools, library, municipal pool, recreation fields, and city and school administration center. The planned complex included a building of 51,000 square feet that was divided into a 31,000-square-foot library, a 14,000-square-foot city administration center, and a 6,000-square-foot "commons" space.

Joint use of a facility may be made necessary because of a crisis like that in Des Moines or because of the need to achieve greater economy by combining two or more projects into one. A shared facility can make it possible for a library to obtain funding for construction when funding might otherwise be impossible to raise. Although such marriages of convenience must be approached with care, they do not necessarily mean an adversarial relationship. When these partnerships work well, they allow you to combine forces and share the burden of maintaining a building. If the administrators of the other facility are team players, you will have the advantage of their experience and influence.

A congenial partnering of two or more complementary facilities can also allow you to enjoy economies of scale not possible when building just a library or just a recreation center. Site costs as well as architect and contractor fees may be reduced. The Des Moines project gives residents a library they might otherwise have waited years for. Phase I provides space for 140,000 items (well over the size of their collection at the time of construction), while Phase II will hold 220,000 items. In return, the library staffs an information desk that directs traffic to and from five city departments, collects city bills and payments, and provides training on the OPACs. The building has the advantage of close integration with other similar facilities. For example, fiber optic cables connect the library with the community schools' learning resource center next door.

Cost savings is usually one of the major reasons why the multiuse model is so popular, but you will probably find that your funding agency expects far greater savings than can realistically be achieved. For example, a new library project may be tottering on the brink of approval when some community leader speaks up and says something like, "Why don't we spend a little more and build an athletic complex as well?" Your community leaders will soon discover that such a facility involves major capital expenditures. When the discovery is made that the shared facility will cost far more than anticipated, conflicts invariably arise.

Of course, some librarians have become adept at playing the same game. When that athletic complex is under consideration, librarians may be the ones who pop up with the suggestion that the funding agency spend a little more and include a new library or library addition. If you or your board chairperson is good at this sort of political strategizing, go for it, but don't delude yourself into believing that two facilities can really be built almost as cheaply as one.

Joint facilities may pose unique problems. For example, the library and the swimming pool may be housed within the same complex and may have to share the same ventilation system. Noisy adolescents may have to walk through the library to reach the pool, or shared walls may force library patrons to endure sound from the pool.

What can be even more devastating than the physical inconveniences that result from such strange bedfellows are their political ramifications. If you share a facility, you share planning and decision-making responsibility. Some librarians have found themselves pitted against assertive, politically astute athletic directors or recreation supervisors who virtually take control of the entire project. If this happens, the library may be deprived of funding for even basic needs while the competing activity wallows in luxury. This is, of course, an exaggeration, but it reflects the way battle-scarred librarians may feel after such a project.

Advance planning is a strategy for dealing with any number of difficulties, but it can be especially important with shared facilities. Such planning involves educating decision makers to library needs long before the bickering begins. When a facility is shared, the number of players multiplies, and so do the politics. This makes it even more important to attract politically astute friends for the library. It also means reassessing your own political skills. Some librarians find that they are the ones best able to defend their projects from the onslaughts of rapacious fellow tenants. Others discover it works best to stay somewhat in the background, providing ammunition while their politically experienced board chairperson engages in any necessary infighting.

IDENTIFYING SPACE NEEDS

While different sites are still under consideration, you should also be considering the spaces that make up the new library building. Although the architects have a much better idea of how large a structure can be built with available funds, the way the space will be used can affect site selection, and likewise, the site can affect the way space is organized. As you visit libraries, you'll quickly discover that some new buildings boasting a generous number of square feet of floor space seem cramped and crowded. Others that are actually smaller in their dimensions feel as if they have more available space. Still others feature long, narrow corridors that make it nearly impossible to find a study room or restroom. The way the space is planned makes all the difference in the way your users interact with the library building. Form should follow function, but you'll discover many architects for whom that phrase means little. For example, they may design the exterior of the building first and then chop up the interior space into oddly shaped rooms.

In many libraries you may find yourself wasting a lot of time and effort just trying to find your way around. Even though the signage system may be well designed, the room arrangement is counterintuitive. Therefore, it is important to identify space needs during the planning process. The following sections focus on the space requirements of the overall building and on various internal spaces of the library.

TIPS

Archives are different from other areas of the library and have special needs. Do you need a sink? Do you need long open counters? How are researchers going to access your collections?

For archives, this is the time to plan to have room for your flat files!

Allow enough room for patrons to comfortably browse current periodicals. This is usually a high-traffic area, and patrons usually need time to stand or sit while paging through their favorite titles.

Optimal Floor Size

If you think about the last time you got lost in a Wal-Mart, you'll realize that there is a limit to how large a space a customer can comfortably traverse. In a Wal-Mart or a large supermarket, however, you can push your cart through the store aisle by aisle. It is not possible to approach library resources in this efficient manner. If you were to follow most patrons as they make use of the library, you would realize that they cover a considerable distance, trudging back and forth as they identify the materials they need. First they will probably stop at the OPAC, then zigzag among several stack areas, and then maybe return to the OPAC. Later, they may seek out the media center or the periodicals department with a detour to the reference desk or restroom. For many people, especially the elderly, this can be an exhausting experience. If they are also carrying a stack of books or lugging around twenty pounds of bound periodical volumes trying to find a copy machine, the experience is not one they will want to repeat.

Most public library areas should not exceed 50,000 square feet on one floor. Beyond this size, staff are unable to direct patrons to the resources they are seeking, signage is too distant to be useful, and both patrons and staff exhaust their energy trotting from place to place. When more space is needed, multiple floors are one solution. Patrons can move from floor to floor by elevator without becoming footsore. Many different levels, however, present security problems since a floor to which no staff members are assigned is potentially dangerous. For a period of time, academic institutions were building "tower" libraries with ten or twenty stack levels ascending high above the campus. This layout can be extremely dangerous, isolating solitary patrons and staff members who cannot call out for help and must defend themselves unassisted from theft, assault, or unwanted advances.

Circulation desk, Carmel Mountain Branch Library, San Diego, California

So what is the answer to this "Catch 22" conundrum? How do you design a large library that doesn't either endanger or exhaust your patrons? One way is to attempt to anticipate your patrons' needs and cluster functions that relate to one another. Another is to adopt the hub or spoke design of many airports with a service desk at the center of the hub. If you have staff available, you might design a series of small hubs, each with a service desk and each relating efficiently to other hubs nearby. Increasingly, however, service desks in libraries are being eliminated because of tightening budgets. Your plan should not be overly optimistic about the number of hubs you can effectively service.

As you may recall from your history classes, ancient Greek architecture was in part built around the axiom (or golden mean) that the perfect proportion for a space is a ratio of 2 to 3. With two thousand years' experience under our belt, we recognize that the Greeks did indeed know what they were talking about. The most functional and aesthetically pleasing rooms are half again as long as they are wide. This formula usually meets the most sophisticated modern needs.

Although it may seem unnecessary to point out, a room should also have four walls and four right-angled corners with opposite walls parallel to one another. When you see the first floor plans for your new building, bear this truth in mind. If your architects have designed a round or curvy building, rooms will be fitted in at odd angles. Not only will room shapes not be governed by the golden mean, but they may not even have four walls. Instead they may consist of odd angles and multiple small walls that jog out into the room wasting huge amounts of space. Remember that triangles, trapezoids, pentagons, or hexagons do not work as efficient room shapes. Any circular room wastes nearly as much space as it provides, and fitting furniture into it can be especially challenging.

The shapes and sizes of rooms are issues on which you and your architects must come to a satisfactory agreement. You can certainly be sensitive to their concerns about an ugly "boxy" building. You share their desire to create a beautiful structure—but not at the cost of functionality. A few oddly shaped spaces needed to accommodate an impressive design feature are probably okay, but be sure bizarre geometry does not become a habit. Be certain your architects understand your views before they begin preliminary sketches. Then, check each room space on the plans to be sure it is rectangular, has roughly 2-to-3 proportions, and has no funny little extra walls. If you discover a problem, begin ringing alarm bells early enough so that a major redesign is still possible.

TALES

The three-shelf book counters at the ref desk are too small for most ref books to stand upright, so almost everything sits on edge.

We have a retaining wall in the middle of the reference counter. (It was not on the blueprints.) The contractor neglected to tell us about it during actual construction, and we didn't see it until after the desk area was permanently fixed.

Service Desks

Early in the planning process, you'll want to decide how many service points you will need and where they will be located. Then consider each in turn. After you tentatively position a service desk, ask yourself if users will be able to see it from a distance or will it be obscured by structural elements? Is it located in a logical place near the resources and equipment that patrons will be using? For example, the reference desk should naturally be near the reference collection and the circulation desk near the main exit. If you are planning to have a separate information desk, it should greet your patrons as they walk in the front door so that they waste as little time finding their way around as possible. Consider traffic patterns and avoid service locations that are too far off the beaten track to serve their function effectively.

Stack Areas

Even with the advent of electronic resources, shelving for the collection still occupies more space than any other function. It is therefore vitally important to design a layout that will satisfy the requirements of both staff and library patrons. Gone are the days of those dark, ugly closed stacks that used to be wedged into buildings two levels per floor with most of their light dependent upon slippery glass floors and accessible only by dangerous spiral stairways. Even though most of those horrors are gone forever, many newer library stack areas are almost as inconvenient.

As you discuss stack areas with architects, consider the impact of shelving heights on visual control of public areas. Also consider the impact of those heights and of compact shelving (see chapter 8) on lighting, and remember how difficult it is to see the call numbers on the bottom shelf. Think about the kinds of users who will be seeking materials and the difficulty they may experience trying to reach books on the upper shelves.

Be careful that the architects do not assume that the stacks will neither shrink nor grow throughout the building's useful life since some staff and reading areas may eventually be transformed into stack space. Don't let them try to convince you that you need not plan for collection growth since electronic information will soon be replacing books. Although the proportion of your budget spent on print materials may shrink, there is no evidence that collections will cease to grow. You will be making some educated guesses about the growth of both print and media collections, but allow for flexibility in case your crystal ball is faulty.

Even though the architects are probably far more knowledgeable than you about technical requirements, be sure they understand that all stack areas or possible future stack areas must be able to handle a live floor load of at least 150 pounds per square foot. An earlier section described the Sleeping Beauty complex that seems to be rampant among architects. Five or ten years from now, you may find it necessary to install stacks in a space originally used for some other purpose. This means that most library areas must be able to accommodate the weight of fully loaded book stacks. Be sure that your architects do not create a library that is unable to respond to change. Consider too that compact shelving requires a floor with a live load of about 300 pounds per square feet.

TALES

For archives, don't assume anyone knows how wide shelving should be. Draw up your own plan (no matter how crude), and think about where you plan to put things. Then actually give samples of boxes for those areas to the vendor, architect—whomever. They are always surprised at the variety of sizes and shapes.

Start estimating stack dimensions and aisle widths early in the project so you don't find yourself coming up short of space and having to make aisles narrower to accommodate the required number of stack units. Wider aisles are not only needed for ADA compliance but they facilitate browsing and reshelving.

I recently discovered that our rare book room will unfortunately be open stacks. (It was not my idea, but I knew I wouldn't win that battle.) It also won't have the added security of glass or a metal grating. Although I'll be the one to unlock the door and supervise visitors, they will still be able to take books off the shelf.

Restroom Areas

After an architect has sketched out the larger spaces on the floor plan, a lot of small, oddly shaped spaces will remain. Some will be hidden behind other spaces and can be accessed only down long hallways. Others will take their shape from structural bracing or other functional necessities. Some of these spaces will inevitably become the library restrooms. In still another of your many gentle tussles with the architect, make it clear that restrooms must be easily accessible. A larger proportion of your patrons will be using the restrooms than any other resource or service in the library.

First, restrooms must be well-marked and easy to find. For example, most people expect that if they see a men's room, there's probably a women's room nearby. When the two are on opposite sides of the building, you will inevitably have disgruntled patrons. Libraries that decide to cut corners by locating men's rooms on even-numbered floors and women's rooms on the odd ones are even guiltier of wasting their users' time, sending them searching fruitlessly up and down stairs, investigating every possible nook and cranny.

Be certain that restroom quantity and size are determined by probable use; this is almost always higher than anticipated. The availability of small, unused spaces should not determine the presence or absence of restrooms. Because everyone who comes into your library probably spends some time on the main floor, you will need to provide the largest number of stalls and sinks there. Since the second floor is next in terms of heavy use, it should be next in size and quantity of facilities, and so on as floors go higher. At least one men's and one women's room is needed even on the top floor. The principle of separate but equal does not extend to the planning of restrooms. Instead, anatomical needs should play some role in determining the number of stalls in each restroom, which means that women generally require more.

Fortunately, design professionals are familiar with Americans with Disabilities Act (ADA) guidelines for restrooms, but in making these accommodations, they may ignore the needs of the majority of users. For example, restrooms should be equipped with both wheelchair- and walk-up-height mirrors or with extra-long mirrors that meet everyone's needs. (See chapter 5 for additional discussion of ADA accommodations.)

Speaking of mirrors, be kind to your women patrons by providing good light and large mirrors. There is nothing immoral about using the restroom to comb one's hair or apply one's lipstick, but we sometimes treat such common creature concerns with contempt. Women do, indeed, spend more time than men in library restrooms, and so, rather than making snide comments, it is important to make these spaces as pleasant and inviting as possible.

Libraries are not noted for the quality of their custodial services. It is hard enough to obtain adequate funding to maintain a library, and it is only with great reluctance that we part with our precious pennies. We are most unlikely to expend extra money contracting for quality building maintenance. Hence, custodial expenses are almost always kept to a minimum. At the same time, no one likes a dirty restroom.

If you think back, you have formed some very negative impressions of stores, restaurants, and even libraries based entirely on an unpleasant visit to the restroom. Talk with your architect about building in easy-clean maintenance solutions. Floor tile, for example, should have a flat, nonslip surface with no troughs or valleys of light-colored grout. Otherwise, within a few short months,

TIP

Remember how loud newer power-flush commercial toilets are, so locate them away from offices and reading areas. Even high-performance acoustical partitions won't entirely conceal the sound. On the other hand, locate restrooms close enough to high traffic areas so that patrons don't wander around for fifteen minutes trying to find the women's room.

each tile will be framed in dirt that will eventually become petrified into antique dirt, remaining throughout the life of the building. Partitions should be easy to clean and resistant to graffiti. Bright colors work well because too-dark colors show cleaning smears and too-light ones become message boards.

Storage Spaces

On the one hand, no library ever has enough space for storage. On the other, it may be wasteful to dedicate large areas to this purpose since storerooms do nothing but sit there crammed with other things you're not using. You will fill every inch of space you devote to storage, and the more space you have, the more junk you will find to fill the vacuum. Do you remember the libraries of the past that had "dungeons" where mountains of uncataloged books gathered dust over the decades? Computers largely eliminated those huge cataloging backlogs, but now we store antiquated or cannibalized computers in similar spaces.

It's probably best to have a number of small storage spaces located throughout the building where you can store paper and toner for printers or replacement bulbs for microfilm readers near the areas where they will actually be needed. If a space begins to approach the size of an office, you can be quite sure that sooner or later it will, indeed, be used as an office. Therefore, consider such areas multipurpose spaces, and be sure that they have adequate light, ventilation, and heat and air conditioning.

Stairwells

How many times have you walked through an attractive library, entered the stairwell, and found yourself in the most appallingly ugly space imaginable? Although I think I understand why architects create some abominations, I've never quite solved the stairwell mystery. Just think about the stairwells in most modern buildings. Unpainted cinder block walls, cement floors, and gunboat gray metal stairs are hardly designed to please the eye. I've been told several times that stairwells are the way they are because they must function as fire exits. If you're responsible for fire drills and building evacuation, you know that you're supposed to herd patrons out of open areas and into stairwells that are hermetically sealed with metal fire doors. Hence, the materials used in a stairwell must be fire-retardant.

Why, however, must being fire-retardant mean being ugly? Is gray paint somehow more resistant to fire than purple or blue or chartreuse? (Not that I'm advocating chartreuse stairwells, though it might be an improvement.) If you can paint the stairs, is there some reason why you can't paint the cinder block? Even interior decorators, doyens of aesthetic sensibility, seem to be blind to stairwells. Of course, only a limited selection of materials can be used in a stairwell, but then I'm not suggesting fabric wall coverings or broadloom carpeting.

Perhaps the problem arises because other buildings have stairs located out in the open, but that seems to be true only of older edifices with those grand, sweeping staircases. Do architects assume that everyone rides the elevator? Maybe library users are the world's only physically fit people who actually prefer to walk up a flight or two rather than wait for a slow elevator. Whatever the reason, your patrons will be using those ugly stairwells, and if you don't intervene now, those patrons will take away with them a gunboat gray impression of your library.

TIP

Determine before the project even starts what will be stored in an archive area. This should not change and needs to be supported before even beginning.

Even if you are blessed with a caring architect or are able to negotiate a reasonably attractive compromise, you cannot put the stairwell war behind you. Stairwells are a kind of "no man's land." Custodians don't clean stairwells, painters don't paint stairwells, and remodelers don't appear to realize that stairwells exist. For example, each time the library is repainted, you're going to have to remind the painting contractor that the stairwells should be included and will require special equipment to reach some areas.

Display Space

If your library is like most others, your enthusiasm for exhibits and displays waxes and wanes with the seasons. Colorful, attractive displays attract public attention, increase circulation, and enlist your users in causes near and dear to libraries like American Library Week or Banned Books Week. On the other hand, creating successful displays is a very time-consuming activity, and sometimes your staff simply cannot spare the time. All of this needs to be factored into your approach to display space in the new library. You will also want to consider the community's needs. For example, you may want to provide gallery space for local art groups. Ideally, you will want display boards, cases, kiosks, and panels available when either your staff or your users feel inspired, but you don't want to live with that ugly, "undressed" look in between exhibits. Panels that can be folded up and stored in a closet between uses are ideal for displays. Covered bulletin boards (in other words, those that have some material covering the cork) are also good because when the boards are not in use, patrons needn't view the gouged-out holes left by ancient tacks and staples.

I personally have never been a big admirer of glass cases. They tend to be terribly expensive, gather dust, and block traffic. Nice exhibits are prone to theft, and ugly ones seem to stay forever. The glass can crack or shatter, so staff must spend precious time monitoring them to be sure patrons aren't piling on books or children aren't climbing on them. It always makes me nervous when Mr. Jones wants to exhibit his rare collection of Indonesian beetles. I know that we'll lose the key to the case, or Mr. Jones will be irate because we didn't treat his priceless collection with proper respect. Brightly lit display cases are a terrible environment in which to place valuable manuscripts or rare books, so glass cases don't satisfy any real needs of the library.

A detour into my checkered past at this point: several years ago, the chairman of the college art department and I were attempting to place a collection of rather frightening-looking African masks in one of the library's display cases. Since they were of considerable monetary value and belonged to the art department, I had asked the chairman to do the arranging. Seconds after the first mask was set down on a glass shelf, the shelf shattered. It took several hours to obtain a new glass shelf so that we could try again. After sliding the new shelf into the case, we jiggled and rattled it, but it appeared to be firmly anchored. Once again, the mask was lifted from its box and placed on the shelf, and once again the glass shattered. While the masks glowered up at us, we engaged in a mild altercation about whether the case was defective. However, the library had been using it for years with no problems. I don't recall whether we tried still a third time, but eventually, we gave up for the day and the art professor went back to his studio.

I was still sitting on the floor surrounded by boxes and suddenly found myself talking to the masks. They had an extraordinary presence, and even though

I felt foolish, I assured them of my respect and admiration. Continuing to talk to them quietly, I placed each on a shelf in the case. Each time I positioned a mask, I waited. Nothing happened. No loud, explosive sound filled the reading room. Eventually, all the masks were in the case, and I was still talking to them about the library and whatever else came to mind.

When I arrived for work the next morning the masks were just as I'd left them the night before. In fact, I thought they looked more at home in the case. Soon the chairman arrived to make another attempt. Fortunately, he did not suggest that I was losing my mind. We both agreed that there was probably a perfectly logical reason for the events of the day before. My hands were smaller than his, and I had taken more care to place the larger, heavier masks on the bottom shelf. Nevertheless, I formed the habit of talking to the masks whenever I passed by and was sorry to see them taken back to the art department a few months later.

Artistic staff members, library pages, and student assistants can create remarkably professional displays with inexpensive inkjet color printers, colored paper, and poster board. Copy centers can enlarge color and black and white illustrations and photographs and mat them for surprisingly attractive and inexpensive displays. That way, you can feel more comfortable knowing that the library is not responsible for anyone's prized possessions. Original artwork should be displayed only in a well-supervised area since paintings are subject to theft and alterations by too-creative middle school students. In general, lean more toward graphic displays than real art or realia so the library staff won't get trapped into discussions of what is art or what is appropriate for display. Your community may have other needs, however, so this may be an area in which you must remain flexible.

Staff Spaces

Now that you have the opportunity to design your "dream library," consider what it's been like working in your present building. I once worked in a beautiful library that had wall-to-wall carpeting everywhere except in staff areas. Cataloging, acquisitions, and processing staffs all worked on a cold, hard cement floor. You've probably even known libraries where technical services are squeezed into a dark basement. Why should the people who spend the most time in the library enjoy the least comfort? In an environment in which quiet is almost a cliché, why must staff frequently be consigned to areas that are so noisy that it is impossible to concentrate?

In addition, staff are sometimes the last to be considered when ergonomically designed furnishings are being purchased. Given the long hours they spend at their desks, staff can be the first to experience carpal tunnel syndrome as well as eye strain resulting from poor lighting. Paying special attention to staff spaces will not only have a positive impact on morale but will substantially increase the productivity of your staff. Consideration given to acoustic performance, appropriate ergonomics, good lighting, and just plain comfort should be basic to the design of library staff areas.

TALES

In the old building, we could touch each other just by extending an arm. My acquisitions secretary's desk was only about 3 feet from mine. Papers were passed by just reaching across walkways. The new tech services room is more than 66 feet long and at least 30 feet wide. It is spacious and beautiful—all open landscape. Communication modes have changed. Now you have to walk a distance that is beyond normal hearing range. Written notes are used more. During the first few months, people noticed that they were simply worn out from a lot more walking.

Planning is absolutely essential. Invest in a solid planning effort before doing anything else. We used the first three months of our design process to study the way we work as it affects adjacencies and facilities layout. This has proven extremely valuable.

How Much Staff Space?

How much staff space will you really need, and how should it be organized? Although the computerization of libraries is making existing formulas obsolete, some basic guidelines can help you make your decisions. The spaces in which the library staff will work should

> be large enough to allow each employee to do his or her job correctly
>
> permit logical and efficient organization (For example, staff members who must work together should have work spaces within reasonable proximity of one another.)
>
> be flexible enough to respond to changes in functions and to easily accommodate additional employees or evolving tasks

Think of designing staff spaces as a giant jigsaw puzzle. You need to explore the various ways in which the pieces might be fitted together and then choose the most functional arrangement. As you will quickly discover, space, whether for public or staff use, is becoming more and more expensive, and using available space in the most efficient manner must be a high priority. It is sometimes possible to allocate fewer square feet per person while maintaining staff comfort and increasing productivity. To decide on the design that best utilizes available space, consider that staff need access to information, to one another, and to library patrons.

Are there ways that the floor plan can save staff time? Here is an experiment you might like to try: At irregular intervals throughout the day, make the rounds of all areas where staff are working. Are they at their desks? Seated at work tables? Standing at counters? Meeting with one another? Pushing book trucks? Getting supplies? Be sure everyone knows you will be doing this so they won't feel spied upon. Then meet with staff to learn how they would describe their comings and goings. You'll probably find that by combining your observations and their perceptions you will arrive at a more complete picture of staff space needs.

TIPS

Involve staff in designing work spaces! The circulation area is beautiful in our new library, *but* function did not precede form. We are finding that the area is too small and does not have adequate shelving.

Make staff areas large enough, comfortable, and secluded.

We involved staff heavily in the design stage. Dividing into teams of three or four, each team visited three libraries, took pictures, wrote notes about good or bad features, and put these into a report that was shared and discussed by all. We then wrote our building program to submit to our architect on the basis of that report. That was one very good thing we did. All bought into the final product.

Adaptability

Simply by becoming and remaining librarians, we are affirming our belief in the future of libraries. None of us, however, can be quite sure what the future will hold, and most of us are convinced we're in for a bumpy ride. This will mean that we must be able to adjust to change quickly. When new technologies replace older ones, we must be prepared to change as well. The future may require frequent physical relocation of employees to meet changing library needs, and so we must be able to quickly reconfigure communications, computer services, and workstations.

The Intelligent Workplace, a 6,500-square-foot office of the future at Carnegie Mellon University, provides some excellent suggestions for coping with changing needs. It was designed to provide better solutions for improving the health and well-being of office staff members, providing for technological adaptability, encouraging organizational flexibility, and conserving energy. The Intelligent Workplace makes maximum use of natural light, locating all employee workstations within twenty-five feet of a window that has a high daylight transmission capability and a low heat transmission factor. Workstations are also located within thirteen feet of an exterior wall. Louvers on three sides of the building redirect the light and are activated by electric motors and controlled by the facility's central computer. Perforated metal shades control glare but allow employees to enjoy views of the outside. When the light level falls below a certain level, lighting is turned on automatically. Each workstation also has task lighting that turns off automatically when no one is in the area.

Voice and data connections are accommodated with "home runs" (direct connections without intermediate branches) from utility closets to the point of use. This means that wires need not be fished through walls and ceilings from one junction box to another. Hard wiring in the floor plenum (the space beneath the floor surface through which wires can be drawn) connects distribution panels in utility closets to consolidation boxes that can serve up to six workstations. These are positioned on a fixed grid just below the raised floor. Preengineered, "plug and play" wiring can be connected to modular floor outlets. These outlets have preconfigured slots for power, voice, and data connections and can accommodate fiber optic cable. When new wiring configurations are required, no major electrical work is needed. Connections between utility closets and consolidation boxes can be left unchanged.

Individual Differences

Today's emphasis on team projects, team goals, and team meetings may be causing us to forget individual needs. We have moved so far in the direction of a teamwork-focused environment that the need for individual concentration may be overlooked entirely. As you plan staff spaces, it is important to focus on maximizing individual performance by creating an environment in which each staff member can do his or her very best work. Doug Aldrich, vice chairman of the International Facility Management Association, says that "Just putting people together in an interactive setting is not enough. After working with the team, an individual might need to conduct a study or write a report—a task that requires concentration."[4] Another expert, Phyl Smith, who founded the design firm Working Spaces, believes that "productivity, commonly judged as performance, begins with thinking. Thinking plus acting equals performance. Anything that gets in the way of thinking, gets in the way of performance. Because thinking is internal and invisible, analyzing how effectively workers can concentrate is often ignored."[5]

Individual staff members are very different in their ability or inability to screen out distractions. Some people can easily block out nonwork-related stimuli and can concentrate even when surrounded by noise and activity. Others are easily distracted and, when working in the midst of a chaotic environment, find that their attention is too easily redirected away from the work at hand. Good staff members may be anywhere on that continuum, and their needs should be respected. Those who are unable to screen out extraneous activity need special accommodation to maximize their performance. Also, because libraries have traditionally been very quiet work environments, there may be a larger proportion of library staff members who respond negatively to noise and confusion than in other professions. Proximity of coworkers and loud machines may make it difficult for some staff members to concentrate and produce their best work. The inability to concentrate effectively in the work environment can result in increased absenteeism, illness, restlessness, anger, and a tendency to become overtired.

Ask your library staff about their present work conditions. Find out what they like and dislike most about their environment. You'll get a good idea of how sensitive they are to environmental distractions including noise, temperature, and even odors. Don't criticize their responses. Although it's impossible to create a workplace that will please everyone, problems should be taken seriously or else productivity levels (and of course, personal satisfaction) will be affected. Staff members most bothered by external stimuli may be more productive in inside corner spaces or those having interior walls and quiet views.

The Great Office/Cubicle Debate

If you're a fan of the "Dilbert" comic strip, you're aware of the trend away from private offices in many work places. Among the leaders of the movement toward systems furnishings and individual cubicles were the young, philosophically egalitarian computer companies like Hewlett Packard that sought to escape the hierarchical status games played by hide-bound, traditional businesses. They were interested in accomplishments, not in who got the corner office suite. Even top managers like CEO Andrew Grove of the Intel Corporation worked along with their colleagues in identical "cubbies."

Is such "office landscaping" appropriate for library operations? It offers many advantages but should be viewed with some restraint. On the positive side, systems furniture is usually very well designed, offering a generous work area in a small space. Everything the staff member needs is close at hand, and a quick swivel of one's office chair to left or right brings file cabinet or computer within easy reach. Office landscaping also tends to increase staff camaraderie and the sense of working together as a team.

On the negative side, privacy is almost nonexistent in cubicles. Everyone hears everything. Partitions give workers the impression of privacy where none exists, so hurt feelings may result when staff overhear conversations not meant for their ears. Supervisors must seek out private spaces to discuss confidential matters or to evaluate subordinates, and such quests in search of privacy are obvious to all. Where a manager might once have gently inserted a word of criticism into a nonthreatening discussion, it becomes a full-blown reprimand when supervisor and subordinate must arrange to meet in secret. For this reason, systems furniture is probably not a good choice for supervisors. That, of course, puts you back into the old "corner office competition," but it may be the lesser of the evils.

If you choose to go with systems furniture for some or all staff members, it is possible to design a comfortable, productive environment, but success will require considerable forethought on your part. For example, work areas in which a lot of people are housed in a small space are almost inevitably noisy. Since staff members vary in their ability to tolerate noise in their immediate surroundings, people with loud voices can sometimes drive their colleagues mad. Limiting the number of cubicles grouped together is one way to minimize noise problems. Make it clear to the architect or builder that the ceiling tiles, carpeting, light housings, furniture, and panel systems should be selected to absorb and mask sound.

Be sure that all staff members can retreat to a quiet, unassigned space where they can hide for short periods to concentrate, to have a private conversation, or just to get away from it all. Privacy is a right that we as librarians should never ignore. No staff member should be denied the right to talk in confidence with his or her physician or family member. These spaces, however, need not be assigned to any one person but remain available for use by any staff member as the need arises.

Remember, too, that visual privacy is important, and the glass walls that may be ideal in public areas may not always be appropriate in staff spaces. Flexible spaces that can be opened up for use by a large group or partitioned for multiple smaller groups are a good idea. However, partitions tend to be expensive and difficult to move into place. Cheaper ones also tend to have poor sound absorption characteristics. Remember that group spaces may need phones, projectors, and screens as well as tackable and/or markable surfaces. Some informal spaces should be conducive to teamwork; these can be furnished with coffee tables and comfortable chairs.

Systems furniture can be easily moved and reconfigured over and over again, creating problems for voice and data installation. Some systems units have what is called a "spine" that accommodates wiring, and some partitions have thicker walls with multiple channels for voice, data, and power. Such plug-and-play options provided with systems architecture allow for horizontal and vertical cabling. Wires may run through panels at the work surface level, as well as through horizontal, overhead raceways or raised floors.

If you do choose systems furniture for some library areas, remember that it will affect the ways heat and air are distributed and the type of lighting that is needed. For example, systems furniture panels cast shadows and considerably increase the need for task lighting

Location

In all too many libraries, administrative offices are located on separate floors or in distant wings, far from the madding crowd. This was never a very good idea since the library director and department heads had little first-hand knowledge of what was going on in the library. With the staffing cuts of the 1980s, however, such ivory-tower aloofness has assumed more seriously negative consequences. On the assumption that a great divide existed between public and back-room staff and never the twain would meet, older libraries also tended to isolate technical service areas in distant corners. In a modern library, all library staff members, whether they be administrators or clerks, catalogers or reference librarians, bear a responsibility for a safe and efficient library operation.

Not only are the rigid lines between technical and public services disappearing but library functions themselves are changing as well. Outsourcing of cataloging services is becoming increasingly common, while instruction and computer-related jobs are growing rapidly. As you design staff spaces, consider how back-room spaces can be changed to accommodate future staffing patterns. Load-bearing walls, for example, should not be used to separate staff and public spaces. Some libraries are also moving more tasks to the circulation area to make better use of available staff resources. This means that some creative planning will be needed to accommodate these additional people and work spaces.

Less rigid divisions of labor may lend themselves to glassed-in offices surrounding public spaces. Staff members are visible and available to assist patrons while at the same time they can carry on conversations without disturbing others or being overheard. However you choose to accommodate staff, you will need to think about supplies and reference sources that must be shared, book trucks that must be parked, and equipment used by more than one person. Planning for such interactions can best be done with the library staff, but this may not be the appropriate arena in which to decide who is entitled to a private office.

Loading Dock

While you're planning spaces designed primarily for staff use, you should probably have a talk with your architect about the loading dock. Although you certainly do need one, you will discover that they function quite differently in libraries than in other kinds of buildings. First, you don't store in a room just inside the dock a large inventory of boxes to be sent to customers. Second, not much leaves the building by the loading dock, and most incoming boxes go directly to the technical services area. Therefore, a small loading dock receiving area is probably perfectly adequate for your needs.

Unless yours is a very large library or serves as a central receiving point for several libraries in a system, you don't have a staff working in a receiving room. Thus, you don't need offices and large work areas there. Instead, what you do need is a loading dock that is convenient to technical services. Since boxes are very likely toted around the building by pages, student assistants, and worn librarians with back problems, they should not have to traverse half the library. Of course, you will indeed need storage space, but most of it should be located in convenient places throughout the library. As mentioned previously, many smaller closets are more useful than one big room.

PLANNING A RENOVATION OR REMODELING PROJECT

New construction, whether an addition or a whole new library, gets more expensive every day. Take a good look at the cost of new construction in your area and the likelihood that the library can raise that much money. Maybe you've already sought approval from your county or university—only to be repeatedly turned down. Would a less expensive remodeling project meet most of your needs? Some projects might involve updating the look of the library. For example, you could replace outdated colors (say goodbye forever to avocado green and harvest gold). You might purchase new furniture (although it's become astronomically expensive and your old library oak is probably a lot better made). You might add new millwork like accent panels, built-in cabinetry, and architectural molding. Another change might involve replacing wallboard with glass to give a more open, airy feel and improve supervision. Getting new carpet can make a huge difference in the look and feel of a library. Likewise, lowering ceilings will not only provide a more-modern look but acoustical ceilings will also reduce noise. This can make all the difference if your present ceiling is so high that it makes the library seem cavernous and echoing.

Even though you will still have the same amount of space, you could reorganize workspace to function more efficiently. A more efficient floor plan in public service areas could have a major impact on services at a relatively small cost. For example, you might remove non-load-bearing walls to open up cramped spaces or turn wasted space into conference, meeting, and study rooms. Some other remodeling improvements might be to

replace an inefficient heating, ventilating, and air-conditioning system

increase storage space with new storage closets

replace windows for improved energy effectiveness

upgrade electrical service to accommodate new computer equipment

replace outdated equipment like copy machines and computers

Do you think that these relatively inexpensive changes would meet most of your library's needs? Of course, an extensive remodeling project is never cheap, but depending on the specific changes you have in mind, it can probably be accomplished for approximately $15 to $20 per square foot. Considering the political climate in which your library functions, would it be significantly easier to obtain funding for a remodeling project than for an addition? In some other situations, you might as well go for a whole new building since the effort involved in getting a major project funded is little different from that involved in a small one.

Reallocating Space

Unlike the librarian who has the luxury of planning a new library or addition, the remodeler's challenge is to find ways of making existing space serve present and future needs. Libraries seem to defy the laws of nature in that they appear to shrink a little with each passing year. After a few years of rapidly growing collections and the initiation of new services needed to keep up with modern library developments, you suddenly discover that your library building is full. Looking into the future, you realize that the library desperately needs more space to accommodate public computer areas, video and other media collections, more extensive children's materials, and a host of new or expanded resources. Where are you going to put them all? If you are unable to build a new addition, how can renovating or remodeling give you the space you so desperately need?

Begin by considering how you can use your existing space more effectively. Rapidly escalating construction costs mean that even librarians blessed with relatively new buildings or new additions must reassess existing space and consider how it can be rearranged, reorganized, or retrofitted to accommodate the new requirements. Although it is not possible to find new space in an old building, an increasing number of options such as compact shelving (see chapter 8), remote storage, and industrial storage systems offer the potential for accommodating growth.

Take a cold, cruel look at the collections and services that are experiencing a decline in use. For example, you may have an audiovisual department replete with film strips, eight-track tapes, and 16-millimeter films that is ripe for weeding or reorganization. It may be time to dispose of a good chunk of the collection or store it off-site in less expensive quarters. Online cataloging facilities have also streamlined cataloging procedures and reduced the number of staff members assigned to copy cataloging. If cataloging has not already been merged with other technical services, now may be the time to do it.

Some library systems have moved to a centralized technical services facility or to outsourcing for ordering, cataloging, and processing their materials. This reduces the space needed for behind-the-scenes functions. As libraries reduce their printed periodicals subscriptions and replace them with online full-text services, they often find that there is no longer a need for back room periodicals processing areas. Moving processing functions to a public service desk can result in better use of available staff and improved public services. The large spaces once needed to accommodate these functions can be remodeled into public areas like computer labs, library instruction classrooms, and meeting rooms.

The Unexpected Cost of Asbestos Removal

If your library decision makers have chosen remodeling or renovation over new construction because of cost savings, make sure these savings are not imaginary. A major renovation can actually cost more than a new building for a number of reasons, one of which is asbestos abatement and removal. Asbestos is a mineral substance that has been used in building construction for many years. It was not until 1986 that the Environmental Protection Agency banned the major uses of asbestos, so most library buildings probably contain at least some of these dangerous materials. Exposure to dust and fibers causes the lung disease asbestosis as well as various cancers, among them lung cancer and mesothelioma. If your library was built between the 1940s and the early 1980s, it probably contains at least some textiles, asphalt, caulking compounds, roofing materials, or insulation containing asbestos. Older structures may also be at risk because asbestos-containing compounds were used for remodeling or repair.

Fledgling renovators almost invariably underestimate the cost of asbestos removal, and even experienced contractors sometimes appear to be blind to the potential investment involved. It is not unusual for a renovation contractor to keep finding more and more asbestos as the project continues. What you and your library decision makers really need is an accurate evaluation of the problem before a single worker arrives. You need the information at a point when it is still possible to call a halt to the project and reconsider a new addition or all-new construction. Most larger communities have specialized asbestos consultants who can make building inspections, monitor air quality, and provide complete laboratory analyses. If this service is not available in your community, building inspectors may be able to make a professional recommendation.

Retrofitting Buildings Not Designed as Libraries

Librarians experienced in renovation projects usually advise caution when city councils, school boards, or university administrators have a building on their hands that they don't quite know what to do with. Yes, it may be possible to transform such buildings into functional libraries, but these people probably have no idea of the amount of money and work involved. If this idea is being discussed among your superiors or board members, try to bring in an experienced library consultant as soon as possible. Don't allow the idea to build up steam (and enthusiastic support) before you react.

Few building designs have much in common with the design of a library. For example, most buildings have a plethora of interior walls that make supervision difficult, thus requiring larger staffs and impeding traffic flow. Both staff and patrons must waste considerable time getting from place to place, and such buildings often have multiple entrances that defeat your best efforts to provide adequate security.

The interior architecture of an existing building may not lend itself to change. Schools converted into libraries may have long corridors and cinder block walls that must be tolerated because the cost of demolishing them is so great. How many library functions can you think of that can be entirely contained within a 400-square-foot segment? Your library's collections should be organized with logical breaks, and merely accommodating natural growth in a well-designed library can pose a challenge. When spaces are created for a rigidly defined function, they tend to resist logical rearrangement. Compared with an office building, in which people in different departments tend to "stay put," library users must use a variety of resources located throughout the building. Balconies and central atria can create a ring-around-the-rosy effect, forcing staff and patrons to walk in circles.

Most older buildings do not meet ADA guidelines. (See chapter 5.) Those impressive exterior stairs, for example, were built long before anyone worried about barrier-free environments, and access ramps would require major alterations in the facade. The handsome entrances of the past were flanked by heavy oak doors that are difficult for able-bodied football players to open, let alone people with disabilities. What does one do when confronted with a historical commission on the one hand and ADA guidelines on the other? The result may be a building that pleases no one.

It may not be possible to transform a historic structure into a library. If you are renovating a historic structure, preservation considerations may get in the way of creating a functional library building. Architectural details and artistic appointments may be off-limits, and you may expect political battles if you are thinking of altering a local landmark. You may find that even though the building has long been ignored and allowed to fall into decay, it will have irate defenders coming out of the woodwork to protect their civic treasure. The architectural details that make an old building unique may be too expensive to refurbish but illegal to remove.

If plans call for renovating or adding onto an existing library, someone will have to decide whether the building has sufficient historic importance that its character should be preserved. This is yet another of those political land mines you must approach with caution. Since this is one of the critical points at which your job may actually be on the line, be sure your position has strong support. There should be clear agreement among your board members or key administrators representing your parent institution.

The library director tends to be the person who has day-to-day contact with the architect. Other participants may not be monitoring the project closely and so may be shocked and amazed when confronted by a delegation of preservationists. You will find that people who seem never to have known what street the library is on will rally to protect what they perceive as an endangered historic treasure. Deal with the issue before the first work crew arrives. Don't allow it to become a cause célèbre when it's too late to turn back.

Satellite reading room, balcony level, Thomas Jefferson Building, Library of Congress, Washington, D.C.

Affection versus Practicality

When it comes to updating our own historic libraries, we have an especially difficult decision. Our buildings are like ancient great aunts for whom we feel both affection and irritation. We love our old libraries, and we are daily frustrated by them. These once glorious edifices are fraught with obstacles to modernization, from their ornate gabled roofs to their hand-stenciled stone walls to their elegant marble floors. In addition to all the rational, brick-and-mortar problems they present, we must deal with our own subjective feelings.

On the one hand, we tell our colleagues that we would happily volunteer for the demolition crew. We complain endlessly about the plumbing and the wiring and pine for central air. Librarians who have been forced to endure an old-fashioned, uncomfortable building usually choose function over form. They would like to see preservation enthusiasts devote their efforts to structures that don't require Ethernet cabling at every workstation and walls catacombed with voice, data, and electrical wires. Nevertheless, these annoying buildings are an integral part of our professional history, and a small internal voice urges us to save them if it's at all possible.

On what should such a decision be based? First and most important is the community of which the library is a part. It will usually cost far more money to both modernize and preserve an old library than to build a new one from scratch. Do your board members and administrators understand this? An institution like Harvard or an affluent community may derive great satisfaction from preserving its heritage while at the same time supporting the information needs of library patrons. When funds are less readily available, however, it is often necessary to choose between history and information access.

Anticipating Difficulties

Some libraries have achieved successful compromises by building a high-tech, architecturally compatible addition and leaving the older structure much as it was. Even this is expensive, however, and the lounges, meeting rooms, stack areas, and other lower-tech functions for which the older structure is used may require a substantial financial investment to meet building codes and ADA guidelines. Following are some other problems often encountered when remodeling or renovating older libraries:

Imposing circulation desks may take up far too much room, forcing staff to create makeshift work areas behind them.

Floors may be unable to bear the 150-pound-per-square-foot live loads that library bookstacks require.

Areas originally intended for closed stacks that were often built of metal self-supporting stack sections and had glass-and-metal floors and narrow winding stairs may permit entrance only on certain levels or at the back of the facility.

Telecommunications and electrical cabling may be nonexistent or strung haphazardly throughout the building.

Libraries on the National Register of Historic Places

Although there are no firm rules about which buildings should be preserved, the decision will already be made for you if the library building is on the National Register of Historic Places. However, whole districts are included on this list, so there is still a lot of room for local decisions. A National Register listing does not mean that an entire building should be frozen in time or that each section of the building is equally significant. If it is decided that yours is a historic building that should be preserved, a new addition can damage or destroy the building's character. An addition to a historic structure should preserve significant materials and features. It should be architecturally compatible with the older section yet not pretend to be part of the original structure. In all probability, the building has been added to or altered many times over its history. It is really not necessary to preserve an alteration made in 1954. In other words, your project will require an architect skilled in preservation work to determine what should be preserved and what can safely be ignored.

The National Park Service provides guidelines for determining whether an addition meets the requirements of historical preservation. "A project involving a new addition to a historic building is considered acceptable within the framework of the National Park Service's standards if it

preserves significant historic materials and features

preserves the historic character

protects the historical significance by making a visual distinction between old and new."[6]

Although you will need an expert to tell you what architectural features of a historic building should be preserved, exterior features are usually more important than interior. Features at the level of the main floor or "primary elevation" are more important than those at upper levels. In general, eighteenth- and nineteenth-century society placed more attractive and impressive design features where the passersby could see them and used poorer quality materials higher up where they were less visible. Preservation-worthy features might include window patterns, shutters, porticoes, entrances, roof shapes, cornices, or decorative moldings. Although the building site may determine location, when making an addition to a historic building, consider placing the addition where loss of important historic features will be minimized. To achieve this, the addition will usually involve adding one or more floors or locating the new section to the rear of the present building. An addition to a historic building should also be fully compatible with the original building. Of course, the building is going to be larger after the addition is completed, but the proportions or relationship of the different areas to one another should be preserved.

The main goal of preservation is to protect the characteristics that were responsible for its being listed in the National Register of Historic Places. You and your community will have to decide whether it is possible to meet this goal while at the same time providing the kind of information access that will be needed by citizens of the twenty-first century. If the two goals are really incompatible, now is the time to find an alternate plan. Don't wait until the building's historic character has been lost or you discover that the library cannot possibly support the technical infrastructure required. If your grand old friend will not work as a library, all is not lost. Your building may still have a long and productive life as a community center, as a historical museum, or in some other useful role.

NOTES

1. Will Manley, "The Manley Arts: Clean, Well-Lighted Stacks." *Booklist* 92 (1 Oct. 1995): 215.
2. Harold Hawkins, "The Uncertain Future of High School Library Design," *School Planning and Management* 36, no. 10 (1997): 7.
3. Anya Breitenbach, "Big Debut for Denver's Public Library," *Library Journal* 121 (Jan. 1996), 20.
4. Phyl Smith, "Too Much Togetherness: Is Your Office Design Hurting Productivity?" *Managing Office Technology* 43, no. 7 (Sept. 1998): 27, quoting Doug Aldrich.
5. Smith, 27.
6. Kay D. Weeks and others, The *Secretary of the Interior's Standards for the Treatment of Historic Properties* (Washington, D.C.: GPO, 1995).

Resources

International Facility Management Assn.
1 E. Greenway Plaza, Ste. 1100
Houston, TX 77046-0194
(713) 623-4362
fax: (713) 623-6124

Working Spaces
1228 Montgomery St.
San Francisco, CA 94133
(415) 421-6139
e-mail: pswrkgspce@aol.com

USING SPACE EFFECTIVELY

Axelroth, Joan L. "The Impact of Technology on Library Space Planning and Design." *Legal Reference Services Quarterly* 17 (1999): 1125.

Brewerton, Antony W. "First, Find Some Visionaries: Scenario Planning for Space Management at the University of Reading." *Library Association Record* 101, no. 6 (June 1999): 3546.

Curry, Ann, and Ursula Schwaiger. "The Balance between Anarchy and Control: Planning Library Space for Teenagers." *School Libraries in Canada* 19, no. 1 (1999): 912.

Ensor, Pat L. "(Inner) Space Planning for the Future; or, If It's Going to Be Virtual, Why Does the Furniture Look so Real?" *Technicalities* 16 (May 1996): 89.

Finnerty, Charles F. "Space Planning for the Special Library." *Technicalities* 16 (May 1996): 11.

Fraley, Ruth A., and Carol Lee Anderson. *Library Space Planning: A How-to-Do-It Manual for Assessing, Allocating and Reorganizing Collections, Resources and Facilities.* New York: Neal-Schuman, 1990.

Kiewitt, Eva L., and Lois J. Lehman "Space Planning: Challenges and Opportunities." *Christian Librarian* 39 (April 1996): 603.

To Build, Add or Renovate, That Is the Question. Chicago: Public Library Assn., 1996. Audiotape.

RENOVATING HISTORICAL BUILDINGS

Ferro, Maximilian L., and Melissa L. Cook. *Electric Wiring and Lighting in Historic American Buildings.* New Bedford, Mass.: AFC/A Nortek, 1984.

Jennings, Jan, and Herbert Gottfried. *American Vernacular Interior Architecture 1870–1940.* New York: Van Nostrand Reinhold, 1988.

National Trust for Historic Preservation. *Old and New Architecture: Design Relationship.* Washington, D.C.: Preservation Press, 1980.

Turberg, Edward. *A History of American Building Technology.* Durham, N.C.: Durham Technical Institute, 1981.

4 The Building Shell

Now that the cast of characters is in place and you've decided upon the size and scope of your project, it's time to clothe this imaginary structure in brick and mortar. To be more specific, there are a great many decisions that must be made about the exterior, including the roofing system and the design of the building exterior.

Everyone enjoys being in an attractive library, but don't allow yourself (and your board or committee) to be swept away by design considerations. As you know from your own domestic experience, there's a huge difference in cost between good quality "off-the-shelf" fittings and their custom-made "designer" counterparts. Sure, you'll want to go for a little drama here and there, but don't sacrifice precious library space for a few showy touches. When it comes to priorities, electrical capacity and data cabling must be placed far above a marble entryway.

EXTERIOR MATERIALS

If you are building an addition to an existing library, you will have less flexibility than if you are building a new library, especially with regard to materials for the exterior of the building. Although it is not necessary to precisely match the existing structure, you will want to choose materials that have a similar look and roughly the same degree of formality. Some postmodern architectural styles provide an excellent transition from old to new. Unless you must match an existing structure, relatively inexpensive, functional materials like brick, block, and

Sheetrock will serve you far better than trendy substitutes costing several times as much.

Many librarians report that the selection of the basic materials is the area where they most often come to blows with their architects. Make your priorities clear from the very beginning. Inquire about the materials that will be used, and ask to be consulted about expensive extras that might drive up the cost of the project. When you're assured that a premium material is just a little more expensive, be sure to ask how much more expensive it is.

Make a list of what you consider absolute necessities and only then a wish list for luxuries. Share the lists with everyone involved in building decisions, explain the logic behind your choices, and try to get them to buy into your vision before egos and architects take their toll.

ROOF DESIGN MATTERS

At one time or another, it seems that every library building in which I have worked has had a leaky roof. In some buildings, the leaks persist year after year with no permanent solution to the problem. Paneling has warped, carpeting has been badly stained, and saddest of all, valuable special collections and important reference sources have been damaged. In addition, sensitive electronic systems can be jeopardized, data lost, systems furniture damaged, and other building contents destroyed. The mold and bacteria resulting from moisture inside a building can also produce sickness and disease.

Why is a roof leak allowed to continue happening? Although there are probably as many reasons as there are libraries, perhaps the most common one is poverty. The government unit or academic institution of which the library is a part is simply unwilling to allocate the funds needed to install a new roof. Instead, each emergency is treated in isolation. The roof is patched, the mess is cleaned up, and the problem is forgotten until it recurs the next year. The moral: do it right the first time. While you're involved in the building process, you have a rare opportunity to insist on the best roof you can get. Be sure that your new roof is designed to last at least twenty years or longer if possible.

Proper installation is just as important as the right materials. If the best available roof is installed incorrectly, it will not work right and will soon fail. For example, supports and penetrations for mechanical equipment must be built into the system, so the finished roof does not have to be punctured. It is also a good idea to have an owner's representative, such as a roofing consultant, on the job site during construction. This can help ensure quality and eliminate the need for cutting out part of the roof for tests at completion.

To begin with, a good roof requires a slope that effectively removes water, a structurally sound deck, and good attachments—such as the insulation of the structural deck. The roofing system should

> use lightweight, versatile, and easily installed materials
>
> offer a broad range of design choices, such as roof color, surface treatment, and edge material
>
> have a long life cycle of at least 20 years

be able to resist rot, fire, solar ultraviolet (UV) radiation, and climatic extremes

be easy to maintain and repair

Flexible Membrane Systems

Most of the better roofing systems fit into a category called flexible membrane roofing systems. These are factory-fabricated "sheets" of roofing. Following are the basic types:

Thermosets membrane is a vulcanized, cured material. Thermosets are seamed using adhesive or butyl tape.

Chlorosulfonated polyethylene (CSPE), or "Hypalon," is a synthetic rubber material that self-cures when exposed to ultraviolet radiation after installation. Hypalon is usually seamed by welding.

Thermoplastics (including polyvinyl chloride [PVC], the various blends of PVC, and thermopolyolefins [TPOs]) are almost always reinforced with polyester and are welded using hot air or solvents.

Modified bitumens and styrene butadiene styrene (SBS), often referred to as "mod bit" in professional parlance, uses hot or cold asphalt adhesives or a torch to melt asphalt in the seam area.

"Single-ply" is the term used to describe products that are manufactured and installed as a single layer. However, in reality some of the "single-ply" membranes consist of multiple layers (plies) that have been put together during the manufacturing process.

Catwalks

While your building is still in the planning stage, think about all the workers who will be walking around on your roof. Roofing systems were never really intended to have people walking on them or dragging heavy equipment across them. Think of the satellite dish, antenna, air-conditioning condenser, and other equipment that will require installation. Inevitably, this kind of usage compromises the integrity of the system. Workers will also be walking across one part of the roof to repair another section. Suggest that extensive catwalks be installed to prevent damage. Remember, the catwalks are a lot cheaper than a new roof.

Roofing Information

Be sure that you or the contractor posts a sign by the access to the roof providing the following information:

- roof type
- name, address, and phone number of the installer
- warranty information
- a warning not to damage the roof

Keep a complete set of technical information in the library file, and copy it for workers when the roof is repaired. Such information is vitally important because repairs can create new problems unless workers know what they are dealing with. For example, some types of roofs should not be repaired using bituminous materials, and rubber roofs require special adhesives and special techniques for repair. The same thing is true of plastic roofs.

TIPS AND TALES

If you're in an area that gets a lot of snow, be sure to include enough snow guards on the roof. You don't want heavy snow to melt and slide onto people's heads or nearby vehicles.

Since we had leaks in the old part of the building, the contractor said it would be cheaper to tear off the old roof and install the addition roof all at once. The standing-seam metal roof went up at a much slower rate because each piece had to be cut separately. One worker fell off the roof during all this.

The new roof leaked just like the old one.

EVERYONE LOVES AN ATRIUM (EXCEPT A LIBRARIAN)

Throughout the Tips and Tales sections, you'll notice librarians criticizing the growing popularity of the atrium. Even Elizabeth McCracken, in her book *Giant's House,* advises librarians never to trust an architect because "he will always try to talk you into an atrium."[1] I strongly doubt that architects have any special atrium fixation. They've probably found that they get pats on the back and design awards when they include them and so assume that everyone likes them as much as they do.

Librarians, on the other hand, have a tendency to talk about the *A* word because atria do, indeed, present many practical problems. They tend to leak, they interfere with climate control, and they go hand-in-hand with balconies and open, echoing spaces that amplify noise. Nevertheless, architects are probably right that people are drawn to an atrium. Mortals that we are, we love a sunny, spacious environment. On a cold winter day, we want to bask in the sun, and nothing cheers us up more than these bright, plant-filled spaces.

In my own new library, we have two large atria. Fortunately, the building was actually designed more than a decade before it opened its doors, so no one on the present staff need accept responsibility for the *A* places. The library is also wildly popular with the university community, exceeding attendance projections by an extraordinary number of visitors in its first year of operation. Library colleagues were generally right in anticipating the problems that we encountered with the atria, although recent technology and a commercial "plantscaping" service have reduced these concerns to more manageable proportions. However, every day a student comments on how light and bright and inviting the library is.

If those around you are clamoring for an atrium, you may decide it's best to graciously concede defeat. If you can convince your building professionals to give some thought to the matter, there are a number of ways to reduce problems and make an atrium more energy efficient. Here are just a few.

TALES

We now have a three-story atrium that serves as a combination echo chamber/den of spiders (cool webs, which can be seen from the first floor).

Where the first and second floors of this library "meet" there is an atrium. It is esthetically pleasing, but in the summer it heats up and funnels extremely hot air into the second floor of the library. And in this atrium we have a red brick cube that obstructs our vision through the stacks.

Orient the atrium in an east-west direction. That way you can maximize exposure to light, minimize skylight size, and reduce excessive heat gain.

Install photocells to turn off atrium light fixtures when light level reaches a certain brightness.

If you use clerestory windows on the sides of the atrium, you can have a smaller skylight with comparable light and fewer leaks, less breakage, and less direct sunlight.

Use slightly tinted glass if glare is a problem.

Consider your location and the average amount of sunlight your area usually enjoys. Once you are above a certain light threshold, additional sunlight merely means additional cooling loads.

Take into consideration the natural air convections in an atrium (cooler air collects at lower levels and hot air rises) when designing cooling systems. This means that in summer, hot air can be mechanically vented or naturally exhausted from the roof.

Locate return air ducts near the bottom of the atrium to supply cool air during summer, reducing energy consumption.

In winter, recirculate rising hot air.

Maintain air circulation to keep cool or warm air in the desired areas.

THE LIBRARY ENTRANCE

The front entrance must serve multiple functions in addition to providing a doorway into the library. It should accommodate such security activities as observation, detection, and inspection.

Where should the main entrance be located? If you have a choice, it's probably better to locate an entrance on a side street rather than on a main thoroughfare. Side street access reduces the volume and speed of the traffic approaching the site, thus adding a measure of safety for pedestrians.

Although most librarians are accustomed to a single entrance for patrons, architects are not. Make it clear that additional entrances are needed only in the loading dock area and as emergency exits. Insist on a single public entrance. Since many people, especially administrators and board members, can't understand why this is such a "big deal," it may be helpful to read the following tales of librarians who must live with the problem on a daily basis.

TIPS AND TALES

Provide a safe, dry place for daily newspaper delivery. Libraries get lots of newspapers, and it's no fun to have them disappear or become wet, sodden masses.

Locate outside book drops where the staff can easily get to them. Remember that staff will be wheeling loaded book trucks and can negotiate uneven sidewalks and steps or curbs only with difficulty.

Make sure that the staff entrance is well lighted and protected from the elements. Imagine staff members fumbling for keys in the dark or struggling to swipe access cards through a reader while being pelted by rain.

We have two entrances and the second one, although it is very popular, is a constant problem. We have a circulation desk and security gates there, but making sure we have student staff is not always possible. The tendency, when a student is absent from his or her shift, is to leave the door unstaffed. This is not a good idea because if the alarm goes off, no one can reach the entrance in time. Using permanent staff to sit at this desk is also much too costly, and when they have to stay at the desk they are not doing other things.

When our older building was restored last year there was some pressure to open yet a third entrance. I convinced the administration that purchasing a security gate and hiring a student assistant for 90-plus hours a week was not worth the "convenience" of giving patrons a third entrance. I have had only one complaint about this, and once the patron knew the money situation, she agreed with our decision.

Another argument to use with your administration and planning committee is the issue of security for patrons. As librarians, we always focus on making sure the books don't walk, but security experts will tell you that a building with only one public entrance/exit (where there is a person who notices your entrance) is much less prone to acts of violence and destruction than one that has multiple entrances. While libraries have been relatively safe from this type of tragedy, it does happen. I believe it is our responsibility to help design space that is safe for our students as well as our books.

Our library is located in a large building of offices and classrooms. Prior to getting a security system in the early 1980s, we had two entrances/exits, and the library was like another corridor for people to pass through. We experienced losses of 3 percent to 4 percent of our book collection annually. When we got a security system, the back entrance was made into an emergency exit with an alarm, and we have kept it that way ever since. Our branch campus libraries all have one entrance/exit with a security system, and I hope all our libraries will stay that way, regardless of what remodeling or expansion happens in the future.

One solution is to have campus security (or a branch of it) located at the secondary entrance. We are in the process of building a new library that will have public entrances on two levels. The administration is going to move the security offices to the area of the second entrance, which will allow access twenty-four hours a day. The main reference floor exit will still have the security gates. The floor plan allows the flexibility of having two entrances accessible to the library during normal business hours. When the reference level is closed, access will be through the entrance guarded by security.

Entries for Multiuse Facilities

It is not unusual for the library to be housed in a building that serves other functions. Public libraries are often part of civic center complexes, and academic libraries may be housed in a larger classroom building. These multiple-access points create special security problems that can be extremely difficult to address. Not only do you have to worry about a number of outside entrances but you must also consider internal access through elevators and stairways that connect the library and nonlibrary areas. Once again, the experiences of other librarians will alert you to potential problems.

TALES

We are in a four-story building that serves dual purposes. The library occupies floors two through four with the entrance on the third floor. The first floor is offices and classrooms. The library was not designed with such use in mind. We convinced the administration to install a security code system on the elevator that allows only authorized individuals to get to the first floor from the library.

My library has one entrance but takes up four floors of a six-story multipurpose building. The problems you should watch out for are the stairs and the elevator. The stairways have doors with alarms, but that doesn't stop the walkers. The elevators go to two lower floors, and too many people (staff and students) have keys. They simply bypass the library floor, leave via the lower floors, and go directly to another building entrance. There is no way we can afford to staff or provide a extra security gate. Students go to the lower floors and leave without checking materials out.

Materials and food are often taken to offices accessed through the library. ("I'm just bringing my lunch to my office." "They said this was a brown-bag meeting.") Staff staying late or after the library entrance is closed pose another problem.

Our main concern has always been about how users exit the building. The fact that one can take the elevator into the library from the first floor but not vice versa has been a livable, if not an ideal situation. One thing to keep in mind when configuring traffic flow is the fire code. You need to be aware that certain entrances/exits, even interior ones, may not be locked under your local area code.

NOTE

1. Elizabeth McCracken, *The Giant's House: A Romance* (New York: Avon, 1997).

5

Environmental and Human Needs

As your project team becomes increasingly enmeshed in technical details, it is possible to lose sight of the users who will be spending many hours in the new building. If the library program is to be successful, users' needs, whether for proper lighting or for special accommodation to physical limitations, must be given serious consideration. Since this is indeed a small planet, you will also want to design a building that is not only kind to your users but kind to the environment as well.

BRINGING LIGHT INTO THE BUILDING

When you investigate the subject of lighting, you may find it a little overwhelming. Whether considering natural light entering through windows and skylights or artificial lighting, lighting tends to be the focus of much of our discontent. Can you think of a single library where overhead lights are positioned in such a way that they illuminate every stack range? If by some remote chance you happen to know of such a library, are lights changed routinely as soon as they burn out? You've probably criticized the lighting of every library you've ever visited, and that's only to be expected.

Although your architect will hammer out the details, you should be prepared with very clear, specific lighting recommendations. How can you hope to emerge from the project with a functional design when so many before you have failed? First, get the architects on your side. If at all possible, take them on a field trip, not only through your present library but to other local libraries as well.

(Go on a reconnaissance mission ahead of time to scout out the darkest areas.) Point out the inaccessible lightbulbs that never get changed because the custodians simply can't get to them. Pause below the ever-dark, nonstandard fluorescent tubes that are always on back order or were only available through a supplier in Montana who went out of business three years ago. Ask them to find a call number that's impossible to read because the book is on the bottom shelf of a remote stack range. Let them watch a video or read a computer screen that has been washed out by glaring afternoon sunlight. Then be prepared to discuss these experiences.

Also visit several newer libraries in your region to examine the lighting fixtures used and the kind of light they provide. You might even ask library users how they feel about the lighting. Ask whether light from windows is too bright or glaring. Ask whether conventional output, single-lamp fixtures provide enough surface brightness or whether an area is perceived as being gloomy.

Although lighting decisions for libraries are not so very different from those for other large buildings, there are some ways in which the library is unique. Architects sometimes forget that library users are almost always reading. In fact, architects may tuck lighting fixtures into places where they are out of the way of other design features. This may mean recessing them in the ceiling, thus directing the light straight down rather than diffusing it. It might be a nice, attractive idea in other environments, but such installations simply don't work in libraries. Factors such as building orientation, blinds, and furniture arrangement as well as the type and number of lighting fixtures all affect the lighting of an area.

Avoid decorative lighting fixtures that don't really provide much light. The bulbs they require are often expensive special orders, and your custodial staff will waste a great deal of time changing them. Be sure that any light fixture you have in the library really illuminates the space it was designed for. Also keep the number of different types of fixtures as small as possible so you're not always running out of one type of bulb or another. In rooms where you turn the lights on and off frequently, don't choose fluorescent lamps, which may take several minutes to warm up.

A Brief Primer on Lighting Theory and Terms

Like other aspects of library design, lighting has a language and some basic concepts that you will need to master to discuss the subject with your architects. The following sections provide a very brief tutorial.

Direct Lighting

Light that is directed downward into an area is direct lighting. In general, it is an efficient way to deliver light to work surfaces. It can, however, create problems. For example, bright lamps or luminaires against a dark ceiling can cause reflective glare on computer monitors, glossy magazines, and photographs and can result in a "cave-like" atmosphere. Harsh shadows are another unpleasant effect of direct lighting. Although we usually choose direct lighting for reading, it tends to illuminate unevenly, and scalloped patterns can occur on books and walls.

Narrowly focused lights may highlight an architectural detail dramatically, but they cause irritating shadows outside the small pool of light and make reading extremely difficult anywhere in the library but impossible in the stacks. Also remember that you will eventually tear down and rearrange book stacks as your collection grows and your priorities change. Will you have a crisis if the lights no longer line up properly? Patches of light and dark are the last thing you need in a library.

Indirect Lighting

When a space is indirectly lighted, light is "bounced" off the ceiling and dispersed throughout the space. For obvious reasons, this type of light is also called "uplighting." Both our users and our staffs find this kind of soft, uniform lighting environment very pleasant. Uplighting is frequently the best choice for a library in which people are reading both printed and computer text.

In general, direct lighting systems provide higher illumination levels, and indirect systems supply a higher quality of light at lower light levels. Libraries really need a combination of direct and indirect lighting. Indirect fixtures create uniform illumination throughout the space while direct lamps improve efficiency and light workspaces. The combination also results in a more attractive, inviting environment in which objects have shape without harsh shadows.

Color Perception

The ability to distinguish and interpret different wavelengths of light is called color perception. Color is not really a property of an object but the way that various wavelengths of light make the object appear. A light source is composed of many different wavelengths, and each object will absorb different proportions of each wave. Then the object reflects the rest of the light toward the viewer. It is this reflection that makes an object appear to be red or green or blue. Color perception affects not only the colors users see but their sense of comfort, pleasure, or even anxiety. Light determines color, and color affects your users' experience of the library. Color perception is the reason why librarians often complain that the colors they selected from swatches, carpet samples, and paint chips look completely different as walls, carpets, and upholstery in the new library. Even though the samples match one another perfectly when first viewed in an office or in the interior decorator's studio, they may look totally different in the new environment.

Lighting Sources

Although lighting fixtures come in every imaginable size and shape, the light they emit allows them to be divided into two major classifications: incandescent lamps and gaseous discharge lamps. (The term "lamp" is being used here to mean a light source.) Gaseous discharge lamps can be divided into two subcategories: low pressure and high pressure or high intensity discharge (HID) lamps.

Incandescent lamps were invented by Thomas Edison. These lamps have not changed a great deal through the years. One recent development, however, is the tungsten-halogen regenerative cycle lamp. These lamps are more efficient than traditional incandescent lamps and can produce more light because the bulb is made out of quartz glass, which permits a higher temperature inside the lamp. You will hear them called quartz lamps, tungsten-halogen lamps, quartz-halogen lamps, or just halogen lamps. These lamps are quite a bit smaller than the common lightbulb. The most popular, the MR-16 lamp, is only about two inches in diameter. Halogen lamps produce a whiter light; standard incandescent lamps shed a yellowish glow.

When an electric arc is passed through a gas, the result is light. This is the basis of the gaseous discharge lamp. This reaction can occur directly, resulting in visible light, or indirectly, when ultraviolet radiation causes a phosphor coating to glow. Something must provide the electric arc that starts it all, and that something is called a "ballast." A ballast is primarily a voltage transformer and current-limiting device that provides a controlled electrical input to the lamp. Unfortunately, ballasts make a lot of noise and consume considerable energy.

When we think of gaseous discharge lamps, fluorescent tubes come immediately to mind. These are actually part of the group called low-pressure discharge lamps. Another lamp that falls into this same category is the low-pressure sodium lamp, although it is usually not used indoors since it produces a yellow light that turns everything yellow and brown. In all probability, your library depends almost entirely on fluorescent lamps, as do most stores and offices. The most common fluorescent lamp is usually four feet long and one-and-one-half inches in diameter (although a one-inch-diameter version is becoming more common). They are extremely cost effective since they are several times more efficient than incandescent lamps. However, they can't really be directed to a needed location, and their color rendering properties are not especially good. In recent years, many smaller tubes have come on the market, and some premium-priced tubes are better for rendering color.

The bluish-greenish street lamps popular a few years ago were mercury vapor lamps, the first high-intensity discharge lamps to be developed. They're no longer used because metal halide lamps provide better color rendering and high-pressure sodium lamps have also been greeted with enthusiasm. HID lamps are extremely energy efficient. Their small size (measured in inches, not feet) allows for good control of light. Although they were once used almost entirely for streets and other outside lighting, they are gradually becoming available in small wattages for indoor use.

Lighting Terms

The following are commonly used technical terms for lighting. They are based on either English or metric measurements. Although you probably don't need to understand each term, you will hear them used often.

Candela (cd)   Unit of measurement of luminous intensity; the candela has replaced the standard candle

Foot-candle   Unit of illumination on a surface that is everywhere one foot from a uniform point source of light, the brightness of one candle

Illuminance   Amount of light that strikes a surface

Lambert   Unit of brightness or luminance; equal to the brightness of a perfectly diffusing surface that reflects one lumen per square centimeter

Lumen   Used in calculating artificial light; amount of light from a uniform point source having an intensity of one candela

Luminance   Brightness or intensity of light on a surface

Different Lighting Requirements for Books and Computers

When we consider what good lighting means in the library, it is almost inevitable that we think of the way available light illuminates a book. Books and periodicals continue to be an important part of a library and so we must never forget the user, standing with open book in hand in a shadowy stack area. That same user, however, will probably be spending some time at a computer workstation before he or she leaves, and so we must expand our picture.

Using the library for reading and study has traditionally meant working with black characters printed on white paper on a horizontal surface. Since printed matter is read by reflected light, it has been assumed that the brighter the illumination provided, the higher the contrast between characters and background. Now that many workstations are equipped with desktop computers, users are looking not at a flat sheet of paper but at a vertical screen that emits, not reflects, light. This means that lighting requirements for computer use and paper-focused activities are very different.

At desk level 100 foot-candles of light has been accepted as a normal office standard. Although architects may plan for this level in a library, the result is almost always uneven, with some areas too light and others too dark. Today's computer monitors can be read in almost total darkness. The ambient light in most library and office areas is so bright that it causes glare or washes out computer screens. In fact, there is evidence that given a choice, employees who spend their entire workday at a computer will switch off the lights completely. Obviously, this is not desirable in a library, but it points up the enormous difference between reading a book and reading from a light-emitting screen.

Any decisions you make about lighting computer areas should take into consideration the following visual tasks that your staff or users will be performing:

- reading text displayed on the screen
- recognizing keyboard letters, symbols, and function keys
- reading written or typed text in a book or on a sheet of paper placed nearby
- inputting notes into a computer

Users should be able to perform these tasks with ease and in comfort. Good readability for paper text requires a higher light level than for computers, but that same light actually reduces the readability of the text displayed on the video screen. When the text on the computer screen is light colored on a dark background, the problem is exacerbated. The ambient light actually veils the image on the screen. Since it is impossible to fully satisfy the lighting needs of both computer users and those reading printed text in the same areas, you will inevitably find yourself making compromises. Just be careful that some flexibility is possible. Since you can expect rapid change in the next few years, try to create environments where both activities can be carried on in proximity to each other and in reasonable comfort.

One solution to the problem of lighting for both reading and computer work is having a light installed in each study carrel or workstation that can be turned on or off by the user to suit the particular task. In general, the more control the users have over their environment, the better. Another solution is to select monitors that have improved the contrast of their screens through dark-surround

TIPS

Insist on excellent lighting and no hidden corners.

Settle only for lighting that gives the proper amount of light needed for each task—not what looks dramatic or is decoratively pleasing. I have been in several new libraries lately designed by big-name architects, and they have all had *terrible* lighting.

phosphors, antireflective coatings, and optically coupled built-in antiglare filters. Installing shades on windows and controlling the placement of light sources are still other options.

Light Switch Panels

If at all possible, you will want to control the lights in your building from one central location. Of course, switches controlling individual spaces (such as storerooms and media rooms) are necessary as well, but you don't want staff members bruising their shins and walking into walls while feeling for switches in a dark building. Not only does a central light panel save staff time and reduce the need for first aid but it is needed for security as well. Even more important, your library needs a bank of light switches (or their high-tech equivalent), not circuit breakers. When one circuit breaker looks exactly like another, all sorts of equipment can be shut off accidentally.

Despite your efforts, it often happens that your library ends up with light switches scattered throughout the building. This situation is difficult enough to live with but becomes a great deal worse when switches get put in electrical and mechanical closets. Such things sometimes happen because the electrical contractor is in a hurry to finish the job and looks for shortcuts, paying little attention to the chaos that will inevitably follow. It may also be the architect's error or yet another misguided cost-cutting measure.

Electrical and mechanical areas are dangerous. Huge quantities of electrical current are pouring into your building, and you certainly don't want staff or student pages mistakenly pulling the wrong breaker. These are the very same areas that often bear signs reading "Danger! Keep Out" for good reason. If the light switch panels are in such "off limits" areas, you may even find yourself in the position of being denied keys to turn on your own lights.

TALES

We have a sophisticated lighting system that we don't use. All we really wanted was an on-off switch.

We still have no idea what some of the wall switches do.

I think the most important thing you can do is have your maintenance staff in on the planning, especially if they have experience in reading electrical plans. They will also see that your light fixtures and ceiling tiles are standard.

Take precautions against children turning task lights on and off.

See that switches are sufficiently tough to accommodate heavy usage.

Our restroom lights were tied into a switch that controlled a bank of light in a distant area. This was a problem at closing because we turned the lights out on people who were still using the restrooms.

Exterior Lighting

To a considerable extent, the nature of the site determines the kind of exterior lighting needed. Security lighting is needed for observation, inspection, deter-

TIPS

Outdoor lights should be low enough to change bulbs easily but not be in or near the ground. We have had a lot of trouble with in-the-ground fixtures, from vandalism (smashing lens covers) to water leakage when seals were not tight enough. One fixture a couple of feet above the ground has been hidden by shrubbery (our fault), and another was broken by a patron who tripped and fell into it.

Flagpole lighting should be mounted on the building, not in the ground.

rence, and safety. The choice of lighting fixtures and their locations depends on site size, vegetation, topography, and building location. The aim should be to provide a uniform level of lighting with overlapping cones of light and with a minimum of shadow areas. If you plan to use closed-circuit television cameras, the lighting system should provide the correct level of intensity for the cameras. Exterior lighting fixtures should be resistant to vandalism and sabotage. Wiring should be concealed, and access to equipment should be via locked cabinets or receptacles.

Before deciding on the type and the extent of external lighting, be sure that your architects have considered the following questions:

What is the present level of light in the area and on neighboring buildings? Is the library in a populated area where existing lighting will help illuminate the building?

Do you plan to illuminate the facade of the library?

Where will the fixtures be placed?

The placement of fixtures plays a major role in determining the mood and effect created by illumination of a building exterior. Lighting fixtures should be located as unobtrusively as possible. Because they are very bright and can get quite hot, they must be placed where people are unlikely to touch them.

The Library's Windows on the World

In a nutshell, here is the truth, the whole truth, and nothing but the truth about natural light:

- sunlight is bad for books
- sunlight is bad for viewing computer monitors
- sunlight is bad for viewing television and other projected images
- sunlight is bad for carpets
- sunlight is bad for upholstery
- users love sunlight
- users win

After grim years in the 1960s and 1970s when libraries, classroom buildings, and corporate headquarters were built without windows, architects have finally realized that windows are essential to our human sense of well-being. Look around the reading room. Tables and study carrels by windows are occupied first. The attraction is not simply a matter of light and ventilation; these can be dealt with artificially. Rather, there is something about sunlight that we crave, and we will put up with all sorts of inconveniences to get it.

One might say that librarians have a love-hate relationship with windows. Yet the windows you select for the new building will determine to a large extent how both the library staff and the library's users react to it. Depending on your part of the country, large windows on all sides of the building are probably not advisable. There can actually be such a thing as too many windows. The orientation of a window really matters, and northern lighting is usually best for reading and general lighting, although windows on any side of the building, if they are well designed, may meet your needs.

Children's Library, Queens Borough Public Library, Flushing, New York

To Open or Not to Open

Windows that do not open provide greater climate control than the type that can be opened and closed. However, it is not uncommon for air-conditioning systems to fail, forcing staff and patrons to swelter. Modern buildings are very nearly airtight, and inadequate ventilation all too common. Sick building syndrome (discussed in detail in chapter 7) results when air is merely recycled and pollutants that are emitted by construction materials are not carried away from the building. Under these circumstances there are few luxuries that surpass being able to open a window and breathe in cool, fresh air. Unfortunately, books do not thrive in fresh air. They respond adversely to dust, mold spores, and pests that commonly enter through open windows. It is, therefore, essential that your library depend for most of its climate control on a high-quality HVAC system. (See chapter 6 for more information on HVAC systems.)

TIPS

Don't let design engineers talk you out of installing operable windows! If your windows don't open, and your air conditioning goes out, you close your library (unless it is small enough to be ventilated by opening doors). It doesn't have to be very warm outside to become unbearably hot inside without air conditioning.

Make sure that the architect has planned for the cleaning of skylights and clerestory windows, both inside and outside. For example, the addition of a rail at the sill of the clerestory

Carrel detail, Carmel Mountain Branch Library, San Diego, California

windows can make cleaning easier and reduce cost. Too often, relatively new buildings have dirty windows. The regular window cleaners have concluded that the windows are too difficult or dangerous to reach and have abandoned them to the elements.

We had huge, beautiful windows with low-E glass (holds heat in), but no safety bars outside. The decision makers insisted on windows that opened so that on nice days we could have fresh air. (Yankee frugality, but no thought of little kids falling out of the windows.)

Daylight Harvesting

A concept that is becoming popular in the lighting industry is daylight harvesting. The idea is that fluorescent dimming ballasts adjust energy output according to the amount of natural lighting that is available. Dimming systems may work in conjunction with energy management systems, daylight sensors, occupancy sensors, or time clocks.

Room Darkening

Most windows will require some way of controlling light. Blinds are probably the best choice for most areas because they provide the most flexibility and can be adjusted for different times of day and varying light conditions. However, they may not darken a room sufficiently for film, video, or computer projection. Specially fitted shades are made just for this purpose. Be careful that you do not go to the effort and expense of installing light-blocking shades only to realize later that you forgot about the glass doors or clerestories through which light pours in.

It will be necessary to turn off the lights in any room in which media is projected, so be sure your building professionals are given a list of all rooms that require separate lighting controls. Since people may be taking notes when films, etc., are being shown, you will also want to be able to darken a room without plunging it into total darkness. Ask that emergency lights be located away from projection screens or the resulting glare will reduce visibility.

ENERGY EFFICIENCY AND NEW BUILDINGS

Whether your hypothetical crystal ball predicts hard times or times of plenty, energy conservation should be part of your building's future. Not only do reduced energy costs mean more money for library resources but our environment profits as well. Unfortunately, the librarian is often not consulted about energy matters in the design of the building shell, HVAC, lighting, and other energy-consuming systems. Ideally, your building's various systems should interact with one another in a synergistic manner. This may require more cooperation among building professionals than normally occurs. If, however, you make your concerns about energy efficiency clear from the start, you are more likely to emerge from the experience with an environmentally responsible building.

As mentioned earlier, construction funds are often more generous than ongoing operating budgets. It makes good sense to pay a little more for systems and equipment that lower your energy costs later. In other words, it is not really cost effective to make decisions on the basis of initial cost. Long-term or life-cycle costing takes into account the initial cost as well as the costs associated with operating and maintaining the building during its useful life. In the case of lighting, for example, the cost of the fixtures and lamps really accounts for only about 10 percent of the real cost. The rest is the cost of electricity and the ongoing labor costs involved in changing lamps and repairing fixtures.

Convincing your building team to invest in energy efficiency is not always a battle you can expect to win since most people involved in the project do not envision themselves being around to reap the savings created by energy conservation. However, the more dramatically you can present the long-term savings, the greater your chance of success. During the construction phase, the cost of making the building more energy efficient is really not as high as commonly believed. Because new lighting, heating, cooling, and cooling equipment is being purchased anyway, there is no need for expensive retrofitting.

New buildings are inevitably more energy efficient than those built in the past. Code requirements and new materials ensure better insulation, more efficient water use, etc. However, new buildings also use far more energy than in the past due to the increased amount of equipment guzzling power and water to meet contemporary expectations.

The Energy-Efficient Building Shell

The design and orientation of the building itself can make a big difference in energy consumption. The building's shell should be compact in form, requiring less energy for heating and cooling than buildings with complicated shapes. Furthermore, the long axis of the building should have an east/west orientation to minimize solar gain in the summer and maximize solar gain in the winter. Windows on the north and west sides of the building should be fewer and smaller. Of course, you will want to keep the amount of air coming into or leaving the building to a minimum. Also make sure that interior wall cavities; chases for plumbing, electrical, and HVAC systems; and drop ceilings are all sealed or thermally isolated.

Insulation

Few energy savers can make as much difference in energy consumption as insulation. The following guidelines will contribute substantially to an energy-efficient building:

> The amount of insulation needed for one-story buildings where the interior is mainly influenced by the flow of heat through the building envelope is greater than for multistory buildings.

> Drop ceilings should not be treated as part of a building's thermal envelope, so insulation should not be placed on top of a drop, grid-type ceiling.

> Fiberglass batts should not be placed between roof rafters with a drop ceiling below. Use blown insulation instead of fiberglass batts where possible.

Passive Solar Design

Using the sun's energy without the use of mechanical collectors, commonly referred to as passive solar design, can reduce use and operating costs significantly and help save the environment at the same time. Daylight can

- allow artificial lights to be dimmed or turned off
- reduce summer cooling caused by heat from artificial lights
- reduce winter fuel consumption through passive solar heating

However, passive solar design requires knowledgeable building professionals to integrate heating, cooling, and daylight in such a way as to maximize the efficiencies and cost savings. The pieces must interrelate with one another so architect, engineers, and contractor must all be involved.

Encourage your architect to consider incorporating passive solar design into your building plans. Not only is it more environmentally friendly but it can reduce energy bills by from 30 to 70 percent. Building components such as windows and masonry can be used to collect, store, balance, and distribute heating, cooling, and lighting. For example, if much of your light is natural, you will not require as much air conditioning to counteract the excess heat given off by artificial lights.

Approaches to passive solar heating can be divided into three basic categories: direct gain, indirect gain, and isolated gain.

With *direct gain,* solar radiation enters a space directly through large areas of glass. When it's sunny, heat is stored in floors and walls and released when it gets cold. It is most effective when glass and storage capacity are correctly balanced.

Indirect gain means that solar radiation is collected and stored in a thermal wall separating south-facing windows from the rest of the library. The heat is distributed through the building over a period of several hours.

With *isolated gain,* solar radiation is captured by a separate space, like an atrium, and distributed by natural airflow or by other methods.

Careful attention to site conditions and the orientation of the building is essential. For example, shading is an important component of both heating and cooling passive solar facilities. Overhangs or natural landscaping can prevent harsh sunlight from entering a facility in the summer and can direct winter sunlight into the building due to the angle of the sun's rays in different seasons. The building should be oriented in such a way that overhangs can shade high summer sun while allowing low winter sun to enter the building.

Windows should be considered when incorporating passive solar design elements. Low-E coatings can increase a window's thermal performance. Some coatings block solar gain or allow solar energy to pass into a building, depending on the climate and the orientation of the building. Selecting appropriate windows can be a complicated matter since east and west windows typically require different glass than south windows if they are to contribute effectively to the overall energy management of the building.

Lighting

More light does not necessarily mean higher energy consumption. First, you will need to determine the proper illumination levels for each space. For example, a lighting power density of about one watt per square foot is adequate for a typical building; however, you may require more in some areas to ensure adequate reading levels, especially in the stacks. Explore the possibilities of task/ambient lighting systems. (Task lights are used to provide higher illumination levels at the work surfaces.)

One common-sense lighting efficiency measure is to install motion-sensor controls where the lights are likely to be left on in unoccupied spaces. (As mentioned earlier, controls should be incorporated into the lighting design from the beginning.) Another is to use light-colored surfaces on modular furniture, wall coverings, ceilings, etc., to minimize the need for artificial lighting. Yet another energy-efficient measure is to install LED exit signs. (They use just a few watts and last for 25 years or more.) Of course, you can also use natural daylight to supplement the artificial lighting.

Fluorescent lamps are approximately five times more efficient than incandescent lamps and three times more efficient than halogen (tungsten-halogen) lamps; therefore, use fluorescent fixtures where appropriate. Use compact fluorescent lamps instead of incandescents for recessed cans, wall sconces, table lamps, pendants, and other wall/ceiling fixtures. Avoid the use of 2-by-2 fluorescent fixtures because the tubes are expensive. Use 4-foot, single-tube fluorescent fixtures where applicable. Specify high-power-factor ballasts in all compact fluorescent fixtures.

Following are some more-technical energy-savings suggestions. Use

lamps with a color rendering index (CRI) of 84 or more

tungsten halogen flood lamps instead of incandescent floods

high-pressure sodium or metal halide lamps instead of mercury vapor (Metal halide fixtures can be used indoors in high ceiling areas and outdoors where color rendering is important.)

high-pressure sodium fixtures in parking lots and on the exterior of buildings for security lighting

Natural Cooling

Natural ventilation or convection can also make a big difference in the long-term costs of energy consumption. For example, holes in the bottom of a facility can allow cool outside air into the building. As the air warms, it rises to the top of the space and exits through holes near the roof. Living in the Southwest, I became accustomed to the humble "swamp cooler," a simple evaporative cooling apparatus composed of a fan blowing air through what looked like a wet doormat. In a more-sophisticated design, the water is sprayed in a downdraft cooling tower on the library's roof. The air filters through the tower and into the building. In dry climates, evaporative coolers can sometimes replace air conditioners entirely. Any of these cooling methods is well worth investigating.

Mechanical Systems

Your present HVAC system probably gobbles up enormous quantities of energy. Newer equipment can produce more comfort with less energy. Specify high energy efficiency for HVAC units, heat pumps, and water heaters.

Be wary of oversized HVAC equipment—it will not achieve its purpose any better than equipment of the right size for your library. Consider using multiple, modular boilers to better match the equipment size to the varying loads. If possible, use natural gas equipment, as it is generally more economical.

In addition, following are some things to remember when planning mechanical systems.

Avoid using heating appliances such as electric resistance wall mount, baseboard, or unit heaters in stairwells, vestibules, utility rooms, and hallways.

Consider unconventional HVAC equipment like absorption cooling, thermal storage for heating and ground cooling, source heat pumps, and/or infrared heating.

Specify insulated steam and hot water pipes in unconditioned spaces.

Call for all ducts to be sealed with mastic (not duct tape) and gaskets to be used between sections.

Specify a timer or a programmable thermostat to turn off the boiler, or consider an energy management system to add more-sophisticated control.

Include in the plans controls to close the system when the building is unoccupied.

Specify low-leakage dampers on all applicable systems.

Consider the use of heat recovery ventilators to pull the heat out of the out-going air.

See also chapter 6 for additional discussion of HVAC systems concerns.

Plumbing Systems

Limiting water consumption controls energy usage. Restrooms can contribute considerably to the conservation effort if you specify fixtures that limit water usage. For example, modern toilets use 1.6 gallons to the flush as compared with 3 gallons and even 5 gallons for older units; urinals use 1 gallon or less per flush. Faucet flow rates can be restricted to 1 gallon per minute.

For water heaters, specify those with a high energy efficiency factor (EF). Gas-fired water heaters should have an EF of 0.62 or more. Electric heaters should have an EF of 0.93 or more, and oil-fired heaters should have an EF of 0.60 or more. Avoid specifying electric water heaters unless they can be on timers to minimize heating during off-peak demand periods. Specify small instantaneous-type water heaters if there is need for them in a location that is remote from the main water heater.

ENERGY EFFICIENCY AND OLDER BUILDINGS

You may be amazed to discover that the buildings with the poorest energy efficiency are actually those built between 1940 and 1975.[1] Surprisingly, really old buildings actually use less energy for heating and cooling than buildings of this "in-between" period. Therefore, buildings built before 1940 or after 1975 may require fewer weatherization improvements. Historic buildings were built at a time when craftsmanship was important, as was the desire to achieve maximum physical comfort by making the most efficient and effective use of natural heating, lighting, and ventilation. If you are confronted with the task of modernizing a historic building and have been agonizing over wiring and plumbing dilemmas, take comfort that there are some bright spots on your horizon.

Among the most obvious (and often ignored) energy savers are windows that open and close providing natural ventilation and light. Your building may also include interior light/ventilation courts, rooftop ventilators, clerestories, or skylights bringing in fresh air and light and ensuring that energy-consuming mechanical devices are used only to supplement natural energy sources.

Historic buildings were constructed long before climate control became a buzzword. However, before making sweeping changes and installing massive HVAC equipment, consider that such structures may be naturally energy efficient. Even though the windows in historic buildings usually have poor thermal properties, their number and size is limited, and the ratio of glass to wall is often less than 20 percent. In other words, the windows are just what is needed to provide adequate light and ventilation. Another energy-friendly characteristic of older buildings is their use of exterior shutters or exterior awnings to effectively control the amount of light and air entering the building.

In the South, exterior balconies, porches, wide roof overhangs, awnings, and mature shade trees are often part of the design of historic buildings. Their exterior walls are light colored to reflect sunlight away from the building. In the

North, heavy masonry walls, fewer windows, and the use of dark paint colors had the opposite effect. In recent years, engineers have come to realize that masonry walls can considerably improve thermal performance, and walls of large mass and weight possess high thermal inertia, known as the "M factor." Inertia can alter the thermal resistance or "R factor" of the wall, increasing the time it takes to absorb heat at its outside surface and transfer it to the interior. This is why many older buildings without air conditioning feel cool when you enter them on a hot summer's day. It takes most of the day for the heat to penetrate the building, and by then it is evening so the heat has plenty of time to dissipate.

Making Simple Changes

Begin making your historic building more energy efficient by initiating passive measures to permit existing systems to function as efficiently as possible. You may find that you need to make fewer major alterations than you thought necessary. For this purpose, however, you will need an architect who has a real appreciation for older buildings and not one who wants to rip everything out and start over. Preservation retrofitting is another course of action, which involves taking appropriate weatherization measures to improve thermal performance.

Passive measures might include better control over how and when a building is used. Such measures can include any or all of the following:

controlling the temperature by using less energy when rooms are not in use, more when they are

lowering thermostats in winter, raising them in summer

lowering illumination levels and the number of lights in use

taking advantage of existing operable windows, shutters, awnings, and vents

seeing that mechanical equipment is serviced regularly for maximum efficiency

making sure radiators and forced-air registers are kept clean

It is surprising what an enormous difference such simple changes can make in energy efficiency. You can save as much as 30 percent on energy usage at virtually no expense. No building alterations are needed, and very little additional staff time is involved.

Preservation Retrofitting

Retrofitting older buildings must be done with care and sensitivity so that it does not jeopardize the historic character of the library. In general, limit your efforts to those that achieve the most energy savings at a reasonable cost, while at the same time altering the character of the building as little as possible. This is why these activities are usually referred to as "preservation retrofitting." Your architects should take special precautions that retrofitting measures do not increase deterioration by trapping moisture. Depending on their location, old buildings usually contain large quantities of moisture in their interiors. In winter, moisture can condense on cold surfaces such as windows; it may also condense as it passes through walls and roof, creating potential problems. A common solution for making modern buildings more energy efficient is to incorporate vapor barriers into interior and exterior walls. In older buildings, such thoughtless, ill-considered solutions can spell disaster.

Another problem that frequently occurs in the course of retrofitting an older building is introducing materials that are chemically or physically incompatible with existing materials. For example, some cellulose insulating materials that use ammonium or aluminum sulfate as a fire retardant can react with moisture, forming sulfuric acid. This is an extremely powerful acid that can damage lumber and wiring as well as building stones, brick, and wood. One particularly distressing horror story concerns a building insulated with cellulose that collapsed when sulfuric acid weakened the metal framework.

Your architect and/or engineer should check to determine how your building was constructed, and what kind of insulation, if any, was used. Your building professionals can determine what sort of retrofitting has been done in the past, and whether it is the source of any problems.

Before your architects begin planning extensive new systems, be sure they have given full consideration to the smaller changes that can be remarkably effective in increasing the energy efficiency of historic buildings. Following are some basic concerns that can be addressed by preservation retrofitting. Not all of them may be appropriate for your building, but you may wish to use it as a checklist when you're talking with your architect.

storm windows	doors and storm doors
attic insulation	vestibules with tightly fitting
basement and crawl space insulation	doors
	replacement windows
duct and pipe insulation	wall insulation
awnings and shading devices	waterproof coatings for masonry

In addition, controlling air that infiltrates the building through loose windows, doors, and cracks in the outside shell of the building can be a very effective energy-saving measure. Consider weatherstripping doors and windows as well as caulking open cracks and joints to reduce this infiltration. You don't, however, want to completely seal and prevent moisture migration in the building. Air infiltration is essential to prevent condensation problems. In addition, don't use too-colorful caulking and weather stripping materials that alter the look of the building. In general, air infiltration might be a good place to begin a retrofitting plan since it is low in cost, requires little skill, and results in substantial benefits.

If it is necessary to replace existing HVAC equipment, ask your contractor to install any new equipment and ductwork in such a way that it can be easily removed later and will not cause irreversible damage when it is installed, updated, or removed later. Weigh the merits of invisibility, which involves hiding piping and ductwork within wall and floor systems, against the damage that such installations may cause.

Remember that the technologies involved in retrofitting and weatherization are quite recent. Little research has been done on the impact of new materials on old buildings, so caution should be a byword.

ACCESS AND AMERICANS WITH DISABILITIES

Like energy efficiency, planning for adaptive technology must be considered at nearly every stage of the building design process. Adding a few last-minute modifications to meet local codes is all too common, and despite the Americans with Disabilities Act (ADA) and numerous volumes interpreting its provisions, new library buildings often fail to serve users with special needs. The old saw about walking in someone else's shoes certainly applies. Again and again, architects and contractors fail to view the building through the eyes of someone with a disability that requires special accommodation. The following parable illustrates this point:

> In a library on a planet not very far away, an auditorium was designed in a bowl shape with descending tiers of seating and a stage at basement level. An elevator was built just to accommodate wheelchairs. In theory, people with physical disabilities would have access to the stage and could also choose to sit in either the first or last row of the auditorium. The intent was praiseworthy. Too often people in wheelchairs are relegated to what amounts to "the worst seat in the house" and are unable to get to the stage, even when they are on the program.
>
> However, when the elevator was built, it allowed just barely enough room to get a large wheelchair or motorized cart inside. Once in the elevator, wheelchair occupants discovered that the controls were on the wall directly behind them and thus totally inaccessible. Had some way been found to operate the controls, the elevator would still have been useless because the stage-level exit opened to the side and not to the rear, as had been the case on the upper floor. There was, of course, no way that patrons in wheelchairs could propel their chairs sideways in the tiny space to get onto the stage.
>
> Naturally, the library director was chagrined when she first saw the elevator. It should have been obvious to anyone that the design was unusable. However, when she brought the problem to the attention of the architect and the contractor, she was met with a stone wall. Nothing, she was told, could be done because the elevator met code. The building professionals were under no obligation to produce an elevator that could actually be used by people in wheelchairs. Their responsibility involved merely meeting building codes intended to implement the Americans with Disabilities Act.

The Spirit of the Law

The implementation of the Americans with Disabilities Act has been fraught with frustration for people whose quality of life depends on access to workplace, school, libraries, and other buildings. The act, signed into legislation on July 26, 1990, prohibits discrimination on the basis of disability in employment, state and local government services, public transportation, public accommodations, commercial facilities, and telecommunications.

In an excellent article, H. Neil Kelley suggests that "The best approach to compliance with the ADA is the golden rule. Offer modifications and accommodations that will yield the access for others that you would like for yourself."[2] Try not to be overwhelmed with the difficulties. Remember that only 20 percent of people with disabilities need any special accommodation. Although some ADA requirements are costly and difficult to meet, the majority of accommodations are relatively inexpensive. You might even think of it as enlightened self-interest since simple modifications can help keep you and your staff comfortable and productive for many years to come. Many people will experience a disabling condition at some time during their lives.

TALE

We had bathrooms that were supposed to be built to ADA specs, and someone at the architect's office made a mistake, so they weren't to spec. These were the bathrooms for the meeting room. We had doors so heavy and hard to open that no one in a wheelchair could open them. They opened the wrong way, and the trustees were obstinate about changing or putting in a sliding door with an electric eye.

Under Title II of the ADA, state and local government units, which include most libraries, must eliminate accessibility barriers that restrict their services by moving services and programs to accessible buildings or by making changes to existing buildings. Most of the few libraries not covered by Title II come under Title III guidelines, which require that owners of public accommodations make "readily achievable" changes that improve accessibility. These may include installing a ramp, creating accessible parking, or adding grab bars in restroom facilities.

The "Checklist for Buildings and Facilities," prepared by the Barriers Compliance Board, is one of the most comprehensive interpretations of the ADA, and it is well worth getting a copy. The checklist is intended as a supplement to the Barrier Compliance Board's *Minimum Guidelines and Requirements for Accessible Design.* It was created "to assist individuals and entities with rights or duties under Title II and Title III of the Americans with Disabilities Act (ADA) in applying the requirements of the Americans with Disabilities Act Accessibility Guidelines (ADAAG) to buildings and facilities subject to the law."[3] Not until you've read the checklist will you realize how many seemingly small details affect access. Although use of this checklist is voluntary, you can bet that in any dispute its provisions will probably be upheld.

Structures Covered by the ADA

The ADA applies to all new construction. That is, it applies to a facility that was designed and constructed for first occupancy after January 26, 1993. In other words, the last application for a building permit or permit extension for the facility was certified to be completed by a state, county, or local government after January 26, 1992. According to the act, exceptions to its provisions are permitted only "where the alternative designs and technologies used will provide substantially equivalent or greater access to and usability of the facility."[4]

Remodeling or renovations, referred to as "alterations," should "be done in a manner so as to ensure that, to the maximum extent feasible, the altered portions of the facility comply" with the guidelines.[5] This means that most of the alterations of specific parts of a facility must be completed in compliance with the requirements for new construction, but full compliance is not required where technically infeasible. If yours is a qualified historic building, it must comply with restrictions unless it is determined that compliance would threaten or destroy the historic significance of the building.

Although it is impossible to include all the issues raised by the checklist in this brief summary (and it frequently becomes extremely technical), it will be useful to just mention some of the most basic considerations. The following is a very small sampling of some of the points you should be aware of:

Outside pathways should be level, or no steeper than 1:14 gradient.

Pathways should have a level rest area every 9 meters (about 29½ feet) or less.

Pathways should have an unobstructed width of 1,000 mm (about 3¼ feet).

Entrances should be sheltered from inclement weather.

Landings in front of entrance doors should have a clear circulation space of 1,550 mm (about 61 inches) in diameter.

Doors should be at least 760 mm (about 30 inches) wide, although 820 mm (about 32¼ inches) is preferred.

Lever handles are preferred to doorknobs.

Thresholds should not have steps.

Floors should be of slip-resistant vinyl sheeting, low-pile carpet, or unglazed tiles.

Corridors should have an unobstructed minimum width of 1,000 mm (about 39⅜ inches).

Corridors should have adequate lighting levels, at least 300 lux.

Accessible bathrooms should have side and rear grab rails fixed at a height of 800 mm to 810 mm (about 31½ inches).

The space beside accessible toilets should be at least 950 mm (slightly more than 37 inches).

Doors and drawers should have "D" handles, not knobs.

Access to Historic Buildings

In one sense, libraries bear a unique burden when it comes to complying with ADA guidelines. Our heritage is integrally tied up in our nineteenth- and early twentieth-century Carnegie libraries that are nightmares of inaccessibility. The multistory structures seem to have steps everywhere, especially the steps averaging eight in number at front doors. The library at Galena, Illinois, for example, has two dozen steps. On the other hand, many people would like to affirm the public library tradition by restoring their Carnegies to their former glory. Most laypeople know little about the modifications that need to be made to a structure to permit access. The clamor to save the old building is likely to arise long before a professional analysis has been performed. If you (or your board) are inclined to renovate a Carnegie library, you should be prepared for a difficult ordeal.

Not only Carnegies but most libraries of the period, especially those with classical facades, suffer from major access problems. Older buildings may have no accessible route from parking lots, and if there are any entrance ramps, they are too steep. Elevators are also nonexistent or too small for most wheelchairs. Wheelchairs are also unable to move among the stacks in many historic buildings, and seating, water fountains, and restrooms are inaccessible.

If your board or administration is considering a renovation project, be sure it is aware of the difficulties involved in making an older structure ADA compliant. For example, exterior stairs may leave no room for ramps, and elevators and automatic doors may be difficult if not impossible to install. Old-fashioned stack areas with their tortuous spiral stairs and narrow aisles usually must be completely removed. Still other features like steep terrain, monumental steps, narrow or heavy doors, decorative ornamental hardware, and narrow pathways and corridors make access difficult if not impossible. Older buildings also often have multiple levels with a single step separating each stack area or reading room from the central area. There may be inadequate space available for ramps, and disabled users may be forced to travel long distances merely to reach a ramp that takes them up or down a step.

Although the unique characteristics of your particular historic structure will determine the specific modifications that must be made, you would do well to use the following list of critical elements to do a personal assessment of your building. You need not even enter the building to get an idea of the scope of the difficulties that may lie ahead. If any of the following statements is not true of your site or structure, you can anticipate problems. This advance warning will allow you to be prepared and, hopefully, to head off poorly informed enthusiasts.

The width, slope, cross slope, and surface texture of walkways permit easy wheelchair access.

The distance between arrival and destination points is short.

Landscaping does not hinder wheelchair access.

Parking is provided conveniently close to the building (libraries serve many older patrons who may use canes or walkers).

Walkways are a minimum of 91 cm (3 feet) wide and preferably wider.

Pathways are appropriately graded and have a firm and slip-resistant surface.

Patrons who use wheelchairs are able to come into the library through the main public entrance. (This may involve changing elevation, steps, landings, doors, or thresholds.)

Space is available to position ramps at public entrances and at every location where one or more steps prevent access. The steepest allowable slope for a ramp is 1:12, or 8 percent, but gentler slopes are preferable. Such ramps should not significantly alter the historic character of the building.

It is true that wheelchair platforms and inclined stair lifts can be installed and used to overcome changes in elevation ranging from .9 meter to 3 meters (3 to 10 feet) in height, but local building codes may restrict their use. It may also be possible to create an entirely new entrance without significantly altering the look of the building. For example, you might make use of a not-too-prominently placed window opening. However, if such major changes are needed, it may be an indication that the structure is not really accessible enough to be used as a library.

On the other hand, there are many ways you can increase access while doing little damage to the original building. For example, creating designated parking spaces, installing ramps (where ample space exists), and making curb cuts are all reasonably straightforward. Inside the building, raised markings can be added to elevator control buttons, flashing alarm lights can be installed, accessible door hardware can be added, and offset hinges can be used to widen doorways. Restrooms lend themselves to fairly easy alteration, and few zealots will argue that they should remain in their original antediluvian state. For example, grab bars and higher toilet seats can be added to stalls, partitions can be rearranged, and pipes under sinks can be insulated to prevent burns. Even repositioning the paper towel dispenser can make a big difference.

Most historic buildings are equipped with ancient elevators or, more probably, no elevators at all. Although it's certainly preferable to install a new elevator, control panels can be modified with a "wand" on a cord to make the control panel accessible. The timing device regulating the doors can also be adjusted. Historic interior doors also pose serious access problems. On the one hand historic buildings are often chock full of fire hazards, so the local fire inspector may insist that interior doors be kept closed. On the other hand, antique door hardware, needed to preserve the look of the doors, severely limits accessibility. Power-assisted door openers can be installed, but they too alter the look of the door.

An inspection of the building and its potential ADA-compliance problems may require the assistance of an accessibility specialist who is trained to identify and assess barriers and who is an expert on local codes, state codes, and federal laws. Together, the accessibility expert and architect should develop a plan that pro-

TIPS

ADA rules *do* apply, and don't forget it. This makes a huge difference in how wide your aisles are going to be and will affect the number of shelving units you can put in. A good vendor knows this and won't fudge but will make the most of the space you have. ADA also affects the width of your doors, hallways, etc.

ADA works well for archives in this regard because the wider halls and doors work better for carts loaded with boxes and odd sized items. You don't have to convince the architect that your carts are going to be heavy and need a wider turning point.

Follow the ADA codes religiously.

vides the greatest amount of accessibility without threatening or destroying the features that make the library a historic building. This plan should be completed before any final decision is made to preserve the building as a library. The historic building under consideration must be able to support a sophisticated technical infrastructure, and it must be able to provide convenient access to all library patrons. If it cannot meet these two basic requirements, the project should be abandoned. It is far too costly, both in human and monetary terms, and it is doomed to failure.

The U.S. Park Service provides a list of priorities when making modifications to a historic structure. They are

1. making the main or a prominent public entrance and primary public spaces accessible, including a path to the entrance

2. providing access to goods, services, and programs

3. providing accessible restroom facilities

4. creating access to amenities and secondary spaces[6]

NOTES

1. Baird M. Smith, Preservation Briefs 3: Conserving Energy in Historic Buildings. Available online at http://ewingrestoration.com/Briefs/brief03.htm.

2. H. Neil Kelley, "ADA: Relax, Take a Deep Breath, and Do It Well." *Illinois Libraries* 74 (May 1992): 302–3.

3. U.S. Architectural and Transportation Barriers Compliance Board, *Minimum Guidelines and Requirements for Accessible Design* (Washington, D.C.: The Board, 1993).

4. U.S. Architectural and Transportation Barriers Compliance Board, *Americans with Disabilities Act: Accessibility Guidelines, Checklist for Building and Facilities* (Washington, D.C.: The Board, 1996). Available online at http://adata.org.

5. *Americans with Disabilities Act,* Public Law 336, 101st Cong. (26 July 1990). Available online at http://www.usdoj.gov/crt/ada/pubs/ada.txt.

6. National Park Service, *Historic Structures and Cultural Landscapes* (Washington, D.C.: GPO, 1999).

Resources

American Council for an Energy-Efficient Economy
2140 Shattuck Ave., Ste. 202
Berkeley, CA 94704
(202) 429-0063

Americans with Disabilities Act Document Center
http://www.janweb.icd.wvu.edu/kinder

Disability and Business Technical Regional Assistance Centers Department of Education
National Institute of Disabilities and Rehabilitation Research
(800) 949-4232
http://www.adata.org/index_dbtac.html

E Source, Inc.
50 Walnut St.
Boulder, CO 80302-5140
http://www.esource.com

Human Factors and Ergonomics Society
P.O. Box 1369
Santa Monica, CA 90406-1369
e-mail: hfes@compuserve.com

Illuminating Engineering Society of North America
120 Wall St., 17th Fl.
New York, NY 10005-4001
(212) 248-5000

Job Accommodation Network (JAN)
(800) 526-7234; TDD in Canada:
    (800) 526-2262
fax: (304) 293-5407
www.janweb.icd.wvu.edu

National Fenestration Rating Council
1300 Spring St., Ste. 120
Silver Spring, MD 20910
(301) 589-6372

Rocky Mountain Institute
1739 Snowmass Creek Rd.
Snowmass, CO 81654-9199
(970) 927-3851

Society for Information Display
1526 Brookhollow Dr., Ste. 82
Santa Ana, CA 92705-5421
(714) 545-1526

**U.S. Architectural and
  Transportation Barriers
  Compliance Board**
1331 F St. NW, #1000
Washington, DC 20004
(800) USA-ABLE or (202) 272-5434
TDD: (202) 272-5449

Beck, Susan Gilbert. "Wayfinding in Libraries." *Library Hi Tech* 14, no. 1 (1996): 27–36.

Carpenter, Scott A. "The Americans with Disabilities Act: Accommodation in Ohio." *College & Research Libraries* 57 (Nov. 1996): 555–6.

Cirrillo, Susan E., and Robert E. Danford. *Library Buildings, Equipment, and the ADA: Compliance Issues and Solutions.* Chicago: American Library Assn., 1996.

Goldman, Nancy, ed. *Readily Achievable Checklist: A Survey for Accessibility.* Boston: Adaptive Environments Center, 1993.

Gunde, Michael G. "Working with the Americans with Disabilities Act." *Library Journal* 116 (Dec. 1991): 99–100.

———. "Working with the Americans with Disabilities Act: Part II." *Library Journal* 117 (May 1992): 41–2.

Hayward, Judith L., and Thomas C. Jester, comps. *Accessibility and Historic Preservation Resource Guide.* Windsor, Vt.: Historic Windsor, Inc., 1992, revised 1993.

HBW Associates, Inc. "Checklist for Barrier Free Access." *Illinois Libraries* 67 (Nov. 1987): 804.

Jester, Thomas C. *Preserving the Past and Making It Accessible for People with Disabilities.* Washington, D.C.: Preservation Assistance Division, National Park Service, U.S. Department of the Interior, 1992.

Natale, Joe. "Done Right: East St. Louis Accessibility Project." *Illinois Libraries* 73 (Dec. 1991): 597–9.

———. "The Next Step: The ADA Self-Evaluation." *Illinois Libraries* 74 (May 1992): 284–90.

Pack, Nancy C., and Donald D. Foos. "Library Compliance with the Americans with Disabilities Act." *RQ* 32 (winter 1992): 255–67.

Uhler, Scott F., and Philippe R. Weiss. "Library Building Alterations under the Americans with Disabilities Act." *Illinois Libraries* 78 (winter 1996): 5–7.

6 Technology and Modern Building Infrastructures

If an early twentieth-century builder could be transported to the twenty-first century for a tour of a modern building, he would be astonished at the changes that have taken place over the last one hundred years. However, to the casual visitor, the majority of these changes are invisible. Modern technology has transformed practically every building system, and library buildings have been affected by technology even more than most structures. If you were to choose the most difficult part of planning your twenty-first-century library, it would probably be that of correctly anticipating technology needs. The mention of the word "technology" probably brings to mind the vast expanses of computers found in many libraries. However, if you look a little closer, you'll discover that the entire library is run by computers, and these aren't the ones that are used by your staff and patrons. Computer chips can be found in the library's climate control system and in controls regulating most of the library's systems.

As you have gone about your work, you have been aided by a wealth of books and articles on library planning. You have been able to examine other libraries, picking and choosing the features you want to incorporate into your new library. Most important, you have been able to take advantage of a network of librarians who have already gone through the process and are usually delighted to share their experiences.

No matter how helpful all these resources may be, no manual and no experienced individual can tell you exactly what technical requirements should be incorporated into a twenty-first-century library. By the time you read this book, any state-of-the-art solutions suggested will undoubtedly be obsolete. All that library literature can do is point out general considerations. The rest is really up to you.

TECHNOLOGY IN TODAY'S LIBRARIES

Superficially, most library buildings look fairly similar. Most have lots of computers and lots of telephones. Television monitors are sometimes visible, as are fax machines, printers, and scanners. All this really tells you nothing. Two installations that look similar to the outsider can be worlds apart when it comes to functionality. However, it is possible to identify and interview the technicians who take care of a building's electronic innards. You may even be able to hold a reasonably intelligent conversation with your newfound wisdom. Such conversations will require a shared language, so before proceeding farther, it would be a good idea to spend a little time sprucing up your vocabulary.

Terminology

As you talk with architects and contractors, you will discover that there's a whole new language devoted to the bits and pieces that compose the technical infrastructure of a modern building. In some cases, the words have been specially coined for this purpose but more often, they are words that sound familiar and comfortable until you hear them used in a strange new context. The following is a very brief glossary of just a few of the most commonly used terms:

Backbone   High-speed communications network that connects smaller networks

Bandwidth   Volume of sound, text, graphics, or video that can be transmitted through a wire; that is, the amount or portion of the frequency spectrum needed to transmit the information

Baud rate   Measure of the transmission speed at which information is sent from one device to another; at a rate of 9600 baud, each bit has a duration of 1/9600 second

Bridge   Device that connects two or more physical local-area networks (LANs) and forwards packets of data from one LAN segment to another without changing it

Cable trays   Channels into which cables are placed; cable tray systems are bonded together

Ethernet   Most widely used method to access a local area network; connects up to 1,024 nodes over twisted-pair, coaxial, and optical fiber cables; fast Ethernet (100 Base-T) increases transmission speed to 100 megabytes per second (Mbps)

Fiber-optic cable   Bundles of glass threads, each capable of transmitting light waves; used to transmit data at a much higher capacity than metal cables

Hub   Part of local area network equipment that allows multiple network devices to be connected to a cabling system through a central point

Local area network (LAN)   Group of computers, printers, and other devices connected to one another through network interface cards, hubs, bridges, routers, and switches allowing computers to share resources, such as information stored in files, and hardware, such as printers and fax modems

100 Base-T   Refers to the speed and capacity of a communications line; for example, the Institute of Electrical and Electronic Engineers (IEEE) 802.30 standard for 100 Mbps Ethernet, also referred to as "fast Internet"; 10 Base-T is slower

Plenum   Lined cavity through which cables or conditioned air is routed

Router   Device that directs e-mail and other information between a local network and the Internet

T-1 line   High-speed digital connection that can transmit data at a rate of approximately 1.5 million bits per second (bps)

T-3 line   Digital connection that can send/receive data at 44,736,000 bps

TCP/IP (Transmission Control Protocol/Internet Protocol)   Somewhat informal rules of the Internet that allow PCs, mainframes, and networks with different operation systems to communicate with one another

Twisted-pair cable   Type of cable used for LANs and other in-building voice and data communications applications; the design helps to reduce cross-talk between the pairs

Overview of a Typical New Library's Technology

Bearing in mind that technology is changing rapidly, it may be useful to take a look at the present state of library technology. For example, the following description might be applicable to a recently built library:

Computers are located throughout the building, not just in the back room and OPAC corral. They are connected to one another through a local area network (LAN), and client-server architecture permits computers of various configurations and operating systems to communicate easily with one another. A "backbone"—probably consisting of fiber-optic cabling—is installed vertically in risers or elevator shafts and horizontally in cable tracks or conduits, connecting different parts of the building and possibly extending to other buildings.

Columns provide numerous terminations for electricity and network access. Future change is anticipated in the floor layout with a conduit grid that can create as many additional access points as may be required. Because cabling is a long-term investment, it has been chosen to permit the highest bandwidth and transfer rate possible given fiscal realities. Provisions have been made to distribute data from a central computer room to sites (possibly communications closets) throughout the building with data, video, and voice accommodated over the same cable.

Specifications for cabling, connectors, hubs, and other network components are standard, widely accepted, and compatible with most hardware and software of the same generation. In addition, the number of nodes, hubs, and ports composing the network can be doubled or preferably tripled without a major change to the basic configuration or extensive rewiring.

Six-hundred-amp electrical service or higher is designed to meet all future power demands. Parallel-port connectors are integrated into work surfaces, and duplex power outlets are part of every workstation. Redundancy is incorporated into the system, reducing down time. An uninterruptible power system (UPS) provides time for the network to shut down normally, thus avoiding having information lost and programs corrupted because of power outages.

Satellite Reading Room, Thomas Jefferson Building, Library of Congress, Washington, D.C., with hollow beams and columns for wiring flexibility

Technology does not exist in a vacuum. In a modern, well-designed library, every element works in unison with every other element. Because technology is changing so rapidly and needs vary across libraries, it is not possible to dictate what should be included in a specific library. Instead, the best way to approach the subject is probably to analyze individual libraries and the configurations they chose. Some aspects of their plans might be applicable to your new library. Other solutions address the specific needs of the local environment. Mayo and Nelson, in their book *Wired for the Future,* provide excellent step-by-step analysis for developing a technology plan.[1]

The Preeminence of the Web

Whatever the specific components of your technology plan, the World Wide Web should be a primary focus. In the last few years we have witnessed one resource after another being made available on the Web. Newer OPACs are Web-accessible, allowing users to dial in from home. Indexes and full-text journals are also available on the Web, as are cataloging and acquisitions utilities. These developments simplify your planning in some respects, but they also make greater technical demands on a library. The description of a modern library provided in the previous section is only the beginning. Libraries have unique requirements when it comes to meeting the information needs of their users. Here, for example, is a description of a sophisticated university library emphasizing the broad access to information resources on the Web:

Technology is designed to support and facilitate the research process.

Study carrels are equipped with Ethernet jacks. Library-owned and personal laptop computers can be connected to the Internet at any workstation.

The network offers a variety of information resources including local and regional tape-loaded resources, Telnet, FTP, World Wide Web, CD-ROM, productivity software, graphics, and statistical packages as well as scanners, fax, laser printers, and other hardware and software to serve the library's user and administrative needs. From a single Web-based menu, users can connect to a wealth of networked utilities including both local and remote resources. Wiring technology allows the digital transmission of data, graphics, and audiovisual resources to all parts of the building.

Library standards for linking computer systems such as Z39.50 are supported.

The university library is an extension of the campus information network and ably supports electronic scholarship. Information technology is a natural, fully integrated part of the public library environment.

Comfortable furniture encourages users to spend extended periods of time studying, researching, and writing using electronic equipment and resources. Carpeting incorporates antistatic properties needed for use with computers and creates an aesthetically pleasing environment. Sophisticated window technology permits exterior vistas and natural daylight without interfering with visibility of projected images or posing a hazard to paper resources. Heating, ventilating, and air-conditioning (HVAC) systems offer zone control, providing comfort for human users and adequate cooling for heat-generating computer servers. Noise is controlled with an appropriate level of comfort-inducing "white noise," facilitating study.

Spacious user instruction rooms are equipped to teach groups how to use online systems. Computer stations are conveniently positioned for the use of speakers or instructors. Teaching spaces are wired to accommodate twenty or more workstations having access to the campus information network. High-quality, easy-to-operate projection equipment is mounted to the ceiling with controls adjacent to the instructor's workstation.

Contracts with suppliers of reference databases permit sufficient simultaneous connections to accommodate groups of users. Sophisticated system software limits the number of simultaneous users to contractually agreed upon numbers; provides a firewall between public and administrative functions; protects against viruses; and routinely monitors, adjusts, and redirects system traffic.

Computers for Staff

When choosing hardware for staff workstations, you will want it to be compatible with the computers in the rest of the library. Here, however, are a few guidelines to use when making your selections:

Choose PC clones unless your environment is dominated by Macs because software is more widely available for PCs.

Avoid dumb terminals or even the new network computers. A PC is both more flexible and more functional.

In your RFPs, specify that computers should come with Windows, Microsoft Office, and other desired software preloaded.

Network all staff computers as part of the larger library network.

Purchase as much RAM memory as you can afford since multitasking saves time and is more functional.

Select software that supports the full ALA character set for display, input/update, and printing.

Provide access to the World Wide Web, e-mail, the LC Cataloger's Desktop, Telnet, and OCLC's Passport for Windows and/or RLIN Passport.

Steering Clear of "Bleeding Edge" Technology

Now that we have a basic description of a modern, technically sophisticated library, let us look at what should *not* be included. If you are a frequent reader of computer magazines, you have already discovered that many pages are filled with enthusiastic descriptions of the next generation of computer technology. Usually some new and amazing breakthrough is described as the way of the future and the obvious direction in which technology will advance. However, if for some reason you should be leafing through last year's back issues, you would find many similar articles describing innovations that in the short space of a year have had their brief moment of fame and then quickly become dinosaurs on the computer landscape.

No one, not even the most highly trained computer engineers, can predict the equipment that will become next year's standard. This means that you can't extend the useful lives of your equipment by betting on technology that isn't here. If it's not fully developed and widely accepted, it's not for you.

Looking back, you probably can count at least half a dozen trendy new technologies that turned out to be a waste of money. In the past, you could usually banish these disasters to the top shelf of the storage closet without any dire consequences. However, today's serious automation error can cost millions of dollars and permanently affect your library's ability to function effectively. You will want to wait until the last possible moment to make computer decisions by keeping an eagle eye on technological developments. Nevertheless, your selections must be based on current, not future technology. No library has the financial or human resources to take chances on "bleeding edge" technology.

PLANNING FOR A HIGH-TECH FUTURE

Although it may not be possible to anticipate tomorrow's technology, there are some steps you can take now to ensure that your library will be able to accommodate the needs of tomorrow's library users. For example, you should allow more space for wiring closets and ventilated file-server maintenance areas than you will need immediately. If there is any prediction you can make with certainty, it is that computers and other media will increase rapidly and will have ever-greater power requirements. Conduit and cable should be laid throughout the building, even in places where there will be no immediate need for it.

Bear in mind that with technology changing so rapidly, it is probable that there will be a long line of workers reconfiguring conduit and cable, upgrading the electrical service, and otherwise accommodating the technical developments of the next century. It is, therefore, important to avoid designing a building in which the cable installer will have to drill holes in walls or knock down walls to get to the building's "innards." Although it is inevitable that technology will change rapidly, the pathways and spaces allocated to the technological infrastructure will remain for the life of the building and should be designed to support many generations of technological change.

Above all, you don't want your building to be obsolete the day you open. Retrofitting is an extremely expensive procedure and one you certainly want to postpone as long as possible. For example, twenty feet of four-inch conduit designed into the initial building will cost approximately $200 to install. If you must later initiate a change order to install it after construction, that same conduit could cost $6,000.

Wiring an Older Library

Certainly, one of the most important reasons for renovating an older facility is to accommodate a sophisticated electrical and data infrastructure. The modern library will require a data networking environment facilitating Internet access and even an asynchronous transfer mode (ATM) network for increased bandwidth demands. If your computing needs are extensive, you may need a high-speed Ethernet network served by a fiber-optic backbone and horizontal cabling.

Installing modern cabling and wiring technologies into existing walls and floors can be extremely difficult. However, it is possible to core-drill holes through the existing floors to receive poke-through devices. Cabling can also be routed through cable trays, in plenum space below, with data cables on one side of the tray and voice lines on the other. Cable trays save a lot on labor costs as well. It is also possible to cut channels in the floor slab and install an in-floor cellular pathway (or channel) on the ground floor. Cutting into a hardwood floor is painful, but it may be necessary. Later, the floor can be replaced and refinished above the pathway.

If, however, you are attempting to preserve the historic interior of the library building, the problem becomes even more acute. One solution is to "fish" a metal-clad cable between the inner and outer walls. Flexible cabling is available for threading electrical circuits into existing walls, plenums, and anywhere that mechanical protection is required. Although traditional pipe and wire cabling may be preferable in most instances, flexible, prewired, metal-clad cable can allow you to keep the beautiful old paneling in the reading room or the charming mural in the children's area.

Raised Access Floors

Cable management has become an important element in modern library design, and a number of methods have been developed to deal with the cable jungle that erupts when many computers are brought together. These include poke-throughs, duct systems, and especially raised access floors. Although quite expensive, raised access floors provide an open space beneath a floor level that makes it possible to easily bring new technology to an area. Raised access floors are designed to accommodate computer, telecommunications, and electric power cabling plus under-floor air delivery systems. In addition, future equipment and network upgrades can be accomplished with much less difficulty than would be the case with a conventional floor. Commercially produced flooring systems are available for this purpose and should be investigated, especially if you are renovating an existing building or if your installation poses other unusual technical challenges.

The following example illustrates how one library used a raised access flooring system to deal with its somewhat inflexible building design. First, the building team identified areas with the most extensive technical needs. They excluded potential stack areas since most raised access flooring systems are not intended to support the weight of book stacks. Next, they chose a 125-millimeter raised floor, which allowed sufficient space for telecommunication cables, small electric power distribution lines, and building-control systems. The building team might have chosen other raised-floor designs with shallower depths at a somewhat lower cost. However, it was the consensus of the group that the extra height was worth the added cost because of its increased functionality. The team was especially concerned that the floor should be stable, even with heavy foot traffic, so they chose carpet tiles, which made it even easier to do electrical work in the floor and made it easy to rearrange workstations. Carpet tiles, however, cost as much as one-third to one-half more than broadloom carpeting.

Just installing a raised access floor does not ensure efficient cable management, however. Therefore, shallow cable trays organized telecommunications cabling and maintained designated routes up to end-user termination points. Otherwise, the raised floor would quickly fill with obsolete cabling. The team chose a plug-in, flexible cabling arrangement consisting of clip-together connectors that allowed for quick cable relocation.

Hewetson Floors is one company that offers fairly economical access floor systems. Its flooring panels are made of press-formed galvanized steel that encapsulate a high performance particle board core. Corner location points ensure accurate positioning and rigidity. Hewetson Floors has a six-minute video intended to provide building professionals with an understanding of the physical construction of raised floors. You might ask your architect to obtain a copy of the tape. Tate Access Floor Systems is another manufacturer of access flooring systems; it has a brochure that can be obtained free of charge directly or from Alumasc Interior Building Products. (Contact these vendors for their information; see Resources.) Tate also uses a modular panel and pedestal system. Its Concore GCS is composed of 600-millimeter-square welded-steel panels with an inert cement core supported by an understructure of adjustable pedestals. Be sure that the system you choose conforms to the requirements of ISO 9002.

Wireless Networking

If you are renovating an older facility or are limited in wiring options, you may find that wireless networks are an excellent way to avoid tearing down walls or coping with a cable jungle. Where major rewiring is impractical or historic design features cannot be tampered with, many libraries are finding that wireless local area networks are the best solution. Wireless LANs eliminate the necessity to wire around obstacles and can save a considerable amount in retrofitting costs. Such networks use electromagnetic airwaves instead of hard-wired connectivity. The frequency bands used by wireless LANs do not require an FCC license or approval for installation, so there is considerable freedom possible in designing a configuration. Wireless and wired equipment can coexist in most situations, and wireless components can take the place of any segment of a network.

At present, some international standards have been developed for wireless technology, so compatibility among vendors is becoming common. However, wireless technology is an area in which change is especially rapid, and products and configurations are appearing on the market almost daily. In recent years, a variety of wireless networks have emerged such as the wireless local area network (WLAN), the wireless personal area network (WPAN), the LAN/LAN bridge, and the wireless wide area network (WWAN). WLAN is in most respects like a hard-wired local area network. It uses the same network operating systems, such as Windows NT or Novell Netware communications protocol, so it is fairly easy to combine wired and wireless networks in the same library. The LAN/LAN bridge allows wired and/or wireless LANs in separate areas to communicate to each other with radio airwaves.

WPAN is not as useful in a library environment. It consists of a limited number of computers located a few feet away from one another. Apple Power-Book computers, for example, come equipped with built-in infrared communication capability. WPAN makes it possible to transfer files, synchronize computers, and access peripheral devices like printers.

Most wireless systems begin with a central "access point" transceiver (a term that combines the concept of a transmitter and a receiver), which communicates with both the network and with each workstation client. The transceiver is very much like a hub of an Ethernet network and communicates with a wireless adaptor or plug-in card in each network computer. Each adaptor comes equipped with an integrated antenna, and software converts data into radio signals and back to data again. The network operating system is completely unaware that this is happening. Protocols developed for the purpose minimize interference among transmissions and ensure reliable communications. Although wireless systems are somewhat slower than wired systems, the difference is not great; in most situations, users are unaware of the difference. The distances over which the radio waves can travel vary with the particular situation—walls, metal, and even people can get in the way. A typical range for a WLAN is 500 feet in a normal library environment or 1,000 feet in open space. One access point usually provides approximately 50,000 to 250,000 square feet of coverage depending on the library's design.

Because wireless technologies began with military applications, security is an integral part of their design. Sophisticated encryption techniques, password authorization of users, and digital authentication of each station make wireless networks more secure than many wired LANs. Some people occasionally ask whether it's safe to have all those microwaves passing back and forth. In actuality, the power output of wireless LANs is quite low and is typically only about a tenth or less of that of a cellular phone. Since radio waves fade over distance, users experience very little exposure to radio frequency energy, and the energy emitted is called nonionizing, meaning that it does not damage cells if it is absorbed by the human body.

Although the cost of the wireless network components is higher than for a wired network, the total cost of hardware, software, cable, conduits, and installation may be significantly below that of wired networks. In new construction, wired LANs are usually preferred, but in the case of an existing building, savings in labor alone can more than compensate for the increased cost of equipment.

Computer Classrooms and Conference Rooms

Although sophisticated electronic equipment is finding its way into every corner of the modern library, certain areas deserve special consideration. Technology-equipped classrooms, meeting rooms, and conference rooms are now standard in new libraries and have quite different requirements from the islands of individual workstations found in most other areas. Traditionally, library instruction has been integral to the mission of academic and school libraries; therefore, instruction spaces have been included in most library plans. With the advent of computers, however, all libraries, no matter what clientele they serve, need space to teach basic computer skills and database searching techniques. As the number of computers in libraries increases, so does the need for instruction in using these resources effectively and efficiently. Internet training is especially popular among library users, and any librarians planning a new or renovated building will find that they must make provisions for multimedia-equipped classrooms.

As you plan special spaces like "smart" or electronic classrooms, you will need to consider recent innovations such as satellite uplinks and microwave transmitters that allow librarians and users to bring together television, the Internet, and the full range of telecommunications technologies. Our users have come to expect these technological marvels, so they must be considered when designing information facilities.

Of special concern is the problem of noise in an electronic classroom. In a room full of computers, the sound that we normally think of as unobtrusive "white noise" from a single computer can become almost deafening when multiplied by a factor of 25 or 30. Make sure the architect has considered potential noise problems and investigated special acoustical wall materials.

A related concern is heat, which also usually goes unnoticed with a single computer. However, the heat generated by a single computer is significant. When that heat is multiplied by the number of computers in the classroom, it can easily exceed the capability of most HVAC systems. Also, don't forget that teaching spaces have unique requirements for lighting, furniture, ergonomics, wiring and cabling, and, of course, computer equipment. Of special concern when viewing a film or an Internet presentation are viewing angles, distance of the viewer from the image, screen size, light level, workstation requirements, and classroom space configurations. (Covered later in this chapter and in the ergonomics section of chapter 8.)

If possible, spaces should be designed so that they can be used as computer labs and can also accommodate seminars and meetings. Consider computer desks that allow monitors to be recessed below the surface with glass panels in the work surface so that equipment does not obscure sight lines with a speaker or instructor. Be careful, however, that furniture is not custom-built around the proportions of today's computer equipment because the size and shape of computers has changed radically in just a very few years and probably will do so again in the future. Having two seating areas—one for computers and one for meetings—is another alternative. This makes it possible to see the speaker or the projection screen without having to peer between computers.

Both classrooms and meeting facilities have some requirements in common. For example, both need storage space for equipment, and both usually require projectors mounted in the ceiling with easy-to-reach controls located near the spot where the speaker or instructor is standing. Both also may require room flexibility that allows a gathering to break up into collaborative work or discussion groups. This might be achieved by the use of movable partitions. Furthermore, both will need soundproofing.

Conditions that are especially conducive to learning don't just happen, and many spaces intended for this purpose just don't work. Of course, budget constraints must be considered, but wall surfaces and finishes, mechanical fixtures, audiovisual systems, projection booths, media equipment packages, and even the lecturer's workstation lectern are points for discussion when planning such spaces.

TELECOMMUNICATIONS AND THE MODERN LIBRARY

Although a number of librarians quoted in this book think they might have been happier with less high-tech ingenuity in some of their building systems, telecommunications is the one area where they almost universally wish they had more. Extensive telecommunications facilities are needed, and most newer libraries provide distance education classrooms and teleconferencing centers. In fact, most library areas should be equipped to provide expanded voice, data, and video services throughout the building. Changes in the telecommunications arena are affecting libraries even more than most other organizations, and keeping up with them can be an overwhelming task.

For the librarian involved in a building project, telecommunications pose some unique problems. Whereas you can assume that your HVAC system is not unlike thousands of others, and both your architect and contractor can be expected to have a firm grasp on essential information, this is not necessarily the case with telecommunications. It is entirely possible that neither building professional has ever worked on a project as sophisticated as yours, and they may need your help.

In contrast to your role in selecting heating/cooling equipment, which may be confined simply to an occasional reality check (not always, unfortunately), the buck really stops with you when it comes to telecommunications. To at least some extent, it's up to you to decide whether your building professionals are prepared for their task. Do they possess the expertise to design and construct the infrastructure that will support your computer network, Internet site, telephone system, and multimedia information delivery? Naturally, you cannot become an instant engineer, but it will be necessary for you to become more knowledgeable about this subject than about most other construction matters. (You will probably find the following subsections rougher going than the others in this book, so grit your teeth and prepare to be painfully enlightened.)

Fact-Finding Missions

Perhaps an education in telecommunications sounds like more work than you're really willing to take on. Once you've plowed through this section (and several recent articles as well), what can you possibly do with the information? First, you'll need it when you are helping to select the firm to plan your new library. In fact, you'll need the information for those many building visits you will be taking. In addition, you'll need extensive background information to discourage elaborate technology plans that have little use in a library environment.

Chapter 1 emphasized the importance of visiting new buildings, and chapter 2 made a case for visiting buildings designed by the design firm being considered for your project. While making your rounds, seek out the technician who is responsible for maintaining the computer network to get the "inside" story. Of course, you'll never find technicians who are blissfully happy with their buildings' infrastructures, but all things are relative. Ask questions like the following:

Does the communications network criss-cross the entire building, or are there large areas bereft of network access?

Are there voice and data ports at every staff workstation?

Is there ample space for servers and other communications equipment?

Are equipment rooms and distribution closets well designed and located conveniently?

Has sufficient attention been paid to ventilating and cooling computer equipment?

Are telecommunications spaces large and numerous enough to allow for future expansion?

What kind of cabling was used?

How difficult is it to replace defective cabling?

How fast and reliable are communications within and outside the building?

As you might expect, the answers to your questions will be in a language totally unlike English. It would help to bring your own library technician along as a translator, but ultimately, you're the one who's going to have to make a judgment about the architect's familiarity with today's technology.

Take a look around an architect's building projects. Does it appear that money has been lavished on design features at the expense of the infrastructure? You don't win architectural awards for cabling or conduits. Then, visit the newest, most technically sophisticated library in your region and talk to the technician in charge of the network. (You might want to check out this building first to have a standard for comparison.) How do the two facilities compare?

TIP

Provide free in-library or campus phones so patrons on upper floors can speak with a reference librarian. Make sure that the phones are solidly attached to the wall since otherwise, they will quickly disappear.

A Working Telecommunications Plan

Give consideration to the special needs of each area. For instance, consider equipping conference rooms for teleconferencing, and bear in mind increased use of voice and data communications for meetings. While you're planning the telephone system, remember that in-house or campus phones are an important security precaution. They should be readily accessible on all floors and in every wing of the library. Not only are they essential for communicating with security guards and other emergency personnel but they can extend reference services to areas where no service desk is available.

All areas of the library should be designed to support multiple voice and data configurations. As emphasized before, never imagine that the way you plan to be using a space on opening day is the way it will be used in the years to come. Your library's needs will change—probably much sooner than you imagine. Communications outlets should be almost as numerous as electrical outlets. Following are some general guidelines for distributing them:

Equip all offices with a minimum of two data and two telephone outlets. They should be located on opposite walls and preferably near electrical outlets. Install multiple communication outlets (one per 75 square feet) in larger offices and suites. A good rule of thumb is to be sure you have no fewer than one data and one telephone outlet at every other electrical outlet. In the case of rooms longer than 12 feet, install one or more floor outlet boxes to provide power and to connect to the building network and control other equipment.

Provide a switch-activated power outlet at the front of the room for projection and other multimedia equipment as well as additional video outlets in conference rooms, lounges, collaborative studies rooms, meeting rooms, and other areas where groups of staff or users gather. Configure conference rooms for teleconferencing with additional acoustic material on the walls and additional power, data, and lighting controls.

Equip bibliographic instruction rooms and meeting rooms with outlet boxes containing power, signal/control, and communication connections. The librarian providing instruction must be able to obtain, review, display, and distribute information in whatever medium is appropriate. Make it possible for librarians, instructors, and speakers to cue up all needed media, including TV monitor/receivers and VCRs loaded with videotape, PCs, 35-mm slides, and 16-mm projectors.

Assume that several pieces of equipment will be needed for the same presentation. Install communication outlets at fixed intervals around the wall (minimum of one per wall) and linked to the speaker's or librarian's location. Locate video drops or outlets so that the display and lighting system provide optimal viewing. Provide enough public address system speakers so announcements can be heard in every area of the library but in such a way that users working near the speakers are not blasted with sound.

Allocating Space for Telecommunications Equipment

Modern libraries are built with an extraordinary maze of channels or mouse-sized passages that traverse the entire space. These are usually called pathways, although you'll occasionally hear the term "raceway" or "tunnel system" used to

TIP

Be sure you have complete plans for any buried conduit. These plans tend to disappear shortly after the building is completed, and you don't want workers digging up your parking lots looking for buried cable.

describe the same structures. If you have the luxury of planning a new building or addition, you will be able to include spaces created just for telecommunications equipment and pathways. Pathways carry the cabling and wires that connect computer and media equipment with the central distribution system which, in turn, links to phone and data connections outside the library.

If your building will be linked to others on your campus or within your governmental unit, you will need an interbuilding distribution system consisting of the utility tunnel, conduit, manholes, and/or direct buried cable. You will not want to dig up the same area every few years to add conduit, so every effort should be made to design conduit for future construction sites. Between four and nine four-inch conduits are required to serve the needs of a medium-sized library building. Entrance conduits allow the placement of various types of cables, including large copper cables, fiber-optic cable, and coaxial cables. Manholes or utility vaults should allow the conduit to enter the building with no more than two 90-degree bends.

If you are renovating a building, it is wise to make the sacrifice and allocate adequate spaces for equipment and pathways even if you must borrow from other library functions. In many existing buildings, you will find telecommunications equipment jammed into janitors' closets and other spaces that are not suitable for housing sensitive electronic components. Such environments can cause equipment failure and can limit access to the services users need as well as endanger the people who must maintain the equipment.

The spaces you need for telecommunications equipment include rooms and facilities to bring cable into the building and to house specialized equipment. You should always include a service entrance, a central equipment room, and distribution closets. (See the following sections.)

A backbone or "riser" refers to horizontal and vertical pathways in a building distribution system used to deliver cable from the service entrance to the equipment room, then to the distribution closets, and finally to the workstation outlets. The backbone accommodates copper, fiber-optic, and/or coaxial cables. Backbone conduits and sleeves are normally four inches in diameter and should be bent no more than twice to turn corners or otherwise change direction.

TALES

It was interesting to discover that our architect had included nothing in the building budget for data wiring, even though he'd included conduit and pathways for it. Having never done a library as fully wired as ours, it never occurred to him to include that in his budget. And so it turned out that all the building contingency fund went to buy data wiring.

I became hysterical over the computer wiring for my area: I have been vindicated by the fact that the talking book computer network has never crashed and still works perfectly while the main library has spent thousands of nonexistent dollars on replacing and upgrading its automated systems.

A library just moved into a new facility with a state-of-the-art internal LAN. On dedication day no terminals were operating, and the library was not open for business because no provision had been made for connection to the consortium central site. I guess everyone assumed someone else had taken care of that little detail.

Service Entrance

As the name implies, a service entrance is a room in which outside cable connects to the building's internal telecommunications backbone. The entrance must provide sufficient space and structural elements to support the installation of a variety of cables and devices. Typical fittings include splice containers, cable termination mountings, and electrical protectors. The service entrance should be located on the lowest level of the library within 50 feet of an outside wall. It should allow direct access to the entrance conduit, the point at which feeder conduits enter the building. The service entrance should also be close to the equipment room and to the vertical backbone pathway. Repairers should be able to enter the room directly from a central hallway, not through another room.

For a 125,000-square-foot building, the service entrance room should be a minimum of 12 feet by 16 feet. It must be dry, not subject to flooding, and out of the path of overhead water, steam, or drain pipes. In addition, the room should be clear of other equipment. The walls should be covered with ¾-inch A-C plywood, painted with fire-retardant paint. Be sure that lighting is adequate in the room, a minimum of 540 lux (50 foot-candle) illumination. Conduits entering the building from outside should be plugged with reusable stoppers to keep out water or gases. Conduits leading toward other areas of the building should be "fire-stopped" after the installation of cable. To reduce airborne contaminants, flooring material should be sealed concrete or tile and should provide a minimum of 150-pounds-per-square-foot loading capability.

Central Equipment Room

Although architects and contractors use a variety of terms to designate this area, a space should be reserved for the telecommunications equipment room. It should be a central space used to house equipment that may serve devices used throughout the building. Examples of equipment include video distribution equipment, Centrex or PBX switching nodes, local area network hubs, and backbone network routers.

The room should be located preferably near the service entrance and the vertical backbone distribution pathways. It should be designed with future expansion in mind so that access to the space from outside can be provided for large equipment. Like the service entrance, the equipment room should not be subject to flooding or other hazards. It should be away from electrical power supply transformers, motors, generators, elevator equipment, radio transmitters, and other sources of electrical interference.

A fully functional air handling system is essential for controlling temperature and humidity affecting the sensitive electronic components housed here. They generate an amazing amount of heat all day every day, and they can suffer extensive damage if not kept at a constant cool temperature. Although some library systems are shut down for periods of time, during the night, on weekends, or during break periods in the case of academic libraries, it is essential that the air handling system for your equipment room provide positive air flow and cooling even during these down times. This may mean the installation of a small stand-alone cooling system designed just for this purpose. To ensure uninterrupted cooling, the unit should be connected to the building's backup power generation system. Temperature change should be closely monitored and should not vary more than 8 degrees Fahrenheit, and humidity should not vary more than 20 percent. Ideally, normal operating temperature should be between 64 and 75 degrees or normal room temperature.

Allow approximately 1 square foot of equipment room space for every library staff member and user workstation. For example, if you have 25 staff members and expect to house 300 workstations, your equipment room should be 325 square feet. In addition, the room should provide for auxiliary power and any systems that provide service to other buildings. Be sure it's fully enclosed and separated from other areas. Because of the weight of much of the equipment, a minimum floor loading of 150 to 200 pounds per square foot is essential, although some specialized services, like major uninterruptable power supply systems and batteries, may require floor loading of more than 400 pounds per square foot.

Be sure that there is adequate ceiling space to accommodate water pipes and air-conditioning ducts. Do not use false ceilings, and to protect the room from flooding, do not position drainage pipes directly over the room. Any accidental leaking should be directed around or outside the room. Nevertheless, make sure a floor drain is installed in the middle of the floor as a fail-safe backup measure.

Like the service entrance, walls should be covered with ¾-inch A-C plywood and painted with fire-retardant paint. To protect the room from fire, install a fire sprinkler system and link it to the equipment electrical panel so that power can be disconnected automatically if the sprinkler system is activated.

Distribution Closets

Once again, terminology may differ, and some architects and contractors still refer to distribution closets as telephone closets. Distribution rooms or closets, however, are spaces that support the cabling and equipment necessary to transmit data between the building's backbone system and user workstations. As the name implies, they are small spaces, usually about 5 feet by 8 feet in size. They are used to terminate cable from workstation outlets and backbone systems and to house video distribution and local area network equipment, multiplexors, and system-monitoring equipment.

You will need at least one distribution closet on each floor. They should be stacked one above the other and centrally located within the building so that the distance from the room to the most distant user locations is roughly the same. Stacking is necessary to provide space for the in-line placement of backbone conduit. Larger buildings may require more than one distribution closet on each floor since the average distance from user station to closet should normally be approximately 100 to 150 feet. Closets must be dedicated to telecommunications lines and should not be shared with electrical, janitorial, or storage functions.

Architects are occasionally tempted to "fit in" a distribution closet wherever there is room left over after all other spaces have been defined. This attitude will create endless problems later on. It is important that a fixed location be identified, similar to an elevator or mechanical shaft. Technicians should be able to access rooms directly from hallways, not through other rooms.

Like the equipment room, distribution closets should not be designed with false ceilings, and air flow and cooling must be constant to deal with the considerable heat generated by the electronic equipment. The floor should be sealed or tiled but definitely not carpeted.

Expandability

When planning horizontal pathways between the distribution closets and workstation outlets, assume that over the course of time many more cable connections will be required. Conduits or cable trays are often installed to meet the current need with no thought to future repairs, replacements, and additions. They are often installed over fixed ceilings and become useless once the ceiling is complete. Floor trench and duct systems are especially likely to deteriorate over time with broken tiles and screws blocking the pathway and water flooding into ducts. Raised access floors are an excellent solution for renovation or high-tech areas but may be considered too costly for extensive use.

Although contractors espouse a variety of different solutions, one of the best is to mount cable trays in conjunction with plenum cable in a false ceiling. If you have an opportunity, encourage the use of plenum-rated workstation cable over nonplenum cable because of its improved electrical characteristics and increased flexibility.

Recent technical advances in both audiovisual equipment and computer hardware make it possible to use less wire and so, less space. Full broadcast-quality sound and visual images until recently required three T-1 lines. Digital-compression technology has made it possible to transfer the same amount of data with only one-third of the cable. Fiber-optic technology provides the ability for multiple signals to travel on one fiber rather than a separate cable for each signal, as is the case with traditional wiring. The connection between the fiber-optic and the twisted-pair cable, however, is quite expensive, so it is usually best to provide fiber-optics in a building's risers with connections to twisted-pairs at every floor.

Be sure your architects overdesign the capacity of your cabling to accommodate your needs ten years from now when your voltage requirements and telecom requirements will, no doubt, be much higher. They should provide abundant electrical access points with high-voltage capabilities so that you can add voice and data ports as needed. Wiring and cabling may be strung inside ceiling plenum or strung inside partitions and in flooring. (See the section on raised access flooring earlier in this chapter.)

Today's patron workstation may require outlets for multimedia, data, and video connections. Outlets should be designed to meet possible future needs, not just today's applications. If the connections are not needed immediately, they can be capped for use at a later date. It is wise to think in terms of potential telecommunications locations as well as those you will use immediately. As with other telecommunications and computer considerations, if the infrastructure is already in place, your library will save a great deal of time and money later.

ELECTRICAL SERVICE

A building's basic electrical system consists of transformers, generators, circuit breakers, wiring, outlets, and transfer switches. Other components of the system may be transient voltage surge suppressors, power factor correctors, and power conditioning equipment. Because your building will be brim-full of computers and other electronic equipment, it presents special challenges to electrical contractors.

TIPS

Make sure that more than enough wiring (for electricity and computer networks) is available in all possible locations.

Be sure to wire for future growth of data and phone lines. Make sure that there is an easy way to add electrical or phone lines when needed.

My advice is to spend as much money as possible on technical details without worrying if the carpet coordinates with the shelving.

With the advent of new systems furniture with partitions that can be reconfigured over and over again, permanent walls are even less in evidence than in the past. Therefore, you cannot limit the installation of electrical outlets to walls alone. One solution is a grid of recessed electrical floor outlets underneath carpet, which can provide power almost anywhere in the building.

"Clean" Power Is Essential

Harmonic currents or distorted electrical waves (electrical interference) generated by large electrical equipment like HVAC blowers and chillers can cause transformers and wiring to heat and burn. They can also cause computers that have "switch-mode" power supplies to fail. Since computers are an important part of a library, a distinction must be made between clean and dirty power. PCs need power that is clean enough to do away with the little disturbances that affect distributed computer equipment. Dirty power creates many such disturbances, even though it may be perfectly adequate for most of the library's electrical needs.

It is important that power-conditioning equipment be installed to ensure clean power to operate computers throughout your building. Proper grounding is also important since grounds can return electrical noise to its source. Grounding also provides a zero-voltage reference to safeguard sensitive equipment. This is important because just a few volts of electrical noise can interfere with computers' low-voltage logic signals.

Computer equipment not only needs special treatment but it also creates problems for other equipment by generating its own electrical "noise." This means that you must pay special attention to segregating it with grounding and double-sized neutral wires so that the noises don't affect the entire system.

Choosing an Electrical Contractor

Be sure that your electrical contractor is experienced with large-scale projects. This is not the place to cut corners and hire the low bidder who lacks experience with a variety of sophisticated, high-tech buildings having heavy data requirements. Although discussions with an electrical contractor may resemble a conversation in a foreign language, the responses (as best you can interpret them) will give you some idea of whether your electrical contractor knows the business.

You might ask the contractor, for example, whether cables will be placed together in wire trays. This is a bad practice; a separate conduit should be used for each circuit. Another important issue is whether an experienced electrical testing firm will inspect the electrical system, test circuit breakers, and use thermal-scan equipment to find "hot spots" due to bad connections or faulty equipment. These inspections are in addition to the ones required by your local government authority and are usually at the discretion of the electrical contractor. Once again, this is a pretty reliable indicator of whether you're dealing with a real professional because the inspection is a vitally important precaution. Electrical wiring has changed drastically in recent years, and you want to be sure that your electrical contractor has been keeping up with all the new ways of delivering power.

HEATING, VENTILATION, AND COOLING

Few people realize that climate control—a term that encompasses temperature, humidity, and air circulation—can have an enormous positive or negative impact on the library's ability to serve the needs of its users. The following parable is based on the experiences of librarians across the country. It represents a fairly realistic picture of what happens when "the best laid schemes o' mice and men gang aft a-gley."

Once upon a time—well, actually it was several years ago—it was decided that the moment had come to erect a new library building. While the elderly library director amassed architecture books and drew feverish floor plans, legions of other interested parties gathered. The university president needed a gracious space in which to entertain generous benefactors; the chair of the board anxiously awaited the oak-paneled rare book room to be named in his honor; the architect, whose sights were set on a grand and glorious architectural award, was busy designing a magnificent staircase; and contractors from near and far were singing the praises of state-of-the-art heating and cooling systems.

At length the building was complete, and it was indeed a sight to behold. The president had her gracious space, and the board member had his oak-paneled memorial. Soon after, the architect won an award, enabling her to raise her fees and join the country club. Unfortunately, the library director did not share in the general warm glow. Possibly his disenchantment began when it was discovered that the state-of-the-art air conditioner, which could easily have chilled a small city, inflated the electric bill to such an extent that it had to be shut down. The sun's rays, shining through vast expanses of glass, heated the building to egg-frying temperatures, a condition that may have accounted for the librarian's less-than-sunny outlook. The state-of-the-art heating module might have worked as predicted if cost overruns had not resulted in a decision to reduce the number of temperature zones. The same quantity of heated air spewed forth in the already toasty window area as in the basement.

Luckily, the library director was a born survivor. He swallowed his disappointment and set to work making the new building livable. First he disconnected half the gizmos and, since he possessed quite a flair for mechanical gadgetry, tinkered with the rest. Each summer evening he descended to the cavernous mechanical room and threw on all the blowers. In the morning, when the cool night air filled every nook and cranny, he shut the system down. When irate mechanical engineers railed, the librarian smiled pleasantly and went on his way. When the frustrated maintenance staff changed the lock to the mechanical room, the librarian picked it with a paper clip and plastic library card. In winter, he simply set some thermostats at 90 degrees, others at 50, and taped plastic drop cloths over outside air vents. When he retired, he passed these life-saving strategies on to his successor.

All went well (or reasonably so) for a few years, until an electrical consultant arrived on a (figurative) dashing white steed to rescue the librarians from their dysfunctional building. Computers, he promised, would save the day. All the dampers and vents and valves would open and shut; all the fans and motors would spring magically to life at the bidding of the amazing automaton.

After weeks of workers strewing lengths of wire and electrical conduit across the carpet and the constant ringing sound of metal striking metal, the project was complete. The entire heating/cooling system would be controlled from a console located in the maintenance or physical plant office. (Naturally, the consultant reasoned, librarians lacked the high-tech know-how to twiddle the computer keys properly, so it could not be located in the library.) Never again would staff need to adjust a thermostat, so the thermostats were removed. In their place appeared electronic sensors labeled with a zone identification number. Yes, unfortunately, they were the same old zones. Once again, funds had been exhausted before new zones could be added.

It so happened that the new system went into operation in the fall, so there was no immediate noticeable effect. Soon, however, winter descended upon the library, and the temperature in the cataloging room fell to 50 degrees. Librarians in woolen gloves typed MARC records into frosty computer terminals. Since all thermostats had been removed, staff learned the actual temperature only after a trip to the nearest hardware store to purchase thermometers. These they carried from room to room accompanied by exclamations of amazement.

When the library director, standing amid shivering down-jacketed staff members, phoned the maintenance or physical plant supervisor, the latter, eyeing the building plan on his computer screen, announced confidently that the temperature in the cataloging room was 75 degrees. Not until the staff threatened, through chattering teeth, to abandon ship did the supervisor agree to personally inspect the premises. Eventually some adjustments were made, and life went on.

A year passed and then another. The much-heralded system just needed a little fine-tuning. However, the temperate nirvana that had been prophesied remained just beyond reach. Finally the staff grew tired of promises. Why were conditions no better than in days of old? Why, in fact, were they actually somewhat worse?

At last the maintenance physical plant supervisor (not the one mentioned above, but his successor or possibly his successor's successor—turnover was a serious problem) made an astounding admission. No one on the present maintenance staff understood how the computer software program worked. Actually, since the computer that monitored the computer that operated the equipment had ceased to function quite a while back, this didn't matter a great deal. The system was on "autopilot." Like Hal in the film *2001: A Space Odyssey*, a runaway computer was calling the shots.

Couldn't the software be loaded onto another computer? Possibly, except that the disks had been packed in a box that somehow disappeared in an office remodeling project. Then couldn't the computer program be manually overridden? This elicited the blankest of stares. How? No one on the present mechanical staff possessed any experience with the system, but a custodian remembered the heaps of scrap metal when the manual controls were torn out. Couldn't they get in touch with the engineering firm that installed the system? Yes, of course, that is, if anyone could remember who installed it. Those records too had been lost in the remodeling project.

Was this a no-win situation? Faced with such overwhelming odds, is there anything we librarians could do to improve such matters? Yes indeed! There's a great deal we can do, but only if we see the library building with all its frustrating physical complexities as part of our jobs. Look at that horror story again, and see if anything might have been done to save the day. At the beginning, we see the interested parties gathered to plan the new library. The director did an excellent job fulfilling what he considered his planning responsibilities. In other words, he correctly estimated the amount of space needed for the library's collections. He identified convenient locations for offices, computers, microfilm machines, and photocopiers. However, he quite reasonably saw the technical requirements—what you might call the building's innards—as someone else's responsibility. In conferences with architect, library board, and others, it was impressed upon him that he need not concern himself with these matters. They should be left to the professionals.

As you're touring other libraries, looking for ideas, you'll encounter almost as many philosophies about heating and air-conditioning as there are libraries. In warmer climates, air-conditioning the entire building may be a foregone conclusion. In other areas of the country, however, an architect, builder, or board member may think that money can be saved by selectively cooling only certain areas, for example, air conditioning reading rooms but not the stack areas. Storerooms are often designed without vents for air or heat. Inevitably, those are the rooms that are converted into offices two years after the library opens.

The Basics of Climate Control

The term HVAC encompasses all heating, cooling, and ventilating equipment in a building. The purpose of an HVAC system is to control temperature and humidity at levels that human beings find comfortable, distribute outdoor air to meet ventilation needs of library staff and users, and isolate and remove odors and pollutants. Systems vary from very simple to ultrasophisticated. In some areas it is possible to rely only on natural ventilation; there may be no need for mechanical cooling equipment, and humidity control may not be part of the system.

Following are some basic classifications of systems. Each type has endless variations, but almost all systems fit into one category or another.

WATER OR HYDRONIC SYSTEMS   You probably have plenty of experience with water or hydronic systems that are characterized by fan coils or radiant pipes. These systems use a network of pipes to deliver water to hot water radiators, radiant pipes set in floors, or fan coil cabinets. Boilers produce hot water or steam; chillers produce chilled water. Thermostats are usually used to control the temperature by zone. Piped systems are easy to install because the pipes are smaller than ductwork. However, they are subject to hidden leaks and to burst pipes in winter.

CENTRAL AIR SYSTEMS   Most central air systems distribute air rather than water, as in the previously described systems, and are designed for low, medium, or high pressure distribution. Compressor drives, chillers, condensers, and furnaces are usually components of the system, depending on whether the air is heated or chilled or both. Ducts are usually made of sheet metal or flexible plastic and can be insulated. Registers can be installed in ceilings, floors, and walls, and thermostats control temperature in each zone. Central systems control interior temperature, humidity, and filtration. Heat pump systems extract latent heat from the outside air and use it to evaporate refrigerant vapor under pressure. When heat is needed, the condenser and evaporator trade functions.

COMBINED AIR AND HOT WATER SYSTEMS   These systems combine the ease of installation of piped systems with the control of ducted systems. Air handling units may be located throughout a building and are served by a central boiler and chiller. Water is sometimes delivered from a central plant that takes care of a complex of buildings.

HVAC Terminology

Like so many of the specialized trades involved in constructing a new building, climate-control professionals have a language of their own. To talk intelligently with your building team, you will need to be familiar with at least some of the most frequently used terms.

ACCA (Air-Conditioning Contractors of America)   National trade association in the field of heating, ventilation, air-conditioning

AFUE (annual fuel utilization efficiency)   Measure of furnace heating efficiency

Air handler   That part of a central air-conditioning or heat pump system that moves air through ductwork

ARI (Air-Conditioning and Refrigeration Institute)   Nonprofit, voluntary organization of heating, air-conditioning, and refrigeration manufacturers that publishes standards for testing and rating HVAC equipment

BTU (British thermal unit)   Amount of heat required to raise the temperature of one pound of water one degree Fahrenheit

COP (coefficient of performance)   Ratio calculated by using the total heating capacity and the total electrical input in watts

DOE (Department of Energy)   Federal agency charged with setting industry efficiency standards

EER (energy efficiency ratio)   Calculated by dividing the cooling capacity by the power input

Efficiency   Method of rating HVAC equipment; the higher the rating number, the more efficient the system and the lower your fuel consumption

Heat source   Solid, liquid, or gas from which heat is collected

HSPF (heating seasonal performance factor)   Measure of heat pump efficiency; the higher the HSPF rating, the more efficient the heat pump

Kilowatt   1,000 watts

Sound ratings   Higher sound levels mean more noise when the HVAC system runs; measured in decibels (To get an idea what a rating means, think of the human voice as about 7 decibels and an electric blender at 8 or 9 decibels.)

Ton   Each ton equals 12,000 BTUs; unit of size for heat pumps and air-conditioners

Watt   Unit of electric power used to rate electrical appliances and equipment

Zone   Area that one thermostat controls

The following tips represent a variety of perspectives from librarians all over the country.

TIPS

I am in favor of air-conditioning all spaces—both for the sake of the materials and for human comfort. Setting temperature and humidity levels requires some thought and consultation with like institutions. If humans are using the space routinely (for example, if they have desks in the storage area), their needs should be considered. Just because conditions can be tolerated doesn't make them acceptable.

Building interiors get hot and humid for reasons other than weather, such as proximity to the mechanical plant and use of equipment in a confined space. It may be desirable to locate storerooms near the building's mechanical plant.

Unlike ponderous mainframes of the past, today's computers can tolerate a fairly broad range of temperature and humidity levels. It is sometimes useful to use equipment as an excuse for better climate control, but humans are sometimes less flexible than machines in what they can tolerate.

Working in 60-degree workspaces may seem reasonable to management, but for staff, bitter resentments can accumulate that lead to seemingly unrelated personnel problems.

It is a fact that pH rises with temperature. This is true of any material. Every ten degrees Celsius in temperature doubles the pH. Acid in the items in your archives, whether in paper, microform, or plastic, becomes more caustic in higher temperatures. By maintaining the temperature at a lower level, you reduce acid levels and lengthen the life of your records.

One thing I would strongly recommend is that there not be a combined HVAC system. It is much better if the heating and air-conditioning/humidity systems are separate. Having worked in repositories with them combined and with them separate, the latter has a much better track record. Indeed, if a building has structurally separate areas, I would advocate running each area off a separate small system. Systems that are less complex and closer to domestic scale (i.e., small-scale commercial) give fewer problems and are easier to understand and maintain. If one component goes down, it doesn't compromise conditions in the entire facility.

Technology, Ecology, and Comfort

As you investigate various types of climate control, you will soon discover that some of your priorities are actually in conflict with one another. For example, computer equipment generates an extraordinary amount of heat, and it is especially important to continuously cool the rooms containing LAN file servers. However, in too many library buildings the LAN file server is housed in a small closet, often with no thought given to cooling and ventilation. If electronic equipment is to be housed in a small, confined area, install fans to blow the warm air out of the closet into the ceiling plenum. In addition, you will need a chilled water source year-round, twenty-four hours a day for cooling.

Maintaining the optimal environment for your equipment can mean increased energy consumption. The equipment itself consumes considerable energy, and additional energy is used to cool it down. The federal government now requires that energy consumption data be available for most appliances and machinery. Ask to see the literature for any piece of energy-consuming equipment under consideration.

The use of climate control systems has implications for many environmental and quality-of-life issues beyond simple energy conservation. (For example, see chapter 7 for a discussion of sick building syndrome.) As you consider the advantages and disadvantages of various systems, the federal Environmental Protection Agency (EPA) recommends that you consider the wide spectrum of related issues. These might include

ozone depletion	exposure to toxic emissions
global warming	other ecological effects
energy efficiency	flammability

TIPS

If it is at all possible to heat/air condition with a number of home-sized furnaces and air-conditioners, opt for that in preference to the large, electronically controlled commercial HVAC systems. (Check with other comparably sized libraries to determine this; do not depend on the architect or design engineer's assertions.) Libraries as large as 26,000 square feet operate on multiple furnaces. Having multiple furnaces is so much less expensive to maintain than one furnace. This way, if one unit goes out, the others are still working. Furthermore, local technicians can service the units. We have spent almost nothing in the 11 years we have had small units in our 6,000-square-foot building. We have spent thousands of dollars on the two units for our 17,000-square-foot buildings built 5 years ago.

If you have a central HVAC system, a computer room will need a separate air-conditioner to cool the room if the HVAC system is out of service.

Pay attention to air handling systems. Closed file rooms, processing areas, and office areas can be too cold or too hot or have too much or too little air blowing around.

MANAGING HUMIDITY

If there is any one problem that afflicts most libraries, it is excessive moisture. In the course of my own career, moisture in one guise or another has seriously imperiled or even destroyed important collections in my library. For example, one time the entire reference collection sprouted a summer coat of mold that quickly proceeded to infest nearly every page of every volume. It proved to be impossible to make the physical plant director understand that this was an emergency situation. He was accustomed to removing mold from restroom walls, and throughout the course of a long and bitter battle, he never really understood that hundreds of thousands of dollars worth of materials, some irreplaceable, were in jeopardy. In another library, seepage coming through the walls of the vault destroyed other valuable materials.

There is no real agreement on what constitutes an ideal environment for printed materials and computers, but you might think in terms of a humidity level in winter of around 40 percent (plus or minus 5 percent) and about 50 percent to 55 percent (plus or minus 5 percent) in the summer. Humidity, however, must be correlated with temperature. To preserve materials and provide an environment in which computers can function effectively, temperature should not rise above 72 to 73 degrees Fahrenheit.

I hesitate to throw these numbers around because in the enormous amount of research that has been done on the subject, some of it is conflicting. Since the floods that devastated the treasures of Florence, preservation studies have become one of the most active and exciting specializations in our profession. Take the time to peruse some of the literature. It is truly massive, and you will only be able to read a small sample. Nevertheless, excellent information is available both in print and on the World Wide Web. Your only difficulty will be in convincing your building professionals of its importance.

Too little humidity should also be avoided. Modern library buildings frequently have computerized building systems that calculate the moisture content of the air and the dew point and adjust the humidity accordingly. Another recent innovation, the water-atomization system, uses compressed air and water, mixing and spraying it out through a nozzle to raise humidity to recommended levels.

Archival Collections and Humidity

Rare books, manuscripts, art, and historic artifacts require special climate controls. At the same time, library users want comfort and sufficient light for reading. Separate archival facilities usually place the needs of the materials first and have considerably more options for protecting materials. A special collection housed within a larger, multipurpose facility has considerably less control over its environment. Even our own staffs will complain that we are trying to give them pneumonia when we turn down the heat, so compromises must be made.

According to the Smithsonian Institution's Conservation Analytical Laboratory Research Group, humidity in archival institutions doesn't need to be controlled as tightly as we've been taught.[2] Considering that even the most sophisticated climate-control systems with every conceivable bell and whistle often don't work, this is very comforting. It is going to take every ounce of determination you have to achieve even relatively minimal climate control for your archival collections. Even under the best of conditions, we know that all we can hope for is a compromise between protecting and preserving fragile collections and serving the public.

Climate control in special collections may require humidification to maintain a constant moisture level. Therefore, you will need to be aware that adding humidification to a building can cause major problems. The most frequently encountered difficulty is that condensation occurs when humidified air comes into contact with a surface that is below the dew point temperature. Many drier areas in the United States are in the West where high-altitude temperatures may plunge at night. The need for a continuous insulation and vapor barrier system is especially important where humidification is a function of the HVAC system. Be sure that the mechanical engineer who is designing the HVAC humidity control is in close communication with the architect designing the vapor barrier system.

TIPS AND TALES

You must make it very clear when working with architects and engineers that there will or will not be people working in the archives. Otherwise, they will base their temperature estimates and levels on the fact that people will be working in the area on a consistent basis. We couldn't get it through the engineer's head that the media was the determining factor for appropriate temperature levels.

We should have gotten the specs on ultraviolet light emissions from windows and lights and on the separate controls for the HVAC system for archives. (The professional literature tells us we need to be in control of this, yet every place I've ever worked it's not possible.)

Cold conditions will slow down the inevitable degradation to a snail's pace. Dry conditions will prevent mold, mildew, and chemical breakdown.

AC doesn't just keep the room cooler and more comfortable for you but also for the bibliographic items in your archive. By controlling the temperature you can control mold growth, and the cost of cleaning mold off items in an archive can be very high. I work in a very small archive/special collection and have had to deal with this problem first hand. One of your primary jobs is to preserve your materials, and you are not preserving them if they are being eaten up by mold.

While it is true that the northern British Isles do not often have prolonged periods of heat by American standards, they can have prolonged periods of elevated humidity. The difference is that the greatest humidity is in the winter, not the summer. So although air-conditioning may not be needed so much as in most of the U.S. to control heat, it is certainly needed to control humidity. And anyone who thinks you need temperatures above 70 degrees for active mold growth has never encountered British mildew!

Because of excessive moisture, most of our rare books won't be shelved in the rare book room, as planned! They'll have to move to the Archives, which means there will be less room for growth than I thought! I'll also have to spend more time supervising visitors.

Mold and Mildew

Whether it affects the interior or the exterior of your new building, mildew can cause serious problems. Although especially troublesome in damp, humid areas, mildew can become a problem under a wide range of conditions. Not only can it scar the building's facade but the enzyme produced by mildew can cause structural damage to some materials, including wooden and painted surfaces. In addition, mildew can affect indoor air quality by producing an unpleasant odor and triggering allergic responses from susceptible individuals.

Mildew is a mold, the spores of which are present almost everywhere. It grows and spreads rapidly when

- organic materials such as soil, grease, or food are present
- temperature ranges from 77 degrees to 86 degrees Fahrenheit
- the relative humidity (RH) ranges from 70 percent to 93 percent

If mildew is a problem in your area, be sure that mildew prevention is considered in both the site plan and the landscape design. Avoid planting trees and shrubs too close to the library building, since plants can block air circulation and sunlight, preventing the exterior from drying out after a rainfall. In recent years, high-tech finishes have been developed that have built-in mildew-resistance. For example, the exterior insulation and finish (EIF) system results in a finish that inhibits the growth of mildew itself and that repels airborne dirt and pollutants, cutting off mildew's food supply. For controlling interior mildew in a wet climate, your building engineer may need to use air-conditioners, dehumidifiers, and exhaust fans during much of the year to keep temperature and humidity out of the optimal ranges for mildew growth.

Tracking Down the Source of Moisture

It is often extremely difficult to tell where moisture is coming from. For example, what is assumed to be a leaking roof may actually be condensation coming from any one of a variety of sources. Whatever its source, excess moisture can not only cause collection damage but also result in rot, corrosion, peeling paint, water stains, and eventually building structural failure.

As was mentioned previously, some geographical areas are more prone to mildew than others. If you live in an area where the humidity remains high for long periods of time, ask your contractor what precautions are being taken to keep the building dry. Rain leaks are frequently the culprits, especially with hilltop and waterfront sites where driving wind makes every instance of caulking and flashing failure a potential time bomb. Remember that caulk has a limited life expectancy, and your physical plant personnel or a private contractor must inspect it regularly. HVAC systems include louvers and exterior exhaust grilles that require caulk around each exterior mechanical penetration. Flashing is also essential around HVAC penetrations. It is not uncommon for a contractor to take shortcuts, leaving these openings unprotected.

Failure to properly install moisture barriers or house wrap is another source of moisture and can cause extensive rotting within a year or two of a building's construction. These wraps, composed of such materials as spun bonded plastic fiber sheets, provide good rain protection and act as an infiltration barrier. In addition, roof overhangs may not provide sufficient protection from rain leaks. Sloped roofs must have substantial overhangs or walls may become sponges, sopping up rainwater.

Doors and windows are yet another source of unwanted moisture due to poor design and inappropriate specifications. Windows are made to differing code standards for wind/rain velocities, and your architects should require tests to determine which standards are appropriate for your specific site. Your building may be more vulnerable to rain and wind damage than those at a site a block away.

While high humidity may be a problem in warm southern states, ice dams caused by water runoff unable to get past ice-clogged gutters are responsible for many leaks in northern climates. Sometimes HVAC equipment installed in attic spaces generates so much heat due to uninsulated flues, ventilation exhaust ducts, and poorly sealed duct joints that the temperature of the attic area rises to room temperature or higher, melting snow on the roof and creating ice dams. Such simple solutions as attic fans for better ventilation are usually inadequate. It may be necessary to remove all the shingles, tape the roof sheathing joints airtight with a rubberized asphalt tape, and insulate the entire roof with 1½- to 2½-inch thick isocyanurate foil-faced insulation board. This is certainly not a project you want to undertake a year or two after the building is completed.

Groundwater and Condensation

Groundwater that leaks into basements or crawl spaces is another source of excessive moisture. Where groundwater is a problem, it may be necessary to hire a geotechnical engineer to prepare a report on the soil and water table around the building site.

Occasionally, a crawl space is left unprotected by a concrete slab to cover the earth below. This is a near-catastrophic error that can create endless problems. Dirt floors in crawl spaces, except in very dry climates, are almost always a culprit when water damage occurs. In addition to making sure there is a concrete slab, one very effective precaution against moisture is the installation of a cross-laminated, high-performance polyethylene film under the concrete. When installed at the appropriate point in construction, it is extremely inexpensive and almost guarantees a dry slab.

Concrete block foundations are usually more prone to leakage than poured foundations because of problems at joints and cracks. Underground waterproofing systems such as rubberized asphalt sheets and bentonite clay panels can help prevent these problems.

Condensation is most commonly found in modern buildings. In older structures, the use of minimal insulation and the average buildings' tendencies to leak large quantities of air meant that moisture was not easily trapped in inaccessible places. Good thick insulation is essential for an energy-efficient building, yet air flows easily through insulation, bringing with it unwanted moisture. A vapor barrier must serve as an air barrier as well. The best kind of wall insulation system is probably a combination of foam insulation, glass fiber, and a good, sealed vapor barrier.

It is not uncommon for contractors and architects to forget that insulation systems must be continuous. In other words, any place there are openings or holes, there will be air leaks. The insulation system includes not only the insulation itself but also the vapor barrier, adhesives, tapes, and fastening clips that hold everything in place. The system is continuous only if the wall vapor barrier is sealed to the floor and to the roof or ceiling vapor barrier. Special precautions must be taken any place that the system is penetrated by structural elements. All electrical, plumbing, and HVAC elements—even sprinkler protrusions—must be sealed and impermeable to air and vapor. Folds and staples in the vapor barrier also destroy the seal. Furthermore, unless the vapor barrier joints are sealed with a suitable adhesive, the barrier is all but useless.

Chilled water running through pipes throughout the building is still another cause of condensation. Piping requires properly installed foam insulation systems with vapor barrier protection, or you will find yourself coping with ceiling drips and stains from the pipes above the ceiling.

If your public library is being planned as part of a community complex and will share a wall, roof, or ventilation system with a swimming pool, the best advice is probably to campaign against such incompatible bedfellows. If, however, funding depends upon togetherness, bear in mind some of the potential problems. In winter, for example, the facility will be bringing in outdoor air, which can create a cloud inside the building. Using air-to-air heat exchangers can improve humidity control as well as energy conservation. Dehumidifying heat pumps can provide year-round humidity control, allowing waste heat to be reused to heat pool water.

If your environment requires special humidifiers to maintain a constant moisture level, you may discover that you have still other problems to worry about. Condensation occurs when humidified air comes into contact with a surface, the temperature of which is below the dew point temperature. Again, the only way to prevent serious consequences is to ensure an absolutely continuous insulation/vapor barrier system. If a mechanical engineer is designing your HVAC humidity controls, do your best to see that adequate communication takes place with the architect who is designing the insulation/vapor barrier system.

As a rank amateur, you are certainly not going to presume to tell your architects how to moisture-proof the building. However, it is not out of place to have a chat about the terrible damage that moisture causes in libraries. It is also acceptable to suggest that extra precautions need to be taken, and to nod wisely when the architects enumerate their brilliant and innovative solutions. The point of the discussion is simply to raise the issue to the level of a high priority.

A QUIET ENVIRONMENT

As HVAC and other building services equipment become ever more powerful, they also become louder. Some buildings even use diesel-powered generators to provide standby power backup for building services. Such generators can create noise in the 100 decibel range and cause excessive vibration and noise in adjacent spaces. Solutions to such acoustical problems are few, so look carefully at the location of your mechanical room and other spaces where service equipment will be running.

The current practice to include atria and other spaces that are open from ground floor to roof in new library designs means that on each floor, stack and reading areas are separated only by balconies from the open space, thus allowing noise to be heard throughout the building. We librarians are extremely sensitive about the "shush" stereotype and may feel guilty enforcing quiet zones. However, we are finding that our users are not so reticent. "For heaven's sake, this is a library!" they complain. This has been quite a surprise for modern, liberated librarians who thought their "quiet" signs should go the way of the dinosaur and the dodo bird. You will be amazed at how traditional your users are in this regard, and you should include several quiet areas in your plans. Bear in mind that a quiet area means full-height walls, sound-baffling carpet, and the absence of loud mechanical noises.

Since the advent of systems furniture, the wall barriers that we traditionally relied on to decrease noise are no longer adequate. Modern management and learning theory encourage people to work together in groups. Therefore, increased sound absorption is needed at the ceiling. "Quiet zones" or separate rooms to provide quiet and privacy are another option. As you're investigating different manufacturers of systems furniture, be sure to check the barrier rating or the amount of sound that can penetrate through the panel.

Rather than permanent walls, you may want to consider mountable partitions that are roughly equivalent acoustically to drywall. Nevertheless, these may not be appropriate for quiet areas since sound can penetrate at the joints between panel and panel, between panel and ceiling, or between panel and wall. To keep out noise, consider having some spaces built with multiple layers of construction and insulation materials including several insulating "sandwiches" of drywall, lumber, and fiberglass.

NOTES

1. Diane Mayo and Sandra Nelson, *Wired for the Future: Developing Your Library Technology Plan* (Chicago: American Library Assn., 1998).
2. Michael Kernan, "Around the Mall and Beyond: Work of the Conservation Analytical Laboratory Research Group of the Smithsonian Institution," *Smithsonian Magazine* (March 1996). Available online at http://www.smithsonianmag.si.edu/smithsonian/issues96/mar96/ around_mar96.html.

Resources

Alumasc Interior Building Products
White House Works
Bold Rd.
Sutton St. Helens
Merseyside WA9 4JG
+44 (0) 1744-648400
fax: +44 (0) 1744-648401

American National Standards Institute
430 Broadway
New York, NY 10018
(212) 642-4900
http://www.ansi.org

American Society for Testing and Materials
1916 Race St.
Philadelphia, PA 19103
(215) 299-5400
http://www.ia-usa.org/k0043.htm

Building Industry Consulting Services Intl.
10500 University Center Dr., Ste. 100
Tampa, FL 33612-6415
(813) 979-1991
http://www.bicsi.org

Electronic Industry Assn.
2001 Pennsylvania Ave. NW
Washington, DC 20006
(202) 457-4900

Federal Communications Commission
455 Twelfth St. SW
Washington, DC 20554
(202) 418-0190
e-mail: ccinfo@fcc.gov

Hewetson Floors Ltd.
Marfleet, Hull HU9 5SG
+44 (0) 1482-781701
fax: +44 (0) 1482-799272
e-mail: @hewetson.co.uk

Institute of Electrical and Electronic Engineers, Inc.
Service Center
445 Hoes Ln.
P.O. Box 1331
Piscataway, NJ 08855-1331
(201) 981-0060
http://www.ieee.org

National Electrical Manufacturers Assn.
2101 L St.
Washington, DC 20037
(202) 457-8400
http://www.nema.org

Tate Access Floors, Inc.
7510 Montevideo Blvd.
Jessup, MD 20794
(410) 799-4200
fax: (410) 799-4207

**Telecommunications Industries
    Assn.**
2001 Pennsylvania Ave. NW
Washington, DC 20006
(202) 457-4934
http://www.tiaonline.org

Underwriters Laboratories, Inc.
333 Pfingsten Rd.
Northbrook, IL 60062
(847) 272-8800
http://www.ul.com/

Davis, Peter, and Craig McGuffin. *Wireless Local Area Networks.* New York: McGraw-Hill, 1995.

Geier, Jim. *Wireless LANs: Implementing Interoperable Networks.* Indianapolis: Macmillan Technical Publishing, 1999.

Lopez-Hernandez, F. J. *Wireless LAN Standards & Applications.* Norwood, Mass.: Artech House, 1999.

Male, Mary C. *Creating Exceptional Classrooms: Technology Options for All.* Needham Heights, Mass.: Allyn & Bacon, 1993.

Managing Technology in the Computer Classroom. Westminster, Mass.: Teacher Created Materials, 1999.

Mayo, Diane, and Sandra Nelson. *Wired for the Future: Developing Your Library Technology Plan.* Chicago: American Library Assn., 1999.

Pahlavan, Kaveh, and Allen Levesque. *Wireless Information Networks.* New York: John Wiley, 1995.

7 Security and Safety

Security is an increasing concern among librarians. Although libraries are certainly not hotbeds of crime and violence, they do provide unique opportunities for the criminal elements of society. Therefore, the personal safety of patrons and staff must be an important consideration when planning a new building. Because libraries are among the most public of public buildings and are often the only buildings open during evening and weekend hours, they also tend to attract people who have no place else to go.

The newspapers occasionally report sensational library violence like the Sacramento Public Library staff members who were gunned down by a mentally deranged patron or the eighteen Salt Lake City patrons and staff members who were taken hostage by another disturbed user. Such dramatic events are rare, but lesser crimes have become uncomfortably frequent. Patrons often seek out remote nooks and crannies because they are well suited to reading and study, but such areas are extremely difficult to monitor. With small library staffs responsible for large areas, purse snatchers, book thieves, and exhibitionists may have what amounts to a golden opportunity.

Safety, however, is not simply a matter of protecting people and property from criminal activity. Mother Nature, in the form of tornadoes, hurricanes, or floods, can be even more destructive, and preparing for these and other natural disasters must be an integral part of your planning process. Depending on the terrain and the part of the country, your building professionals will evaluate these threats differently, but all should take seriously the possibility of fire. Whether the work of nature, arsonists, or careless patrons, fires are far more common than other major types of disasters. In addition, the building itself may contain materials that are hazardous to library staff and visitors. Chemicals like formaldehyde, which are an integral part of the manufacturing process, can cause serious illness if care is not taken.

DESIGNED-IN SECURITY

As discussed in chapter 3, the library's site can have a major impact on building security; so too can the basic design of the library building. Think back to the old Carnegie libraries. With their central rotundas and clear sight-lines into stack areas, they permitted good control of a large area. Of course, such monumental architecture does not appeal to today's patrons, but you can plan to arrange stacks and other furnishings in such a way that you don't create secret hideaways. Avoid creating poorly lighted areas, and take care that changing lights throughout the building will be relatively easy. (One librarian complained that the maintenance staff has not changed hard-to-get-at bulbs above a stairway since his library first opened.)

In your planning think about how you will station staff around the building in spots where they can see what's going on, but be careful that you don't isolate them. A lone office on the top floor can serve as a magnet to petty thieves or worse. Some areas may require surveillance cameras; even highly visible "dummy" cameras can discourage potential troublemakers. Take time to learn about today's high-tech security systems including electronically accessed entryways and motion detectors.

When making plans for building security or selecting surveillance equipment, be sure to involve the people who will be charged with protecting your facility. If you are building a college or university library, your campus security head would be the logical choice to include in the planning process. In a public library, you might ask your city or county police chief to appoint a representative to work with you. These experts have an excellent idea of what works and what doesn't. Depending on the circumstances, they can save you a surprising amount of money on unnecessary hi-tech equipment, while pointing out unsecured entryways or design features that are especially vulnerable to vandalism.

Take a good look at the other people involved in orchestrating your building security. Modern computer-monitored systems are becoming so sophisticated and complicated that it really takes an expert to design an effective system. No matter how expensive and elaborate the system, obvious entrance and exit routes are sometimes forgotten. For example, since you (and your architects and contractors) have limited experience with crime, it may not dawn on anyone that the equipment storage room is accessible through the suspended ceiling from the room next door. Try to get all the free advice you possibly can, and if there isn't enough good free advice available, be prepared to pay a security consultant.

Plan on centralizing all financial transactions at one desk, and invest in a safe (the kind with a slot so the last person on duty needn't know the combination). You will want to arrange to empty the safe daily and keep money at the desk to the minimum needed to make change and handle refunds. Most libraries need two safes. In addition to the one for everyday transactions, one should be fireproof and be used to protect valuable objects. Both safes should be large enough and heavy enough to discourage theft.

In addition to these security precautions, carefully consider the placement of vending machines since these are often broken into. Also look into copy cards instead of coin-operated photocopiers, computer printing stations, and microfiche printers.

An Integrated Security Plan

As you develop a security plan for your new building, think in terms of a total system. Security involves personnel, facilities, communication, and electronic systems. Your objective is to make the thought of committing a crime as unattractive as possible. Potential wrongdoers are looking for opportunities in isolated locations where they can come and go freely and where a criminal act can be completed quickly and easily. To thwart their machinations, you will need to take a multipronged approach that includes all of the following.

CONTROL ACCESS   Fences and intrusion-detection systems can help control access to the facility, but building layout can be even more important. Design the building in a way that restricts public access to staff and storage areas. It might help to think in terms of security zones with a variety of access levels.

ENHANCE VISIBILITY   Position staff workstations where staff can best see what's going on. Make good use of glass partitions. You will probably need to hire security guards, at least for certain hours, but you can reduce the need for security personnel simply by positioning staff workstations effectively. Windows can also inhibit theft, vandalism, and improper behavior. The idea is to make people believe they will be seen if they do something wrong. Outside the building, plan the landscaping to minimize hiding places, and use exterior lighting to illuminate other places of concealment.

INCREASE THE PROBABILITY OF DETECTION   Delay can sometimes be as effective as prevention. Thieves and vandals don't want to be caught, and any delay increases the probability of their being discovered. If a criminal act looks like it will be difficult and time consuming, it may not seem worth the effort. If such delaying hindrances do not dissuade the criminal entirely, they may at least provide time for security forces to arrive.

REMOVE THE APPEARANCE OF OPPORTUNITIES   Bear in mind that criminals do not always know what is worth stealing. They may cause considerable damage breaking into a cash register or vending machine that holds only a few dollars. Look at your building as an "outsider" might. Where might money or valuables be stored? You might find yourself protecting—or to use the industry term, "hardening"—areas that in themselves don't really need protection to prevent expensive vandalism. Announce the presence of security measures with signs, highly visible locks, and other obvious security additions.

CONSIDER HIRING A CONSULTANT OR SECURITY ENGINEER   If funds are available in your budget, you might hire a security engineer to evaluate risks, assess terrain features, and select appropriate security hardware and equipment. Working with the engineer or other public safety and security professionals, set up an organized plan that identifies all the issues that must be considered. The plan should cover everything including site selection, perimeter barriers, exterior lighting, facility layout, and access control.

Security System Considerations

As the new building takes up more and more of your time, it's easy to lose track of what is really happening in the library. You may find yourself comparing the features of various security systems with little thought to how they would really function in your unique library environment.

EASE OF USE   While you're listening to the architect or vendor describe the bells and whistles of their space-age, super high-tech security systems, stop a moment and ask whether you and your employees will really be able to use the system on a day-to-day basis. If the library staff will have a hard time figuring out how to use the system, they are very likely to disable it or find other ways of preventing it from doing its job. If the system gives false alarms repeatedly, you will grow angry. Your staff, who probably know considerably less about the system than you do, will have even shorter fuses.

OBSOLESCENCE AND COST   Another important question to ask is how soon will the system become obsolete? How long has the vendor been selling this particular system? If it's too old, your system will be obsolete before your building is completed. If it's too new, you're taking a chance on a system that may not have all the kinks out of it. How stable is the vendor? Is the company likely to be around ten years from now? If so, will it be committed to maintaining your geriatric system? Security is one of those high-tech industries that are in a constant state of flux. However, the costs associated with purchasing, installing, and learning to use a new security system are great enough that you must be prepared to live with your system for a good many years.

How much additional electrical wiring will have to be done to accommodate the new system? How much will it cost? Remember to add this amount to the equipment, installation, and maintenance costs when comparing the costs of various systems.

SERVICEABILITY   Does the vendor you're considering rely on a third-party company to service the system? If the answer is yes, which it often is, you will want to ask similar questions about that service company. Is service locally available, or will you have to pay expensive travel charges? Does the company promise to be on-site within a certain number of hours or days? When your system goes down, you will need help quickly. Now's the time to find out what you can expect.

TRAINING   What kind of training does the vendor provide? If the library staff never fully masters the system, you've wasted a lot of money. An hour's walk-through and a voluminous, incomprehensible manual do not constitute adequate training.

SIMPLICITY   The more magnetic locks, security gates, card-accessed closets, motion detectors, vibration detectors, cameras, monitors, and other controls there are, the more confusing the system becomes. Don't allow yourself to get carried away. Just remember all those passwords you've forgotten, those keys you've misplaced, and the instruction manuals that have disappeared over the years. How much information can you reasonably expect to pass on as library staff members come and go?

Planning Doors and Locks

If most of the projects designed by your architects are office or classroom buildings, you may be surprised to find that the first round of drawings include far too many outside doors. It may take some time to convince them that you need only one public entrance, a loading dock, and the minimum number of emergency exits required by code. On the other hand, it's very easy to get into a library with its long hours and open access. Our problems are more like those of grocery or computer store managers, who must take precautions against thieves getting away with merchandise.

Before your project is complete, you will have uttered dozens of oaths (minced and otherwise) at the multiplicity of doors and locks you must contend with. The number can easily run into the hundreds. In the case of each door, you must answer a complicated set of questions and make decisions about whether the lock is needed.

- Does the door in question require a lock? If the answer is yes, then on which side must you insert a key? Inside and outside are not always readily evident.
- Should the door lock automatically or remain unlocked until a staff member remembers to relock it? Self-locking doors may be a sensible security measure or the bane of your busy staff's existence.
- Should you be able to lock the door without a key by punching in a button on the knob or latch? These are not usually appropriate for public areas where children can create pandemonium by locking themselves into restroom cubicles, broom closets, or study rooms.
- Should there be an alarm for the door? If so, should the alarm be turned off when the library is open, or will it require its own keypad to activate and deactivate?
- Does the hardware on the door comply with your local fire code?
- Will the location of the door and the door's hardware deter thieves from running off with valuable equipment while still serving as an emergency exit in case of fire?

Determining the best door for stairwells can be particularly confusing. In case of fire, patrons should be able to enter any stairwell on any floor. However, the same stairwell that opens into a public stack area on one floor may lead into a rare book room, media storage space, or staff processing area at other levels. Therefore, you will want to safeguard these areas and possibly allow the public to exit the stairwell only on the first floor. Remember that auxiliary locking devices like barrier bars, slide bolts, and padlocks may violate fire codes. If such devices require that patrons have special or prior knowledge in order to exit, patrons could be trapped in the event of fire. One good solution to the problem is a dead bolt mechanism with a fifteen-second delay. Although that may not seem like much time, it does serve as an effective deterrent.

You may decide you don't want to use keys on some doors because if a key is lost, it will compromise security and require expensive rekeying. Increasingly, electronic access card readers are being installed wherever it's important to restrict access. Such systems may be a good choice, but they can be both expensive and temperamental. Here are some issues that should be considered before you rush to install card readers throughout the library:

the kind of door (single or double)

ADA requirements

"tailgating" (what happens when someone without a card enters behind a card holder)

the problem of ice, which may keep the magnetic lock from functioning properly

Although it's an exhausting process, the best way to secure the building effectively is probably to make a list of all the doors. Identify them from the floor plan and consider who will use them, whether they will protect anything of value, or whether they could allow an intruder to leave the building unobserved. Most library doors will need lockable hardware; choosing the right lock configuration can be as effective a deterrent to crime and vandalism as any high-tech security system. You might want to develop a form to make the review process easier. Such a form could identify each door, possibly with a number that corresponds to a location on the blueprint. It should also indicate the rooms on each side of the door, when and why the door would be kept locked, and which side allows people to exit in case of fire. If the door should lock automatically, indicate this as well. Involve your staff in a virtual tour of the library, imagining each door (complete with hardware) through which they pass. Ask them to pretend that they're burglars attempting to escape with a VCR or staff members carrying a precarious load of books from one area of the library to another. It's a good idea to involve your staff in your lock-and-key quandaries from the very beginning since several heads are better than one.

You will probably want to consult with a locksmith long before any firm decisions must be made. Give yourself time to change your mind frequently before placing hardware orders. It is all but inevitable that you will make some mistakes, but preplanning will keep them to a minimum and prevent a full-blown nightmare on opening day.

FIRE SAFETY

Planning for fire safety is not just a simple matter of requesting sufficient sprinklers and fire extinguishers. Fire safety requires an integrated approach to protection, and these preventive measures must be orchestrated in such a way that they permit the detection of and rapid response to fires that may break out anywhere on the premises. Every building system is involved. For example, the telecommunications system should provide for direct fire department notification, and the HVAC system should be programmed to shut down some operations and start up others. It is essential that a fire be detected at the earliest possible stage and that library staff members be alerted immediately, enabling them to evacuate the building without injury or loss of life.

If you have been a librarian for any length of time, you're probably aware of the arguments that have raged over the years about the best method of protecting the library from fire. To sprinkle or not to sprinkle: that has become the question. Libraries and archives have experimented with almost every new system available, usually with mixed results. For example, fire-retardant gases were in vogue for a number of years, and gas-flooding systems may still be the best choice in certain situations. However, many gases are harmful to the environment, depleting ozone levels and contributing to global warming. Some gases produce thermal decomposition products that are corrosive or toxic. They may even cause certain cardiac reactions if used in sufficient concentrations to extinguish a fire. Since fire-retardant gases are also expensive and the ongoing costs can be high (especially when false alarms cause discharges), they are no longer a frequent choice for library installations.

Sprinkler Systems

Early water sprinkler systems doused large areas when staff members burned their toast and set off smoke alarms. The technological improvements of recent years have finally provided a fairly satisfactory product. However, librarians, by this point, have become gun-shy, and architects may have a very limited understanding of library needs. Though the thought of introducing water into a library is the stuff of nightmares, modern automatic sprinklers are probably the most important component of a good fire management system. Such systems are not without problems. Librarians still worry about the potential for inadvertent operation—as with burned toast incidents. The most important question, however, is how the damage due to water release compares with the damage to the library building and danger to patrons and materials if sprinklers are not installed.

Sprinkler systems can generally be divided into three broad categories: wet pipe, dry pipe, and preaction systems. The *wet pipe system* is perhaps the simplest of the three and in recent years has become known for reliability. Since wet pipe systems have the smallest number of components, they tend to malfunction somewhat less often than the other systems. Because a sprinkler system often gathers dust for years before it is needed and library maintenance schedules are often years behind, reliability is especially important. Wet pipe systems are also relatively low in cost, requiring less time and expertise to install as well as fewer service calls. Following a false alarm or even a real fire, wet pipe sprinkler systems need less time and labor to restore—simply replace the fused sprinklers and turn the water supply back on. These systems are not, however, a good choice for subfreezing environments.

In a *dry pipe sprinkler system,* pipes are not filled with water. Instead, they contain pressurized air or nitrogen that holds a valve in a closed position. When a fire occurs, the heated air escapes, and the dry pipe valve releases, allowing water to enter the pipe. Dry pipe systems offer protection in spaces such as unheated warehouses where freezing is possible. Some library and museum professionals think dry pipe systems better protect water-sensitive areas from leaks, but this has not turned out to be a significant concern. Since dry pipe systems are more complex, they require additional control equipment and more maintenance and can be less reliable. In addition, they do not offer the design flexibility of wet pipe systems and take up to 60 seconds longer to respond to a fire.

TIPS

Is the bathroom next door and does it get flooded (or is it above you)? Is there a kitchen below that lets greasy fumes through the air handling system? Has anything in the kitchen ever caught fire? Could it? Just know and consider what you don't want to live with but can and what you simply can't accept. Sometimes you have to live with these things anyway, but the construction plan can take these things into account or your disaster preparedness plan can.

Fire protection is vital for archives. (We built out of concrete, even the roof.) Fire suppression is also vital.

Unless the system is completely drained and dried after use, sprinklers may corrode, causing them to malfunction.

The *preaction sprinkler system,* the third type in common use, is like the dry pipe system in that water is not kept in the pipes but is held in check by an electrically operated valve called a preaction valve. To release water, the preaction valve must operate and sprinkler heads must fuse, thus providing greater protection against accidental discharges than with the wet pipe system. Smoke or dust that is not the result of fire causes an alarm to sound, but water will not flow.

DISASTER PREVENTION AND PREPAREDNESS

Although the threat of fire affects all libraries, natural disasters tend to single out libraries in specific areas of the country. One library may be situated near an earthquake fault; another is located in a coastal area regularly visited by hurricanes. The structural adaptations that should be incorporated into the plans of each of these libraries are quite different but equally important if the libraries are to continue to serve the needs of their users for years to come. Disaster prevention and preparedness should, therefore, be an integral part of your planning process.

Flooding

Where flooding is a problem in your area, buildings should be constructed from materials such as concrete, steel, and brick that are resistant to water damage. If at all possible, don't build your library in a flood plain. If you are not successful in this campaign, then be certain that a flood wall is included in the plans. Ask if a back valve will be installed to prevent water from backing up into a building. This ingenious gadget works because the pressure of water backup in pipes closes it. If a soggy basement is a distinct possibility, an automatic sump pump in a recessed area of the floor can expel water before your flood bears any resemblance to Noah's.

If you live near a coastal area, you may need to plan for flooding from the ocean during heavy storms or hurricanes, and you will need some sort of protective structure between your building and the ocean. Tidal surges are another problem and may require openings at lower elevations so the water can run right through the building.

Earthquakes

If earthquakes are a source of concern in your region, seismic building codes exist to protect against loss of life. However, they do not really prevent or even minimize building damage. Structural failure and damage caused by the architectural, mechanical, and electrical systems are not uncommon. A number of factors may make a building more vulnerable to earthquake damage. These include

- precast, pretensioned, or posttensioned concrete
- tilt-up designs with weakly connected load-bearing members
- timber framing with severe irregularities
- first floors without adequate support

Hurricanes and Tornadoes

During a hurricane, winds can rush in and destroy everything inside. Storm shutters can be useful for protecting windows. A track at the top and bottom of windows and doors or recessed in concrete slabs at their bases allows the shutters to be slipped into place quickly. Electronic shutters similar to garage doors can be used to roll down and protect the main door and windows. Storm-resistant windows that offer protection from flying projectiles are another good idea, as are recessed windows that can deflect the impact of flying objects. Bracing installed behind doors is still another option.

To a considerable extent, risk depends on how well a building is tied together. A weak link can breach the "envelope" of the structure. It's important that the building act as a unit, not have many vulnerable pieces. The foundation in a high-risk area should support a lot of pressure, so concrete footings should be made bigger than average to keep the library building from becoming unattached to the ground. Concrete used should have a higher than normal compressive strength, as high as 4,000 pounds per square inch. Steel columns should also be designed for higher stresses.

Tornadoes can occur almost anywhere, although there are areas known as tornado corridors. Experts recommend fewer windows if tornadoes are a particular problem in your locale since it is important to keep the wind from getting inside the building. If windows are important to you and your users, they can be inset to keep debris from hitting them. Storm windows also give additional strength to deflect debris.

In hurricane- and tornado-susceptible areas, be sure your roof is well connected to the rest of the building since it can fly off exposing the building to interior damage. If a door opens out, it is less likely to be blown open. Where fire codes permit, something as simple as a doorstop can keep doors in place, again protecting the building from interior damage.

Be sure to include in the building design safe places where staff and patrons can wait out the danger. A safe room should have several walls between you and the outside. Since innocent objects turn into unguided missiles when they are hurled by the wind, a safe room should not have any windows. Floor, walls, and ceilings of safe rooms should be fastened together with metal ties, and the floor plate should be securely fastened to the foundation.

SICK BUILDING SYNDROME

In recent years, we've been hearing a lot about sick building syndrome or SBS. Since the term has been embraced by the media, its definition has become extremely flexible. However, the Environmental Protection Agency (EPA) has defined sick building syndrome as a constellation of "situations in which building occupants experience acute health and comfort effects that appear to be linked to time spent in a building, but no specific illness . . . can be identified."[1] In other words, a building is defined as sick when a significant number of the occupants of a building suffer increased medical problems that are especially severe during the hours they spend at work. Such problems may result from breathing in particles, mainly petroleum-based chemicals emitted by construction materials, cleaning compounds, office equipment, and office furnishings, particularly carpeting.

Sick Building Syndrome ◆ **151**

TALE

We had welding fumes in the basement, causing our cataloger to start having watery eyes. We closed only briefly for that because no one believed me when I told them welding fumes could be toxic. (I consulted a chemical engineer on this.)

Sick building syndrome tends to affect new buildings—bright, shiny, seemingly well-built structures that their occupants have been waiting impatiently to occupy. In fact, the World Health Organization found that polluted air may reside in one-third of all new and remodeled buildings. The energy crisis of 1974 was responsible for new emphasis on building energy-efficient buildings. The determination to reduce dependence on foreign oil resulted in major reductions in the amount of fresh air buildings were designed to circulate through their ventilation systems. This enthusiasm also resulted in the development of modern insulation materials that are almost too efficient at holding this recirculated air inside the building.

Most people are familiar with Legionnaires' disease, which has spread through HVAC systems in some hotels. This is an illness caused by a sick building. Hotels, however, are not the only buildings subject to the malady. A new courthouse in Martin County, Florida, had to be immediately renovated at more than twice the cost of the original building. The cause was mold and mildew allowed to thrive in the ventilation system. Such a disaster to your new library building could ring the death knell to your hopes and dreams.

Symptoms

What are the symptoms of sick building syndrome? Although the problem affects different individuals in different ways, here are some of the most common symptoms reported by employees.

headaches	physical and mental fatigue
respiratory infections and breathing difficulties	allergy flare-ups
	depression
cold symptoms (runny noses, sore throats)	bronchitis
	eye and skin irritations
dizziness	forgetfulness
nausea	nosebleeds
drowsiness	rashes

If such symptoms are ignored, the toxins responsible can weaken the body's immune system, leading to many more serious health problems related to the liver, kidneys, and central nervous system.

Causes

Sick building syndrome is caused by an extraordinarily wide variety of culprits, but the HVAC system is a frequent offender. For example, poor ventilation systems that have leaks or that trap stale air, as well as systems that do not circulate sufficient quantities of air, may be at fault. Air ducts harboring dust, mold, bacteria, and mildew are another frequent problem. As pointed out in chapter 6, when humidity levels are not adequately controlled, mold spores and mildew can collect and circulate through the ventilation system. Sometimes the problem is not with the system itself but rather with the human beings responsible for its maintenance. For example, poor housekeeping may allow dust to build up on ventilation filters, or, in misguided attempts to economize, engineers may set systems too low to allow adequate amounts of air to be circulated. In other situations, the system may not permit sufficient human intervention; therefore, the absence of individual manual controls or dependence on computers rather than human beings to respond to temperature, humidity, and ventilation problems may be at the root of the problem. Inadequate filtration of airborne particles is another frequent problem.

In addition to problems related to the HVAC system, there are a large number of other potential conditions that produce illness.

- radon or asbestos present in the building
- urea-formaldehyde foam used as insulation
- pesticide chemicals that are not adequately ventilated from the building
- cleaning agents containing hazardous chemicals
- airtight buildings that can't "breathe" and so entrap indoor air pollutants
- high levels of hydrocarbons and carbon dioxide

Precautions

The cost of a sick building in terms of delay, renovation, staff absences, and medical costs is astronomical. What can you do to prevent sick building syndrome? Your efforts should begin with your initial discussions with the design team and continue throughout your tenancy of the building. The problem does not end when the workers leave and you open for business. Attention to the problem is required day in and day out, and a good motto to tack up over your office door might be "Eternal Vigilance." Following are just a few important precautions, many of which lie within your control:

Be sure your HVAC system can control humidity independent of temperature.

Provide local environmental control.

Use high quality materials like rubberized asphalt membrane and copper flashing around window openings to prevent leakage.

Increase the use of outdoor air.

Keep green plants around. They give off oxygen and absorb harmful impurities in the air.

Balance air flow throughout the building.

Select windows that can be opened for ventilation.

Install ceiling fans.

Use nontoxic paints.

Install carpeting made of natural fibers.

Use tacks, not glue, to keep carpeting in place.

Select office furniture covered or made of nontoxic materials.

Place copiers near windows to ensure that ozone is directed outside.

Place ventilation ducts on or near the ceiling.

An adequate HVAC system should be able to meet the standards of The American Society of Heating, Refrigerating, and Air-Conditioning Engineers (ASHRAE). These specify the exchange of between 15 and 60 cubic feet of outside air per minute per occupant.[2]

Modern HVAC technology has given us very sophisticated energy-recovery systems. They are capable of returning exhausted heat and humidity back into the building's ventilation in the winter. In summer, cool air is returned. This can mean a savings of up to 75 percent in heating and air-conditioning costs. In other words, the system will recover 75 percent of the energy expended. These systems also allow you to reduce the size of your air-conditioning equipment, further cutting costs. Even though the system is capable of such savings, you really don't want to have such large quantities of used and even contaminated air circulating through your building. Outdoor air is essential for a healthy building and for healthy occupants of a building. Fresh air needs to circulate throughout an entire building, not just a few areas. Your building may require a control system to monitor and control air distribution. Such equipment includes sensors that can detect contaminant levels. Not one but a series of filters is also important for reducing contaminants. Some experts recommend 30-percent prefilters for large air particulates followed by 90-percent final filters for fine particulates. Both filters should provide antimicrobial treatments to inhibit and control the growth of organisms the filters catch. Good filters make good sense economically since high-efficiency filtration will mean reduced cleaning of ductwork and other system components.

NOTES

1. U.S. Environmental Protection Agency, Office of Air and Radiation, *Indoor Air Facts* no. 4 (April 1998). Available online at http://www.epa.gov/iedweb00/pub/sbs.html.

2. American Society of Heating, Refrigerating, and Air-Conditioning Engineers, *Guideline for Commissioning of HVAC Systems* (ASHRAE Standards, 1-1989).

Resources

American Society of Heating, Refrigerating, and Air- Conditioning Engineers
Public Relations Office
1791 Tullie Circle, NE
Atlanta, GA 30329

Building Owners and Managers Assn. Intl.
1250 Eye St., NW
Washington, DC 20005

Indoor Air Quality Information Clearinghouse
P.O. Box 37133
Washington, DC 20013-7133
(800) 438-4318; (202) 484-1307
fax: (202) 484-1510

National Institute for Occupational Safety and Health
U.S. Dept. of Health and Human Services
4676 Columbia Pkwy., Mail Drop R2
Cincinnati, OH 45226

All of the following publications are also available from:

National Clearinghouse for Educational Facilities
National Institute of Building Sciences
1090 Vermont Ave. NW, Ste. 700
Washington, DC 20005
(202) 289-7800; (888) 552-0624

Blue, Don. "Safety by Design." Paper presented at the International Crime Prevention through Environmental Design Association Conference, Washington, D.C., Dec. 14–16, 1998. Available online at http://www.arch.vt.edu/ crimeprev/ pages/confpapers.html/blue.html.

Crime Prevention from the Ground Up: CPTED (Crime Prevention through Environmental Design). National Crime Prevention Council, 1999. Available online at http://www.ncpc.org/2add4dc.htm.

Designing Safer Communities: A Crime Prevention through Environmental Design Handbook. National Crime Prevention Council, 1997. Available online at http://www. ncpc.org/8how1dc.htm.

Superintendent of Public Instruction, Virginia Department of Education. *Checklist for the Safety and Security of Buildings and Grounds,* 1997. Available online at http://www.pen.k12.va.us/VDOE/Instruction/safety.html.

8

Flooring Materials, Wall Coverings, and Furnishings

Although the furnishings and floor coverings in a library serve an important practical purpose, their practical functions can easily be forgotten by those project participants who want the new library to make a statement; that is, they are far more concerned with the way the library looks than with its philosophy or with the services it provides. This same failure to focus on function comes into play when selecting flooring materials and wall coverings. For example, it would be nice to match the blue in the upholstery pattern, but it is far more important that the chosen floor surface does not send patrons skating perilously across the entryway when it becomes wet. Although you and your staff are not immune to such superficial concerns, you are far more aware of the role each chair and workstation must play in supporting the services of a new library.

On the other hand, a cheerful, attractive building is very important to your patrons. Librarians across the country report that an up-to-date, even trendy, interior can have a major impact on their attendance and circulation statistics. Especially in public libraries, circulation figures may go steadily downward as the library building gets older and seedier. When the same collection, services, and staff are moved into their new quarters, usage skyrockets. Most people are very aware of their surroundings and want to be in a bright, welcoming environment with a harmonious color scheme. This chapter will attempt to balance functional and aesthetic concerns. However, because fashions in decor change so frequently, most discussions will focus on more practical matters.

It is probably safe to say that few things irritate our compatriots more than the whole subject of decor. On almost every building project, there is someone in a position of authority who considers himself or herself the ultimate arbiter of taste. Someone—maybe a trustee, college president's wife, or library board member—

who knows nothing about the functions of a library will happily sabotage your efforts and inflict all manner of horrors on you and your users as long as the results are color coordinated.

Unless you are willing to purchase lavender computers with raspberry printers and spend your every moment refereeing battles between tasteful factions, you are going to have to come to grips with the problem of differing decorating tastes. While you were worrying about high-pressure exterior lighting, Ethernet cabling, and dry pipe sprinklers, you were probably left blissfully alone. However, the instant the words "color," "style," or "fashion" are publicly uttered, you will be besieged with opinions. Everyone is a self-styled expert on interior decoration. Unfortunately, you will never find two people in total agreement on the subject. Taste is highly subjective, depending upon culture, social affiliation, age, eyesight, and dozens of other variables.

IMPORTANT VERSUS UNIMPORTANT DECISIONS

There are some decisions that don't really matter and others that are vitally important; don't get the two categories mixed up. For example, furniture must be designed for living, breathing human beings. There's nothing wrong with attractive chairs, but first and foremost, they must be comfortable. Library patrons will be sitting on them for hours at a time, and I doubt that your staff includes a chiropractor. Decisions about fabric and wood stain can safely be delegated to those taste-makers and trendsetters in your boardroom or preferably to your project task force under the watchful eye of a design professional. You will want to be sure, however, that any chairs under consideration are "sit-able" for long hours of study and strong enough to stand up to the wear and tear of a real library setting.

Be as generous as possible in delegating decorating decisions. You really don't want to pick the color of the restroom walls. Everyone will hate it, and you'll be crushed or seething. Let someone else take the rap. You will want to have lots of similar decisions handy to delegate. They serve as a smoke screen that allows you to take care of more important matters.

Trendy Color Schemes

First, clear your brain of some of your mental pictures of your beautiful new library and concentrate on what really matters. For example, many contemporary color schemes would probably be acceptable to your users, but in a few years they will tire of them. Think about how you feel when you enter an avocado and gold building reminiscent of the 1970s. Having endured just such a library complete with shag carpet, I'm convinced that nothing makes a building look old and depressing like yesterday's color scheme. Therefore, you may not care what color your modish associates decide upon, but you will want to be certain you can get rid of it when it is no longer au courant. That means that accent walls are fine, but furniture intended to last for thirty years should not be rainbow hued.

TALE

We will be putting up with our inadequate but color-coordinated building for many long years. My advice is to spend as much money as possible on technical details without worrying if the carpet coordinates with the shelving.

Although you should steer clear of the battle over colors, it is true that color can have an enormous influence over the way people feel. For example, Bill Marriott, who owns countless Marriott Hotels, refuses to decorate his guest rooms and public spaces in blue because he believes it's depressing and anxiety-producing. In general, warm palettes are probably best used in cold climates and vice-versa.

Hiring a Decorator or an Interior Designer

Though it may seem cowardly, it's usually a good idea to have an interior designer on hand to take the brunt of the aesthetic criticism. The designer can perform useful services like presenting a choice of color palettes and limiting choices to reasonable alternatives. The decorator or designer is also a professional whose judgment carries weight. It can't be just any decorator, however. As the accompanying tale shows, decorators can be almost as fiendish as architects. They can be quite as narrow-minded as any interfering trustee and may exhibit terrifying tunnel vision when they are obsessed with creating their elegant masterpiece. It is hard to coexist peacefully with someone who wants to hide the copy machines because they are not aesthetically pleasing.

On the other hand, a decorator or interior designer does more than just take the blame for unpopular color choices. If you are fortunate enough to have one involved in your project, you may have access to a wealth of practical advice not only about decor but also about the efficient use of space and flexible floor plans. A good decorator is even aware of relevant building codes, fire and life-safety requirements, and accessibility guidelines.

Despite stereotypes, decorators do not usually begin by choosing paint or carpet colors. Instead, they develop a program—a comprehensive list of specifics based on library functions. They make note of the number and size of workstations, conference rooms, service desks, and storage areas, considering practical and aesthetic requirements. Some interior designers are part of the design-build team and may develop preliminary layouts of the space, loosely blocking in public study areas, book stacks, work areas, and traffic patterns. Such design professionals can be very helpful. You might think of a decorator as an interior architect who selects appropriate materials, fixtures, and furniture to achieve the best integration of aesthetics, efficiency, and cost effectiveness.

If you will be working with a decorator, be sure to have the following information available. (This is yet another of your written handouts.)

total square feet planned for each function and how you see it being used

library organization chart with staff positions including titles and functions as well as department relationships

adjacency requirements—who needs access to what areas

furniture and equipment requirements for each function

electrical, acoustic, lighting, or other requirements

Be sure your decorator is sensitive to your area and its architectural traditions. One need not be slavishly "Santa Fe" in the Southwest, for instance, but a color scheme appropriate for a New York skyscraper will be unlikely to travel well.

TALE

We had an egotistical interior designer who insisted that everything match whether it was functional or not. Make sure you have a decorator who puts function first.

SELECTING FLOORING MATERIALS

The floor coverings and surfaces selected for a library or archive should not simply be left to planning professionals. These materials will have far more impact on the library's ability to function effectively than any architect realizes, and one size does not fit all. Each area must be considered separately, and most buildings require different materials for different purposes, such as restrooms, entryways, meeting rooms, etc.

Consider carpeted areas, for example. Patrons like to walk on carpet, especially on cold, biting days. Staff members who must be on their feet during much of the day find that carpet reduces leg pain and other discomforts. Printed materials, however, are endangered by the dust and other pollutants that inevitably come from carpets. No matter how frequently it is cleaned, a carpet is a comfy home to all sorts of creepy, crawly things that may peacefully coexist with people but not with paper. There are, indeed, types of carpets that release fewer pollutants into the air than other types, but where collections are the priority, carpets really cannot be considered safe.

One library was carpeted with thousands of yards of broadloom, laid down everywhere except in staff spaces, where tile and cement reigned supreme. Don't let this happen in your library. Staff members spend eight or more hours a day in the library and have every right to be comfortable. Walking through the technical services departments of some libraries, I'm reminded of the uncomfortable servants' halls of yesterday. (Though if one is to judge by Public Television's *Upstairs Downstairs,* they may have been considerably cozier than many modern library backrooms.) Yours may be a repository in which the collection is considered too precious and fragile to tolerate any carpeting at all. However, if you are planning to use carpeting in public spaces, it is almost always appropriate for offices and workrooms.

So considering these factors, where will you use carpeting, and where are other materials more appropriate? Look carefully at your present library building. When patrons enter through the front door in sodden raincoats and muddy boots, those first sloppy steps should not be taken on carpet. What is needed is a surface that is easy to clean and does not become slippery when wet. The best choice is probably some type of slip-resistant tile.

If your elevator doors open into a carpeted area, you may live in fear of mishaps caused by book trucks and constant foot traffic that gradually scuffs up the carpet edge, leaving it exposed and dangerous. The difficulty encountered when rolling book trucks through the library will give you a fairly good idea of the obstacles experienced by users in wheelchairs who must navigate thresholds, high-pile carpeting, and barriers created by the transition from one surface to another.

Restroom flooring presents additional maintenance considerations. You probably have seen restroom tile that always looks dirty because dirt becomes lodged in grout crevices and is difficult to remove.

What about stairs? Carpeting can make them less treacherous, but it will receive heavy wear. Carpeting with rubber treads may be a good choice. Carpet tile would be a poor one since tiles coming unglued represent accidents just waiting to happen.

One of the most important considerations is the nature of your collection. If you have large archival or rare print collections, then you may wish to keep car-

Biomedical Research Library, Vanderbilt University Medical Center, Nashville, Tennessee

peting to a minimum. You may even need a separate ventilation or air handling system to keep carpet pollution away from collections. In fact, if this is a major consideration, you may wish to forgo carpeting altogether. This is a rather radical position, however, since other options are somewhat limited. Vinyl tile tends to give a "cafeteria" look to a space. Ceramic tile, reminiscent of the Southwest, can be lovely, but it is hard, slippery, and agonizing for anyone pushing book trucks. Hardwood floors are usually well beyond the budgets of most libraries.

You might think about where your library or archive might be placed on a continuum with concerns for patron comfort at one end and concerns for preservation at the other. At one end might be a repository where the preservation of the collection is the prime consideration and patron use is confined to one or more small reading rooms. In such a facility, carpet might be totally absent. One of several excellent, modern sealants might be applied to the cement floors in place of tile. That way, there are no cracks in which dirt can breed. Book trucks can roll smoothly over such a surface too, but staff will find it far from cozy.

At the other end of the continuum you might find a public library branch with lots of programs, children's activities, and an easily replaced popular collection. Here, you would choose floor coverings based on programming needs and patron preferences. Young children are constantly falling down and need a soft surface on which to land. They may be quite noisy, and hard surfaces serve to echo and magnify the hubbub. Since the collection will not be around long enough that you need concern yourself with preservation issues, carpet is clearly the best choice.

Carpet tiles are a very attractive option when you have large numbers of voice, data, and electrical outlets installed in the floor. Although carpet tiles can cost 30 to 50 percent more than broadloom carpeting, carpet tiles make it much easier to add computers and media equipment as well as repair and upgrade the data infrastructure than with broadloom. It's also easier to replace tile in heavy traffic areas without turning it into a major project. Ultimately, when you consider the long-term cost of having to replace either carpet tile or broadloom, the cost is about the same.

Whether you choose carpet tiles or broadloom, it's a good idea to purchase more than you need and store the extra carpet for future use. Some areas wear much faster than others, and you may find yourself replacing certain relatively small sections more often than you will purchase new carpeting for the whole library. Furthermore, it may be hard to match small sections with new carpet because dye lots vary considerably, and manufacturers frequently discontinue textures, colors, and patterns.

Static Electricity

Since the modern library has so much money invested in computers, it is important that they remain in good working order for as long as possible. Static electricity is produced by walking across carpeting. It builds up gradually until finally when patrons touch something metal, they notice a slight (or somewhat more severe) shock. Static electricity poses a much greater hazard in dry climates and during the winter months when heating systems remove most of the humidity from the air. Not only is it annoying and a little painful but it can cause serious damage to delicate electronic equipment. For example, static can cause printers to spew out unwanted toner, burn out tiny spots in a monitor screen, and interfere with the computer functioning so that frequent rebooting is necessary.

Over the last few years, the practice of treating carpeting with an antistatic solution has become common, and most of the static problems have been alleviated. Furthermore, some newer varieties of carpet effectively reduce static electricity. Nevertheless, it is necessary to remain on guard against static and exercise restraint in selecting carpeting for electrical and equipment closets as well as in areas where servers or other hard-to-replace equipment is kept. It's a good idea to require that library technicians wear antistatic wrist straps whenever they work on the inside of a piece of electronic equipment; in addition you may want to attach grounding devices to the equipment.

TALE

The beautiful blue-green carpet started developing runs in the children's department two weeks after the grand reopening.

Safety and Wear

Attractive flooring materials can add a great deal to the ambiance of a library, but aesthetics should not be the most important consideration when making selections. First and foremost, consider safety. In addition, you will want to consider how well the materials will wear over time. Following are some things to think about when you compare various flooring materials.

Is there a safe "transition" area in front of the elevator to prevent patrons from tripping over the edge of carpeting and injuring themselves?

What happens to the flooring material you're considering when it gets wet? Does it become dangerously slick? (Marble, for example, becomes positively treacherous.)

How difficult is the flooring material to clean?

Is the floor sloped?

How much traffic do you expect in a particular area? (Carpeting will not long survive in your central lobby area.)

Will ugly black marks or permanent indentations result when you move stacks and other heavy pieces of furniture?

What are the product's antistatic qualities?

Does carpeting comply with fire regulations in your area?

For how long is the flooring material guaranteed?

Will you be rolling book trucks through an area? (They can make a terrible racket on ceramic tile and should not be rolled across studded resilient flooring.)

Have you given special consideration to high risk areas like ramps, stairs, and potential wet/damp areas?

Have you planned a "runoff" area at the entrance where patrons can clean their shoes?

Are your stair landings safe, slip-proof, and equipped with color strips to call attention to different levels?

Other Flooring Materials

For those areas where carpeting is not a good choice, you and your team will have a variety of materials from which to choose. The following sections provide a brief overview of the general categories and classifications. This is definitely one of those topics that will require long hours leafing through manufacturers' catalogs, but before anyone gets carried away by an aesthetically pleasing material, take time to learn a little about industry specifications and standards.

Resilient Flooring

Resilient flooring includes commercial sheet goods as well as vinyl composition tile. Librarians are sometimes surprised that commercial resilient flooring does not have an easy-to-clean urethane surface like the residential vinyl floors do. The increased traffic of a public area makes such a surface impractical, although it may be perfectly satisfactory for home use. Unlike the no-wax floor in a kitchen, resilient flooring materials for a library need to be polished regularly. Installation also takes longer than in residential applications because the adhesive used to install commercial flooring must set up properly before heavy equipment can be moved across it. If it hasn't set, adhesive displacement can result in unattractive dents that your contractor will never be able to remove. If it is essential to bring in heavy objects, place sheets of plywood or underlayment over the flooring to spread the weight.

If a resilient floor covering is installed over a concrete slab, take moisture and pH tests since the vinyl acts as a moisture barrier. Since most adhesives used are water based, moisture can be trapped in the concrete slab, making it impossible for the adhesive to set up properly. Then adhesive can ooze up between tiles, or tiles can pop loose.

Ceramic Tile

Ceramic tile has been in use for thousands of years. It is a mixture of different clays and other minerals that have been shaped and fired at high temperatures. The higher the temperature, the harder the tile. This "hard body," sometimes called "bisque," is given a glazed wear layer or left untreated. A glaze is actually glass that is fused to the bisque by intense heat. The fewer air pockets in the clay, the denser, and thus, stronger the bisque. The ceramic tile industry measures density by the amount of water the tile absorbs. Nonvitreous tiles are those that absorb 7 percent or more of their weight in water; semivitreous tiles absorb between 3 percent and 7 percent water. Vitreous tile absorbs 0.5 percent to 3 percent water; and impervious tiles are the densest and strongest, absorbing between 0 percent and 0.5 percent of their weight in water. These distinctions are extremely important when deciding which types of tiles are most suited to a particular installation. In general, when you're given a choice, you will probably find that denser tiles are the best choice.

Another common choice is between glazed and unglazed tile. Unglazed tiles, like porcelains and quarry tiles, are baked pieces of clay in which the color runs through the entire clay body. Unglazed tiles are usually thicker and denser than glazed tiles. Although color selections for unglazed tile may be limited by the colors of the clay, it is usually an excellent choice for areas where there is a lot of wear and tear.

The Porcelain Enamel Institute has developed a system to rate the durability of each type of tile. The following is a very abbreviated outline of the system:

Group I: This category includes tiles that are suitable for only residential bathrooms. They cannot stand up to the wear that characterizes public buildings.

Group II: This category is also appropriate only for residential installation.

Group III: These are tiles suited for commercial areas that experience light traffic, such as offices and reception areas.

Group IV: Tile in this category is appropriate for medium commercial and light institutional applications.

Group IV+: This is the category that, in most cases, you will want to choose for the new library. Tile in group IV+ is suitable for heavy traffic and wet areas where safety is a major concern. It can also be used for walkways and building entrances.

Monocottura technology is a ceramic technology that is in common use today; this Italian word means "single-fired." That is, the tile is shaped, glazed, and fired in one step, thus speeding up production and reducing costs. The process can produce tiles in less than one hour compared with days in the past. The result is a denser body and harder glaze. In addition, tiles produced with this method have a flat back that makes them easier to install than tiles produced with older processes.

Laminate Flooring

Most librarians are familiar with laminates like Formica used in countertops, but they don't think of it as flooring material. A good way to define a laminate floor is an interlocking tongue-and-groove flooring system that floats on top of the subfloor (a concrete slab, an existing vinyl floor, or a hardwood floor). This means that the new floor is not attached to the floor underneath. A bead of water-resistant glue placed between the tongue-and-grooves of every plank holds planks together and seals the edges from moisture. Before the floor is installed, a polyurethane padding is placed over the subfloor to prevent glue from sticking to the subfloor. The laminated material is composed of a hard-core material with a laminated printed layer and backing secured to the core. The sandwich of materials is saturated in a resin called "melamine" in much the way that Formica countertops are produced. Of course, the amount of resin applied must be much greater to produce a flooring material that resists wear and tear. The result is a floor that can work well in certain library areas.

Hardwood Floors

Because of escalating costs and environmental concerns, hardwood floors are becoming an infrequent choice for libraries. However, hardwood floors are still the preferred option when a touch of luxury is needed, such as in a boardroom or rare-book reading room. Solid wood floors use planks that are one complete piece of solid wood from top to bottom. Most often, they are ¾″ or ⁵⁄₁₆″ thick and 2¼″ or 1½″ wide. One of the most serious problems experienced with this type of flooring is its reaction to moisture. Winter heating dries the wood, making it contract or leave gaps between the boards. Summer humidity will cause the wood to expand and cup.

Oak is perhaps the most common hardwood floor. Unfinished solid oak comes in several different qualities.

- clear (no visual blemishes or knots; extremely expensive)
- select (some small knots; very little dark graining)
- better (similar to select but slightly less desirable)
- #1 common (more knots and more dark graining)
- #2 common (even more knots)

"Engineered" is a term that refers to laminated boards that have 2, 3, or 5 layers of wood laminated together. They range in thickness from ¼″ to ⁹⁄₁₆″ and in width from 2¼″ to 7″. The process involves cross-graining (in other words, the grain of each layer is perpendicular to that of the layer above and the one below), so it is more stable and less affected by moisture than solid planks. Because wood always expands in one direction, solid planks expand across their width, not their length. By changing the direction of wood graining it is possible to greatly reduce expansion and contraction. Parquet was once the ultimate in luxury floors, but today parquet is often an engineered floor, usually composed of 12"-by-12" squares. The term "long strip" means an engineered floor characterized by extra-long planks (usually 84") and separated "sliced cut" slats that are glued together to produce the face of each plank.

The planks of most solid wood floors are sawn from the tree trunk, cutting through the tree's circular growth rings. In an engineered floor, veneers are cut with sharp knives as the trunk is spun in a circle, producing a much larger, aesthetically pleasing surface area. When the veneer has dried, it is laminated to other layers to make wood flooring planks.

SELECTING WALL COVERINGS

Walls are, of course, integral to the structure of the building and serve a variety of essential functions. In addition, however, they also provide an unparalleled opportunity to alter the look and feel of the building—most importantly, the image it presents to your users. As you're considering the look and feel of interior spaces, remember that modern computer environments can seem coldly dehumanized. Wall treatments can be your most important ally when it comes to creating the kind of welcoming environment you envision, and paint, plaster, and wood paneling as well as paper and cloth wall coverings can enliven any interior. For example, you may wish to incorporate some soft, homey wall coverings into both public and staff spaces and use colors and textures that are pleasing and restful. Flooring materials and textiles as well as wall coverings can provide a unifying background and complement the library's architecture for a warm, restful image.

Although colorful, highly textured wall coverings can be extremely effective in small areas, it is best to be sparing in your use of these materials. Painted Sheetrock is much less expensive than other wall coverings, and it can be repainted again and again with whatever colors are in vogue. Paint may be your most valuable weapon in your war to keep the building from looking antiquated and boring. A splash of bright color or a striking design may create exactly the kind of ambience you are going for, but don't get carried away.

The majority of the flexible wall coverings sold for commercial applications in the United States are of fabric-backed vinyl construction. The rest includes coated paper, textiles, solid sheet vinyl with paper backing, and grasscloths. Wall coverings are especially useful in retrofitting older structures to hide cracked walls or unsightly wiring installations.

Wall coverings are divided into two basic types: type I includes wall covering weights of 15 ounces and under, while type II includes up to 22-ounce weights. To a large extent, the weight of the wall covering is a good indicator of quality and depth of texture and finish as well as a predictor of performance. Some wall coverings are available unbacked for light duty. Such materials are not usually appropriate for libraries, however. A good polyester backing is usually essential for good performance and durability.

Be sure that the wall coverings chosen are free of solvents, biocides, and stabilizers that damage the environment and produce allergic reactions. Off-gassing and volatile-organic content emissions from some adhesives used during installation are another source of pollution and sick building symptoms.

It is inevitable that your library walls will be the recipients of considerable deliberate and accidental abuse, whether from college freshmen or from children with crayons, who look at your walls as a vast canvas on which they can exercise their creativity. High-abuse areas may require using coatings of Teflon, Scotchgard, or acrylics to resist stains. If the wallcovering is in an area that receives direct sunlight, investigate the product's color-retention properties.

If you are asked to look at samples of wall coverings being considered, be sure that you see the samples under the same conditions as those in the new library. Determine whether each will be viewed under natural or artificial lighting conditions. Try to identify the type of artificial lighting that will be used in a particular space for which you are selecting the wall covering, and find a similar environment in which to view the sample.

SELECTING LIBRARY FURNISHINGS

When you begin thinking about furniture for your new building, consider the activities that will be conducted within the building. Imagine what your patrons will be doing. Get out of your office and look around. Then consider the opportunities the new facility will offer for expanding your services and resources, and picture your patrons using those resources. You might even create an inventory of activities that will take place in the library.

Even though the future is unknowable, try to imagine what patrons will be doing in the library ten or twenty years from now. Consider preparing a written, room-by-room activity description for the whole building. Once you have a complete list, translate these activities into equipment and furniture selections. Some libraries have begun their planning with just such a list of activities. They have first identified the furniture and equipment to support the activities and then wrapped them in walls and spaces until they have a building.

As you're considering furnishings for the new library, you might check out a commercial Internet page titled "WorkSpace Resources." Here, you'll find a resource index of commercial and institutional furniture and accessories. Not only will you discover information on vendors and consultants but also on concerns like ergonomics and space planning for business, industry, and education.

Whether you're working with a decorator or selecting furnishings yourself, look for correct ergonomics, comfort, durability, safety, looks, and value. No one of these factors can be ignored or given priority over the others. Providing a warm, welcoming environment is as important as choosing study carrels that can survive the abuse endured by high-use facilities. Chair design and construction must minimize both the danger to the patron and the damage to furniture when some clever kiddie decides to impress his friends by pivoting on one chair leg. The process of selecting furniture and furnishings for a library/media center varies with each library's individual requirements.

Begin by talking with staff from all library departments about their furniture needs. Discuss how patrons use and abuse existing library chairs and tables. If you have children's and young adult sections, are sizes and shapes appropriate for the different age groups? Were the chairs in your adult reading room built for children? Remember that five-foot-tall women and two-hundred-fifty-pound men will be using your resources. How well does your existing furniture meet their needs?

Next consider colors, fabrics, and finishes that can unify and add interest to library spaces. As you talk with decorators and others, consider that people have very strong likes and dislikes. You're going for a look that many people will find pleasant and attractive, not a decorator showcase.

Find a way to see any furniture line under serious consideration. Visit local libraries or ask for samples of chairs or other smaller pieces. Analyze their construction to decide which kinds of furniture will last longest. Furnishings must last a long time, and almost any librarian in a new building will tell you that much furniture construction is remarkably shoddy. Look for signs of good craftsmanship. For example, the well joints on file drawers and steel desks should have double-sided walls for strength and stability. Sometimes the company with the big name is living off its reputation and you can find better values from number two or three. High-end knockoffs for chairs and desks can be as well made or even superior to the brand-name equivalents. Some of the better library furniture vendors are Buckstaff, Worden Company, Luxor, Gressco, Fleetwood, and Virco. However, it is a good idea to look further and consider where you can use less specialized and often less expensive office and computer furnishings.

Look for surfaces that resist fading and moisture, especially if the furniture will be in direct sunlight. Stay in close contact with your contractor and be sure he or she has samples of colors and finishes. There are many different finishes called "oak," or "warm oak," or "sunny oak," or some similar meaningless name, and every one of them clashes with all the others. Unless your contractor has samples and understands that wood finishes must be coordinated, woodwork, doors, and furnishings will all be at odds with one another.

Cleaning and Maintenance Issues

If you were to don your cloak of invisibility and follow the custodial staff around your library, you'd probably discover that their carts are equipped with two squirt bottles, sometimes referred to as "blue juice" and "red juice." Every offending surface is zapped with the contents of one squirt bottle or the other. Blue juice is the milder of the two concoctions, while red juice is intended for heavy duty jobs. Both are industrial strength, however, and can disintegrate delicate surfaces. After years of frustration, I have finally concluded that nothing should be purchased for the library that cannot be safely "juiced." I've witnessed the demise of too many lovely study tables to take any further chances. Not only do I require that every wood surface be protected with polyurethane, but I get nervous if I can even *feel* the grain of the wood.

CHUCK CHOI

Lobby and Reading Area, Scholarly Communication Center, Rutgers University, New Brunswick, New Jersey

TALES

We told the architects what kinds of office furniture we needed, but not specific brands or models, and left it to them to get what we needed. That was a mistake. Based on our descriptions, they selected desks, filing cabinets, chairs, lockers, etc., that they thought were what we wanted but weren't, and then put together a bid package. Based on the bids, orders were placed. Fortunately, I happened to find out about one piece that I knew was totally wrong. When I looked at the entire order, I was dismayed to discover that we were spending tens of thousands of dollars more than we needed to in order to buy furniture that would not meet our needs.

A major factor in promoting respect (among 2,400 students) may be the high quality that was designed into the building.

Custom Furniture Issues

As you've discovered when shopping for personal needs, any item created for a specialized market usually costs more than similar mass-marketed equivalents. This is definitely the case with library furniture. You may be able to get better buys with standard office furniture if it fits your need. Even consumer products can be good buys if they're built for the kind of wear and tear you can expect in a public environment.

Think hard about what you gain with specially designed library furniture. Atlas and dictionary stands, for instance, are extremely well designed for the purpose they serve and probably cannot be duplicated in an office furniture catalog. Tables and computer work stations are another matter entirely. Compare catalogs aimed at a variety of different markets like tables produced for restaurants, schools, and offices. You'll discover that the size of the market affects price, as does the perceived affluence of the buyer. For example, prices escalate noticeably when furnishings are intended for use in a hospital or doctor's office.

Every library has some built-in furnishings that must be custom built. These might be counters, service desks, oak bookcases in the boardroom, or any of a number of special-function structures that you simply can't buy off-the-shelf. These units tend to be fraught with even more than your daily quota of problems because you and your architects must create them. When you choose a piece of furniture or equipment from a library catalog, you can have at least some assurance that the manufacturer understands (more or less) library needs. This is emphatically not the case with a custom furniture builder. Since you're always reinventing the wheel, communication between you and your furniture builder is especially important.

Service Desks

If reasonably acceptable service desks are available from library furniture vendors, definitely take advantage of this opportunity. Whatever else is wrong with them, they have been standardized over the years to meet most library needs. Their heights are standard, their kneeholes are standard, and their book-drop slots are at the right height to accommodate book bins. Most are modular and can be arranged in a wide variety of different configurations. In addition, no matter how astronomical their prices, they usually end up being cheaper than their custom-made equivalents.

You may, however, require custom-millwork service desks because they must fit into oddly shaped spaces or because the architect insists that off-the-shelf units will not be compatible with the rest of the building. If so, plan to spend hours in other libraries measuring and remeasuring their service desks. Don't stop at measuring height and breadth; also measure how much space is available for drawers, knees, shelves, and so on. The functionality of service desks really matters and deserves substantial planning. If you'd rather not spend the time yourself, appoint a small committee with representatives from your library's circulation and reference desks. They would probably be delighted to right some of the wrongs they have been living with.

Every so often, a battle erupts on one of the electronic library discussion lists about the height of the reference desk. One school of thought holds that the desk should be at table height to encourage reference interviews and permit staff member and patron to sit comfortably across from one another. The other school holds that the desk should actually be a high counter behind which staff either stand or sit on stools. This faction contends that the high desk is more visible and that most questions do not require a sit-down reference interview. Amid all the philosophical and psychological arguments, you might remember that librarians will more readily take their turn at the desk if they are comfortable. Few methods of torture have been invented to equal an hour or so perched on one of those high swivel stools.

Although they are an integral part of our library lives, our minds tend to go blank when we begin planning this important workstation. In a sense, this is the hub of the library—a sort of action central that can contribute to the library's efficiency or cause endless problems. Following are some of the many items that may need to be accommodated at the desk:

computers	book detection sensitizers/ desensitizers
computer printers	
scanner	equipment storage
card reader	mobile files
security monitors	drawers
security video recorders	shelves
cash register	telephones
credit card charging machine	book-return slots
public address system	mobile depressible book-return carts
enunciator panel for monitoring building activities	reserve collections
fire alarm pull	

Specific Requirements

If you're sending out RFPs for custom furniture, be sure that the requirements are extremely specific. This is one area where you definitely do not want the low bid unless quality standards are assured. Bid specifications should include all the necessary information for the furnishings, as well as bonds and installation requirements. When the bids come back, make sure you are comparing apples with apples. Use a spreadsheet to create a table of prices and features. If a vendor hasn't been specific enough, ask for more information. Don't give serious consideration to any vendors until you have complete information about their products.

Once contracts have been awarded, make arrangements to review any alternate finish materials and to approve mockups, if available. Remember that delivery must be timed precisely, and you will need solid assurances that the vendor can deliver the furnishings on schedule. You will not want furniture around while construction is still going on since it is almost impossible to store and is subject to loss and vandalism. Similarly, a completed building is almost useless until the furniture arrives. Library furniture usually arrives looking like a vast Erector set. Installation must be carefully coordinated and integrated into your project schedule. You will want installers to begin their work as soon as possible without getting in the way of construction workers.

TALE

Make sure you *see* shop drawings of workroom cabinetry, etc. Shop drawings are typically sent by the subcontractor to the architect for approval. The owner is often left out of the loop. We received cabinets that were not what we asked for as a result, and there was a considerable time delay while cabinets were remade to our original specifications.

Wiring Issues and Library Furnishings

Whether your furniture is custom-made or selected from a catalog, it must accommodate the plethora of computers that are an integral part of any new library. You may occasionally feel as if you're designing the entire building around the special requirements of electronic equipment, but in doing so, you are also serving your users. Computer workstations not only require large amounts of clean, conditioned power, but the wires for that power pose other challenges as well. Even though recent systems furniture and library carrels may appear to be well designed, you can end up with the same old octopus electrical cable configurations and spaghetti wiring that characterized your old library. Following are some basic points to consider when selecting and installing computer workstations:

Select workstations that permit easy installation of cable and have ample space for cable storage. Electricians should be able to separate and store cables by function.

Store wires in channels to eliminate excess wires cluttering work surfaces. (This also reduces the cost of floor ducting.)

Select workstations that don't require wiring to be accessed from behind panel base plates, thus requiring the workstation to be disassembled when changes or repairs are made.

Be sure outlets are located conveniently, preferably at desk height, not below work surfaces or behind storage units.

Select workstations that allow users to plug in to electrical receptacles and phone/data junction boxes located within the wire-access cavity.

Locate cable access cutouts on all work surfaces to allow electronic equipment to connect above and below the work surface without requiring special grommets.

Be sure panels are at least 4″ thick with a 2″ hollow center. This allows cables to run both vertically and horizontally throughout the workstation. If you are installing a fiber-optic or Category 5 network or plan to do so in the future, the 2″ panel thickness commonly encountered can interfere with the ability of the cabling to make right-angle bends to maintain data integrity.

Allow space for a transfer box needed with fiber-optic cables to move signals to equipment. These are usually 2¾″ deep by 2⅛″ wide by 4″ high, so the transfer box cannot be mounted inside the frequently encountered 2″ panels.

Encourage electricians to store "goof loops" (extra wire) in workstations to avoid rewiring when changes are made or equipment is added. Running cables through the panels protects the cables.

Be sure workstations use lay-in cable management rather than conventional string-through methods. This makes future changes easier and protects wires from damage. Cables should be placed in a trough positioned at the top of the panels so wires are supported. They can then be dropped down to desk height wherever needed.

User Workstations

More and more reading and stack areas in a modern library are equipped with computer workstations for public use. As you select computer furniture, you will naturally be looking for work surfaces large enough to accommodate the equipment. You will be looking at the size and positioning of shelves, provisions for the cable jungle bulging out behind any PC, and all the other considerations described previously. What you may not consider, however, is what the patron is doing at the computer workstation in addition to using the computer. Students require space for notes, pens, and textbooks. Women need a safe place for their purses, and many readers carry books and magazines from other areas of the library. All of these encumbrances require space on the work surface.

If you walk through many computer areas, you will see personal possessions piled on the floor or notebooks perilously balanced on student laps. A computer workstation should accommodate all the same paraphernalia that patrons have always needed for their library activities in addition to providing space for equipment. The space traditionally allotted to a reader is not sufficient for a computer-equipped workstation. The exact size will vary depending on your equipment. For example, more work space is available to the user if tower-cased computers are installed below the work surface, and more space will be needed if workstations include printers, scanners, or other peripherals. However, a good width for computer-equipped study carrels is five feet, allowing space for books, equipment, data ports, power outlets, and locks where appropriate. Multipurpose tables should also be spacious with data and power provided at every seating space.

Staff Workstations

When designing staff spaces, consider the wide variety of tasks that are performed in a library. As much as possible, build in flexibility with adjustable chair and work surface heights. Many library tasks are highly repetitive, so take care to minimize strain. Consider the following suggestions when selecting furniture and equipment for staff spaces:

> The ideal work surface can be adjusted from 22 to 45 inches high, although normal desk height is 26 to 28 inches.
>
> People with back injuries may find it more comfortable to work and use equipment while standing, so provide a few workstations at the appropriate height.
>
> Several people may use the same workstation, since libraries are open days, nights, and weekends, so workstations need to be easily adjustable.
>
> Adjustable levers on furniture should be readily accessible and easy to use.
>
> Lots of space should be available for book trucks.
>
> Ample shelving should be provided.

As you investigate specifications for the ideal staff workstation, you will encounter many differences of opinion. Such conflicting information arises from the difficulty of trying to satisfy the needs of the average staff member. Why not design staff work spaces especially for your existing staff? Of course, staffing will change with the years, but so will the equipment. Specific modifications have a lot to do with the age of staff, whether they wear glasses, and other considerations. Ask the library staff to conduct experiments with one person viewing a screen at the most comfortable height and distance while another staff member measures.

Compact Shelving Issues

Although electronic resources are becoming numerous in libraries, print collections continue to grow rapidly as well. Early in the planning stages, you will want to decide whether you will install compact shelving now or possibly some time in the future. The decision needs to be made now rather than later because compact shelving requires significantly higher loading capacity than regular shelving. Although a capacity of 150 pounds per square foot live load is adequate for many stack areas, compact shelving requires about 300 pounds per square foot.

Since the additional cost of shelving and installation can mount up (a few dollars per square foot), you may wish to designate certain lower floors for this purpose. On the other hand, it is possible to designate a section or a quadrant on all levels within which the floors will be reinforced and additional load-bearing columns installed. Chicago's Harold Washington Library chose to accommodate heavy floor loads on several floors at the ends of the building to provide more flexibility when reorganizing the collection in the future.

If funds are tight, you may just elect to pour a thicker slab for the ground floor, as long as your subsoil can support the weight of fully loaded shelving. Just be very certain that your soil has been tested and found to be satisfactory. Horror stories abound about ill-fated buildings that begin sinking into the earth soon after the contractor departs. If you are not planning to install compact shelving now, be sure that the floor-to-ceiling height is sufficient to take into account both the shelving itself and the track assemblies needed.

It's a sad fact that light is considerably reduced by fully loaded compact shelving units. In fact, light from ceiling fixtures may not shine directly into aisles even if you have given careful attention to stack lighting. It is worth the additional cost to specify that lighting fixtures be attached to moving shelves. Most manufacturers of newer compact systems can provide such fixtures.

All compact shelving manufacturers are not equal. A number of librarians complain that they were forced to use the vendor who came in with the low bid even though the product was less than satisfactory. If compact shelving is in your future, spend some time researching the alternatives. If you decide that some types are unacceptable, put it in writing. Be certain that the RFP provides solid grounds to reject unacceptable vendors.

TIPS AND TALES

We wrote the specifications for a Spacesaver compact shelving system. The general contractor, overseeing this construction as a subsystem, opened the bids and awarded the contract to a competing bid that was all of $200 under the Spacesaver bid. As library director, I learned of this after the contract had already been signed by the general contractor. Our university facilities planner, overseeing the project for the university, also was not consulted by the general contractor before the contract was awarded and signed. Surprise!

Recently on my mailing lists there have been comments about the pros and cons of automatic versus manual-crank compact shelving. All I can say about this is that you get what you pay for. I talked to many librarians and archivists and interviewed several compact shelving manufacturers. I recommended Spacesaver. The director balked because of the higher price, bid it out, went with the lowest bidder, and now we live with the results. This place had one foreman of sorts, shipped the materials here, then they hired temp workers to do the assembly!

We decided to go with manual-crank compact shelving since it is in a staff-only area. From what I've read, I think that's good. I was concerned, however, if for instance, we hire a disabled librarian—the aisles are not wide enough, he or she would have to get a wheelchair over the lip up onto the platform, etc.

Be sure you have the weight load specs for compact shelving.

Ergonomics Issues

One way of defining ergonomics is "the study of the human body at work." Although the industrial revolution and World War II contributed to our understanding of the way human beings interact with machines, it has been only in recent years that we've become aware of the dangers of bad ergonomics, such as repetitive stress injuries. With the move in recent years from blue collar to white collar jobs, emphasis has moved from factories to offices and on the way human beings interact with computers: the new discipline called the human-computer interface.

Libraries are in a unique position in that they must consider not only staff members, who spend long hours at their computer screens, but also library patrons, who may spend nearly as many hours reading and doing research. From the staff point of view, increased use of computers has been associated with increased absenteeism, muscular discomfort, eyestrain, and reductions in job satisfaction.

Human beings are not comfortable when they are forced to freeze in one posture for a long period of time. The computer screen is seen as one of the main culprits because it requires that users work within a very restricted posture range. You can move a book or stack of papers up or down as well as to the left or to the right. You simply can't do this with a computer screen. Not only do humans come in different shapes and sizes requiring adjustments to their environment but they must move frequently to remain comfortable. Such needs can be difficult enough to accommodate for staff members, but they become almost overwhelming when multiplied by the thousands of patrons who use the library. Ignoring ergonomic requirements can inflict considerable pain on the library community and can cause long-term disability.

When you select computer desks or tables, be sure you can place monitors, keyboards, and other input devices at heights that encourage proper posture and straight wrist positions. The correct monitor height can reduce eye and neck strain. Especially for staff working at service desks, workstations that permit both sitting and standing are desirable because they can promote improved circulation and reduce back strain.

Research has shown that workers using computer equipment more than one hour per day complain twice as often of neck and shoulder discomfort as a control group that did not use computer equipment. Computer users also reported eye strain three times as often as the control group. When workers were permitted to participate in the selection of furniture and the development of layouts, absenteeism dropped from 4 percent to less than 1 percent, and error rates in document preparation fell from 25 percent to 11 percent even when the amount of computer use was actually increased.[1]

Eye Strain and Work Station Design

Eye strain is becoming a frequent complaint from both staff and patrons who use the library's computers for long hours at a time. Symptoms include tired and dry eyes, difficulty focusing, and frequent headaches. The use of monitor screen filters and film coatings that reduce annoying flicker can help minimize strain, as can lowering overhead lighting levels to avoid glare and shadows. However, the combination of print and computers in libraries makes eye strain an increasingly serious concern.

As discussed in chapter 5, we librarians have been so concerned with raising light levels in order to penetrate shadowy dark stack areas that we sometimes forget that the modern library's lighting needs are much more complex than they used to be. Staff find that task lighting fixtures with adjustable, articulated arms provide focused light on whatever needs to be illuminated while reducing glare on computer screens. Window coverings can also eliminate VDT glare, and computer screens can be positioned in such a way that they don't catch reflections from uncovered windows. Background and character colors with a high level of contrast can also be helpful.

Distance is the key consideration when positioning computer monitors. When we read or look at an object near-at-hand, the ciliary muscle in the eye changes the shape of the lens. Then the lens bends light rays in such a way that they strike the retina at a single point and produce a sharp image in the brain. The image is blurred if this point is too far in front of or behind the retina. When the eyes are resting and looking at nothing (sometimes called "staring into space"), they are actually focusing an average of about 31½ inches away. The closer the position of the monitor approximates this resting distance, the less eye strain. With age, the lens changes and this ideal point gets farther and farther away.

When we read a book, we direct our eyes downward, which just happens to be an excellent way of increasing our ability to accommodate a wider range of distances. In other words, we can read an open book on an elbow-height horizontal surface more easily than we can read the same information if presented vertically at the same distance from the eye. In fact, people prefer to look downward at an average angle of 29 degrees below the normal computer-work position, and the closer the object, the further down people want to look. A downward gaze also reduces the need for head movement.

Still another cause of pain is "neck tilt," especially when it is increased to 30 to 45 degrees. Ideally, a forward neck posture of 15 degrees is considered best. Although this may not always be possible with user workstations, it is desirable to at least provide separate surfaces to support the keyboard and monitor. Where possible, the screen should be at a level where the user looks slightly down to the center of the screen. As you're positioning monitors, bear in mind that anyone who wears bifocals probably needs the visual display screen as low as possible since they very likely read through the bottom part of the lens.

Because most of your patrons are not experienced computer users, it is desirable to reduce the distance between the keyboard and display screen since they will probably move their eyes constantly between keyboard and screen to make sure they are pressing the correct keys. In the past, you might assume that the people who regularly used typewriters had been formally taught (often in high school or business school) to type correctly. This meant not only learning key strokes but also correct posture and hand positions. Now most people who type on a computer have no formal training, so patrons may feel more discomfort after an hour at a computer than yesterday's typists experienced after several hours at a typewriter.

Physiology and Workstation Design

One study of performance conducted on employees of the State Farm Insurance Company showed as much as a 15 percent increase in productivity with ergonomically designed workstations and seating.[2] A study of back discomfort by the Norwegian State Institute found that back-related absenteeism was halved after improvements to workstation layout and seating.[3] Years ago, it was decided that a standard height of twenty-nine inches for working desk height and twenty-six inches for typewriters met the physical requirements of the "average" individual. Although chairs may be adjustable, these fixed heights mean that shorter-than-average individuals must raise their chair to reach a comfortable working position at a too-high work surface and either leave their legs hanging with their feet off the floor or endure discomfort from pressure under the thigh where it presses against the chair. Since many nerve endings and veins pass through this part of the leg, such a position forces the user to sit forward in the chair to avoid discomfort, leaving the back without support.

Since desk heights were determined before large numbers of women joined the workforce, the "average" individual was really an average male. It is, therefore, more often women who fall victim to repetitive stress injuries. Taller people are also affected, however, when the work surface is too low, causing them to slouch with a curved spine and their knees near or approaching the chin level. When a tall person sits in a chair, the chair will tilt back, so the sitter must then sit forward away from the back support. This may cause back pain, fatigue, or aggravated tension.

Ergonomically Correct Chairs

What do people do in libraries? They sit! Of course, that's not the only thing they do, but seating is certainly an important consideration when designing a library. Therefore, ergonomically correct chairs are especially important. When staff or users are working in front of a computer screen, their body parts (back, thighs, elbows, and legs) should be at right angles with their feet solidly planted on the floor. Chairs should support the natural S-shape of their spines. When they are reading or writing, it is easier on their backs if the chair seats can follow their body movements forward to prevent pressure on their thighs and the leg arteries.

When selecting chairs, look for resilient padding that reduces contact stress on hips and thighs and provides even weight distribution. Look for adjustable height, sliding seat depth, back supports, and adjustable backward and forward tilt as well as height and weight-adjustable arm supports. Ideally, users should be able to sit back in their chairs with their thighs parallel to the floor and weight evenly distributed across the chair. Sitting straight upright may look healthy and alert, but it rotates the pelvis backward, thus straightening the lordosis (curvature) that is natural to the spine. A chair that reclines somewhat is better for reading text from a terminal with its large characters, while leaning forward is more appropriate for paper copy and other work involving fine detail. In the case of library staff work areas, integrated library software, e-mail, Web browsers, and other networked communications programs eliminate much of the walking from the work day, resulting in dangerous semi-immobility.

Choose chairs with recessed or sloping arms rather than chairs with high and prominent arms because high arms prevent users from being properly positioned at their desks. Armless chairs, however, are usually an even better choice, especially at angled workstations. Historically, typists never had chairs with arms, but somehow we've come to see chair arms as a status symbol. The exalted boss had a "papa bear" size executive chair with fixed arms that distinguished his work space from that of the lowly typist. It is hard to accept the fact that the typist had the better deal. Footrests can be helpful for maintaining proper back posture and some even include a back-and-forth rocking motion that exercises the feet, ankles, and legs.

The renowned architect Mies van der Rohe once described a chair as more difficult to construct than a skyscraper. The people who will use your library come in all shapes and sizes. No matter where they choose to sit, whether at a computer terminal, television screen, table, or study carrel, they should be able to find a convenient chair where they can sit comfortably for several hours.

Few people are willing to stand for more than a few minutes, yet libraries frequently equip stacks, reference collections, and OPAC terminals without a chair or stool in sight. Possibly it is because patrons once walked from drawer to drawer while using the old card catalogs that librarians fail to realize how uncomfortable patrons become when using modern online catalogs. A patron may spend half an hour or more at an OPAC station marking records, printing bibliographies, and accessing resources at remote libraries. Surely, we don't want to discourage users from taking their time with the catalog to narrow their search to precisely the materials they really need. The modern trend toward fully functional personal computers located throughout the library is gradually solving the OPAC problem, but the number of users uncomfortably camped out on the carpet in stack and reference areas has not declined. Chairs are essential for most library activities.

Be sure your architects know that you want to test any chair under consideration. Ask for sample chairs from vendors, and have your library staff test them. Ideally, chairs should be passed around so staff can sit on them for several hours at a time. Among the things they should be looking for are

> separate chair seat pan and back if the chair is adjustable
>
> concave seat
>
> solid foam cushioning that holds its shape
>
> "waterfall" edge that's rounded so circulation will not be restricted in the back of the thigh
>
> seats wide enough to accommodate a variety of people shapes (seats that for most people extend at least one inch from the hips on either side)

TIP

A building with all old stuff (furnishings and materials) won't inspire people. Make the chairs comfortable but practical.

armrests that don't prevent users from getting close enough to the work surface

appropriate height (low enough so women's feet reach the floor and high enough to allow older users to rise without difficulty)

Repetitive Stress and Work Station Design

When most people think of repetitive strain injuries (RSIs), the first thing that comes to mind is carpal tunnel syndrome or possibly tendonitis. Many of us have friends and associates who are suffering from some condition causing pain in the wrists or fingers. Workers with hands bent to any extent away from a straight hand in line with the wrist position are prime candidates for an RSI. Bending or arching the hand can stretch or compress tendons, ligaments, and nerves.

A common problem with computer keyboards is that they are too high, so users are forced to raise their arms. If shorter people must raise their arms from the shoulders to support the weight of both the upper and lower arm, they strain the muscles across the top of the shoulders and at the base of the neck.

Ideally, the keyboard should be at the same level as the elbow when users drop their arms to their sides while sitting. This allows them to work in a comfortable sitting posture with their forearms at right angles to their bodies and parallel to the floor. Keyboards that are too high cause people to drop their wrists or palms onto the surface that supports the keyboard to relieve their discomfort.

Of course, your first concern must be library staff who, unlike patrons, cannot get up and leave if they are uncomfortable. However, senior genealogists, students writing papers, or any number of other avid patrons can easily log more consecutive hours in the library than a staff member. The needs of all these people should not be ignored. If workstations allow all keyboards to be adjustable, the home row of keys can be adjusted to elbow height, making possible a straight hand in line with the wrist position that can be maintained without shrugging.

NOTES

1. "Deploying an Effective Ergonomics Process: Part 1: Risk Management," *Ergo Advisor* (spring 1998). Available online at http://216.70.129.103/cw/a08.html# Proc1.

2. Franz M. Schneider, *Ergonomics and Economics* (Calgary, Alberta: Allscan Distributors, 1999). Available online at http://www.combo.com/ergo/ergoecon.htm.

3. Schneider.

Resources

American Society of Interior Designers (ASID)
608 Massachusetts Ave. NE
Washington, DC 20002-6006
(800) 610-2743
http://www.interiors.org.

American Society of Testing & Materials
Committee on Resilient Floor Coverings
100 Barr Harbor Dr.
West Conshohocken, PA 19428-2959
(206) 822-2423

International Interior Design Assn. (IIDA)
341 Merchandise Mart
Chicago, IL 60654-1104
(312) 467-1950
fax: (312) 467-0779
http://www.iida.com

Chaffin, D. B. "Localized Muscle Fatigue—Definition and Measurement." *Journal of Occupational Medicine* 15 (1973): 346–54.

————. *Occupational Biomechanics.* New York: Wiley-Interscience, 1991.

Grandjean, E. *Ergonomics in Computerized Offices.* London: Taylor & Francis, 1987.

Grandjean, E., and others. "VDT Workstation Design: Preferred Settings and Their Effect." *Human Factors* 25 (1983): 161–75.

Heuer, H. "Vertical Gaze Direction and the Resting Posture of the Eyes." *Perception* 18 (1989): 363–77.

Jaschinski-Kruza, W. "Visual Strain During VDU Work: The Effect of Viewing Distance and Dark Focus." *Ergonomics* 31 (1988): 1449–65.

————. "Eyestrain in VDU Users: Viewing Distance and the Resting Position of Ocular Muscles." *Human Factors* 33 (1991): 69–83.

9

Surviving the Construction Phase

At this point, let's imagine that plans have at last been finalized, funds have been raised, and ground has been broken. The contractor is on site, equipped with the largest, loudest machinery you've ever seen. You feel as if you and the library staff have survived enough crises, pitched battles, and misunderstandings to last a lifetime, but you have more "adventures" ahead. Eventually, your library building will emerge from the clutter and chaos, and interior partitions will be in place. It is at this point that you and key staff members will need to walk through the building. This is necessary both to catch unforeseen problems and to determine the wording and positioning of your signs. You will inevitably find that your contractor will attempt to dissuade you, but although a signage contractor can be chosen earlier in the process, it is not until you can see the new library through the eyes of your users that you can make these final decisions.

CHANGE ORDERS

Since this is probably your first library construction project, you're still a neophyte when it comes to reading blueprints. No matter how diligently you study the plans, you will almost inevitably fail to recognize problems that your contractor will insist are clearly indicated. There are also a number of vital necessities that the architect solemnly promised to include but were somehow forgotten. This means that as construction on the new library progresses, change orders will become the scourge of your existence. You will discover that assumptions any ten-year-old could be expected to take for granted have eluded your building professionals. To be honest, it is sometimes your own fault for having failed to ask enough questions or spend sufficient time digesting the information you've been given. Change orders almost always cost money unless you can clearly establish that you made your needs known in advance (usually in writing) and your request was ignored.

There is probably no way of avoiding change orders altogether, but they can usually be minimized. In addition, better documentation of your requirements may mean that the library need not pay for all change orders. Don't trust yourself to catch every problem. Ask the library staff to review floor plans and imagine themselves performing their usual tasks in the new spaces. Request extra copies of the blueprints, but be prepared to pay for them. The relatively minor cost of extra sets of plans will be compensated for by the savings on change orders later. Ask staff to think about the locations of closets, positioning of light switches, and placement of doors. Each person could be made responsible for identifying potential problems in an assigned area.

TIPS AND TALES

We are getting a closed, windowless stack and vault area with compact shelving on the lakefront of the building. They did not care that the lakefront was unsuitable for document storage because of a previous history of dampness. Offices and workroom are also windowless. The reading room has one window facing the A/C compressors.

When I realized that I was regarded as a Donna Quixote, I kept my mouth shut and made plans how to make the best of an unchangeable situation.

Contractors don't always (perhaps usually) build what's on the blueprints. I've met a number who couldn't read them—they just build what they think is needed, or easiest, regardless of what the architect designs. This leads to light switches in the wrong place, plumbing running through vaults, open sewer pipes in offices and vaults, air-conditioning fan-coil units draining onto shelving, and ductwork penetrating vaults rather than being routed around them. The costs go up and up as you find them after signing off.

"To engineer is human," and humans make lots of mistakes. Be sure to encourage both architect and contractor to communicate with you frequently, discussing any potential problems they have identified. If you can catch the problem early, a change order may not be needed. Hiring a watchdog early in the project can also help to anticipate difficulties and make needed adjustments before they require tearing out walls and ductwork or making other expensive changes.

Don't assume that people will inform you of changes made to your area. Keep your nose in the action, even if people try to play political games with you. Keep asking questions, and verify what has changed or not changed over time. Sometimes those in charge will "OK" what they think is a relatively minor change and not bother to check with the person who will be working in the area.

Make sure you know what the deadline for "free" changes is. At some point in time, any changes made cost a lot of money. Usually the people in charge of the money bags will refuse to make a change if it costs them any money.

Be a "hands-on" owner during the construction so you can check each day to see if things are getting done the way they should—even if you have a construction manager on the project. The CM will make sure you are getting done on time and budget what you requested, but you may need to make adjustments. If you don't look, you will never know!

Keeping your eyes open helps a lot. I encountered two men standing in a hallway with a set of blueprints looking at the ceiling outside the film vault at an institution where I used to work. When I questioned them, it turned out they were running new ductwork for a group of rooms occupied by a different department. They were discussing cutting holes in the walls of the refrigerated vault and running the ductwork through the vault into the next building. They planned to do this work in the middle of the night when no one was around so as not to disturb anyone. This would have destroyed the environmental integrity of the vault. When I suggested that there might be a better way, we examined the plans and discovered that we could route it through the ceilings of a general office, avoiding the vault entirely.

You need to go over every detail of every plan. Architects "forget" the necessities to make their overall plan work. This means measuring and remeasuring, counting wall sockets, checking door openings, keeping track of plumbing lines, researching fire-control systems, checking sight lines for staff who oversee public areas, etc.

The finished measurements of rooms are smaller than sizes shown on plans. This can make a difference when planning the size of work tables and the placement of furniture.

Know your building. I stopped a contractor from installing compact shelving over a service tunnel because I knew the tunnel was there and it wasn't on the plans he was supplied. I also discovered a contractor had led a hazardous waste fume duct into the building's cold air return rather than to a chemical waste duct because I examined all of the building plans.

It sounds like we had a terrible time, but I found the whole thing (for the time I was involved) to be rather interesting. It has taught me to keep a close eye on projects that are being handled by others outside the library.

THE SPECIAL PITFALLS OF A RENOVATION

If you are renovating an older library rather than building from scratch, you can expect a pretty harrowing experience. You will be living with constant banging, clanging, and confusion. You and your staff will be asked to vacate areas crammed with books and equipment with less than twenty-four hours' warning. You may knock down and reassemble the same stack sections three or four times during construction. Although surviving such an ordeal is difficult, you can at least minimize the disruption.

If you're renovating an existing space, be very sure that the architect and contractor fully understand the expanded electrical needs of a modern library and have given due consideration to the source of the additional electrical power. To provide for the additional power needed while construction is under way, a new breaker panel should probably be added even before the project begins. It is not uncommon for a project to come to a screeching halt while change orders are filed for the new panel.

To minimize problems, here are some other things to consider if you are renovating an existing facility.

Work should be planned in phases and, when possible, during low activity times to minimize disruptions to patrons and staff.

Cleanliness is vital. It may be necessary to install temporary drywall partitions in work areas to reduce noise, dust, and dirt as well as to keep people out of the hard hat area.

Be careful that the project does not grow out of control. Renovation was probably chosen over new construction because of cost. You will inevitably find more and more that needs renovating, but you have a budget to think about. If funding is really flexible, then maybe a new building or at least a new addition would have been a better choice. You don't want to start confusing frills with functionality.

Don't do a little here and a little there. Renovation is disruptive, so you will want to concentrate on the neediest areas.

Since your general contractor is responsible for performance, give him or her the freedom to choose mechanical and electrical subcontractors (if such is consistent with local policies).

Be sure that the carpet and wall coverings specified by decorators or interior designers are readily available. Insist they avoid custom choices that can cost up to 50 percent more than standard styles.

Remaining Open for Business

Closing your library during renovations places a heavy burden on your user community. No matter how nerve-racking, it's usually better to stay open while construction is under way. First, identify your priorities. Which areas of the library must remain open throughout the period? Which services and backroom activities are essential? How can you maintain convenient and safe access to the library? Be sure your contractor understands your priorities and the need for minimal disruption of power and water. Work together to find ways to avoid excessive noise, vibration, fumes, dust, and debris.

You may have some difficulty getting your building professionals to see the library operation through the eyes of the staff and users. They may imagine that the inconveniences will be much less intrusive than turns out to be the case. They are accustomed to working in environments in which noise is not as great a problem as in a library environment. Reading and study are not activities that can take place in the presence of constant loud noise. It is important that the architects and contractor be honest and identify the true scope of the renovation and its impact on the existing building.

One reason that disruption is so extensive is that building professionals cannot assess the existing situation without opening spaces in walls and ceilings to examine structural, mechanical, electrical, and plumbing systems. Exploratory demolition may seem unnecessarily disruptive, but early investigative work is essential. It is far better to uncover hidden conditions as soon as possible and solve problems early in the design process rather than later when expensive surprises result in expensive remedial work.

Library Services and the Project Schedule

How will your contractor sequence the project schedule? Will crews be working horizontally floor-by-floor, vertically, or randomly as space becomes available? Discuss these plans at length. Don't be taken by surprise each time you are asked to vacate a space. Try to look at the library as a builder might. Plumbing, for instance, might be done vertically with plumbing risers and floor penetrations, while other segments include horizontally adjacent spaces.

Tactfully encourage your builder to spend time on a phasing study to help avoid problems, such as running piping or ducts through an area that has already been renovated or performing disruptive work near occupied areas. A good phasing study is in the contractor's interest as well as yours since an accu-

TALES

rate schedule minimizes delays and costly change orders as well as allowing subcontractors to submit more accurate bids.

Try to identify the most frequently used areas in the library and request that, if possible, your contractor schedule work on those areas during low traffic periods. In an academic library, summer is an excellent time but not always convenient for the contractor. You can probably win more compromises if you and your staff vacate areas on time with a minimum of grumping. Ideally, only one wing or area should be under construction at a time.

The safety of your staff and users is your most important consideration during this grueling period. Construction is a dangerous activity, and you should work with your contractor to ensure that your facility remains a safe place throughout the project. For example, emergency exits must be maintained; construction activity must be segregated from patron areas with barriers and signage. Noisy and unusually disruptive activities should be specially scheduled.

There will probably be times when you may have no alternative but to close the library. These times, for example, when connections are made to water, electricity, gas, and other utilities, should be kept to a minimum with careful planning. Get into the habit of having brief chats with the construction manager. Make the chats as upbeat as possible so he or she doesn't start avoiding you. Communication is possibly the most important ingredient in a successful project. Communicate what you learn to your staff and patrons through meetings, e-mail, newsletters, signs, and notices. Patrons will be forewarned and can schedule their visits at the most opportune times.

Ask about subcontractor activity and how it will affect the library's operation. Are any power outages scheduled? Be prepared, however, to lose data, power, or water unexpectedly. Such crises will probably occur sooner rather than later, so a contingency plan for dealing with the consequences is essential.

Temporary Quarters

After weighing various options, you may decide that it is not possible to continue to provide library services when construction activities are taking place. In a smaller building, for example, there may be no way to separate the construction activities from library activities, and the entire building may become a hard hat area. It may be that library activities can comfortably coexist with the construction of a new wing but may be impossible when extra floors are being added. Each project is different, of course, but major renovations are unlikely to be complete in less than a year. Your challenge will be to find a way to function as normally as possible during this period and to close your doors for the briefest time possible. University students obviously must have access to their library's collection, and public libraries will be under considerable pressure from their boards and borrowers to do business as usual.

Just as boards and administrators approach a building project with little understanding of how libraries work, they may have unrealistic ideas of what constitutes adequate temporary quarters. Many facilities will not make satisfactory "ad hoc" libraries, and the cost of even minimal refitting is usually much greater than most people imagine. You will probably need every bit of tact and negotiating skill you possess to reach consensus on an acceptable facility.

Be sure you are prepared well ahead of time with a list of minimal requirements for a facility. Use your online discussion groups to identify a network of colleagues who have superintended a move to temporary quarters. Find out if it is possible to hire a library consultant specifically for the task of identifying a suitable facility. Be sure you have access to information about such vital matters as the floor's live-load capacity. Proposed temporary facilities are often old, and technical information may have been lost along the way. If in doubt, hire an engineer to be sure the building can accommodate not only the weight of book stacks but the data and power needs of a library.

An excellent source of information on managing a move to temporary quarters is the ERIC document "Planning and Strategy for Setting Up and Operating Academic Libraries in Temporary Quarters: Experiences of Two Northeast Colleges."[1] The libraries of both Skidmore College and Lyndon State College moved temporarily to gymnasiums on their respective college campuses. In both cases, the new space was much smaller than what had been available in their library buildings. The staffs of both libraries were forced to cope with very stressful conditions before they could at last move into their expanded and refurbished buildings. Although the two staffs went about their Herculean task in somewhat different ways, the following is a general outline of the procedure they recommend:

1. Measure the stack areas, work spaces, and seating areas to determine the minimum space needed for each function.

2. Ascertain that the live load of the floor in the temporary facility is at least 150 pounds per square foot.

3. Create a preliminary stack layout using computer-aided design software.

4. Calculate the total linear shelf space available in the temporary facility by taking into consideration the maximum number of stacks and shelves that can be accommodated in the space.

5. Subtract the total linear shelf space available in the temporary facility from the total linear shelf space in the library to determine how many books will need to be placed in storage.

6. Work with the architect (if possible) to lay out spaces for circulation, reference, patron seating, technical services, and the other areas that must be accommodated. If the architect is not available, create preliminary layouts for spaces using computer-aided design software.

7. Identify any areas where you can squeeze out space by moving stacks closer together or doubling up on staff spaces. Stack areas will probably not be wheelchair accessible in the temporary location. You may wish to consider closing the stacks or identify ways in which you can more effectively serve the needs of users in wheelchairs.

8. Design areas in such a way that furniture such as stack units and file cabinets can substitute for walls and can be used to control access. You will probably need to use the temporary space more or less as is and will be unable to construct or tear down walls.

9. Determine where additional power outlets and phone and data jacks must be installed. Keep these to a minimum since they will be temporary and may use up funds needed for more urgent matters.

10. Identify storage areas for restricted materials and equipment.

11. Decide upon a method for identifying books for storage.

TIP

Be ready with figures if a city council or manager or county commissioner wants the library to move into an old building that doesn't have the proper foundation to hold the weight of books.

12. Determine how much seating space is absolutely necessary. Remember that other spaces are available for reading and study. You will probably need to sacrifice seating space for collections.

13. Consider using a larger portion of the acquisitions budget for online resources to make up for unavailable printed materials.

14. Prioritize services and decide which ones will continue to be available throughout the transition period. For example, service to outside groups may need to be restricted.

SIGNAGE SYSTEMS

Whether you are spending your last weeks and months in the old building or camped out in temporary quarters, construction workers are rapidly (you hope) approaching the completion of the job. Once the new building or addition has achieved its final shape and the interior partitions are in place, it's time for you and your staff to start thinking about signs. Since the building and its environs are still a hard hat area, this will very likely mean increased stress for both you and your contractor.

Signs are custom-made for your particular library, and there is no way you can anticipate precisely what will be needed until you're actually inside the building. Blueprints cannot really tell you what is visible from which position. It inevitably turns out that a sign that looked great on the floor plan is actually hidden from view by a column, stairway, or ceiling fixture or visitors may approach from an unexpected direction. Until you can walk the length and breadth of the space, you cannot know for sure which signs are needed and precisely where they should be mounted. On the other hand, if you delay ordering signs until the contractor gives the "all-clear," your patrons, instead of exclaiming about the wonders of the new building, will be wailing in frustration as they unsuccessfully search for the restrooms or the video section.

Imagine for a moment your newly opened library. Your first users enter through the pristine front door, proceed into the lobby area, and look around. What now? How will you make it clear that the periodicals are straight ahead and to the right, that the computer lab is behind the reference area, and that the literature books are on the second floor? "Signs," you answer quickly. But just as you utter the word, an image of your present library pops into your head. Signs are plastered everywhere; some are professionally produced but most are homemade and dog-eared. The thought of all those beautiful new walls marred by ugly signs is too painful to contemplate.

Why must you provide signs anyway, argue some librarians (and architects)? Nobody ever looks at them. Patrons ask directions to the restrooms when signs are in plain view. Just remember what you know about information-seeking behavior. Your users respond differently to visual stimuli but most find simple, clearly worded signs helpful. However, color blindness, spatial perception, and many other factors all influence the effectiveness of your signage.

How do you provide enough signage without cluttering up the place? How do you design signs that harmonize with the decor yet stand out sufficiently to be noticed? How do you decide which areas your users will find on their own without difficulty and which will require several signs at different points to keep them from becoming confused?

Organized Approach

A systematic approach to signage allows you to communicate information effectively to your users. You are able to base the design process on a careful analysis of your user needs using standardized terminology, layout, color, and other design elements. The appropriate use of signs can considerably reduce the number of simple directional questions asked at service desks as well as make users aware of the full range of available library services and facilities. A complete signage system can include changeable floor signs, hanging and wall-mounted directional signs, room-identification signs, and point-of-use instructional signs where appropriate. The keys to a really good system, however, are its abilities to respond to the user's need to progress from general to specific information and to provide directional information at decision points where a choice of routes must be made. The point is to identify the best means of displaying information at the point of need, taking into consideration the unique challenges of your proposed building and using signage to overcome them. Then work with your vendor to draw up a "sign schedule" or detailed, sign-by-sign list keyed to locations in the building. A professional sign designer can provide invaluable assistance in deciding upon graphic standards like typography, colors, layout, and other characteristics.

Each signage installation is different because of the unique configuration of the library building. You will want to take advantage of the design features of the new building that lend themselves especially well to signage. Although your old library will be physically quite different from the new one, you can still gather information about the behavior and needs of your users. You can also keep track of the most frequently asked directional questions at your service desks and conduct on-site tests to be sure that proposed solutions actually work. Nevertheless, no matter how careful you are, you are bound to make some mistakes. Be sure that you reevaluate signs after opening to decide whether they should be relocated or additional signs purchased.

The task of designing a signage system is a task fraught with potential problems, but the following suggestions will help you avoid many of the most common ones:

Use durable materials that can stand up to long-term use but allow for changing needs as the library grows.

Retain information on the vendor and on the style, colors, and materials of the signs to make sure new signs will be compatible with existing ones.

Use symbols and terminology that users have become accustomed to in other public spaces such as airports and hospitals. When using specialized library terminology, develop a "controlled vocabulary" of library terms. Don't, for example, refer to magazines in one sign and periodicals in another. Select the most readily understandable names for rooms and services. For example, the term "checkout" means more than "circulation" to most users.

Place building directories in lobby areas and near elevators. List library resources, areas, and services shown in relation to a building map, and provide additional information closer to the destination. Provide self-guided tours, in print or on tape, that are keyed to marked locations on the building directory.

It is helpful if users can identify areas from a distance, so large signs or over-size graphics are effective to mark major areas. Facilities for handicapped users should be visible from a considerable distance.

Provide signs to identify specific library tools. Display "how-to" information at major tools like OPAC catalogs, public-access computers, and reference sources. Present such basic information clearly and in as few words as possible. Use signage to reinforce library instruction or to provide simplified explanations of various library procedures.

Carry the sign system's graphic elements to bulletin boards, suggestion/response boards, and fliers. Bulletin boards in high-traffic areas can be very effective for posting current information.

Keep regulatory signs to a minimum, but clearly communicate smoking, food/beverage, noise, copyright, and security policies. In addition, provide signs for fire exit routes, emergency procedures, meeting room capacities, and other information required by law.

Provide changeable signs to notify users of temporary conditions, library hours, and special events.

Signage System Schedule

If you've ever had the job of designing a sign system, you'll realize that it is far from an easy job. Plans for the sign system should be included as part of the overall library building design, and the basic components of the system should be developed as part of the interior-design and space-planning process. Get bids from sign vendors early in the construction process. You need not provide the actual wording and an estimate of the number and size of the signs needed. As mentioned earlier, until you can actually walk through the building and approach each area from different directions, you will not be able to decide on the exact wording and placement of signs. Even then, unless you are clairvoyant, you cannot possibly imagine every wrong turn your users are likely to make until you actually move into the new facility. Nevertheless, signage is usually included in your capital outlay budget, and you will need to get started designing and locating signs long before opening day.

Perhaps the best solution may be to divide your project into two stages, leaving funds in your budget to purchase additional signs from your vendor after you have had a chance to live in the building for awhile. This is sometimes impossible if all capital funding disappears in a puff of smoke on a given day.

Even if you somehow manage to open your library with the right signs in the right places, this blissful state will not long continue. Libraries are changing at an astounding pace. We librarians seem to spend half our work lives moving things around. One area may begin its existence as a listening area, then be converted to a space for young adults and ultimately become a computer lab. Somehow your signage must keep up with these transformations. Changeable elements are needed to keep pace with your changing floor plan. Modular signs with panels that slide in and out are useful for this purpose. Individual letters that slide in and out can be handy or they can be extremely frustrating if your more-creative patrons make a habit of rearranging the letters. When you're considering purchasing signage components from a vendor, ask your staff to take on the roles of troublesome patrons and see how difficult it is to disassemble modular signs.

Easily Updated Signs

Directories will probably be the most expensive signs you purchase. Most directories include floor plans for each level and indicate the collections and rooms in each area. For example, the word "literature" may be screen printed on the floor plan in the northwest corner of the second floor. When you reorganize and move the science collection into this area, the directory will become obsolete. Since the library is unlikely to have funds to replace the directory, it is likely to remain as it is, misleading users who are seeking the literature collection. Rather than include complete location names, why not label the floor plan with a series of numbers or letters? To the side of the floor plan, include a space where you can insert modular (changeable) letters that spell out the location names. Take a look at the directories in your local shopping mall. Theirs are probably far more elaborate than you can afford, but they have the same problem of accommodating change. Think of how many stores come and go in a short period of time.

Sign vendors seem to go out of business with disturbing rapidity. This can become a major problem when your modular signage components are unique and cannot be used with components supplied by another vendor. Some incompatibility is probably inevitable, but think twice if you hear a vendor touting a "revolutionary new design."

Invest in a modular system to display the call numbers at the end of stack ranges since nothing looks worse than typed or handwritten index cards, even if they are displayed in small metal frames. Before you contract with a vendor, request samples of their product so that you can see how tamper-resistant the pieces are. You will discover that an enterprising child or college student can dismantle the poorly designed ones with a minimum of effort. The words can be rearranged to spell out messages you do not want to inadvertently communicate to your users. Since these systems are made up of thousands of little pieces, be sure that someone in the library is in charge of storing the components in an organized manner and changing the pieces as locations become outdated.

Much of the sign clutter in your present library results from the need for temporary signs explaining a policy, advertising an event, or associated with a display. Fortunately, color ink-jet and laser printers do an excellent job of creating professional looking, spur-of-the-moment signs. The problem is that they quickly become dog-eared and dirty if tacked or taped to your walls. A wonderful solution is a wall-mounted window sign that most sign vendors keep in stock. These signs consist of a frame, usually color coordinated with your other signs, that surrounds an 8½-inch by 11-inch glass or plastic window. The frame may be large or small, come with screen-printed library logos or text like "Coming Attractions," and portable or permanently mounted. Laser-printed paper can be slipped into the window where it stays clean and protected.

Soon after you open your doors, you will find yourself at war with users who try to post their own signs. Within less than a week, you will have pieces of paper taped to your doors, windows, elevators, and on every blank wall. Although you may feel tempted to stalk through the library ripping off the offending sheets of paper, it is probably best for public relations and your own mental health to find another solution. Bulletin and message boards help keep clutter to a minimum, and tack strips also allow users to post flyers in a limited, controlled space.

It may be that libraries have too many signs reading "Staff Only" or "No Admittance." With recent staff downsizing, it's becoming harder and harder for patrons to find someone to help them. Ask yourself (and your staff) why you really want to keep patrons out of a particular area. If valuable materials are lying around unsupervised, the signs make sense, but if staff just don't want to be bothered with the public, you may want to reconsider. Most of us no longer have the luxury of hermetically sealed backrooms, and I'm not sure this was ever a useful policy. Most staff members nowadays have some interaction with the public and should be available when needed. Of course, there will always be areas that must be kept closed to the public, but instead of a negatively worded sign, maybe you might have one that reads "Please knock before entering" or "This door is kept locked. Please see librarian for assistance."

NOTE

1. Garet Nelson, Laurel Stanley, David Eyman, and Peggy Seiden, *Planning and Strategy for Setting Up and Operating Academic Libraries in Temporary Quarters: Experiences of Two Northeast Colleges,* 1996, ERIC, ED 410956.

10 Moving and Getting Settled

By this point in your project, you and the staff are probably showing signs of wear. Your tempers may be somewhat frayed, and you've probably joined the International Association for the Annihilation of Architects and Interior Designers. You may need to stop periodically and make yourself realize that things are really going pretty well. You've averted innumerable catastrophes, and you feel some assurance that a reasonably functional library will soon emerge.

Remember the comment in the "Tips" section about keeping lots of chocolate on hand? You and your staff need plenty of TLC. Be sure you don't take your frustrations out on staff, and in the midst of your agonies, don't separate yourself from their world. Of course, their usual complaints and frustrations are going to seem petty when compared with yours. However, you may not be delegating enough of the new building oversight duties to make them feel fully involved. Just because the building phase is over, there's still a lot to be done. The staff will feel much more ownership in and appreciation for the new building if they have a "piece of the action."

If you have been imagining that once moving day is over, you will be able to sink back in your new color-coordinated executive chair and relax, I'm afraid I have some rather unpleasant news for you. This chapter begins with moving day, but as with the real world, it does not end there. The first year in a new building can be almost as stressful as the year or years leading up to the move. No new building is free from flaws, and you will probably be shocked at the number of construction mistakes you will be dealing with. In my own library building, which has now been open for about two and a half years, we are still dealing with poorly designed restroom sinks. There have now been so many "fixes" that I have lost count, but vanities still are getting waterlogged, causing them to warp and separate from the walls.

MOVING DAY

Did you know that in business and industry, studies indicate that many of the staff responsible for their companies' relocation plans are fired, demoted, or have to take a leave of absence due to stress-related illness after the move? If you've ever been a key player in a library move, you probably won't blink an eye at this fact of work life. Even though moving a library may be one of the most stressful experiences known to man or woman, careful planning can minimize the gray hairs and contribute to a smooth transition.

TALE

We went to great effort to find a company that could provide us with cardboard boxes that were long enough to hold one full shelf of books. The plan was to have two students carrying each box. They would carry the box from the old library to the new library, which was about a block away. Other students would be loading the boxes and unloading them onto shelves. The plan seemed very well organized. Nothing would get out of order. We even did some trial runs with a few student teams to determine how long it would take per trip, and from that we estimated how long the total move would take. The big day arrived. The early morning hours went fine. By late morning we noticed that many of the carrying teams began to drop out. Some students had volunteered for the whole day. We quickly had to go to "plan B" and called in trucks, etc.—and then, of course, the flow of boxes got all out of order. In retrospect, we did not anticipate that students would just get worn out walking back and forth, and we should have tightly scheduled students for blocks of service of no more than two hours. The boxes were wonderful; some got ragged, but we had the good ones around for many years afterward, using them for a wide variety of temporary tasks. The bottom line: make sure trial runs take every possible factor into consideration.

Every move is of course different. You may be moving across town or merely down the hall. However, there are basic axioms applicable to most moves. First, allow sufficient time to plan the move. Moves to libraries of less than 50,000 square feet need six months of planning; those greater than 50,000 square feet take at least twelve months. Considering that you probably have many other full-time duties, it may be necessary to begin planning even earlier.

Second, identify ways to streamline the operation. Weed the collection before the move. Get rid of old files and equipment. Decide what furniture and equipment will be left behind and what will come with you.

You will need to establish clear goals and a concrete, step-by-step plan so you can explain what is happening to movers, construction workers, customers, vendors, and others. If at all possible, hire professional library movers, even if this means additional costs associated with bringing them in from out of town. If you are unable to hire professional library movers, at least contract with an experienced, reliable local mover, and work with the supervisor to develop methods for keeping boxes in order. Assign staff to work with movers and to see that boxes and shelves are clearly labeled.

The preceding tale makes it clear that it may not be wise to depend on volunteers or conscripted custodians who lack the training, experience, and stick-to-itivity to do a professional job, but you may not have a choice in the matter. If professional movers are out of the question, work out a clear, detailed plan for boxing, transporting, and reshelving the collection, and give it the time and attention of the D-Day landing. Meet often with library staff to plan the move and to make sure they feel personally involved.

Finally, delegate as much responsibility as possible. Set up a staff committee on moving to define issues, set priorities, identify schedule conflicts, solve problems, and disseminate information. Be sure that all the details of telephone and data lines have been worked out long before the actual move and that the lines are ready to be activated on the move date. A week in a new building with no phones is not an experience anyone would like to have.

TIPS

There's a great Web page—Moving Library Collections. [See Resources at the end of this chapter.] This site documents the University of Oregon's Knight Library move from three separate library buildings into a new facility. The problems with shifting its collection as well as info regarding the $27.4 million, 3½ year project are discussed.

First I obtained a blueprint of the shelving area in the new construction and made a shelving chart, giving each shelf a number. Once the construction was far enough along for the contractor to have the shelves up, I checked them to be sure they matched the blueprints I had. They didn't, so I adjusted my shelving plan accordingly. Then all the new shelves were numbered. Once that was done, we tagged each individual box with a little note listing its new shelf location in the new stack area *before* we began the physical move.

After the contractor released the building, the staff supervised the loading of all the boxes onto book trucks. Then we supervised the unloading in the new area. After completing the move, we checked the physical location of the boxes on the shelves with the shelving list.

We were closed to the public for a week during the actual move, but otherwise we offered minimal service for a week on either side of the move.

Ideally, if you can close during the move, you should do it. If you have to provide service, try to keep it to a minimum during the move. Our patrons were very understanding, and we were able to keep the worst of the disruption to one week.

Don't be misled by a "move-in date"—this will definitely be shoved back at least once and probably two to three times. Once you have moved you are still not finished; you will soon discover all the "little" things left undone: scratched, dented signage that can't be read or that is in the wrong place, etc. Contractors will be interrupting you for several weeks or months after you've moved in. Be prepared.

Temps make great book movers and are *much* cheaper if you have a good supervisor.

HEALTH HAZARDS OF A NEW BUILDING

As you prepare to move into your beautiful new building and begin joyously inspecting its nooks and crannies, your nose suddenly twitches and you come down to earth with a thud. The building smells! If it were not so crude, you might even say it stinks! What you are smelling is off-gassing from many of the construction materials used in a modern building. These include

- carpet pile releasing irritating microscopic fibers
- carpet adhesives
- carpet backing with styrene butadiene latex
- volatile organic compounds such as paints
- glues used to bind pressed-wood products
- copy machines that discharge carbon monoxide and nitrogen dioxide

Paints, adhesives, and carpets all exude gases as part of the curing process. Though unpleasant, the smell is not really the problem. Paints and some adhesives may smell quite strong, but in a short while, the odor will disappear without creating any major problems. What can be far more dangerous, however, are materials having a high volatile organic compound (VOC) content like bromide and formaldehyde.

If curing proceeds at its own pace, most of the gases are gone by the time you move into the new building. Unfortunately, however, many materials are covered up soon after they are applied, thus decreasing the air flow. Exposure to air is essential to the curing process, but in modern construction, paint that might cure in twenty-four hours under normal conditions may take several days depending upon temperature and humidity. For example, the colder the material, the longer it takes to cure.

Your contractor is probably under a lot of pressure to finish the job quickly and move on to another construction project. You and your administration are undoubtedly contributing to the pressure because you have made your plans around specific dates. For example, the new school year is about to begin or there's only a very small window when the movers are available. When you add to these pressure points the realization that your project will almost inevitably be behind schedule, you have a recipe for environmental illness. In those last few weeks, of course you're anxious to move. You're in a sort of limbo, and every delay makes you more frustrated. Talk with your contractor about a realistic move date. Of course, you will still have work crews in the building, but don't try to move in the day after the carpet is laid down.

In chapter 1, you were advised to collect printed matter about all the materials and equipment that would be used in your building. Among the most important of these are material safety data sheets (MSDS). Manufacturers are usually required by law to make these available and to include information on total off-gassing and volatile components. Once your building is complete, don't lose track of these data sheets. Preservation literature is abundant, and a little research will help you interpret the information you find in the data sheets. It is also important to have this information available for use by local fire departments in case of an emergency. Work with your contractor to identify sources of off-gassing and decide if small schedule adjustments can help keep your staff and users healthy.

If you have extensive collections of rare books, manuscripts, or other fragile materials, some emissions could cause a reaction. PVC glue, for example, affects most plastics and can ruin paper products as well. (To reiterate, if you're building a separate repository to house a substantial collection of fragile materials, this book is not adequate to meet your needs. A problem like this one, which is usually just a small annoyance in most libraries, may have devastating consequences in an archive or rare book center.)

If you have the impression that yours is an unusual situation with uniquely valuable materials or with problems during construction that might have let excessive moisture seep into construction materials, you might want to discuss the matter with your contractor. Rental equipment is available for VOC removal that is not extremely expensive. The air in your building can be rapidly recirculated. Desiccant wheels that are coated with a VOC-absorbing material can remove most of the contaminants.

Even if construction has been uneventful and your building is curing on schedule, you might wish to hold off awhile before moving in valuable materials or archival collections. In his book *Solid, Safe, Secure: Building Archives Repositories in Australia,* Ted Ling suggests that "Before you start bringing records into your new building, you should allow it the opportunity to acclimatise and 'breathe'."[1] He goes on to recommend that you keep your HVAC system operating normally for at least a couple of weeks before you move in so that any contaminants that were accumulating during the construction phase are removed.

THE SHAKE-DOWN PERIOD

TIP

You and your staff should take vacations before you open—because you'll wish you had.

The first few months in a new building are by far the most trying. All kinds of unexpected things occur, and you discover dozens of problems you never anticipated. As you walk through the new building each day, you'll probably be mentally kicking yourself that you didn't think of this or that potential problem. Each space will stimulate guilt pangs or feelings of hostility toward the architects or contractors who misinterpreted or deliberately ignored your requests. Don't! Stop! Let it go! The building is finished, and although there are still many small improvements you can make, such unproductive musings can destroy your pleasure and sense of accomplishment. You've accomplished a truly Herculean task, and the best thing you can do is congratulate yourself and your staff and then go on to serve the needs of your users.

It is not unusual to find that something that looked fine on paper really doesn't work when paper gives way to bricks and mortar. Of course, you will want to change as little as possible, but control your tendency to be defensive. You can't be right all the time. You also cannot anticipate the reactions of your users. For example, Chicago's Harold Washington Library Center ended up making major changes after opening day including the addition of their famous Winter Garden and the reorganization of special collections on the top floor to accommodate the addition of another exhibit room.

Over the years, I have become convinced of one particular law of nature. Any new basement will leak or flood the day after you stack boxes in it. After a burst pipe destroyed computer equipment and administrative records in my present library, we decided to hold up the move of a half-million-volume storage collection until everyone was fully assured the basement was watertight. Hence, the collection was not moved for six months, during which time absolutely nothing more went wrong. Then at last, the first thousand boxes were delivered and stacked to await shelvers. Within less than twenty-four hours, water came cascading down a wall, puddling over a sizable portion of the basement.

Sooner or later, of course, you're going to have to use the basement for its intended purpose. You can't keep on waiting indefinitely for the evil below-ground gremlin to go away and leave your new building in peace. Hold off as long as possible, and then take precautions. Be sure that all boxes are up on skids or pallets. If you're installing book stacks or warehouse-type shelving, leave the bottom shelves empty. Maybe if you spoil the gremlin's fun, it'll go find some other basement to beleaguer.

Progress toward a Functional Building

Everything will go wrong during your first year of operation. The roof will leak, the HVAC system will be set incorrectly, keys will not open doors, and sewage will erupt into the restrooms. Therefore, you will need to view this entire period as a construction phase. If you imagine that you will be moving into a finished building in which everything will go smoothly, you are dooming yourself and your staff to a year of misery.

Count everything that does work correctly as a blessing, and face the fact that this is not the norm. Long before you ever move in, decide how you will deal with the traumas that will soon be greeting you daily. You will be busy developing services and procedures tailored to the new building. In addition, there will be staff to hire, hordes of new patrons to accommodate, emergency plans to devise, and generally enough work to keep you busy twenty-four hours a day. That means you will not have time to argue with the painters who forgot the finish coat in the meeting room or the building engineer who insists your frigid lobby is cozy warm. You will need to appoint a staff member as the official contact with contractors, engineers, security gate vendors, and all those other people who will be trooping into your building, playing loud radios, and dropping cigar butts on new carpet.

The Building Coordinator

The first year of operation is the time when tempers flare. Library staff members feel as if they are running on a treadmill, trying to reestablish services, rethink procedures, placate dissatisfied users, and locate hundreds or thousands of missing items. Patrons expect the new library to open with all systems functioning perfectly and all the limitations of the old library magically gone.

By this time, the tendency of architects and contractors to blame one another for mistakes has become all but intolerable. When librarians are confronted by errors that would be obvious to a six-year-old child, no one will take responsibility. Repeated incidents can create an atmosphere of resentment and hostility. Ideally, we should all realize that these conflicts are inevitable and that the best thing to do is to forgive and forget. (I've tried to remember this but I've never managed to become one of those paragons of virtue.)

Inevitably, the project is behind schedule. Construction crews have not finished their work and they resent the usurpers who have taken over their building. Annoying people are telling them to wipe their shoes and lower their voices. In my own library, a worker came in with his radio on. The poor man had been repeatedly frustrated by the fussy rules of the newly arrived building occupants, and when an irate staff member demanded that he work without the inspiration of his favorite radio station, it was the last straw. He snarled, turned the radio up to full volume, and stomped off.

Some of my colleagues insist that there is a basic, even primeval antagonism between librarians and construction workers. Interpersonal eruptions like the one previously described are not uncommon. In most cases, the building is not really ready for occupancy and the presence of outsiders slows down and complicates every task. Treat such problems with professionalism. After all, your common goal is to get the building completed quickly with as few problems as possible.

You need a staff member who will serve as your building coordinator and who will deal with every problem that arises, one migraine at a time. Don't try to do this yourself. You don't have the time, and besides, your nerves are already shot. Choose someone on your staff who will be charming but tenacious, who can stay on the telephone from dawn until dusk reporting leaky pipes, broken windows, wobbly chairs, defective cabling, arctic temperatures, and all the rest. Take your coordinator with you when you do the punch list, or to-do list for the contractor, and involve the coordinator in meetings with the contractor.

Ask that all subcontractors check in when they come to make repairs on the building. This means that your library paragon is going to have to be assertive but nice. A good "come hither" trick is to have a pot of coffee brewing for good little workers who make their presence known. Keep a sign-in sheet by the coffeepot for times when the building coordinator is out of the library.

Mold

If the area in which your library is located is one afflicted by high humidity and dampness, you already know all about that gooey gray stuff that poses a constant threat to your collections. Mold, however, does not require a damp environment to prosper. Even if the interior of the new library is exceptionally dry, mold can still thrive on the moisture stored in materials used to finish interior areas. New materials can retain moisture for a surprisingly long time, and since everything in the building or addition will be new, it already may be providing first-class accommodation for the all-too-common fungus. Thermal insulation is an especially likely host and may already be providing succor to the enemy.

Throughout your first year in the new building, check frequently for signs of mold even if it is not a common problem in your area. Purchase a high-quality humidity gauge to measure moisture levels, and keep moving it from one area to another. Don't make assumptions about where dampness problems are greatest. Instead, keep track of the locations where you're getting the highest readings, and do a little detective work to try to discover the source of the humidity. Make sure your contractor understands what a serious problem moisture poses for a library, and report excessive levels while the building is still under warranty.

TIPS

Keep a careful record of maintenance after the building is completed. That way if you have to replace the automatic doors or heating system, that record can be used to get the construction company's insurance to pay for the replacement, or failing that, to disqualify that vendor from supplying the replacement item even if that vendor has the lowest bid.

Remember that some things won't work and may require replacements. One library got the architect's insurance to pay for the replacement of their entire HVAC system—they proved that it had been faulty from the start.

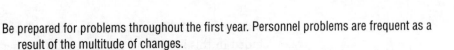

Be prepared for problems throughout the first year. Personnel problems are frequent as a result of the multitude of changes.

Your new space will be so wonderful and such an improvement over the old that you will eventually forget just how you suffered during its construction.

THE DEDICATION

After years of planning and daily crises, the actual dedication or grand opening may come as an anticlimax. If you are like most librarians, you are exhausted, having worked day and night to be ready for the festivities. Then you must sit through a ceremony in which everyone else is thanked and congratulated while you and your staff are almost an afterthought.

Anne Turner and Margaret Pelikan's humorous article in *American Libraries* really tells it like it is. They describe the excruciatingly correct behavior required of a library director during the sometimes-painful proceedings. They recommend that you wear a "blank expression, varied occasionally by a polite smile" while "listening to the mayor explain how he/she has always loved libraries." They also caution against snarling "when you overhear the board chair telling local reporters how hard he/she personally worked to get the building built." A frosty smile is appropriate for the architect with whom you were "last on friendly terms eighteen months ago when the construction contract was signed."[2]

As you have already discerned, the dedication is unlikely to be the high point of your architectural odyssey. Don't get depressed; get some sleep. Tomorrow is another day, and the worst is over. Sure, you still have contractors in the building, supposedly attending to the myriad items on the punch list. More likely, they're deliberately hammering on drainpipes to hear the melodious notes ringing through the quiet study area, but so what? This too shall pass. The job is nearly done, and the time to begin enjoying your new attractive, spacious, and highly functional library building is at hand.

Be prepared for an anticlimax. Will Manley, probably the funniest man in the library profession, has a wonderful column about the library director who has just completed a building project. She has been observed "sitting in her office and crying for no apparent reason; complaining of numbness . . . reading Dr. Kevorkian's latest 'how-to' book; laughing hysterically . . . and wearing weird clothing." Will advises the concerned secretary that the director is merely experiencing post-building depression syndrome. He chronicles the lofty peaks and valleys of despair characteristic of building projects, like being gradually reduced to accepting a stucco-and-chicken-wire building half the size originally planned with the nonfiction stack area eliminated. He cautions that the illness may last from two months to two years but promises complete recovery.[3]

It's time now to start putting aside all those frustrations and accusations and guilty qualms that have been a part of your life for the past few years. You did the best you could. You rescued the building from dozens of potential catastrophes and probably failed to prevent quite a few others. If only you knew three years ago what you know now! Well, you couldn't possibly have known. The mix of human, technical, and circumstantial ingredients in your building project was unique. Nostradamus himself couldn't have anticipated all the omissions and commissions and interactions that took place. They could not have all been included in this book, and no amount of burned midnight oil would have made much difference.

Anyway, you were magnificent! Your skill at locating information paid off. Imagine what a handicap it must be to be anything but an information professional. However, just because you could locate gigabytes of information on lighting, heating, roofing, and all those other specialty areas, you were under no obligation to consume it all. You had neither the time nor the training to become an instant architect or instant electrician.

Speaking of architects and electricians, and all the other building trade professionals who've been involved in your project, it's probably time to bury the hatchet, especially if they've at least made an effort to be somewhat responsive to library needs throughout the project. Their jobs have become increasingly complex in recent years, and they're probably finding it very difficult to remain up to date. Most never imagined when they entered the business that they would have to become computer experts, and they certainly didn't expect that much of their knowledge would become outdated every year.

When you stop to think about it, they're really not so different from you. How could you possibly have predicted when you entered library school that you would someday need such sophisticated skills in such a wide variety of subjects? It never ceases to amaze me that we manage to pull off our building projects so successfully. Unfortunately, this is no time to rest on your laurels. Your new library will require a whole new approach to services and collections. You have a library that will serve your users well into the twenty-first century. Now it's time to develop a dynamic program that will do the same. Best of luck!

NOTES

1. Ted Ling, *Solid, Safe, Secure: Building Archives Repositories in Australia* (Canberra: National Archives of Australia, 1998).

2. Anne M. Turner and Margaret Pelikan, "The Proper Dedication Day: Two Directors Who Have Been There Review Excruciatingly Correct Behavior for the Uninitiated," *American Libraries* 21 (1990): 354–6.

3. Will Manley, "Facing the Public: Diary of a Library Building Project," *Wilson Library Bulletin* 63 (1988): 62–3.

Resource

Moving Library Collections
http://libweb.uoregon.edu/acs_svc/shift

Index

Jeannette Woodward is assistant director of the David Adamany Undergraduate Library at Wayne State University in Detroit. She has held other positions in library administration in both North Carolina and Santa Fe, New Mexico. Another book, *Writing Research Papers: Investigating Resources in Cyberspace,* was published in 1998 by NTC/Contemporary. Other publications include "The Fairfax County Wars: A Chronicle of Engagements on the First Amendment Front" (*Public Library Journal,* 1996) and "The Tale of the Terribly High-Tech Library Building" (*American Libraries,* April 1995).

DATE DUE

HIGHSMITH #45230

Printed
in USA

Dad,

HAPPY BIRTHDAY!

This book brought back
such great and fun memories
that you and mom gave me
growing up. I think you too
will enjoy it

Happy Trails
and many more

I love you

Jean

11/19/2009

Ladd

Minnesota Vacation Days

An Illustrated History · Includes 90 Vintage Recipes

Kathryn Strand Koutsky and Linda Koutsky

MINNESOTA HISTORICAL SOCIETY PRESS

THE AUTHORS WOULD LIKE TO THANK the Minnesota Historical Society for safe harbor of the state's photos and treasures—many of which we feature in this book. Among the countless staff at the History Center and MHS Press who helped us, we are grateful to Eric Mortenson for his masterful photography and to Mark Haidet, Patrick Coleman, and Bonnie Wilson, who shared their insightful knowledge of the tourism industry. But especially, we'd like to thank our editor at the MHS Press, Pam McClanahan, who patiently helped us develop our vacation road map and guided us on our journey—figuratively and literally. Her encouragement and dedication kept us running on the right track, full steam ahead.

Throughout the state, we also met with staff at regional historical societies who sifted through their archives for historic tourist information. Many of the state's individual collectors enthusiastically shared their historic artifacts and vintage photographs, including Alan Bakke with his rare Minnesota-made fishing equipment and Paul Mikkelson, who provided information on Minnesota marine companies. Our sincere appreciation also goes to the Minnesota resort owners who took time during their busiest season to provide us with photos and recipes to complete our story.

Friends and family put up with us being distracted and "one-dimensional," or downright unavailable for months. Luckily we managed to rope a few of them into this project. For photos from the 1950s and '60s—not readily available in historical society collections—friends and relatives dug through family albums and swamped us with scenes of holiday times gone by. Uncle Vic took stunning vacation photos at his woodsy north woods cabin and cousin Janet Strand saved them all for us to use in this book. We are indebted to our "volunteer research assistant," Madeline Betsch, who spent hours contacting county historical societies to identify important tourist destinations. David Steinlicht created our logo designating national register properties.

The frosting on our cake is due to the talents of Ann Burckhardt, who edited and adapted our vintage recipes. During her long career in food journalism, Ann produced eleven cookbooks as a Betty Crocker ghostwriter at General Mills and wrote thousands of features in over twenty-four years for the popular Taste section of the *Minneapolis Star Tribune* newspaper. Her recent publications include five ethnic cookbooks for grade school students and the highly readable *A Cook's Tour of Minnesota*.

But the closest person to our project—often unwittingly—was husband and father Dean Koutsky, who put up with a house strewn with piles of paper and photos. He happily agreed to document his favorite subject of boating and, with the patience of an angler, researched information on fishing. Without him, we might have missed the boat.

And to all the others who made this an insightful Minnesota vacation experience—we extend our grateful thanks.

www.mhspress.org

The Minnesota Historical Society Press is a member of the Association of American University Presses.

Manufactured in China by Pettit Network, Inc., Afton, Minnesota

10 9 8 7 6 5 4 3 2 1

♾ This book is printed on a coated paper manufactured on an acid-free base to ensure a long life.

Library of Congress Cataloging-in-Publication Data

Koutsky, Kathryn.
Minnesota vacation days : an illustrated history /
Kathryn Strand Koutsky and Linda Koutsky.
p. cm.
Includes index.
ISBN 0-87351-526-9 (alk. paper)
1. Minnesota—Social life and customs. 2. Minnesota—Social life and customs—Pictorial works. 3. Minnesota—Description and travel. 4. Minnesota—History, Local. 5. Vacations—Minnesota—History. 6. Vacations—Minnesota—History—Pictorial works. 7. Tourism—Minnesota—History. 8. Tourism—Minnesota—History—Pictorial works. I. Koutsky, Linda. II. Title.

F606.K69 2005   977.6—dc22   2005041673

This book is funded in part by the Joseph and Josephine Ruttger Descendants Fund of the Minnesota Historical Society.

Photographs: p. i, Fireplace of States, Bemidji; p. ii–iii, Slone's Pine Cone Lodge, Park Rapids; p. iv, G & G Souvenir Mfg. Company

Introduction

MINNESOTANS ARE LUCKY! American vacation choices are abundant, but our own diverse Minnesota landscape offers many extraordinary escapes. We have long stretches of lakeshore lined with resorts and cabins, vast expanses of water for boating and fishing, and rugged forests for hiking and camping.

Since territorial days, Minnesotans have headed out across the state in search of relaxation and invigoration. Our own family retreat was called Hodge Podge Lodge and it was the epitome of cabin kitsch. The cleaning, cooking, maintenance, and repairs that came along with owning a spot on a lake never daunted our enthusiasm. Touristy souvenirs, quirky cottage furnishings, and down-home cabin cooking were part of our nature. Summers were meant for the lake and we fancied ourselves classic north woods cabiners.

As we set out to re-create one hundred and fifty years (1820–1970) of Minnesota vacation history, we quickly discovered others who were downright passionate about the subject. Reminiscing relatives charmed us with stories of rough-and-tumble cottages and old-timers chatted about local resorts—and gossiped about resort keepers—

Golden Hill Cabins, Rochester

sometimes for hours! Third- and fourth-generation family members running hundred-year-old Minnesota companies dug through their archives for time-honored products. We leaned on friends who dusted off old family photo albums for vacation snapshots, and collectors found vintage artifacts in attic hideaways. To them, we are thankful. We also owe a debt of gratitude to volunteers at county historical societies and the knowledgeable staff at the Minnesota History Center who helped us assemble a remarkable panorama of past vacation destinations and experiences.

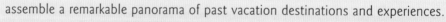

The mountains of information we gathered provided us with intriguing discoveries that made this project fascinating. We were surprised that tourists stayed in rooms at Fort Snelling as early as the 1830s and that industrial steamboats evolved into fabulous floating hotels. Bubbling mineral springs spawned health resorts that were recognized nationwide and hotels on Lake Minnetonka were known around the world. By the turn of the twentieth century, our famous local railroads expanded the horizons for tourists and created a huge tourism industry in the state and beyond.

To make our vacations easier, Minnesota companies invented or revolutionized travel products. Backpacks, tents, boats, canoes, fishing lures, and even mosquito spray were designed and manufactured locally. Souvenir companies turned out remembrances of vacations past, while American Indians crafted beautiful beadwork and birchbark keepsakes. And tourists around the country bought Minnesota products because they were made with creative imagination and enduring workmanship by Minnesota's best. Throughout these pages you'll see many of these items that helped—and humored—the traveler.

Famous homegrown food companies perfected our flavorful north woods cooking style and we found vintage recipes, from sizzling camp fare to savory railroad cuisine to sweet pie breaks. Kids who like to cook, or moms who want a day off, will find vacation recipes marked with a green pennant ▄▄◀. Staples in cabin kitchens, like wild rice, morel mushrooms, blueberries, and walleye, became state icons. We're grateful to food historian Ann Burckhardt, who precisely and patiently adapted all the recipes for today's cooks. And we couldn't resist wacky collections of salt and pepper shakers to animate the recipe pages!

Vacationers found haven at homey hotels, modern motels, picturesque resorts, rustic lodges, quaint cottages, cozy cabins, and sprawling summer homes. Many of the state's early resorts and cabins survive today in one form or another and some of those that retained their original historic integrity have been listed on the National Register of Historic Places. We've designated them throughout the book. But sadly, as time goes on, the classic Minnesota vacation is changing. Many of our vacation accommodations are disappearing as lodges and resort cabins are sold off to private owners.

Many notable people have enjoyed our vacation destinations. America's famous— and infamous—found Minnesota vacationland inspiring. Bing Crosby, Bob Hope, and Clark Gable all cast their lines on our clear blue lakes, while Chicago gangsters hid out nearby in secluded cottages. Local architects graced our shorelines with classic retreats and rustic getaways. Minnesota artists had no end of beautiful landscapes to paint and writers were never at a loss for words to describe them.

To help depict our state's vacation history, we used antique and vintage postcards from our personal collections as well as those from the Minnesota Historical Society. The first scenic sights were documented in rare stereograph photos and *cartes de visite*, or "calling cards," of the 1870s, and in scenic view cards of the 1880s. Then, in the 1890s, came the first mass-produced postcards! Millions were produced for tourists to mail or to keep in albums to show friends back home. Postcards became the most comprehensive documentation of the times—until decades later when the vacation slide show illuminated our living rooms.

Maps and brochures published by the state, towns, resorts, and auto clubs were another source of visual record. The ephemera of the travel industry is a tribute to the state's artists and illustrators who depicted the romance of a Minnesota vacation in a wide range of artistic styles.

In the end, it was a daunting task to pick the images that best illustrated the vast array of styles and activities people cherished for their vacations. We could feature only a fraction of the thousands of resorts that prospered over the hundred and fifty years. And all those fish! *Everyone* showed us pictures of long strings of fish. Alas, we could only land a few of the best to display in the fishing chapter.

We hope you'll relax with this vacation-in-a-book and, by the end, feel like you've had a few days off. We've had a great time and we're glad that you're here!

Enjoy your visit!

"All roads lead to Bemidji"

Douglas Lodge, Itasca State Park

Cass Lake

Lake City municipal boat harbor

Thief River Falls

CHAPTER ONE

Pioneering Tourists

MINNESOTA WATERS have long been associated with vacations. Steamboats began passenger expeditions on the Mississippi River as early as the 1820s. They chugged upstream through muddy waters and marshy backwaters—often narrowly avoiding treacherous sandbars—into a land called Minnesota. Amidst the cargo were curious traders, excited explorers, and anxious settlers whose imaginations had been fired up by stories of fabled woods and clear blue lakes and paintings of great waterfalls. The new land would never be the same.

By the 1850s, steamboat companies promoted tours specifically designed for the Upper Mississippi River valley. Inquisitive excursionists from around the country booked passage. On board they found sumptuous dining and luxurious appointments unknown by earlier travelers. As steamboats reached the upper river valley, passengers watched in awe as gentle riverbanks transformed into towering overlooks and soaring bluffs on the way to Fort Snelling. Journalists aboard were fascinated and returned home to pen breathless descriptions of the newfound territory.

Painters, poets, writers, and composers rushed to the valley, inspired to create works of art and literature that became legendary throughout America. Longfellow conjured up poems of Minnesota's crashing waterfalls, Thoreau extolled the beauty of its unspoiled forests, and Currier and Ives published romantic engravings. To entice travelers to the area, public halls of Eastern and Southern cities exhibited delicate paintings of Indian villages alongside hundred-foot-long panoramas of wagon trails leading into endless prairies.

St. Anthony and Minneapolis attracted visitors by the thousands who came to view the increasingly famous sights. In St. Paul, side-wheelers docked stem to stern in the now-bustling river port. Enterprising innkeepers provided comfortable accommodations and arranged exhilarating excursions into the countryside.

More and more tourists arrived and many stayed. Rising population and new industry soon forced vacationers to head away from the congestion—to Lakes Calhoun and Como. Crowds quickly came to these newly discovered watery havens and summer vacationers took refuge at Lakes Minnetonka and White Bear. Here small, intimate resorts and great hotels, petite cottages and grand summer homes all shared shorelines. Then the railroads came along and sped vacationers further away to new attractions all over the state. Minnesota became a national tourist destination.

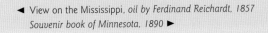

◄ View on the Mississippi, *oil by Ferdinand Reichardt, 1857*
Souvenir book of Minnesota, 1890 ►

Forts and waterfalls

As early as the 1830s, Fort Snelling offered safe lodging for adventurous travelers. Although considered a frontier outpost, the garrison provided visitors with rooms for the night, healthful food and beverages, evening social activities, and access to nearby cold springs. Horse and carriage excursions sallied forth from the fort accompanied by experienced Army officers who were said to be both hospitable and gentlemanlike. Daytime outings included exploration of local Indian life and expeditions into the scenic countryside.

Fort Snelling, Upper Mississippi, *watercolor by F. Jackson, 1857*

Tennis players at Fort Snelling, 1885

Woman and child seated near spring at Camp Coldwater, Fort Snelling, 1885

Dusty trails from Fort Snelling brought visitors to the nearby laughing waters of Minnehaha. Further along the Mississippi River were St. Anthony's thundering falls, often compared to Niagara Falls for its sheer drama. These locations were Minnesota's first tourist attractions and represented the romantic values of nature and wilderness so in fashion with travelers in the early 1800s.

The Song of Hiawatha by Henry Wadsworth Longfellow, 1858. Watercolor illustration by Harrison Fisher

Henry Wadsworth Longfellow's book-length poem, *The Song of Hiawatha*, written in 1885, memorialized Minnehaha Falls. Though he never actually visited the falls, his poem was inspired by images and stories brought back by many other admirers. The romanticized tales of Indian lore caught the imagination of tourists who came in droves to hear the poetry of Minnesota's wistful waterfall.

St. Anthony Falls, 1778

2

Life revolved around the Mississippi River, and St. Paul had the advantage of an accessible and extended river landing. Steamboats transported multitudes of travelers and traders who arrived right along with cargo and goods destined for the new settlements. In some years the busy port welcomed more steamer passengers than residents who lived in the entire city of St. Paul.

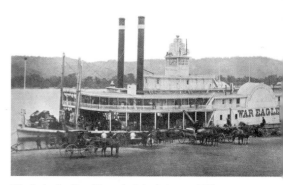

War Eagle, *the Grand Excursion's lead steamer, 1865*

St. Paul levee, 1865

Steamboat Alex Mitchell, *1875*

In 1854, the Grand Excursion, a flotilla of five steamboats, arrived in St. Paul. The all-expenses-paid, six-day trip was sponsored by the Rock Island Railroad in honor of their new line connecting Chicago to the Mississippi River. Over a thousand people, mostly from the East Coast, including newspaper reporters, politicians, artists, and ex-president Millard Fillmore, joined the festivities. The publicity was far-reaching. Spirited accounts of the Grand Excursion piqued national interest for the Upper Mississippi River valley and the number of tourists increased daily.

Deck hands, 1870

Steamer Morning Star *on Mississippi River, 1900*

Passenger steamers that also carried cargo arrived at St. Paul with coffee, tea, tobacco, spices, corn, flour, potatoes, and lard. They returned downriver with grain, cranberries, beets, onions, hay, whiskey, and ice.

Steamer and packet Morning Star, *1912*

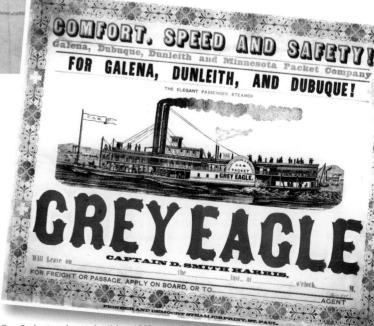

COMFORT, SPEED AND SAFETY!

Galena, Dubuque, Dunleith and Minnesota Packet Company

FOR GALENA, DUNLEITH, AND DUBUQUE!

THE ELEGANT PASSENGER STEAMER

GREY EAGLE

CAPTAIN D. SMITH HARRIS.

Will Leave on _____ the _____ inst., at _____ o'clock _____ M.

FOR FREIGHT OR PASSAGE, APPLY ON BOARD, OR TO _____ AGENT

PIONEER AND DEMOCRAT STEAM JOB PRINT, ST. PAUL.

Grey Eagle *steamboat advertising, 1858*

The *Grey Eagle* was one of the earliest steamboats docking at St. Paul's levee. Comfort and speed were important, but safety was also a concern to those contemplating Mississippi River travel.

3

Floating hotels

Early tourists joined popular excursions called "fashionable tours" to the new frontier, and steamboat companies accommodated them by becoming fashionable floating hotels. Tour arrangers planned visits to picturesque ports along the route. Educational excursions to famous sites in the countryside included frontier tales from one-time explorers and adventurers. Travel to Minnesota was suddenly in vogue.

Photos from the E. W. Tallmon Steamboat Album, late 1800s

E. W. Tallmon collected photographs of Mississippi River steamboats. His fragile and historic albums provide rare views of life on a steamer.

Interior of steamer Grand Republic, *1870*

Interior of steamer Phil Sheridan, *1872*

The steamer *Phil Sheridan* was typical of the new generation of steamboats plying the Mississippi by the 1870s. Well-appointed cabins lined the perimeter fore to aft. Cabin doors opened into intricate lounges where passengers relaxed under fluted columns and fancy fretwork. Elegant dining halls held tables set with fine linen, bone china, and sparkling crystal and meals were prepared using the abundant, fresh bounty gathered from river stops along the way. Anyone with time and money to spare wanted to join in the fun!

Lakeside Hotel, Lake Pepin, 1910

Winona, Wabasha, and Red Wing were important stops along the Mississippi in the 1850s. People living in river towns were connected to the rest of the world almost entirely by steamboat. When packet steamers arrived, crews delivered the town mail first, then replenished wood to fire up steam engines and restocked the galleys with fresh local provisions.

General Israel Garrard created Minnesota's only resort on the Mississippi River. St. Hubert's Lodge, his 1855 hilltop hideaway, was located in the little hamlet of Frontenac where he provided lodging on beautiful Lake Pepin for friends and acquaintances. Describing his settlement as the "Newport of the Northwest," Garrard was confident the area would become a popular summer holiday destination. In 1867 he converted the town's grain warehouse into the Lakeside Hotel complete with boating facilities, breezy porches, ladies' parlors, a billiard room, and a ballroom. The general's wealthy friends and other affluent travelers, including General Ulysses S. Grant, arrived on riverboats with maids, servants, even horses and carriages. It remained one of the Upper Mississippi River valley's most elegant resort hotels for decades.

Steamer St. Paul, Diamond Jo Line, 1895

Office of the Diamond Jo Steamboat Line, St. Paul, 1900

Diamond Jo Reynolds was a colorful river man. He established his Diamond Jo Packet Line in 1880 to run between St. Paul and St. Louis. Packet boats carried passengers and mail and Diamond Jo's became the most popular line. However, by the turn of the century, railroads had siphoned passengers away from the river and the company became the last to operate scheduled steamers from St. Paul.

Steamer Mary Morton, Diamond Jo Line, 1895

Bustling St. Paul and St. Anthony

Once steamers arrived at the St. Paul levee, horse-drawn buses, called omnibuses, transferred weary wayfarers to their hotels. Along the way drivers related colorful descriptions of local landmarks. For a grand tour, including the distant towns of Stillwater and St. Anthony, sightseers booked seats on stage lines. Teams of horses ambled off to the tune of wagon wheels on cobblestone streets and straight onto stagecoach roads leading through prairie grasses and oak savannahs.

Winslow House, St. Paul, Minnesota

The Winslow House trademark cupola provided a familiar beacon to weary travelers arriving in St. Paul.

American House, St. Paul, 1858

Windsor Hotel, St. Paul 1870

John Summers's busy boarding house was always full. His guests complained and he built a brand new sixty-room hotel. When that hotel burned, he replaced it with the two-hundred-room Windsor Hotel. Vacationers and businessmen loved it—until 1910, when the Windsor Hotel was torn down and the St. Paul Hotel was built on its site.

City omnibus line, St. Paul, 1880s

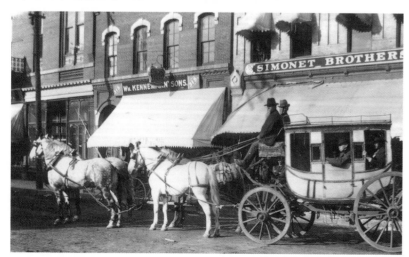

First stagecoach between Stillwater and St. Paul, 1864

Girl standing in omnibus, St. Paul, 1880s

Falls of St. Anthony and Winslow House

Entrance to Winslow House, St. Anthony, 1860

St. Paul hotel owner James M. Winslow took advantage of a site near St. Anthony Falls and built the elegant two-hundred-room Winslow House in 1857. It was styled in the manner of fashionable Eastern summer resorts and Winslow added his trademark cupola on the roof. Pleasure-seekers came in droves to participate in lawn games, croquet, bicycling, and carriage rides. Many sought the benefits of a cool climate away from the heat and illness of big Southern cities. The Winslow House enjoyed a lively, yet short life as peaceful tranquility survived but a few decades at St. Anthony Falls.

By midcentury, well-to-do Southern and Eastern travelers arrived in such large numbers that hotels and boarding houses in St. Anthony, and Minneapolis across the river, were full all summer long.

Mineral Springs

Promises of health-restoring waters enticed visitors to promenade on boardwalks to the famed Chalybeate Springs located on the riverbanks.

St. Anthony Falls

First mills on Hennepin Island at St. Anthony Falls, 1860

By the 1860s, the falls that had inspired poets and artists also inspired millers and lumbermen: sawmill racket, milling debris, and waterpower contraptions began to obscure the pleasant view. With the start of the Civil War, Southern travelers stopped coming to the state and many hotels ultimately made way for industry.

The Lakes of Minneapolis

Along with out-of-state tourists, Minnesota's urban dwellers fled the din of growing cities, noisy crowds, and muddy streets for beautiful lakes only a buggy ride away. Campers loaded up their big white tents, tables, chairs, and fish-fry pans for a week's stay.

Lake of the Isles campsite, 1897
Excursion boat on Lake of the Isles, 1912

Lyndale Hotel, east shore of Lake Calhoun, 1883

The Lyndale Hotel established the city lakes as a first-class resort area. Elaborate furnishings included Brussels carpets and interiors finished with mahogany wainscoting and gas lights. Its seventy-five rooms had hot water and electric bells. The dining room, ladies' ordinary, and conservatory overlooked Lake Calhoun. Men made use of the billiards hall and barber shop, and a sixty-foot-long frescoed music hall had maple floors for dancing. Wide verandas on each floor offered views in all directions and a livery stable housed elegant vehicles for touring, including glass landaus, phaetons, coupes, buggies, and eight saddle horses for trotting on pathways around the lakes. The grand opening was the social event of the decade.

Cedar Lake campsite, 1885

Oak Grove House hotel, south shore of Cedar Lake, 1870

Innkeepers had high hopes for city lakes as early as the 1880s. The Oak Grove House offered resort-style amenities and became a popular vacation spot.

Guy Baltuff's camp, Lake Calhoun, 1900

Guy Baltuff entertained his city friends with sailing and fishing excursions on Lake Calhoun—where the big fish were plentiful.

University of Minnesota law students at Lake Calhoun, 1898

8

By the 1890s, city lakes were crowded with people from shore to shore. Lurline Boat Club members set their sails to the wind or paddled canoes over calm waters. Fanciful pavilions provided entertainment for multitudes of land lovers and rooftop musicians serenaded evening crowds who simply did not want to go home. Campers and vacationers seeking rest and tranquility started looking for a new utopia!

Lyndale and Lake Calhoun Railway and Steamer Hattie, *1880s*

Street railways provided efficient transportation around town and were an especially popular ride to the lakes. They eventually caused the demise of quiet local hotels by shuttling thousands of active day-trippers to the shores of Lakes Calhoun and Harriet. The Minneapolis, Lyndale and Lake Calhoun Railway's steam train brought riders to the 36th Street dock for a cruise on side-wheeler *Hattie*.

Lake Calhoun public bathing beach, Minneapolis, 1911

Architectural rendering of Lake Harriet Pavilion

The first Lake Harriet pavilion and streetcar station was designed in 1888 by architects Long and Kees, known for their work on Minneapolis's Lumber Exchange and Masonic Temple.

The second pavilion at Lake Harriet, 1895

The second pavilion was designed in 1891 by Harry Wild Jones with a first floor dining room and upper level concert seating.

Lake Harriet's third pavilion's roof garden at night, 1909

Lurline Boat Club, Lake Harriet, 1887
Lurline Boat Club, Lake Calhoun regatta announcement, 1887

9

The Lakes of St. Paul

St. Paul lakes were convenient stops for city residents looking for close-to-home vacations. A horse-and-carriage ride from town took no time at all and out-of-towners came by train to depots located beside the hotels.

Lake Elmo Resort, 1888

The 1870s Lake Elmo Resort was built in fashionable Eastlake style. The gently curving beach held a small pavilion, sturdy docks, and easy-gliding boats. Lake Elmo's only hotel burned while still in its teens and private cottages soon overtook the shore.

The Saint Paul Boat Club held its first annual regatta on the tranquil waters of Lake Elmo in 1887.

Aldrich's Hotel, Lake Como, St. Paul, 1870s

Boys gathering nuts, White Bear Lake, 1908

White Bear Lake was surrounded by woods where boys gathered nuts along with the usual sticks and stones.

White Bear Lake, along with nearby Bald Eagle Lake, tempted St. Paul society with crystal clear expanses of water and secluded resort hotels. In early years locals competed for rooms with outsiders from the big cities of Chicago, Kansas City, and New Orleans. But the locals lasted it out, and White Bear Lake surrendered to cottagers building summer houses and tending their wind-filled sails, occasionally sprinkled with an early night of not-too-raucous entertainment.

The Hotel Leip offered 125 rooms in various suites and cottages. Guests strolled through nearly forty acres of shady paths and lush lawns. Fishing guests had their pick from a fleet of rowboats while loungers rocked on steamers cruising around the lake. Health seekers were reminded of "the lack of swampy shoreline without the faintest suggestion of malaria or other fevers so common at the time!" Rates were $2.50 per day in the 1880s.

Hotel Leip, White Bear Lake, 1885

Williams House hotel, White Bear Lake, 1869

The Williams House was one of the few large resorts on White Bear Lake operating during the late 1800s. Resort hotels enjoyed busy but brief lives as most of the land gave way to private summer cottages.

Ramaley's Pavilion, 1906

Newspapers in 1890 reported rave reviews on the grand opening of Ramaley's Pavilion. A special train left Duluth's Union Depot filled with partygoers headed for the celebration—it was reported to be crowded to excess! They joined other Pavilion patrons enjoying exotic food and spirited libations along with elaborate entertainment. An audience of two thousand jammed the elegant second floor auditorium to hear an original musical composition, titled "With Full Sail" by Seibert's orchestra.

Ramaley's Pavilion was a three-story affair with four attention-getting towers. Cafés served refreshments on the ground floor and two hundred hotel-style guest rooms marched around the entire perimeter of the building. Bathhouses, spas, lake excursions, and boat *purchases* were booked at the water's edge—catalogues for the Ramaley Boat Company were available at the front desk!

Pickle Club, White Bear Lake, 1890

Pickle Club members relaxed at their clubhouse and held galas at Ramaley's Pavilion.

Ramaley's Pavilion, 1890

Ramaley Pavilion.

Open for Season of 1892.

CONCERT AND HOP

Every Tuesday and Friday Evening.

Admission, - - 25 cents.

Hall for rent for other entertainments on other evenings

Finest Fleet of sail and row boats on lake. We make a specialty of taking care of sail boats.

J. D. RAMALEY, Manager.

Chautauquas

Chautauquas were summer events held around the country. Their large buildings and huge tents accommodated programs that attracted thousands of vacationers. People gathered for as long as a week to hear stimulating cultural lectures and discussion on social and political issues of the day. Along with an impressive message of self and civic improvement, sessions included opera, elocutionists, and classic theater productions. Famed literary, political, musical, and religious speakers of the times, including politician William Jennings Bryan and writer Mark Twain, were often featured, and they traveled to meetings throughout Minnesota. Located beside quiet lakes, chautauquas broadened the lives of people throughout the country with enlightenment and wholesome entertainment.

Chautauqua Assembly Building, Mahtomedi, 1883

The Mahtomedi Chautauqua Assembly Building was more fanciful than most. It served patrons of the Mahtomedi Hotel and many others who camped in tents on the grounds throughout the summer.

Chautauqua, Green Lake, Spicer

Cottages of White Bear Lake

White Bear Lake was known for quaint summer cottages and tasteful summer houses. St. Paul families moved to the lake for the season where entertainment was a backyard picnic or ice cream social.

The road over an arching bridge to Manitou Island led into a labyrinth of meandering walkways, tree-lined drives, and secluded cottages. When a group of St. Paul businessmen purchased the White Bear Lake island in 1881 for private development, they built family summer houses and a clubhouse intended for socializing. But owners preferred peace and quiet and the clubhouse was rented out. A pair of stone monoliths announced the entrance to Manitou Island.

Entrance to Manitou Island, 1905

Summer house, White Bear Lake, 1907

Summer cottage, White Bear Lake, 1880

Interior of Manitou Island clubhouse, 1895
Manitou Island clubhouse, 1895 ▼

Architect Cass Gilbert leased the clubhouse for his family during the summer months. Since he lived in nearby St. Paul, it was a convenient studio to work on plans for summer homes in the area. He was also the photographer for these family pictures. Gilbert went on to design many buildings, including landmarks such as the Minnesota State Capitol, the Supreme Court building in Washington, D.C., and the Woolworth Building in New York City.

On the porch, White Bear Lake

Truman Ward Ingersoll was a well-known photographer and publisher during the late 1800s. He documented Minnesota scenes in photographs, lithographs, and stereoviews. Ingersoll spent the warm season at White Bear Lake where he captured picturesque images of people sailing, relaxing, and going about their everyday activities.

Ingersoll photograph of girls sailing, White Bear Lake, 1890s

Ingersoll photograph of women, White Bear Lake, 1900

Ingersoll Birch Lodge, Dellwood, 1890

Birch Lodge was Ingersoll's own summer cabin and also housed one of his photography studios—and he invited lots of friends to share in the fun at the lake. Ingersoll sat on his boat after setting the camera's timer for this photograph.

Judge Young's cottage, 1885

Truman Ward Ingersoll's original photos were often made into engravings for commercial reproduction and sale. These etchings of Judge Young's cottage were done from Ingersoll photographs.

Judge Young and his family summered in Eastern Stick-style architecture typical of cottages in the White Bear area. Wood stickwork applied as outlines to the clapboard siding, decorative brackets, and colorful windows personified the fanciful architecture so prevalent at the lake. In 1978 the last owner, the Fillebrown family, bequeathed the house to the White Bear Lake Area Historical Society.

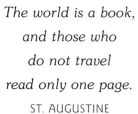

The world is a book, and those who do not travel read only one page.

ST. AUGUSTINE

Hotels on Lake Minnetonka

Lake Minnetonka enjoyed widespread fame and romantic celebrity for its wandering shoreline, picturesque bays, and cooling breezes. By the 1870s, the lake had become one of the major tourist spots in the nation for both affordable and extravagant escapes. Dozens of intimate and homey hostelries encouraged activities from peaceful fishing to downright riotous fun—their secluded bays and cozy retreats mingled happily with noisy casino pavilions and public boat docks. At the other extreme, huge and extravagant hotels offered posh and expensive accommodations—their own onsite billiards and theatrical productions vied for consideration with tennis matches and shore excursions.

Keewaydin, Cottagewood

The Sampson House, Excelsior

The White House, Excelsior, 1892

Hotel Buena Vista, Cook's Bay

Guests arrived at the Sampson House with fishing poles over their shoulders—boat, bait, and bass were close at hand.

With wide porches all around and a location high on a hill, the Hotel del Otero appealed to vacationing Minnesotans as well as visiting Southern families. It is also one of the few hotels to have documented its amenities so thoroughly. A typical day included a morning of fishing or sailing, lunch at the picnic grounds, naptime on a sunny porch, games at the ballpark, made-from-scratch meals in many dining rooms, and dancing at the casino. Then the next day it started all over again!

Hotel del Otero, Spring Park, sunset parlor

Dining rooms

Reception parlor

Casino, Excelsior, 1900s

Lake Minnetonka's bustling town of Excelsior offered varied entertainment for vacationers. Casino porches sheltered lunchtime tourists as they waited for a boat ride or contemplated roller skating or dancing in the pavilion afterward. Dozens of excursion boats waited at spacious docks ready to load up passengers and then steamed away across the lake. Most set their course for Wayzata with stops at sights and hotels along the way. Over the decades, amusement parks on Big Island and Excelsior Park attracted day-trippers who arrived by streetcar. For entertainment, Excelsior was *the* place to be.

Inside the casino, Excelsior, 1905

The Blue Line Docks, Excelsior, 1908

Vacations at Minnetonka were all about the famous lake. Steamers went everywhere and everyone wanted to be on one. Unfortunately, their steam boilers blew up occasionally, which added to the adventure.

The upper deck of the Hattie May, *1885*

Hattie May was one of the first big steamers on the lake, often filled to capacity with 350 happy sightseers aboard.

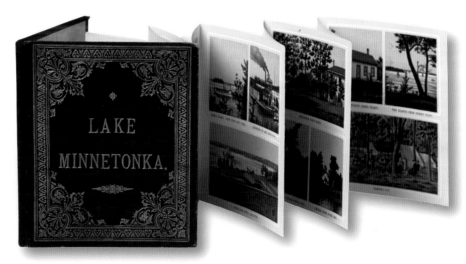

Steamboat Excelsior, Lake Minnetonka, 1903

Lake Minnetonka souvenir pictorial, 1890

The Grand Hotels of Lake Minnetonka

Lake Minnetonka offered the ultimate stop for Southern and Eastern vacationers. Irresistible marketing in national magazines brought tourists in ever-increasing numbers to eloquently described hotels. Families fled their hot cities and endured long journeys to arrive at cool and airy lakeside lodgings. Parents and kids, maids and servants, steamer trunks and tennis racquets all settled in to stay the summer.

Steam train, Deephaven, 1898
Railroad depot, Deephaven, 1890

Belle of Minnetonka, 1890s

Minnetonka's hotels installed private docks and hotel patrons walked but a few steps onto waiting steamboats.

Children on the porch of Lafayette Hotel, Minnetonka Beach, 1890
Lafayette Hotel, Minnetonka Beach, 1883 ▼

Railroad baron James J. Hill's Lafayette Hotel was the largest and most luxurious resort hotel west of the Mississippi River. Furnished with a collection of fine furniture, works of art, and handmade carpets, it rivaled anything in the East. When the hotel opened in 1882, Hill's trains delivered guests right to the door. The mammoth structure was strategically located on a ridge and allowed three hundred rooms on both sides to have sweeping lake views. The vast exterior was an animation of bouncing gables and porches. The interior was orderly and elegant and a staff of 150 employees fulfilled every whim. Waiters served breakfasts on guest room balconies or white-glove dinners for a thousand in dining rooms overlooking the lake. Festive events added color to the Lafayette's history, from opulent galas attended by national celebrities to intimate family picnics.

Convenient passenger rail service was necessary for large-scale hotels to be successful. Trainloads of vacationers arrived at nearby depots or within steps of the hotel front lobby.

Guests arrived on the Chicago, Milwaukee, and St. Paul Railway at the Deephaven depot, where hotel carriages awaited.

Deephaven was home to the first large-scale resort hotel on the lake. Opening in 1879, the Hotel St. Louis set new standards in elegance and catered to the most elite vacationers. Each story was graced with wide verandas and the two hundred guest rooms were furnished with electric lights and indoor plumbing. There was even a bath on every floor! The landscaped grounds were filled with picnic areas, walking paths, and tennis courts. Evening musicals, poetry recitals, and dances enlivened the grand ballroom.

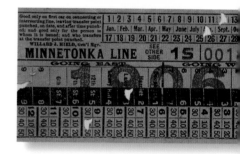

St. Louis Hotel, 1885

Lake Park Hotel, Lake Minnetonka, West Tower.
Office, Dining Room, Pavilion, 1897

Advertised as a chautauqua retreat and health resort, the Lake Park Hotel catered to those in search of intelligent stimulation along with entertainment. Towers and cupolas overlooked nearly five miles of shoreline. Fleets of boats and a large wharf for lake steamers held the attention of a thousand guests. A four-hundred-seat dining room, reading rooms, a barber shop, reception rooms, and parlors sprawled throughout inside. An amusement pavilion held a theater for summer operas and plays, a billiard hall, and soda fountain. An even larger casino building held a roller skating rink and ballroom for dancing. In 1904, the Lake Park Hotel was purchased by the Twin Cities Rapid Transit Company and renamed the Tonka Bay Hotel. The roller rink building was later moved across the lake to become the Danceland pavilion at Excelsior Amusement Park.

In the 1880s, Lake Minnetonka's three largest hotels registered more than 10,000 guests. Those were Lake Minnetonka's glory days. After James J. Hill laid his tracks to the door of the Lafayette Hotel, his rails went on to cities all over the state. Other Minnesota railroads followed the same migration. As trains reached new distant resort areas, so migrated inquisitive vacationers who went to discover what was over the horizon. The height of the Minnetonka resort era had peaked. One by one, the grand old hotels began to close, steamboats began to disappear, and by 1900 private cottages and summer homes began to take over the lakeshore.

17

Summary cottages on Lake Minnetonka

Even before Minnetonka hotels began closing, individuals had their eyes on the beautiful lakeshore to build summer homes. With a relatively short ride from Minneapolis, it was possible for families to move in for a summer at the lake. At first, cottages mingled happily with hotels, then small cottages were squeezed by larger summer homes, and those in turn became grand summer homes. With increasingly better roads and faster automobiles, many eventually turned into permanent, year-round homes.

Linton cottage, Lake Minnetonka

Wood shingles and clapboard siding were reminiscent of East Coast cottage design, but Minnetonka builders developed their own style—a solid farmhouse look accented by airy wraparound porches for lazy summer days.

Crane Island, 1900

At the turn of the century twenty-five Minneapolis families established a Presbyterian community on undeveloped Crane Island. Construction material was transported by boat for fifteen family cottages and a caretaker's cabin. By 1915, the owners could travel to Excelsior by streetcar, then board a ferry to the island.

Kelly cottage, Minnetonka, 1890

Zimmerman cottage, Bowlder Lodge, Enchanted Island, 1900

Fieldstone was not in short supply but it was heavy to move and rarely reached higher than foundations and porches.

For afternoon naps no setting was more perfect than a cool, breezy porch. Then again, sleeping on a porch was better both day and night.

Lake Minnetonka boasted a few very grand summer homes, complete with maids, cooks, and gardeners, but when winter whistled, everyone packed up and moved back to the city. The homes were substantial and charming and boat tours cruising past always included a slowdown to gawk at the big houses at the lake.

Henry cottage, Lake Minnetonka, 1890

Peavey summer home, 1904

Stanton family and friends on porch, Wayzata, 1910

Harry Wild Jones

As lake hotels were closing, Minneapolis architect Harry Wild Jones was designing summer cottages. Prolific and versatile, his cottages ranged from small charmers to large attention-getters. Jones trained with Boston's famous architect H. H. Richardson, then established his own practice in Minneapolis. Notable local projects include Butler Brothers Warehouse, Lakewood Cemetery's Chapel, and the second Lake Harriet Pavilion.

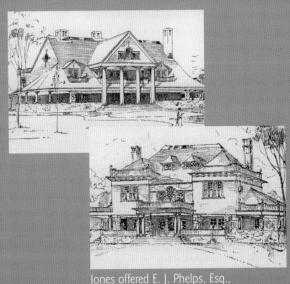

Jones offered E. J. Phelps, Esq., a choice between two very different "cottage" styles.

Camping at Minnehaha Falls and Cherokee Heights

As more people looked for more places to take short vacations, camping became a popular way to take a holiday and still be close to home. Tourist parks and campgrounds took advantage of picturesque sights around the Twin Cities.

Longfellow's eloquent description of the romantic waters of Minnehaha Falls inspired a pilgrimage of sightseers. Parkland surrounding the falls was continuously expanded to accommodate increasing multitudes of devoted admirers. Campgrounds, picnic areas, pavilions, bandshells, and fenced areas of real elk and buffalo drew even more crowds. They came in small groups and enormous gatherings, first by horse and carriage, then by bicycle, streetcar, automobile, and tour bus.

Changing a tire, Minnehaha Park tourist camp, 1925

Permanent sites for mobile campers were established in wooded areas near the park grounds.

Volunteers of America Sunday School picnic, Minnehaha Park, 1925

Girls getting water at Minnehaha Park tourist camp, 1929

1850, 1860, 1880, 1910

To capture the best view of Minnehaha Falls, bridges were built in the glen below. They evolved from the makings of rickety wood to fanciful twig-work to sturdy river rock.

Cherokee Heights Tourist Park, 1924

Cherokee Heights Tourist Park, 1925

Cherokee Heights Tourist Park stretched along a Mississippi River bluff across from downtown St. Paul. Campers unloaded their Model Ts, pitched their tents, and sent the kids to explore the riverbanks. Grown-ups settled in to enjoy the panoramic view.

Tourist cabins in Minnehaha Park, 1955

Thirty-five tourist cabins once provided sanctuary in the midst of Minnehaha Park. They were auctioned off in the 1950s for $125 to $175 each and new owners removed them to make room for further expansion of the park grounds.

Longfellow Gardens

Longfellow Gardens, Minneapolis, 1910

When Robert "Fish" Jones sold his house and land on 16th and Hennepin to make way for construction of the Basilica, he moved his small menagerie of animals to a new park he named Longfellow Gardens across the streetcar tracks from Minnehaha Park. Over the years he added an extravaganza of fountains, statuary, walkways, bridges, buildings, gardens, and a steam train ride. More animals arrived in ark-like pairs of peacocks, cranes, exotic birds, bears, and elephants. Jones himself trained lions, leopards, barking seals, and twelve Russian wolfhounds that performed for the crowds. Camels and ponies stood ready to give rides. He was an equal attraction—he dressed in a silk top hat and Prince Albert suit. People loved the park and came in flocks for thirty years. Except for one replica of Longfellow's Boston home, the gardens and buildings were all removed in 1936.

Robert "Fish" Jones feeding his seals, Minnehaha Park, 1905

Jones and his trained lions, 1920

Riding the camels, 1905

21

One-day getaways

When people living in Minneapolis and St. Paul were looking for one-day vacations, amusement parks or "picnic resorts" provided the answer. In the 1900s, Thomas Lowry stretched his Twin City Rapid Transit streetcar lines from Lake Harriet out to Lake Minnetonka, then to White Bear Lake and Stillwater. At Excelsior he added a fleet of double-decked boats that resembled streetcars gliding on water—and they became the darlings of the lake. Now there was an amusement for absolutely everyone and all they had to do was climb aboard a streetcar. Round-trip fare from St. Paul to White Bear: 25 cents.

Streetcar at Gibbs Lake, Lake Minnetonka
Streetcar boat Minnehaha, 1920s

The Twin Cities and Surroundings
Population over 700,000
Territory Shown: 16 Miles North and South; 48 Miles East and West
Electric Lines ———— 444 Miles. Steamboat Lines ------ 22 Miles

Music casino at Big Island Park, Excelsior

Streetcar boats took passengers to sixty-five acres of fun on Big Island Amusement Park. Merrymakers visited Spanish Mission–style buildings, carousels, roller coasters, and a huge aviary. Song lovers gathered at the music casino to be entertained by local musicians—and many returned week after week all summer long!

Excelsior Amusement Park, 1940s

Excelsior Amusement Park provided an alternative for entertainment after Big Island and Wildwood had closed. People missed the opportunity for leisure activity by the lake and the new park could easily be reached by car and bus. The lively amusements provided entertainment for mobile thrill-seekers for fifty years.

Katzenjammer Castle and roller coaster, Wildwood Park, 1905

Wildwood Park was the site of choice for company parties, club events, and family gatherings. Picnics ruled as the favorite activity in all amusement parks and Wildwood had numerous grounds and tantalizing concession stands. Other temptations included water tobogganing, beach activities, boating, and fishing, followed by trips to the fun house, roller coaster, shooting galleys, and diving pony acts. If energy allowed, a dance contest polished off the night. Then the fireworks started!

Wildwood Park

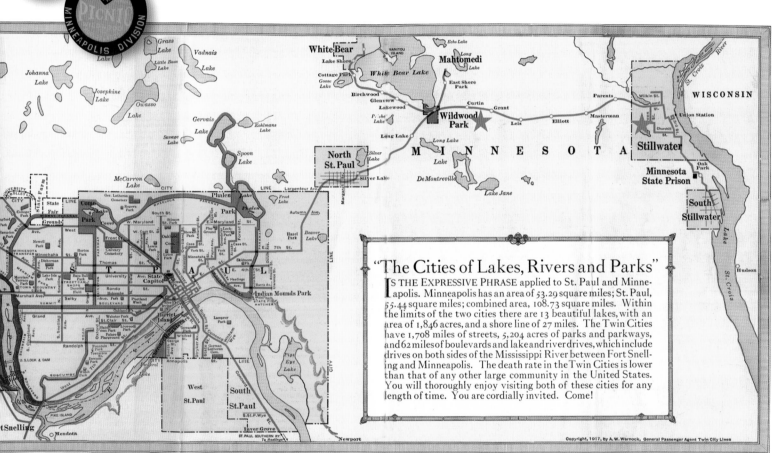

"The Cities of Lakes, Rivers and Parks"

IS THE EXPRESSIVE PHRASE applied to St. Paul and Minneapolis. Minneapolis has an area of 53.29 square miles; St. Paul, 55.44 square miles; combined area, 108.73 square miles. Within the limits of the two cities there are 13 beautiful lakes, with an area of 1,846 acres, and a shore line of 27 miles. The Twin Cities have 1,708 miles of streets, 5,204 acres of parks and parkways, and 62 miles of boulevards and lake and river drives, which include drives on both sides of the Mississippi River between Fort Snelling and Minneapolis. The death rate in the Twin Cities is lower than that of any other large community in the United States. You will thoroughly enjoy visiting both of these cities for any length of time. You are cordially invited. Come!

Copyright, 1917, by A. W. Warnock, General Passenger Agent Twin City Lines

Twin Cities streetcar map, 1917

Wildwood Park

Rattlesnake Curve, Stillwater

Mineral springs

People who were ailing had few medical options in the nineteenth century and many took holidays to seek restoration at mineral springs and mud baths. "Taking the waters" was thought to correct iron deficiency as well as other more serious ailments. With growing industrial pollution in large cities, people felt better with a treatment of cool mineral drinks followed by a sulphur mud bath. The forerunner of spas, Minnesota's abundant mineral springs attracted health-seekers from around the country. Writer Henry David Thoreau, on doctor's orders, came to the state specifically to help cure his tuberculosis in clean air and mineral springs.

Pavilion at Mineral Springs Park, Owatonna, 1880s

Southern Minnesota was brimming in mineral springs. In addition to Owatonna, they were known to exist from Cannon Falls to Big Stone Lake on the western border.

Chalybeate Springs, East Bank Mississippi River, Minneapolis, 1880
Pettingill's Amusement Resort, 1875

Minneapolis boasted an impressive, but fleeting, mineral water resort from 1875 to 1883. Pettingill's Amusement Resort included a hotel, observation tower, ice cream parlor, cigar stand, boat rides, and entertainment. Nearby was the photography gallery of Michael Nowack, who sold his stereoscopic views of the state's early landmarks. But the main attraction was the Chalybeate Springs, which meant "water impregnated with salts of iron." Visitors descended on paths arched with wild grapevines to arrive at a platform with a panoramic view of the river and waterfall. There they found the magic elixir—one of the springs had been fashioned into a fountain and the mineral water could easily be reached with a water glass.

Jordan Sulphur Springs Sanitarium and Shakopee's Mudbaden Sulphur Springs Resort became famous for their sulphur-saturated mud baths. Opened in the early 1900s and billed as health resorts, they attracted both patients and vacationers hoping to restore their health and happiness. The popular resorts provided their unique treatments for nearly fifty years.

Mudbaden Sulphur Mud Baths and Springs, 1900

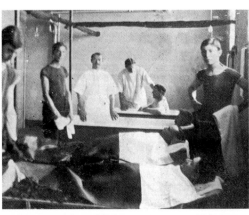

Mud baths at Jordan Sulphur Springs Sanitarium, Jordan, 1914

Spa lunch

Turn-of-the-century lunch was worthy of long hours spent in the kitchen, and artfully arranged fare was presented at Victorian tables set with delicate lace and elegant silver.

The following recipes have been adapted for easy preparation, modern cooking methods, and ingredients that are readily available.

Eggs a la Suisse

Heinrich's Cook Book & Home Doctor, Minneapolis, 1900s

- 1 tablespoon butter, melted
- 1 tablespoon milk
- Grated cheddar or Swiss cheese
- 2 eggs [per serving]

Use a shallow baking dish for each 2-egg serving. Put in the melted butter and milk, then a thin layer of grated cheese. Break eggs into the dish, being careful to keep them separate. Season with salt and pepper. Sprinkle more cheese over the top. Repeat for as many servings as you need. Bake in a 325°F oven about 12 minutes or as soon as egg whites are set but yolks are soft.

Ramekins of Carrots with Green Peas

Watkins Almanac, Winona, 1912

- 1 cup carrots, diced
- 1 cup green peas
- 1 cup milk
- 1 tablespoon flour
- 1 tablespoon butter
- Salt, pepper, sugar to taste

Cook carrots and peas together covered in slightly salted water until tender, 6 to 10 minutes. Drain vegetables dry and return to pan. Add hot milk. Rub the flour and butter together in a bowl to form a creamy paste; add to pan with milk and vegetables, stirring frequently. Season with salt, pepper, and sugar to taste. Mix well, and simmer a few minutes. Serve in bread cases. Makes 6 servings.

FOR BREAD CASES: Cut crusts from slices of bread. Press bread slices down into buttered muffin cups forming a cup. Brush bread cups with melted butter. Heat in hot 400°F oven until browned delicately.

Spinach Soufflé

From a prewar menu by Mrs. Sumner T. McKnight in Food of My Friends by Virginia Safford, 1944

- 1-1/2 cups frozen chopped spinach
- 3 tablespoons butter
- 1 tablespoon chopped onion
- 3 tablespoons flour
- 1 cup half-and-half
- 4 eggs, separated

Cook spinach. Melt butter in large saucepan; add chopped onion and sauté lightly. Blend in flour; add half-and-half to make a smooth sauce. On low heat, put spinach into hot sauce and add well-beaten egg yolks. Stir a few moments until thick; season with salt and pepper. Remove from heat. Beat egg whites until stiff and fold in. Fill greased 6-cup ring mold with spinach mixture. Set ring in pan of hot water and bake in 350°F oven about 35 minutes, until puffed and golden. Plan to serve immediately, inverting ring onto serving plate. Fill center with a bowl of hollandaise sauce. Makes 6 servings.

Chicken a la King

Albert Lea Milk Company Cook Book, 1921

- 3 tablespoons butter
- 1 celery rib, chopped
- 1/4 cup chopped red or green pepper
- 1/2 cup chopped mushrooms
- 1/4 cup flour
- 1-1/2 cups milk
- 1 teaspoon salt
- 1/4 teaspoon ground pepper
- 1-1/2 cups diced cooked chicken
- 2 hard-cooked eggs, chopped
- 5 slices toast
- Parsley for garnish

Melt butter in saucepan. Sauté celery and peppers in butter. Add mushrooms. Stir in flour and cook over low heat, stirring until mixture is smooth, bubbly. Remove from heat. Stir in milk. Return to heat. Bring to boil over low heat, stirring constantly. Boil 1 minute. Season with salt and pepper. Add chicken and chopped egg. Continue cooking until chicken is heated through. Meanwhile, prepare toast; cut in quarters to make toast points. Arrange toast on five plates; pour chicken mixture over toast. Makes 5 servings.

A Delicious Fruit Salad

Albert Lea Milk Company Cook Book, 1921

- 1 bunch celery, cut into one-inch lengths
- 1 cup large grapes
- 3 bananas cut into one-inch lengths
- 3 oranges, peeled and sectioned
- 1 cup English walnut kernels
- 1 head lettuce
- Mayonnaise to moisten

In a large bowl, mix the celery with fruits and nuts. Mix in the mayonnaise and set on ice until just before serving. Line ten salad dishes with lettuce leaves, then heap the salad in the dishes. Makes 10 generous servings. 1920s instructions were included with this recipe: "This salad must be prepared by the housekeeper herself, as it is such a dainty dish that a hireling would be apt to slight it and make a failure of what might otherwise be a temptation to the most fastidious gourmet. The most tedious part of the operation is skinning the grapes." For today's cook, we recommend leaving the skins on!

Bath Buns

Ceresota Cook Book, Northwestern Consolidated Milling Company, Minneapolis, 1900s. This bun recipe originated in the famous spa city of Bath, England.

- 4 cups all-purpose flour
- 1/2 cup sugar, divided
- 1/3 cup butter, softened
- 1 teaspoon salt
- 1 envelope active dry yeast (2-1/4 teaspoons)
- 1 cup very warm milk (120°–130°F)
- 2 eggs
- 1 cup seedless raisins
- 3 tablespoons coarsely chopped almonds

Mix 2 cups of the flour, 6 tablespoons of the sugar, butter, salt, and yeast in large bowl. Add warm milk and eggs. Mix with spoon until smooth. Add enough remaining flour to handle easily; beat by hand forming a stiff dough. Work in raisins, distributing them evenly. Let covered dough rise until very light and double in volume. Then, without further handling, divide dough into 12 portions with a broad-bladed knife. Form each portion into a rocky bun. Lay buns a little distance apart on a greased baking sheet. Sprinkle shaped buns with remaining 2 tablespoons sugar and chopped almonds. Let rise uncovered in warm place half an hour, or until double. Bake in a 400°F oven 15 to 20 minutes, until golden brown. Serve warm or cool. Makes 12 buns.

Peach Melba

From a menu by Mrs. John S. Pillsbury in Food of My Friends by Virginia Safford, 1944

- 1 whole peach per person
- Slivered almonds
- Currant jelly
- Raspberry juice
- Vanilla ice cream
- Brandy

Peel peaches, cut in half and remove stones. Set in individual glass dishes. Stick peaches porcupine-like with almonds. Over all pour a glaze made by thinning melted currant jelly with raspberry juice. Chill in refrigerator. Serve with a sauce of softened vanilla ice cream flavored with brandy.

CHAPTER TWO

Are We There Yet?

AMERICANS' URGE TO EXPLORE their country increased with each and every decade. Fifty years of lively Mississippi river travel had introduced river towns to the rest of the country and provided memorable vistas for travelers. But even though the upper valley held spectacular scenery, steamers were limited to stops near the river. By the late 1800s the golden age of railroading sped into the state and travel on gracious steamboats began to decline.

For the next fifty years, where only wagon and stagecoach trails had existed, rail lines fanned out across the land. They connected towns and cities, states and countries, and by the turn of the century luxurious railroad trains had revolutionized travel for Americans everywhere.

Minnesota railroads offered the best in travel. Trains stopped in almost every Minnesota town and two famous lines linked the state to the East and West Coasts. Journeys over the iron rails boomed as plush coaches brought tourists to new and intriguing recreational areas. Long stretches of modern cars housed elegant dining rooms and comfortable lounges, along with entertainment and scenic narrations along the way. At journey's end, resorts, hotels, and campgrounds appeared to be seamless extensions of the railroad itself. Train travel became the most socially active and exhilarating holiday for decades to come.

While rail lines were limited by economics and geography, a far worse fate would diminish scenic travel on beautifully appointed rail coaches. Americans fell in love with the independence of automobile travel. By the 1920s motor technology had advanced rapidly and the nation's roadways improved to keep pace. Travelers could go nearly anywhere in the state at their leisure and in relative comfort. Conveniently located gas stations provided fuel, repairs, and directions. A stay for the night could be had at any number of either quiet or bustling roadside stops. Travelers found paths to the most remote corners of the state and automobiles bumped and groaned to get them there. Minnesota bus companies expanded to carry travelers across the nation. Comfortable motor coaches joined a growing parade of cars, campers, trailers, and motorcycles taking tourists to vacation spots in all directions.

After native son Charles Lindbergh completed his flight to Paris in 1927, midwestern companies began to provide air travel for the rest of society. Among the first to climb aboard home-based air carriers were passengers looking for timesaving travel to make the most of their limited vacation days. Midwestern airlines expanded and grew to fly high for decades to come.

The residents of Minnesota benefited from progressive homegrown railroads, bus companies, and airlines. Transportation options flourished in the state, perhaps to take residents away, more likely to bring travelers in. Whatever the reason, the land of lakes became a sought-after vacation and an easy-to-reach destination for residents and visitors alike. Only one question remained: Are we there yet?

◀ *The Milwaukee Road advertisement, 1950s*

Promoting vacations

Alluring vacation brochures created by railroads became the benchmark for travel promotion. Commissioned works of art portrayed beautiful scenes along the journey. Lively slogans and colorful graphics promoted excursions to not-to-be-missed tourist destinations—all of which were located near the rail lines. Travelers became enamored with a newfound romance of the rails.

Two of the country's most important railroads originated in Minnesota. Along with providing access to lands for settlers and the state's industries, these railroads literally invented the tourism industry. Well-laid tracks became the link to some of the best vacation activities in the state and country.

In 1864, President Abraham Lincoln signed an Act of Congress creating the Northern Pacific Railway that allowed owner Jay Cooke to connect northern Minnesota towns to the Pacific. In 1870, the first spike was driven in Duluth. Thirteen years later in Wyoming, former President Ulysses Grant drove the same spike as a ceremonial "last spike" and completed Northern Pacific's rail line. Yellowstone Park was a destination for millions of passengers over the next decades. While the shipping of lumber and agricultural products diminished in Minnesota, passenger interest in new vacation areas grew as travelers found rail lines conveniently close to hundreds of lakes.

In 1890 James J. Hill formed the Great Northern Railway by acquiring small Minnesota rail lines and then branching out to Canada and the Pacific. Beginning with the Lafayette and Del Otero Hotels at Lake Minnetonka, he headed west, creating vacation havens along the way. The boldest accomplishment by far was the creation of Glacier National Park, which Hill and his son Louis carved out of the Montana wilderness and became a premiere destination for millions of tourists arriving on Great Northern trains. Eventually the famous railroad carried passengers to Hill's own Great Lakes steamships and ocean-going liners that sailed from the West Coast to ports in the Orient.

Twin Cities' newspapers reminded readers of Minnesota lake activities with appealing cover illustrations on their *Sunday Magazines*.

Riding the rails

Enchanted travelers and curious sightseers eagerly climbed aboard comfortable new rail coaches and headed for unexplored recreation. Passenger trains traveled first to Minnesota's western border. If a town had no resort or hotel, the railroad built one, and towns with up-and-coming tourist attractions received a big, handsome depot.

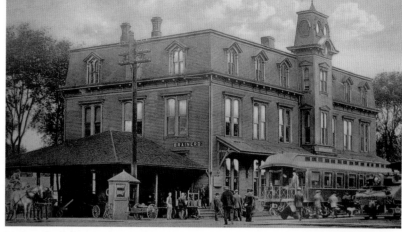

Northern Pacific Depot, Brainerd, 1920s

Heading north of the Twin Cities, ready-made freight rails brought fishermen and vacationers to northern lake areas. Freight still tagged along behind the train, but passenger comfort came first and coaches and dining cars "heading up north" filled up fast.

Depot, Lake Sarah, 1900

Camp Hubert depot, 1930

Waiting for the train, Spicer, 1910

Great Northern Depot, Bemidji, 1914

Bemidji was a popular vacation destination; it was served by five different rail lines—each with their own depot in town.

Coney Island Resort, Waconia, 1899

Coney Island was an 1870s recreational resort with fishing, sailing, shoreline villas, and an amusement center built on a lush island on Lake Waconia. Visitors from the Twin Cities paid just $1 in 1899 for round-trip railway fare to one of the first family resorts west of the growing urban areas.

The monumental architecture of urban depots provided a stunning backdrop in which to begin a Minnesota vacation. As highly visible landmarks, they were grand palaces of an exuberant railroad age. Graceful arches and fluted columns supported sky-high ceilings and these elegant spaces invigorated Victorian-era travelers. It was a magical time for traveling.

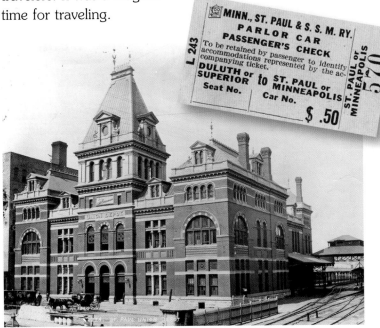

Original Union Depot, St. Paul, 1890

Milwaukee Depot, Minneapolis

Interior of Union Depot, engraving, St. Paul, 1885

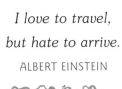

I love to travel, but hate to arrive.
ALBERT EINSTEIN

Passengers on the rear vestibule, 1910

Magnificent rail cars rivaled their steamboat counterparts in ornate interiors and sumptuous appointments. Polished mahogany cabinetry and brass fittings surrounded contented passengers in dining cars and lounges. Seats converted into Pullman sleepers and beds dropped down from above. Rocking with the train made for a cozy night's sleep.

Streamlined vacations

By the 1930s, rail coaches and dining cars became the epitome of streamlined modern design. Engines looked like they were racing forward even when standing still. Passengers rode over smooth rails in stylish coaches designed for genial travel. Dashing waiters served the finest cuisine and porters provided professional service for a smooth journey. A modern way to travel indeed.

North Coast Limited, Northern Pacific Railway, 1940s

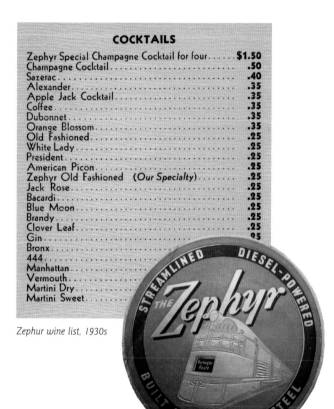

COCKTAILS

Zephyr Special Champagne Cocktail for four	$1.50
Champagne Cocktail	.50
Sazerac	.40
Alexander	.35
Apple Jack Cocktail	.35
Coffee	.35
Dubonnet	.35
Orange Blossom	.35
Old Fashioned	.25
White Lady	.25
President	.25
American Picon	.25
Zephyr Old Fashioned (Our Specialty)	.25
Jack Rose	.25
Bacardi	.25
Blue Moon	.25
Brandy	.25
Clover Leaf	.25
Gin	.25
Bronx	
444	
Manhattan	
Vermouth	
Martini Dry	
Martini Sweet	

Zephur wine list, 1930s

Dining car crew, Northern Pacific Railway, 1930s

In 1893, the Northern Pacific adopted the Chinese yin-yang symbol of a balanced universe.

Great Northern Railway, 1940s

Travel by rail revolved around the delights of the journey itself. Travel experts provided information along the route and life inside the coach was often as interesting as the scenery passing by the windows. Although many familiar vacation destinations were created by railroads, often the journey was the destination itself.

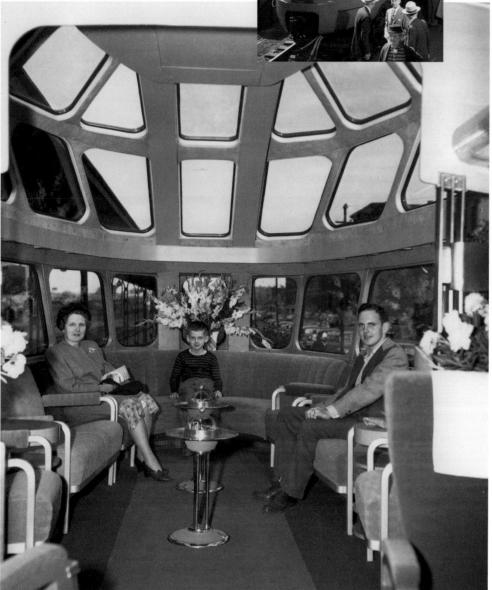

Hiawatha lounge-observation car

Map of the Lewis and Clark trail, 1940s

Northern Pacific day coach on Fargo-Minneapolis-St. Paul line, 1934

Cruising the Great Lakes

A steamship vacation in Minnesota? It was a common occurrence at the turn of the twentieth century. The Great Northern Railway owned the Northern Steamship Company that ran two luxury cruise ships on the Great Lakes. Other steamship companies launched larger ships and competition grew between them, to the delight of summer passengers.

Dining room of the steamship Noronic, *1920s*

Hearty breakfasts started off a smooth day on Lake Superior. Big waves didn't bother this grand dining room since the tables and chairs were anchored to the floor. Round-trip fares on the *Noronic* from Duluth to Detroit in 1940 were $73.20 for an inside stateroom, $83.20 for an outside room, and $119.20 for a parlor suite. Meals and entertainment were included.

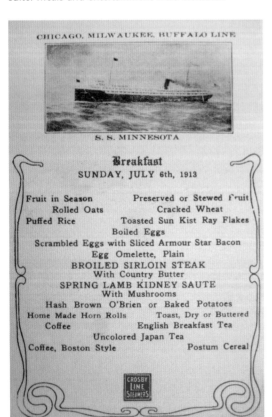

Breakfast menu from the S.S. Minnesota, *1913*

Northern Steamship Company ad, 1900

James J. Hill ran his railroad tracks straight to Duluth next to a gigantic wharf on Lake Superior. There he launched a pair of luxury passenger ships, the *North West* and *North Land*. The high-class steamships cruised on Lakes Superior, Erie, and Huron, with ports of call at various stops between Duluth and Buffalo, New York. Passengers enjoyed unimagined opulence until the 1920s when the pair of Northern Steamship Company ships cruised out of port for the last time.

Steamship North Land, *1905*

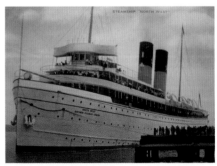

Steamship North West, *1900s*

Steamer Tionesta, *Duluth-Superior Harbor, 1920s*

Stateroom interior, S.S. North American, *1930s*

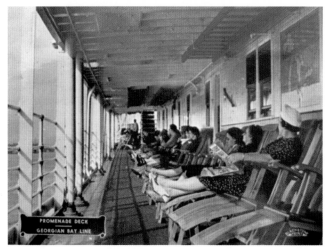

Deck chair lounging, S.S. North American, *1930s*

Sunning on a cool Tionesta *deck, 1920s*

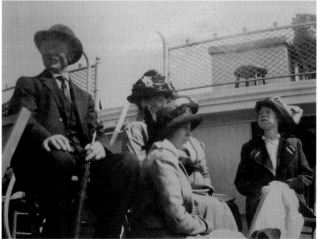

Relaxing on the deck, S.S. North American, *1930s*

Georgian Bay Line ships sailed between Duluth and Buffalo, New York. Highlights of the cruise were views of Isle Royale, passing through the busy Soo locks, and optional stopovers at the Grand Hotel on Mackinac Island in Michigan.

Great Lakes Cruises, 1928

Up, up, and away

In the 1920s few vacationers could afford the luxury of airline travel. Those who could checked in at austere passenger terminals, then boarded propeller-driven aircraft waiting on grassy runways. A climb on a shaky stairway, then up the sloping aisle to a seat, was almost adventure enough. But airlines were dependable, planes were safe, and passengers mustered up the courage to fly to primitive airstrips in popular vacation areas.

Minneapolis/St. Paul Airport, Wold-Chamberlain Field, 1930s

Passengers wait for a pilot, 1930s

Luggage stickers boasted of their owner's travel accomplishments and advertised airlines that served the Upper Midwest.

Jefferson Airways, Wold-Chamberlain Field, Minneapolis, 1928.

Float planes provided picturesque aerial tours and were the easy way to head to a remote campsite or fishing camp in the Boundary Waters Canoe Area. The town of Ely in northern Minnesota saw more float planes per capita than anywhere in America in the mid-twentieth century.

Seaplane base, Ely, 1950s

Seaplane at the dock, 1950s

It was many a fisherman's dream: fly to the lake, tie the airplane to the dock, take an evening boat ride, and return to a fresh fish dinner waiting at the cabin.

Northwest Airways passenger terminal, Wold-Chamberlain Field, Minneapolis, 1927

In 1926, the inaugural flight of Northwest Airways departed from Wold-Chamberlain Field in Minneapolis. The little plane carried a few adventurous passengers along with bags of mail. By 1950, Northwest Orient Airlines was a major Minnesota business and in the decades since, the company has continued to soar into international prominence.

THIS SEAT IS OCCUPIED

Minneapolis–St. Paul International Airport, 1960s

Arriving Northwest Orient Airlines passengers left their plane and walked *outside* to enter the new airport in the 1950s.

Fly the Best! Fly Northwest!

The World's Largest and Finest Luxury Airliner

NORTHWEST *Orient* AIRLINES DOUBLE-DECK BOEING STRATOCRUISER

LUXURY COMPARTMENT

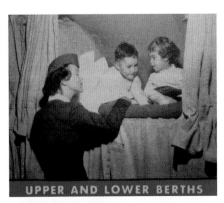

UPPER AND LOWER BERTHS

LOWER DECK LOUNGE

MEN'S DRESSING ROOM

The Stratocruiser introduced unbelievable extravagance in air travel. It was the most innovative, convenient, and comfortable passenger airplane the world had ever seen, and Northwest was the only airline flying the big aircraft at the time. Passengers experienced the latest in sky-high luxury, including live entertainment. "Strato Fashion Flights" between Chicago and Minneapolis featured University of Minnesota students who modeled the latest styles from the Young-Quinlan department store—the aisle became the fashion runway.

Motor coach touring

Minneapolis Journal *sightseeing bus, 1902*

Stretched car becomes a bus, 1917

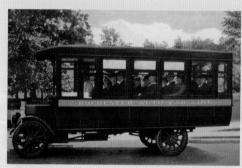

Rochester Auto Car Line, 1920s

Twin City Motor Bus Company, 1935

Touring by bus was a comfortable way to see local sights, explore the countryside, or venture into the north woods. The motto, "leave the driving to us," encouraged people who didn't want to drive or had no transportation of their own to tour inexpensively to their favorite sightseeing places. Tour guides described sights and offered an amusing tale or two along the way.

Twin City Motor Bus, 1940s

Royal Rapid Lines boasted "You will never forget this scenic trip along the beautiful Mississippi River. You get startling views of wide stretches of water—of towering rocky cliffs—of great stands of trees—of quaint hamlets and modern little cities nestling upon the shores." One-way fare, between Chicago and the Twin Cities, $10, round-trip fare, $18 in the 1940s.

Greyhound sightseeing bus, Duluth, 1930s

Two Minnesota transportation companies provided relaxing motorcoach tours and sightseers signed up by the busload. Jefferson and Greyhound bus lines originated in Minnesota and quickly became nationally recognized companies that many people depended on for touring as well as for their basic transportation needs.

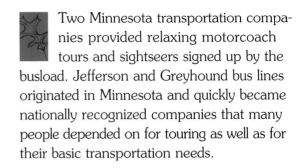

Jefferson Transportation Company bus, 1934

"From our home in America's heartland, we connect people with places" was Jefferson Transportation Company's motto. Founded in 1919, it was a pioneer in the motorcoach industry. The family-owned company has specialized in express scheduled service, charters, and tours throughout mid-America. The company took its name from the Jefferson Highway, which passed through Minnesota enroute between Texas and Canada.

The Super Scenicruiser, Greyhound, 1950s

The Mesaba Transportation Company shuttled miners between Hibbing and other towns on the Iron Range beginning in 1914. Over time, the company expanded by carrying passengers and vacationers across the country under its new name—the Greyhound Lines. Narrated tours, comfortable seats, onboard restrooms, and big windows for sightseeing made the ride on a Scenicruiser a vacation in itself!

Interior of a Jefferson Highway Bus, 1921

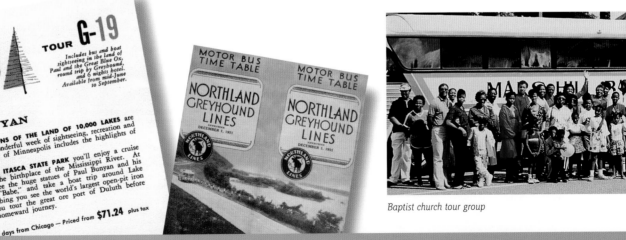

Baptist church tour group

Dusty roads

No other method of travel could compare with the flexibility of driving in the family car. But automobile travel early in the twentieth century was an adventure not without problems. Still, vacationers could turn down any road that piqued their interest and stop for lunch at their pick of roadside cafes.

C. E. Adams Tire Station, Willmar, 1915

Fixing a flat, 1923

Flat tires were commonplace due to road hazards or leaky rims, and inner tubes were fixed on the spot with tube patch. To keep moving, motorists mounted toolboxes on the running board, toted canvas water bags for overheated radiators, and stowed an assortment of fix-it-yourself items in the back.

Rubber repair kits from Permatite Manufacturing Co. and Gambles, Minneapolis

On a bridge at the state line, 1920

Johnson-Erickson Garage, Willmar, 1918

More serious mechanical problems needed the talent of serious mechanics.

Dedication ceremonies at Mississippi River Scenic Highway, 1925

The Mississippi River Scenic Highway was established in 1920. Its humble beginnings evolved into the Great River Road, a series of scenic river byways that winds its way from Itasca State Park to the Gulf of Mexico.

In the 1920s, roads were touring destinations themselves. Interstate highways and scenic routes provided ample opportunities for motorists who followed the colorful graphic signposts—predecessors to the highway number system. These well-traveled routes were important for local communities and civic leaders often solicited road planners to bring routes through their towns. Before federal funding, communities were responsible for road repairs and maintenance.

The Jefferson Highway, sometimes called the Palms to Pines Route, began in New Orleans, passed through Owatonna and Hallock, and ended in Canada in Winnipeg, Manitoba.

The King of Trails stretched from Texas to Canada, rambling through Minnesota at the western edge of the state.

In 1919, the Yellowstone Trail, the first transcontinental highway through the northern United States, passed through the Twin Cities.

Tannery Road, Red Wing, 1919

The first concrete driving lane in Minnesota was laid along a dirt road in 1911 and it proved to be the best solution for early road problems.

Superior Boulevard, Minneapolis, 1916

As traffic numbers soared, concrete provided smooth travel on Superior Boulevard in 1912, later renamed Wayzata Boulevard, and then Interstate 394.

Minnesota highway patrolman, 1925

In 1929 the official State Highway Patrol was created by the Legislature. It authorized a total of thirty-five men to be paid no more than $150 per month. The first training school was held at Highway Patrol Chief Earle Brown's farm in 1930.

Fireplace of States, Bemidji, 1935

The WPA built the Fireplace of States for the Bemidji Tourist Information Bureau. It featured stones collected from all 48 states.

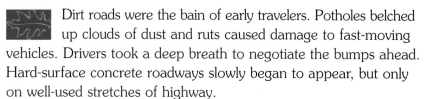 Dirt roads were the bain of early travelers. Potholes belched up clouds of dust and ruts caused damage to fast-moving vehicles. Drivers took a deep breath to negotiate the bumps ahead. Hard-surface concrete roadways slowly began to appear, but only on well-used stretches of highway.

Travel became safer and smoother with the establishment of the Minnesota Department of Highways in 1917 when it began to organize the state trunk highway system. Drivers took to the new roads in daunting numbers.

Highways 7 and 100, St. Louis Park, 1948
Beehive fireplace, Highway 100, St. Louis Park ▶
Roadside spring, Stillwater ▼

The highway department provided safe wayside rests and scenic overlooks for motorists. Built as Works Progress Administration (WPA) roadside parks, many survived both harsh elements and encroaching road improvements.

The Belt Line Highway, or Highway 100, provided a continuous roadway away from slow and congested city streets and changed driving habits forever. A twelve-mile stretch of Lilac Way became the state's first four-lane highway with the country's first cloverleaf interchange. Seven wayside rests were designed by landscape architect Arthur Nichols and featured stone benches, rock gardens, ornamental reflecting pools, and beehive fireplaces for grilling. Another Nichols project is Glacier National Park in Montana.

Fill er up?

Gas stations were roadside beacons and safe harbors for travelers seeking not only fuel and oil, but also emergency repairs and parts. Gas pumps stood on road intersections waiting for weary motorists and thirsty cars— and a tankful of gas in the 1930s hovered around fifteen cents a gallon. The car itself would have set the owner back $485 for a coupe, $500 for a coach, or $650 for a four-door sedan.

Trading Post gas station, Lake of the Woods, 1922

Log cabin service station, Fergus Falls, 1930s
▼ *Minnesota Oil bottle and hand cleaner, 1930s*

Gas ration books were issued by the Federal Office of Price Administration from 1942 to 1945 during World War II. Gas rationing was intended to conserve the rubber used in automobile tires, and no one could own more than five tires or drive faster than the lowered speed limit of 35 mph.

Pan automobiles at the Minnesota State Fair, 1922

Pan automobile with Sam and Anna Pandolfo, St. Cloud, 1918

After Sam Pandolfo built his Pan Motor Company manufacturing plant near St. Cloud, more than seven hundred cars rolled off the assembly line. Pan cars featured patented insulated ice storage compartments and front seats that folded back into a bed—unusual features for travelers at the dawn of the automobile age. The entrepreneurial Pandolfo provided his workers with new California-style housing and a streetcar line into town. After a short run of five years, the Pan Motor Company closed. A decade later Pandolfo opened his next business in downtown St. Cloud: the Pan Health Food Company.

World's smallest gas station, Detroit Lakes, 1920s

Vacationers in Detroit Lakes filled up at the three-by-four-foot smallest gas station in America, according to Robert Ripley's *Believe It or Not!*

Harmonica-playing gas station attendant filled the tank of a Ford Model T, 1923.

Erickson gas station, Minneapolis, 1961

Of the many gasoline brands serving the state's fuel-hungry automobiles, Minnesota-based Erickson gas stations have been a familiar holiday stop. In fact, Holiday became Erickson's name in the 1960s. In addition to selling gasoline, station stores held a vast variety of products. Customers were rewarded for their purchases with Holiday savings stamps—used to buy provisions for the cabin perhaps?

Erickson station gas pumps, Minneapolis, 1956

If all the cars in the United States were placed end to end, it would probably be Labor Day Weekend.

DOUG LARSON

Gas station designed by Frank Lloyd Wright, Cloquet, 1940s

Architect Frank Lloyd Wright's only gas station design featured a copper-clad canopy that cantilevered thirty-two feet over the gas pumps. A panoramic travelers' lounge occupied the second floor.

Co-operative Oil Company, Rochester, 1940s

From single outdoor fuel pumps to eye-catching monumental structures, gas stations reflected evolving motor technology and the latest style of the cars they served.

The American Automobile Association (AAA) began educating, entertaining, and assisting motorists as early as 1902. The Minnesota AAA opened the same year with auto clubs that offered dining and lodging, even garage stalls where motorists could work on their cars. AAA clubhouses went up throughout the state to aid and entertain travelers and were popular stops for early highway enthusiasts. Social events worth the drive were arranged by club staff.

Automobile Club Town House, Minneapolis, 1920s

Automobile Club of White Bear Lake, 1920s

Vacation lures

The best illustrators of the day were called upon to create the beguiling art featured on road maps. While cover illustrations lured enthusiastic travelers to a Minnesota vacation, the routes and highways inside showed them the way to get there—and the maps were free!

Roadside rhymes

In Minneapolis, Clinton Odell invented a travel-friendly brushless shaving cream called Burma-Shave. His son Allan convinced him to spend $200 for small, wooden highway signs that held a series of short humorous verses. In 1925, the first sets went up from Minneapolis to Albert Lea and Red Wing. Orders poured in. Allan recruited brother Leonard to help install signs across Minnesota and into Wisconsin. More orders poured in. Soon there were signs across America, as far as Alaska, and Europe, and even Antarctica. Customers were encouraged to submit their own jingles and Burma-Shave grew to see sales in the millions. In 1966, the new owner, Gillette, thought television would sell more product and every last sign disappeared from America's highways.

BURMA-SHAVE
BUT NOT YOUR CHIN
YOUR HEAD GROWS BALD
OF TOIL AND SIN
WITHIN THIS VALE

Three generations of Odells were asked to pick their favorite rhyme and everyone agreed on this timeless favorite.

DON'T STICK YOUR ELBOW OUT SO FAR IT MIGHT GO HOME IN ANOTHER CAR BURMA-SHAVE	ALWAYS REMEMBER ON ANY TRIP KEEP TWO THINGS WITHIN YOUR GRIP YOUR STEERING WHEEL AND BURMA-SHAVE	HIS FACE WAS SMOOTH AND COOL AS ICE AND OH LOUISE! HE SMELLED SO NICE BURMA-SHAVE	HIS FACE WAS LOVED BY JUST HIS MOTHER HE BURMA-SHAVED AND NOW — OH, BROTHER	IF THESE SIGNS BLUR AND BOUNCE AROUND YOU'D BETTER PARK AND WALK TO TOWN BURMA-SHAVE
TRAILER FOLK HAVE LITTLE SPACE FOR TOTIN' THINGS TO FIX THE FACE THEY USE BURMA-SHAVE	HE'S THE BOY THE GALS FORGOT HIS LINE WAS SMOOTH HIS CHIN WAS NOT BURMA-SHAVE	SHE KISSED THE HAIRBRUSH BY MISTAKE SHE THOUGHT IT WAS HER HUSBAND JAKE BURMA-SHAVE	ANGELS WHO GUARD YOU WHEN YOU DRIVE USUALLY RETIRE AT 65 BURMA-SHAVE	EVERY DAY WE DO OUR PART TO MAKE YOUR FACE A WORK OF ART BURMA-SHAVE
THE CHICK HE WED LET OUT A WHOOP FELT HIS CHIN AND FLEW THE COOP BURMA-SHAVE			AT CROSSROADS DON'T JUST TRUST TO LUCK THE OTHER CAR MAY BE A TRUCK BURMA-SHAVE	FISHERMAN! FOR A LUCKY STRIKE SHOW THE PIKE A FACE THEY'LL LIKE BURMA-SHAVE

SALESMEN, TOURISTS
CAMPER-OUTERS
ALL YOU OTHER
WHISKER-SPROUTERS
DON'T FORGET YOUR
BURMA-SHAVE

THE WHALE
PUT JONAH
DOWN THE HATCH
BUT COUGHED HIM UP
BECAUSE HE SCRATCHED
BURMA-SHAVE

Travelers' dinner

Steamboat dining was a study in glamorous food with fresh ingredients gathered along the route. But delectable dishes from America's railroads soon became the standard for fine dining across the country. And for a time, even airlines continued the tradition of serving interesting food from faraway places to their captive passengers.

The following recipes have been adapted for easy preparation, modern cooking methods, and ingredients that are readily available.

Crabmeat Olympia Hiawatha

Milwaukee Road in *Dining Car Recipes—How to Prepare 130 Specialties Served on the Dining Cars of Famous Trains*, 1940s

- 1 pound cooked fresh crabmeat [or shrimp or lobster]
- 1 celery rib, finely chopped
- 1 green onion, finely chopped
- A small quantity of fresh chervil and parsley, finely chopped
- 1 teaspoon tarragon vinegar
- 4 tablespoons mayonnaise
- Crisp lettuce leaves
- Curry powder
- Pitted olives, sour pickles, and crisp watercress

Place crabmeat in a mixing bowl with celery, onion, chervil, and parsley; toss lightly. Stir vinegar into mayonnaise; pour over crabmeat mixture. Mix well. Line a serving bowl with lettuce, placing crabmeat mixture in center. Dust with curry powder. Decorate with pitted olives and sour pickles cut into fan tails, also with watercress. Serve as an appetizer spread for crackers or salad for 4.

French Onion Soup

Created from a menu on the Northern Steamship Line

- 6 medium onions, thinly sliced
- 6 tablespoons butter
- 1 teaspoon sugar
- 1 teaspoon salt
- 1 teaspoon nutmeg
- 6 cups strong beef broth
- 6 thick pieces French bread
- 1/2 cup dry sherry wine, or to taste
- 1-1/2 cups grated Swiss cheese
- Grated Parmesan cheese

Sauté onion in butter until soft. Add sugar, salt, and nutmeg and toss well. Cook down slightly; onions should be golden brown. Add broth and bring to a boil. Reduce heat and simmer 30 minutes. Meanwhile, toast bread in oven until nearly dried out. Add wine to onion mixture and taste and correct seasoning. Ladle soup into 6 ovenproof casseroles or pots and top each with a piece of French bread. Spoon about 2 tablespoons grated Swiss cheese on top of bread. Bake in 300°F oven 10 minutes or until cheese is melted and bubbly. Serve with additional Swiss cheese, Parmesan cheese, and French bread. Makes 6 servings.

Vinaigrette Sauce for Lettuce or Asparagus Salad

Great Northern Railroad in *Dining Car Recipes*, 1940s

- 1 cup tarragon vinegar
- 2 cups olive oil
- 2 tablespoons prepared mustard
- 3 dill pickles, chopped fine
- 3 sprigs parsley, chopped fine
- 1 tablespoon capers, chopped fine
- 3 red pimientos, chopped fine
- 3 tablespoons onion juice

Mix all ingredients thoroughly in a wide-mouthed bottle. Taste and adjust seasoning. Shake well before each service. Serve in a sauce boat. Good with lettuce, asparagus, and vegetable salads. Makes 4 cups.

Baked Filet of Lake Superior Whitefish au Gratin

Dining Car Recipes, 1940s

- Fresh whitefish filets
- Salt and pepper
- Paprika
- Fresh bread crumbs
- Fresh grated Parmesan cheese
- Butter, melted
- Parsley and lemon slices

Clean and bone whitefish; cut into standard size portions (4 to 5 ounces each). Place filets in a single layer in a well-greased baking pan; season with salt and pepper. Sprinkle paprika, fresh bread crumbs, and grated fresh Parmesan cheese over fish. Sprinkle on a little melted butter. Bake in a 375°F oven uncovered 15 to 20 minutes or until fish flakes easily with fork. Care must be taken not to overcook fish, which would cause it to lose a great deal of its flavor. Place on hot serving dish, garnish with parsley, lemon, and additional melted butter.

Breast of Chicken Cashew

A Northwest Orient Airlines Home Recipe, *Minnesota's Greatest and Best Recipes: A University of Minnesota Cookbook*, 1980s

- 8 boneless, skinless chicken breast halves
- 1/3 cup butter
- 3 tablespoons sherry wine
- 2 tablespoons cornstarch
- 2 cups chicken broth
- 3 tablespoons soy sauce
- 2 teaspoons sugar
- 1/2 teaspoon garlic powder
- Toasted cashew nuts

Season chicken with salt and pepper. Lightly sauté breasts on both sides in butter. Bake in oven for 15 minutes at 400°F. While breasts are baking, blend sherry and cornstarch together; set aside. Bring broth, soy sauce, sugar, and garlic powder to a boil in a saucepan. Slowly pour in sherry-cornstarch mixture as sauce boils. Thicken to desired consistency. Place chicken on platter and pour sauce over. Garnish with toasted cashew nuts. Makes 8 servings.

Big Baked Potatoes

Northern Pacific Railroad in *Dining Car Recipes*, 1940s

Wash large baking potatoes. Pierce with an ice pick or fork at both ends and place in a 350°F oven. The potatoes should be turned several times during the process of baking. In spring and summer they will bake in about an hour and a half; during fall and winter months it requires approximately 2 hours. It is well to place a pan of water in the oven with the potatoes to compensate for some of the natural moisture which has evaporated during the storage period. When the potatoes are done, take from the oven and roll gently to loosen the meaty part from the skin. Cut from end to end, spread open and serve with a large piece of butter in the center.

Floating Island with Custard Sauce

Burlington Lines in *Dining Car Recipes* and *Aunt Jane's Cook Book*, McConnon & Co., Winona, 1940s

FOR FLOATING ISLANDS:
- 3 egg whites (save yolks)
- 1/3 cup sugar
- 3 cups milk

FOR CUSTARD SAUCE:
- 3 egg yolks plus 2 whole eggs
- 1/2 cup sugar
- Dash of salt
- Milk reserved from making islands
- 1-1/2 teaspoons vanilla

FIRST, MAKE ISLANDS: Beat egg whites until soft peaks form. Beat in 1/3 cup sugar, 1 tablespoon at a time, until stiff peaks form. In 10-inch skillet, heat milk to simmering. Drop egg white mixture in 8 portions into milk; simmer, uncovered, until firm, about 5 minutes. Lift these meringue islands from milk, drain and chill, reserving milk for custard sauce.

FOR CUSTARD SAUCE: Slightly beat reserved 3 egg yolks with the 2 whole eggs. Beat in sugar and salt. Stir egg yolk mixture into reserved slightly cooled milk. Cook and stir over low heat until custard coats a metal spoon. Cool pan quickly in a bowl of ice water. Stir in vanilla; turn into a bowl and chill in refrigerator. TO SERVE: Top individual servings of sauce with meringue islands. Makes 8 servings.

CHAPTER THREE

Tourist Courts & Motels

AFTER DECADES OF TRAIN TRAVEL, Minnesotans embraced the idea of flexible trips in their own automobiles. In the early twentieth century, better highways and reliable cars gave birth to the modern road trip. Throughout the state, tourist courts sprang up on scenic highways and were harbors of rest for weary wayfarers. Alternatives to fancy hotels, these informal, one-room accommodations didn't provide much, but they were a place to rest after a long drive. Cars pulled up right next to the room and for tired travelers, metal frame beds, clean sheets, a flyswatter, and shared bathrooms were paradise. No need for luxury—vacationers spent most of their time out and about seeing the sights.

Tourist courts were an inexpensive getaway, a step up from camping, but not as glorious as a resort. Simple rooms were just a place to sleep. Boating, fishing, sightseeing, and dining were done offsite. These tight clusters of small buildings were often located on highways close to shops, restaurants, and lakes. Owners lived on the property, did most of the housekeeping and rental work themselves, and success was dependent on the proprietor's skills as jack-of-all-trades.

As more and more people owned cars, the travel industry began to grow and tourist courts vied for attention. No longer was it enough to include a parking place alongside the room; people were interested in more and better amenities. Postcards and advertisements boasted innerspring mattresses, ice boxes, showers, private toilets, and hot water; and modernization brought radios, thermostats, phone service, televisions, and the latest in tubular steel furniture.

Tourist cabins themselves were wayside advertisements. Quaint or quirky architecture pulled eyes away from the competition down the road. Spanish-style buildings, wigwam villages, and Hansel-and-Gretel cottages were a few of Minnesota's funky lodging choices.

Eventually individual tourist courts and cabins became connected together and the building style evolved into the modern motel—a combination of the words "motor" and "hotel." Swimming pools, shuffleboard, and kitchenettes kept vacationers onsite. Lobbies, cafés, and cocktail lounges were gathering places for families on a weekend outing. While exteriors often stretched off into the distance, interiors ranged from the latest in sleek modern style to colorfully flamboyant design.

For travelers having trouble deciding where to stay, travel clubs came to the rescue. Their logos stood out boldly on huge motel signs and assured lodgers of an approved place to stay. Tourist courts and early motels provided Minnesota travelers with a stopover for a night or a place to stay for a week of local sightseeing.

◄ *Twin Pines Resort and Motel, Mille Lacs, Garrison, 1955*

Uniformly good accommodations

Tourist court, Detroit Lakes, 1950

Usually built on busy roadsides, neat and tidy groupings of buildings were trademarks of early tourist courts. Auto travelers appreciated the convenience of parking their cars in spaces right next to the door of their lodging—and a lake was often nearby.

The Colony, Mille Lacs, Garrison

Typically clustered around a grassy area, tourist courts offered the opportunity to spend a night indoors, but otherwise there were few amenities—and no cooking facilities. A double bed, simple table, and light bulb overhead were enough to make the tiny rooms a welcome respite at the end of a long day on the road. For those who wanted to see the state, it was an easy alternative to camping. Lodgers shared picnic tables and lounging areas, and common showers and restrooms were often tucked in the back. With the addition of steam heat, travelers could stay year-round.

Cal's Cabin Camp, Bemidji

This perfect row of identical cabins is a classic tourist court. Like the aesthetics of the machine age, these units had the precise uniformity that told a traveler these accommodations would be clean, consistent, and reliable.

The Ranch Cabins, La Crescent, 1940s
◄ *Lyonais Modern Cabins, Brainerd, 1944*

RATES
$1⁰⁰ an UP

As more rooms opened for tourists throughout the state owners developed strategies to keep them attractive, modern, and visually appealing. Street appeal was especially important to grab the attention of passing motorists. Buildings appeared larger when individual cabins were linked together with covered archways or extended roof eaves. Cars parked in sheltered carports between the rooms, and tourist courts began to evolve into modern motels.

Park View cabins, Detroit Lakes, 1930

Arriving at a tourist court, 1940s

Twin Pines, Mille Lacs, Garrison

Individually owned tourist courts joined together in associations for publicity and to cautiously assure quality control: *accommodations are not uniform, but they are uniformly good.*

Lakeside Lodge cabins, Detroit Lakes

Rustic tourist courts

Some tourist courts provided travelers with a pioneerlike experience, even if it was just for a night or two. Log and stone construction made customers feel like they were traveling the western plains or driving to a rustic cabin instead of along a busy highway.

Cabin City Court, Riverview Station, St. Paul

Kum-Bak Camp, Duluth

Virginia Tourist Camp, 1930

A vacation should be just long enough that your boss misses you, and not long enough for him to discover how well he can get along without you.

UNKNOWN

Snelling Motor Court, 1951

Knotty pine paneling and bedspreads that matched the curtains found favor with guests in the fifties.

Y Motel, Mille Lacs, Garrison

A lighthouse motif along with the promise of a cocktail lounge next door lured fishermen off the lake and motorists off the highway at the busy "Y" in Garrison.

These stone tourist courts in Perham looked charming and rustic, too.

Lake Winnibigoshish Tourist Camp, Bena, 1925

Gas pumps out front were convenient for guests staying in this Bena tourist camp. Cottages were available out back, but the main building's pagoda-style architecture was an exotic attraction for traveling motorists. A fourth-generation owner now tends a lineup of modern gas pumps.

As road conditions improved and automobiles became more reliable, people traveled throughout the country and further from home. Accommodations with wacky, attention-getting themes became a national phenomenon. Tourists needed more than just a place to stay—they needed to be entertained.

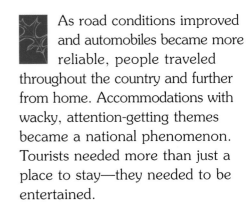

The Tourist Court, Hibbing, 1935

Spanish-style architecture arrived in Hibbing during the fashionable thirties and modern motorists arrived wearing driving knickers and jaunty caps.

Night-O-Rest Cabins, Anoka, 1940s

This enterprising Anoka tourist court owner offered an elaborate folk art grotto in addition to "modern and semi-modern" accommodations. Between the birds and the waterfall, sleep at the Night-O-Rest may have been a challenge.

Native American motifs were popular in the 1930s and many towns across America featured wigwam motels and entire villages of rentable teepees. These wood-frame and galvanized metal structures in Little Falls held a simple bed and dresser. The owners lived in a three-story teepee and were promptly there when a car pulled up to the gas pumps.

The Wigwam Inn, Little Falls, 1930s

Modern motels

By the 1940s, long, linear U-shaped motels entered our culture. The sprawling geometric highway communities catered to modern motorists in modern automobiles. Centrally located office areas often included a café or a patio overlooking a pool or playground. Some motels added deluxe rooms with their own kitchens, and a room for a night could easily turn into a room for a week.

Miller Motel, Austin

Lakes and Pines, St. Paul, 1950s

Kay's, St. Cloud

"Garage services while you sleep or eat."

Never go on a vacation in a car unless the windows outnumber the kids!

MILTON BERLE

Minneapolis Suburban Motel, 1950s

Wilken's Deluxe Cabin Court, Fairmont, 1948

"The best of everything in modern overnight accommodations. On U.S. 16, the direct East-West route to South Dakota Badlands, Black Hills, Yellowstone National Park, and the West Coast." With marketing copy like that, who wouldn't want to stay here?

Voyageur, Duluth; Minnetonka Motel, Wayzata, 1957; El Motel, Hibbing; St. Paul Tourist Cabins, Lake Phalen, St. Paul; Duluth Motel, Duluth

Postcards mailed home to friends were a great source of advertising for early, individually owned motels. Printed on the back was information about location and modern-age amenities that included Beauty Rest mattresses, tile baths, carpeting, television, air conditioning, and phone service.

55

Interior design of the 1950s

Modern motels created an aura of style with clean, attractive rooms. The epitome of contemporary design, minimalist interiors provided clutter-free shelter for the night. Striking pea-green walls, chenille bedspreads, and wildly patterned curtains surrounded tourists as they listened to the radio or watched television in their up-to-the-minute rooms. Spacious lounges encouraged socializing and mingling with other guests—newfound friends away from home.

Cloverleaf Motel, Minneapolis

Hilltop Motel, International Falls

River View Motel, Brainerd

New England Motel, Red Wing

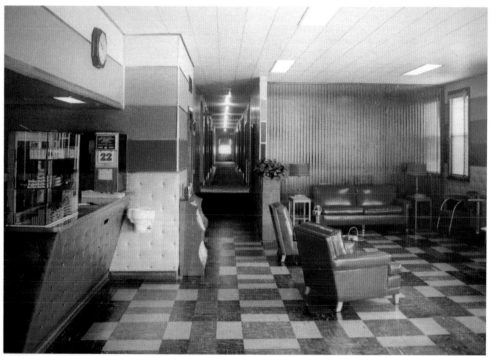

Riverside Hotel, Grand Rapids

Multicolored linoleum floors, tufted vinyl wainscoting, ribbed glass walls, fluorescent lights, a built-in plant stand, and Naugahyde furniture—straight out of *Architectural Digest* 1950.

Bahr's Motel, Deer River

Shoreline Hotel, Grand Marais

Clutter-free, Scandinavian Modern design allowed the lake to be the featured attraction in this Grand Marais motel room.

A vacation is a period of travel and relaxation when you take twice the clothes and half the money you need.

ANONYMOUS

Shoreline Hotel, Grand Marais
Birney Quick, 1965 ▶

Artists have always gravitated to the North Shore. A pristine lobby featured a mural painted in 1954 by Minnesota artist Birney Quick, founder of the Grand Marais Art Colony and instructor at Minneapolis College of Art and Design.

Edgewater Inn, Tofte, 1950s

Edgewater Inn was located on Lake Superior. Every room had beautiful water views and warm weather stopovers seemed like a real vacation. Winter stays also had beautiful views of the big lake's dramatic snow and ice.

Franchised Favorites

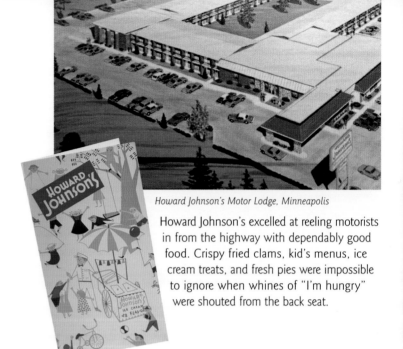

Howard Johnson's Motor Lodge, Minneapolis

As Sinclair Lewis predicted, by the early 1960s the travel industry was becoming standardized and chain motels grew in both room size and amenities.

> "Somewhere in these states there is a young man who is going to become rich. He is going to start a chain of small, clean, pleasant hotels, standardized and nationally advertised, along every important motor route in the country. He is not going to waste money on gilt and onyx, but he is going to have agreeable clerks, good coffee, endurable mattresses and good lighting . . ."
>
> Minnesota's Sinclair Lewis in the *Saturday Evening Post*, January 3, 1920

Howard Johnson's excelled at reeling motorists in from the highway with dependably good food. Crispy fried clams, kid's menus, ice cream treats, and fresh pies were impossible to ignore when whines of "I'm hungry" were shouted from the back seat.

Thunderbird Motel, Bloomington, 1970s

Wild West and Native American themes entertained lodgers at this urban oasis.

Ambassador Resort Motor Hotel, Minneapolis

Special rooms were available for events, meals were served in several dining rooms and lounges, and the domed pool was a perfect winter getaway!

Plymouth Radisson, 1970s

Named for the French Canadian explorer who traveled into Minnesota, Radisson is one of the country's largest hotel chains. Curt Carlson bought the first hotel in downtown Minneapolis in the 1960s and spread the chain across the world and onto the seas with a cruise ship line.

the Radisson

Motel supper

Travel books promoted the best places to eat along America's highways and tourists used them to plan their evening meals. Popular travel writer Duncan Hines visited Minnesota often, and his *Adventures in Good Eating* promoted many of the state's favorite eateries.

The following recipes have been adapted for easy preparation, modern cooking methods, and ingredients that are readily available.

Thunderbird Blue Cheese Dressing

Thunderbird Motel Corporation, from *Minnesota's Greatest and Best Recipes: A University of Minnesota Cookbook*, 1980s. If you enjoy blue cheese, you may wish to add a little more when preparing this recipe. This dressing goes well with all forms of tossed salad.

- 12 ounces blue cheese
- 1/2 cup buttermilk
- 1/4 cup half-and-half
- 1 quart mayonnaise
- 1 pint sour cream
- 1/4 teaspoon celery seed
- 1/8 teaspoon Tabasco sauce
- 1/8 teaspoon garlic powder
- 1/8 teaspoon white pepper
- 1 tablespoon Worcestershire sauce

Crumble blue cheese into small pieces. Mix with buttermilk, half-and-half, mayonnaise, sour cream, celery seed, Tabasco, garlic powder, white pepper and Worcestershire sauce. Cover and refrigerate several hours to meld flavors. Store covered in refrigerator. Makes 3 quarts, 20 to 25 servings.

Spinach Salad

The Ford Times Traveler's Cookbook, Ford Motor Company, 1960s

Toss 1-1/2 cups washed spinach leaves with 2 sliced hard-cooked eggs and thinly sliced red onion rings. Toss again with Thunderbird Blue Cheese Dressing or favorite garlic dressing. Makes 2 servings.

Finger Salad

For a refreshing first course or appetizer that is easy to prepare, set out a selection of these raw vegetables: carrot sticks, radishes, celery, green onions, green and red pepper slices, cherry tomatoes, cauliflower buds, sliced cucumbers, sliced mushrooms, and diced raw turnips. Serve with Thunderbird Blue Cheese Dressing as a finger salad or dip.

Hot Pot of Beef and Potatoes

The Ford Times Traveler's Cookbook, 1960s

- 2 tablespoons vegetable oil
- 1-1/2 pounds beef chuck, cut in small chunks
- 3 or more medium potatoes
- 2 onions
- 1/2 cup beef broth
- Salt and pepper to taste

Grease the skillet with oil and brown the meat slowly, turning often. Peel and slice the potatoes and onions. Put them in with the meat. Stir everything together and add broth. Season with salt and pepper. Cover. Cook slowly 1-1/2 hours or until meat is very tender. If heat is low, it can cook all afternoon. Serve with ketchup. Makes 6 servings.

Beef Stroganoff

Bon Vivant Room, Holiday Inn, Moorhead, Minnesota, in *Holiday Inn International Cook Book*, 1960s

- 3 pounds beef tenderloin tips
- 1/4 cup vegetable oil or butter
- 1/3 cup minced onion
- 1 cup sliced mushrooms
- 1/4 cup whiskey
- 1/2 cup diced dill pickle (optional)
- 2 cups sour cream, at room temperature
- 1/4 cup cognac or brandy
- Salt and pepper to taste

Cut beef into 1/2 inch cubes. Sauté the meat rapidly in oil, but do not overcook. Add the onions and mushrooms and cook until tender, then add whiskey. Cover and cook for 2 minutes. Add dill pickle and sour cream. Heat but do not let boil. Sprinkle cognac on top just before serving. Serve with hot rice. Makes 12 servings.

Peas Bonne Femme

Mrs. Duncan Hines in *Adventures in Good Eating*, 1953

- 2 tablespoons butter
- 2-1/2 cups frozen peas
- 2 cups shredded lettuce
- 1/4 cup chopped onion
- 1 teaspoon salt
- 1/4 teaspoon ground black pepper
- Pinch sweet basil, tarragon, or mint

Melt butter in saucepan; add peas and cook slowly until peas defrost. Add lettuce, onion, salt, and pepper. Add herbs to taste. Mix lightly, cover with a tight-fitting lid and let steam for 5 minutes. Serve at once. Makes 4 servings.

Savory Squash

Variety in Food with Foley, 1946

- 3 cups cooked mashed squash
- 2 tablespoons butter
- 1/2 cup minced onion
- 1/3 cup cream
- 1 teaspoon salt
- 1/8 teaspoon pepper

Bake squash; scoop squash from shell and mash. Melt butter in frying pan, add onion, cook until onion is lightly browned. Add cream and heat just to boiling. Beat in mashed squash, salt, and pepper. Turn into baking dish and bake at 375°F for 15 minutes. Makes 6 servings.

Lemon Velvet Ice Cream

From Otis Lodge, Sugar Lake, Grand Rapids in *Ford Treasury of Favorite Recipes*, 1963

- 2 cups heavy whipping cream
- 2 cups whole milk
- 2 cups sugar
- 1/3 cup fresh lemon juice (2 lemons)

Mix together whipping cream, milk, and sugar. Milk should be very cold. Then add lemon juice, stirring slowly. Mixture thickens as juice is added. Place in freezer container as this ice cream can be made with good results in a refrigerator freezer. Makes about 1-1/2 quarts.

Banana Cream Pie

Family Fare, U.S. Department of Agriculture recipes sent to Minnesota cooks by Senator Hubert H. Humphrey and Senator Eugene J. McCarthy in the 1960s

FOR THE CRUST:
- 15 graham crackers
- 1/3 cup melted butter
- 1/3 cup sugar
- 1/4 teaspoon cinnamon
- 1/4 teaspoon nutmeg

Roll crackers fine to make about 1-1/4 cups. Mix with other ingredients. Turn into a 9-inch pie pan and pat to form a smooth crust. Bake at 350°F 10 minutes. Chill.

FOR THE PIE:
- 1/2 cup sugar
- 1/2 teaspoon salt
- 3 tablespoons cornstarch
- 2 cups milk
- 2 egg yolks, slightly beaten
- 1 tablespoon butter
- 2 teaspoons vanilla
- 2 bananas
- Whipping cream (optional)

In a saucepan mix dry ingredients with a little of the milk. Add rest of the milk. Cook over medium heat, stirring until thick. Simmer 1 minute longer. Add a little of the hot mixture to egg yolks. Pour egg yolks back immediately into hot mixture and cook a few minutes more, stirring constantly. Remove from heat. Add butter and vanilla. Slice bananas into cooled pie crust. Pour filling into crust and chill thoroughly. Serve with whipped cream.

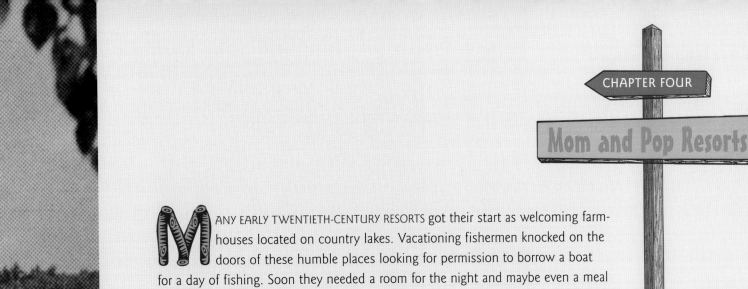

CHAPTER FOUR

Mom and Pop Resorts

MANY EARLY TWENTIETH-CENTURY RESORTS got their start as welcoming farm-houses located on country lakes. Vacationing fishermen knocked on the doors of these humble places looking for permission to borrow a boat for a day of fishing. Soon they needed a room for the night and maybe even a meal or two. All over the state farm families quickly caught on—their beaches were cool and breezy and their beautiful lakes full of big fish. They built a cabin or two away from the barn and many of the state's agricultural lands became the first "mom and pop" resorts.

When automobiles and inexpensive gas became plentiful in the 1920s, families piled into the four-door sedan and headed for a lake. Newly mobile vacationers on the lookout for small resorts spotted a hand-painted wood sign near the highway that pointed to a dirt road disappearing into leafy woods. They bumped along the winding trail to a modest house and a clutch of cottages beside a pretty lake.

Check-in buildings held a front desk and little else. But as time went on and the number of cabins increased, small lodges were built with recreation rooms smartly finished with patterned linoleum floors and woodsy pine walls. Nestled in a corner was a snack counter with stools for perching and the latest in amuse-ments for a rainy day.

Small resorts were made up of homey, whitewashed cottages or honey-hued log cabins. Fieldstones collected in wheelbarrows lined curving walks and horseshoe drives. Stretches of little cabins nestled along shorelines and cars filled with eager lodgers pulled up conveniently behind them. Ready for a boating getaway, rods and reels leaned against the buildings and tackle boxes hid under the steps.

Housekeeping cabins were the heart and soul of family resorts, and "house-keeping" meant cooking and cleaning the cabin yourself—barely a holiday for mom. But unloading the car, hanging up clothes, and settling in for a couple of weeks at a cozy place did feel like a vacation after all. Kids discovered talents for amusing themselves, dad went fishing, and mom began to unwind in a hammock with a book.

By the 1950s, resort cabins featured the look of the times. A-frame construction held sleeping lofts and modern designs boasted huge picture windows. Formica counters stretched between two-burner stoves and Cold Spot refrigerators, while sleek furnishings ambled throughout.

Small, family-run resorts reflected the determination and idiosyncrasies of their owners. Succeeding generations modernized while still maintaining the resorts' original personalities. But short seasons and high operating costs forced many small resort families to sell off their cottages to those who wanted to buy a cabin of their own. The genesis of Minnesota's resort industry, the charming, family-run resorts, are changing and many are disappearing with time.

◄ *Isle O' Dreams Lodge, Park Rapids*

MALMO BAY RESORT
Malmo, MINN. Phone 6-M-30

Checking in

Weary from a long trip, travelers arrived stiff and tired, but happy to be there. Resort owners were waiting by the door and it was time to check in, sign the register, and find the X on a map to the cabin. A key and the rules were handed over.

Camp Van Vac, Ely

Lien's Resort, Ottertail Lake, Richville

Smitty's Resort, Mille Lacs, 1950

BENNETTS'
LAKEVIEW RESORT - RICE LAKE
PAYNESVILLE, MINNESOTA 56362
The Kannenbergs and Stocks

1979 DECEMBER 1979

Bennetts' Lakeview Resort, Rice Lake, Paynesville, 1970s

Bonnie Lakes Farm, Cross Lake, 1940s

Lakeview Resort, Horseshoe Lake, Richmond

Coborn's, Detroit Lakes

Resort signs along the road alerted cars filled with tired passengers that their vacation was about to begin. A long and gently bumpy road led under a reassuring gateway—yes, this was the place.

Ping-Pong on the porch, Mud Lake

Recreation Room, Canadian Border Lodge, Ely

Cee-Ess-Ta Resort, Gull Lake Chain, Nisswa

Big Pine Resort, Big Pine Lake, Perham

Recreation Room, Beaver Dam Resort, Manhattan Beach, 1955

Library, Cool Ridge Resort, Big Sand Lake, Park Rapids

Common rooms at resorts were places to grab a soda and sandwich, play games, and make new friends. Even with the outdoors calling, finding the community television set was comforting—then everyone felt at home.

Evergreen Motor Court, Grand Rapids

Whitewashed cottages

With key and suitcase in hand, vacationers hiked past pleasant rows of cottages to find the right cabin number or clever identifying name hanging above the door. Whitewashed cottages in colorful trim were welcoming, and neat and tidy rooms appealed to returning lodgers like a familiar second home.

Peg's Resort, Nevis

Heading for the cabin

Hill Crest Inn, Ash Lake

Happy to be here

Vi-Lu Resort, Pequot Lakes

Those that say you can't take it with you never saw a car packed for a vacation trip.

ANONYMOUS

Fairyland Cottage, Detroit Lakes

Here at last! Everyone helped to unload the car and open the cabin windows to let in fresh air. Suitcases bursting with shorts and T-shirts were left on the floor while everyone claimed a favorite bed. Bags of groceries waited on the kitchen table as the cupboard was given the once-over and the icebox was filled. Wonder Bread went into the breadbox and everyone went out to explore.

Little cottages were the most common early vacation dwellings. They were cute and cozy places often reflecting the style of the owners who rented them out by the week. Sometimes a boat was included—oars were free, motors were extra.

Huddle's Resort, Leech Lake

Recreation room and boathouse, Thunder Lake Lodge, Remer, 1940

Twin Lakes Lodge, Menahga

Speck's North Shore Acres, Pequot

Log cabins

The architecture of vacation getaways changed in the early twentieth century. A natural aesthetic emerged to replace fanciful cottages in painted clapboard siding, and nothing represented Minnesota's northern landscape more than timber and rock. True log construction harkened back to the days of territorial pioneers when cabins were made from whole trees notched together at the corners.

Jester Farm Cottages, Bemidji

Miller Heights Resort, Mille Lacs

Camp du Nord, Ely

This idyllic roost perched above Burntside Lake was solidly anchored to shore with log pilings in the days before lake setback requirements existed.

Pine Crest Lodge, Blackduck

Horseshoe Lodge, Pine River

Northern Lights Resort, Lake Kabetogama, Ray

At many northern resorts, solid stacks of pine logs became walls, floors, and ceilings, and craggy twigs and branches became furnishings. Stockpiles of stone and rock emerged as the design focus in rustic fireplaces that completed the wilderness package.

Cabin Deluxe, Four Winds Resort, Lake Kabetogama, Ray

Leaning Elm Lodge, Sunset View Resort, Brevik

Becker's Log Cabin Camp, Big Fork

Tomteboda, Grand Marais

Real log cabins were less common at resorts and they were always popular and in demand. Distinctive corner details became creative design elements.

Point of Pines Resort, Lake Kabekona, La Porte, 1958

Cabins with log *siding* were quicker to build, easier to maintain, and had nearly as much charm as true log construction.

Kansas City Resort, Red Lake, Waskish

Resort names sometimes honored the origins of owners or loyal guests from other states who returned year after year. Real logs installed vertically were easy to put together as corner details were eliminated and logs could be smaller.

A quiet smoke by a quiet lake

Cool treats on a hot day

The quiet side of resort life was often the time most fondly remembered. Boating, biking, and badminton were active and fun, but relaxing with friends and family became treasured memories of summers at a friendly resort.

Can I back up a move?

Peace and tranquility in a Lawn chair

Cake walk on the beach

Vacation planning

Resort owners hired local print shops to design their brochures. Eye-catching graphics and bragging rights covered anything that might attract the attention of would-be vacationers.

MINNE-WA-KA LODGE

"ating water-lilies"

A Perfect Vacation In Minnesota

Lake Vermilion

PELICAN INN

Our locatio the Chippewa est betwe

CA LO

GRAND » Reso

CAMP IDLEWILD

MARCELL, ITASCA CO. MINNESOTA

ETROIT - MINNESOTA

Rooms with a view

Contemporary cabin design departed from the quaint and cozy cottages of the past but had its own appeal. Huge picture windows framed sweeping panoramas of the lake and provided the design focus for modern rooms. Simple furniture and minimal accessories did not compete for attention with the view.

Timberlane Lodge, Park Rapids

Swedmark Lodge, Bemidji

Eagle Nest Lodge, Big Cut Foot Sioux Lake, Deer River

Schule's Camp Bowstring, Bowstring Lake, Deer River

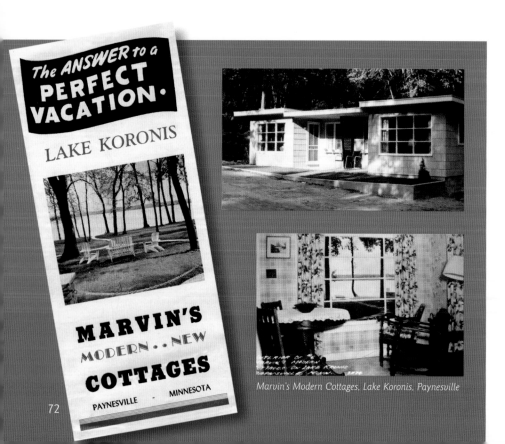

Marvin's Modern Cottages, Lake Koronis, Paynesville

If the view out the window wasn't enough, resort owners could bring nature inside with prints by artists like Minnesota's Les Kouba. His portrayal of deer, birds, fish, and native wildlife enlivened many cabin interiors.

Bayview A-frame cabin, Walker, 1949

Sarkipato Tourist Haven, Ely, 1930s

Wrapped in a knotty pine cocoon, these stalwart bunk beds were reminiscent of tight quarters in a ship's cabin.

Crescent Beach Resort, Big Wolf Lake, 1973

The term "cabin" originally meant a small and tidy room on a ship. Landlocked cabin bedrooms were small and tidy look-alikes. Weary vacationers entered these inner sanctums to collapse on soft springy beds covered with woolen blankets. Bare feet shuffled on wood floors and rag rugs warmed nighttime toes in these unpretentious quarters.

Sherwood Forest Lodge, Gull Lake, Brainerd

Fagan's Resort, Brainerd

Hudson Bay–style blankets provided color and warmth in many cabin bedrooms. Originally used for trade between French Canadian voyageurs and Native Americans, the distinctive wool stripes became coveted by tourists. Established in 1865, Faribault Woolen Mills is the country's oldest manufacturer still making blankets from their own wool.

Cabin kitchens

Cabin kitchens were basic but busy when the family gathered at mealtimes. A hearty breakfast sent fishermen off for the day, lunchtime featured energizing soups and sandwiches for the crowd on land, and if the catch wasn't good, it was ham and potato salad for dinner.

*Time you enjoy wasting
was not wasted.*

JOHN LENNON

Becker's Log Cabin Camp, Big Fork

Logs came right into the kitchen of this rustic cabin while the icebox sat outside on the porch.

Long Bow Resort, Walker

Bugbee Hive, Lake Koronis, Paynesville

Kennedy's Rustic Resort, Cook

Jones Resort, Lake of the Woods

A table under the window was almost a cabin requirement. Scampering squirrels, hesitant deer, and an occasional bear provided dining adventure never found back home.

Lodge lunch

When the weather forecast predicted rain, meals in the cabin became attention-getting events. Until the sun returned, children were kept busy cooking in the kitchen with kid-friendly recipes.

The following recipes have been adapted for easy preparation, modern cooking methods, and ingredients that are readily available.

Mugged Tomato Soup
From a recipe at Hodge Podge Lodge, 1950s

- 4 cups chicken broth
- 2 (10-ounce) cans tomato soup
- 1 teaspoon dried sweet basil
- 1 teaspoon ground coriander
- 2 teaspoons paprika
- 2 teaspoons curry powder
- 1 cup heavy whipping cream
- 1/2 tablespoon salt

Combine broth and soup in saucepan. Add basil, coriander, paprika, and curry powder. Heat to serving temperature. Meanwhile, whip cream with salt until stiff. Pour soup into mugs and top with a generous dollop of salted cream. Drink from the mug carefully—soup will stay very hot. Makes 5–6 servings.

Paul Revere Sandwiches
Red Owl Chicken Cook Book, 1970s

- 1 cup finely chopped cooked chicken
- 1/4 cup finely chopped onion
- 1/3 cup mayonnaise
- 1 teaspoon prepared mustard
- 1/4 teaspoon salt
- 1 can refrigerated biscuits (10 biscuits)
- 1 medium dill pickle, cut in 10 slices

Mix chicken, onion, mayonnaise, mustard, and salt. On floured surface, roll or pat each biscuit to a 4-inch circle. Place a heaping tablespoon of the meat mixture in center of each biscuit circle; top with pickle slice. Fold up all sides of biscuit and pinch edges together to seal. Place biscuits on lightly greased baking sheet; bake in 425°F oven till golden brown, about 10 minutes. Makes 10 sandwiches.

Tomato-Asparagus Cheese Sandwich
The Simplicity of Elegant Cooking, Dairy Council of the Twin Cities/WCCO Radio, 1950s

- Softened butter
- 1 slice bread, toasted
- 4 asparagus spears, precooked fresh or frozen or canned
- 2 tomato slices
- 1 slice American or Colby cheese

Generously butter the toasted bread. Top with asparagus, tomato, and cheese. Place on cookie sheet and set under pre-heated broiler for 5 minutes, or until cheese becomes bubbly. Makes 1 sandwich.

Log Cabin Baked Ham
Towle's Log Cabin Syrup and *Remember the Can,* Hormel, 1940s

- 5- to 6-pound fully cooked Hormel ham
- Whole cloves
- Towle's Log Cabin Syrup

Stud ham in patterns with cloves and spread maple syrup over the outside of the ham. Bake ham according to directions on label, basting frequently with the syrup. Slice thin for hot ham sandwiches or add ham slices to the Tomato-Asparagus Cheese Sandwich. Makes 20 servings.

Reuben Casserole
Minnesota's Greatest and Best Recipes: A University of Minnesota Cookbook, 1980s

- 1-3/4 cups sauerkraut, drained
- 1/2 pound corned beef, thinly sliced
- 2 cups shredded Swiss cheese
- 3 tablespoons Thousand Island dressing

- 2 tomatoes, thinly sliced
- 2 tablespoons butter

FOR TOPPING:
- 1 cup seasoned crumbled Rye Krisp
- 1/4 teaspoon caraway seeds
- 1/2 cup butter

Spread sauerkraut in 9x13-inch pan. Top with corned beef and then Swiss cheese, distributing evenly. Dab dressing on top of the cheese. Add tomato slices in a single layer. Dot tomatoes with butter. For topping, sauté Rye Krisp crumbs and caraway seeds in butter and spread on top of the layered ingredients. Bake at 375°F 30 to 40 minutes or until bubbling. Makes 4 to 6 servings. A favorite dish with the boys.

Cabin Potato Salad
From a recipe at Hodge Podge Lodge, 1950s

- 4 to 5 medium potatoes, boiled in jackets, peeled and cubed
- 3/4 cup creamy red French dressing
- 1 medium onion, diced
- 1 cup mayonnaise/salad dressing
- Salt and pepper to taste
- 1/4 cup chopped chives
- 1/4 cup chopped pimientos
- 4 hard-cooked eggs, peeled

In large bowl, pour French dressing over warm potatoes. Add onion; toss to combine. Cover and chill at least 2 hours. In separate bowl, mix the mayonnaise with salt, pepper, chives, and pimientos. Chop the eggs and add to potato mixture. Carefully add mayonnaise mixture, mixing gently. Chill 2 hours. Makes 8 servings.

Hot Fudge Pudding
Softasilk Cake Recipes, General Mills, 1950s

- 1 cup sifted Softasilk Cake Flour (or all-purpose flour)
- 2 teaspoons baking powder
- 1/4 teaspoon salt
- 3/4 cup sugar
- 2 tablespoons baking cocoa
- 1/2 cup milk

- 2 tablespoons melted shortening or oil
- 1 cup chopped nuts

FOR TOPPING:
- 1 cup packed brown sugar
- 1/4 cup baking cocoa
- 1-3/4 cups hot water
- Whipping cream

Preheat oven to 350°F. Sift flour, baking powder, salt, sugar, and 2 tablespoons cocoa together into bowl. Stir in milk and shortening. Blend in nuts. Spread in 9-inch square pan. Stir together brown sugar and cocoa. Sprinkle over batter, then pour hot water evenly over batter. Bake 45 minutes. During baking, cake mixture rises to top and chocolate sauce settles to bottom. Cut pudding into squares. Invert squares onto plates, dropping sauce from pan over portions. Serve warm with whipped cream. Makes 9 servings.

Dream Bars
King Midas Baking Queens Favorite Recipes, 1950s

FOR THE CRUST:
- 1-1/4 cups King Midas All-Purpose Flour
- 2 tablespoons brown sugar
- 1/2 cup butter, chilled

Combine flour and brown sugar in mixing bowl. Cut in butter until particles are the size of small peas. Pat into 9x13-inch pan. Bake 10 minutes at 350°F.

FOR THE FILLING:
- 2 eggs
- 1-1/2 cups brown sugar
- 1 teaspoon vanilla
- 1/2 cup flour
- 1 teaspoon baking powder
- 1/4 teaspoon salt
- 1-1/4 cups coconut

Combine all ingredients. Spread over baked crust; return to oven and bake 20 to 25 minutes longer. Let cool, then cut into bars. Makes 30 3x1-inch bars.

Fun for kids to make

CHAPTER FIVE

Making a Splash

ITH THE STATE SLOGAN, "the Land of 10,000 Lakes," it's natural to assume water recreation is a high priority with Minnesotans. Our ninety thousand miles of shoreline—more than in the states of California, Florida, and Hawaii combined—have been host to innumerable sand castles, water slides, diving platforms, water-skiers, floating rafts, and sunburned bodies.

Swimming and dock jumping were the earliest water activities. It was hard to do anything else in the late nineteenth century dressed in heavy wool swimsuits or short-sleeved dresses with knickers. As time progressed, hemlines shrunk along with the billowing fabric that made swimming difficult. Minnesota manufacturers responded to the changing styles by producing fashionable and less restrictive swimwear. Minneapolis Munsingwear even held a patent on elastic, formfitting suits in the 1920s.

Other Minnesota entrepreneurs took advantage of the receptive audience by inventing irresistible water toys. Multilevel diving platforms were piled high with waterlogged kids. Rickety wooden toboggan slides flung swimmers down a ramp into a thrilling ride over the water. And these popular contraptions were everywhere. A Faribault company shipped their amusement equipment to resorts complete with installation instructions. Fairie-Bow Water Sport Devices assured "profits for owners, thrills for bathers, and pleasure for spectators." Spring-action waterwheels and roller coaster–style slides offered exhilarating thrills but were not destined to last. The dangers were ever present and these daredevil amusements were taken down by the 1950s.

But other water thrills lurked nearby. In 1922, Ralph Samuelson of Lake City invented an entirely new form of recreation—water-skiing. His trials behind a speeding boat took the state by surprise and soon nearly every lake had water-skiers flying behind speedboats. The White Bear Water Ski Company was the first to manufacture pine boards that were turned up slightly on the front end. The craze swept the state and lake fun would forever be changed as water-skiing evolved from skimming the water with two boards to slalom-skiing on one ski, from multiple skiers behind one boat to multilevel pyramids of water nymphs in flashy multiboat ski shows. Minnesotans became truly amphibian.

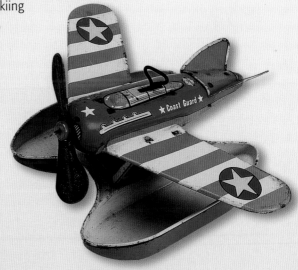

A Department of Natural Resources booklet on water safety sums up the state's love of water by saying: "Nearly every Minnesotan will be involved in some form of outdoor water recreation at one time or another." So go jump in the lake!

◄ Diving raft, Alexandria, 1943

Getting our feet wet

Swim costume, 1890

In the late 1800s, men dipped in the water wearing wool suits loosely fitted from neck to knee. But swimming was not socially acceptable for women because it showed bare skin and promoted exercise, both frowned upon by Victorian society. Plus, it was difficult to swim in restrictive beach costumes festooned with breezy streamers, sashes, ruffles, and bows. Pure silk fabrics in dark colors were rubberized to be waterproof and they shimmered in beautiful iridescent colors when wet. Floppy hats, wading shoes, and girdles completed the cumbersome ensemble.

Lake Lida, Pelican Rapids

Lake Emily, St. Peter, 1900

Beach costume, 1915

Young woman in bathing costume, 1925

Attitudes changed after World War I and suddenly it was in vogue for women to wade. The new water nymphs continued to wear bathing dresses in rubberized satin, but relaxed necklines and shorter skirts allowed more freedom of movement when wet. A stylish beach outfit included bloomers or pantalets with black wool stockings and beach shoes that laced up the leg. Topping it all off was a cloche-style hat, cape, belt, bag, and matching parasol.

Lake Nokomis, Minneapolis, 1914

Lifeguard, 1930

By the 1930s, frilly feminine frocks gave way to fitted suits reminiscent of the decades-old masculine tank. Now called swimming suits, they were shorter and leaner, exposing more skin to the sun and allowing swimmers smooth gliding through the water. As suits became scantier, the body was on parade, and it needed to look fit in clinging fabrics of printed silks, wool jersey, linen, even cashmere. Life at the beach would never be the same. Each decade saw inhibitions and suits decrease in size as beach and water activities increased in velocity. Elasticized knits revolutionized swimwear and pastimes such as water tobogganing, swimming, diving, and water-skiing were plunged into enthusiastically.

Leap frog, 1935

A bikini is the closest thing to a barbed-wire fence — it protects the property without obstructing any of the view.

MILTON BERLE

Munsingwear suimsuit ad, 1930s

Minneapolis apparel giant Munsingwear, known for "taking the itch out of underwear," also patented an elastic swimsuit that was advertised to be a perfect fit. Clingy and racy, swimsuit design entered a new era.

Fashion designers created all manner of imaginative and waterproof headgear. Plain rubber caps were covered with embossed shapes or printed in colorful, geometric designs. Dimensional floppy flowers in bright colors transformed a daring swimmer's head into a moving lily patch, while swirls of lace adorned more conservative women's heads.

Water slides and diving platforms

Water play became wildly popular by the 1930s. Swimmers had a variety of fun—and often dangerous—choices. Thrill-seekers toted wood toboggans up towering stairs to treetop-high toboggan slides, then flew down on bumpy rollers to sail across the water before finally slowing down and submerging. With low side railings, sliders sometimes fell off the slides before reaching the bottom, or crashed into other swimmers at the base. The hazardous slides survived for only a few exciting decades.

Calhoun Beach water slide, Minneapolis, 1925

Water toboggan, Wildwood, White Bear Lake, 1905

Shoot the chutes, Pleasant Point House, Shoreham

Children with wood water toboggan, White Bear Lake, 1903

Diving platform, Fairmont, 1922

Fairie-Bow Water Sport Devices

The Roc-a-Dive propelled divers into the air with rebound-spring bumper action. Fairie-Bow Water Sport Devices claimed their "absolutely safe" products would increase profit for resort owners and provide thrills for bathers and spectators alike. Manufactured in Faribault, these exhilarating amusements were shipped with a set of blueprints, but no liability insurance!

Diving tower, McCarron's Lake, 1929

Waterwheels and diving towers provided sport for summer crowds flocking to Minnesota lakes. Diving became a lively new competition and thousands climbed aboard homemade diving rafts or flocked to towering, tiered structures. Midair crashes and water collisions would eventually force most of them to disappear.

Water wheel, Detroit Lakes, 1950s
Spinning wheel, Detroit Lakes ►

Swimmers enjoyed slipping and sliding on the spinning wheel before being flung into the water.

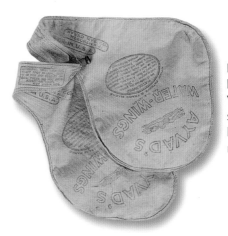

Early floatation devices like Ayvad's canvas Water-Wings were surprisingly effective in keeping a novice swimmer's head above water.

Water-skiing

The world of water sports changed forever on June 22, 1922, in the town of Lake City when Ralph Samuelson finally managed to rise up on the water's surface when pulled behind a boat going twenty miles per hour. A fan of snow skiing, eighteen-year-old Samuelson knew that with the right equipment he should be able to ride the waves. His friends pulled him on a variety of snow skis, barrel staves, and pine boards from the lumberyard. After many failed attempts, he bent the tips of two eight-foot-long by nine-inch-wide planks using a combination of steam heat and iron brackets. The crowd gathered on the shore gasped in awe as Samuelson, upright with his feet attached to the skis by leather straps, zig-zagged back and forth behind the boat.

Ralph Samuelson with flying boat, 1925

Eventually Samuelson perfected the skis and built greased jumps for water tricks and aerials. Faster and faster boats added to the thrills until he found his ultimate partner, a World War I Curtis flying boat. Samuelson took his show on the road, sharing his daredevil stunts with spectators and spreading the joy of his new sport.

Waves from Ski Antics performers, Gull Lake, 1953

Nisswa was home to a most adventurous group of water-skiers. Frank Beddor, who had set a world's record for skiing the length of the Mississippi River, organized a show in 1951 called Ski Antics. Performers mesmerized hundreds of viewers on Gull Lake with a skiing Paul Bunyan, jumps through leaping flames, and numerous other antics. "Ohs and ahs" echoed from the audience as skiers flew over jumps in perfect formation, rarely falling on landing. Ski Antics became the forerunner of Minneapolis's Aquatennial water-ski shows. Nor-Craft Marine in St. Paul manufactured ten different styles of water skis under the name Ski Antic.

Threesome at Detroit Lakes, 1950s

As a short-lived but successful cottage industry, White Bear Water Skis were made by Tom Weinhagen in the 1950s in his Bald Eagle Lake garage. Additional space was soon required and he found manufacturing facilities in White Bear Lake. The esteemed skis delighted fans throughout the state over the next twenty years.

Hit it!

Island View Lodge, Gull Lake, Brainerd, 1958

Hamilton Lodge, Long Lake, Park Rapids

Coming in for a landing, 1960s

Just once around the lake!

SKIING SIGNALS

FASTER

SLOWER

SPEED O.K.

RIGHT TURN

LEFT TURN

BACK TO DROP-OFF AREA

CUT MOTOR

STOP

AFTER FALL

PICK ME UP OR FALLEN SKIER—WATCH OUT!

Jet-Ski Corporation brochure, Grand Rapids, 1962

Grand Rapids sporting goods store owner Art Jetland manufactured water skis for the area's abundant lakes. The small family business survived for fifteen years.

83

Gotcha!

Swimming, splashing,
wading, floating, or
simply dangling feet off
the dock—these are the
irresistible lures of a
Minnesota vacation.

Football anyone?

Bathing beauties

Ouch!

Picnic on the beach

Beach activities and picnics went together like roasted hot dogs and toasted marshmallows. And then there were s'mores. Who could say more?

Lake Superior, 1960s

Lake O'Brien, 1960s

Child toasting a treat over a camp fire

Lake Calhoun swimmers eating toasted marshmallows, 1900

S'mores

Early Girl Scout Handbooks held the first written recipe for this famous campfire treat. In Girl-Scout-speak "gimmesomemore" became "s'more" and the rest is campfire history.

- Marshmallows—big ones
- Hershey milk chocolate bars
- Graham crackers
- Roaring campfire
- Green sticks with forked ends

READY: Break one large graham cracker into two squares. Place a piece of chocolate bar on one square.

SET: Put one or two marshmallows on the end of a stick and roast over the fire to a golden brown, or until the marshmallow catches on fire, at which time you must carefully blow it out.

GO!: Quickly place the hot marshmallow on the chocolate and squish down with the other graham cracker half.

CAREFUL: It's going to be hot and messy and you will want s'more.

Beach snacks

Lake activities could last all day. To keep energy high, water athletes and shore loungers alike filled up on creative snacks and clever cookies.

The following recipes have been adapted for easy preparation, modern cooking methods, and ingredients that are readily available.

Toaster Delights

Minnesota's Tonka Toaster is an example of a unique utensil designed for cooking food over campfires. Made of two pieces of heavy aluminum with long handles, it is similar to brands that may be called a pie iron, a sandwich cooker, or a pudgy pie maker.

- 2 slices white bread, buttered
- 1 slice Swiss or Cheddar cheese
- 1 thin slice onion
- A dab of mustard
- Softened butter

Heat the iron in medium coals. Make a cheese sandwich using the bread, cheese, onion, and mustard. Spread the outside of the sandwich generously with butter. Place in the pie iron/Tonka Toaster; close it and trim off the crusts. Cook 4 to 5 minutes over medium coals, turning occasionally. Repeat, making as many sandwiches as needed.

Or, make a dessert sandwich with 2 slices white bread and 2 tablespoons cherry or apple pie filling.

Saucy Dogs

Let's Eat Outdoors, Hormel, 1960s
- 1 cup dairy sour cream
- 2 tablespoons prepared mustard
- 1 tablespoon minced onion
- 1 teaspoon salt
- Dash pepper
- 1 teaspoon Worcestershire sauce
- 1 tablespoon lemon juice
- Dash Tabasco

- Grilled Hormel Hot Dogs
- Grill-toasted buns

Combine all top ingredients. Serve the sauce on grilled hot dogs in toasted buns.

Bread Twisters or Bayonet Bread

Cooking Out-of-Doors, Girls Scouts of the U.S.A., 1940s
- 3 cups flour
- 2 tablespoons baking powder
- 1/2 teaspoon salt
- 2 tablespoons shortening
- 1 to 1-1/2 cups water (to desired consistency)

Mix flour, baking powder, and salt. (If desired, seal dry ingredients in a bag to take along.) Cut in shortening using two forks. Add 1 cup water mixing to form a soft dough. Keep adding water a little at a time until right consistency. Pinch off a small portion of dough and, using floured hands, mold into a long patty. Wrap dough around the end of a peeled green stick in a spiral twist. Hold over hot coals (turning to bake evenly). Bread will bake quickly with a good bed of coals. The dough can also be wrapped around a grilled hot dog on a stick and then baked over hot coals.

Midnight Fudge

Favorite Recipes, Ginsburg's Grocery and Hubbard Milling Company, Mankato, 1940s
- 4 cups sugar
- 14-ounce can evaporated milk
- 1/2 cup butter
- 12-ounce package semisweet chocolate chips
- 8 ounces marshmallows, about 32
- 2 cups coarsely chopped walnuts

Combine sugar, milk, and butter in a large saucepan and cook over medium heat, stirring constantly until soft-ball stage 240°F on candy thermometer. Remove from heat. Add chocolate chips and marshmallows. Stir until blended. Stir in walnuts. Pour in greased 8- or 9-inch square pan. Cool and cut into squares.

Everybody's Chocolate Soda

Peanuts Cook Book, 1970
- 2 large scoops marble fudge or chocolate revel ice cream
- 2 to 3 tablespoons chocolate sauce or syrup
- 10 ounces club soda

Mix one scoop of ice cream with the chocolate sauce in bottom of tall glass. Fill with soda to 1 inch from the top. Stir gently and add final scoop of ice cream. Makes 1 serving.

Wheaties Ting-a-Lings

Betty Crocker's Good & Easy Cook Book, General Mills, 1954
- 12-ounce package semisweet chocolate chips or equal amount milk chocolate
- 4 cups Wheaties

Melt chocolate over hot water. Cool to room temperature. Stir in cereal until well coated. Drop with tablespoon onto waxed paper. Place in refrigerator until chocolate is set, dry and hard, about 2 hours. Makes 3 dozen. Variation: Use 4 cups Cheerios or Kix in place of Wheaties.

Potato Chip Cookies

Favorite Recipes by Rita Martin, International Milling Company, 1950s
- 3/4 cup shortening (such as Crisco)
- 2 cups brown sugar
- 1/3 cup milk
- 2 teaspoons vanilla
- 2 eggs, beaten
- 3 cups sifted Robin Hood All-Purpose Flour
- 1/2 teaspoon soda
- 1 cup crushed potato chips
- 1 cup chopped walnuts or pecans

Mix shortening, sugar, milk, and vanilla in large bowl. Add beaten eggs. Stir in flour and soda. Blend in potato chips and nuts. Drop teaspoonfuls on ungreased cookie sheet. Bake at 400°F 10 to 12 minutes. Makes 7 dozen cookies.

Salted Peanut Cookies

Reddy Kilowatt's Baking Guide, Home Service Department, Northern States Power Company, 1960s
- 1 cup shortening (Crisco or margarine)
- 2 cups brown sugar
- 2 eggs, beaten
- 2 cups flour
- 1 teaspoon baking soda
- 1 teaspoon baking powder
- 2 cups quick rolled oats
- 1 cup corn flakes or Wheaties
- 1 cup salted peanuts

Mix ingredients in order given. Drop dough from teaspoon onto greased baking sheet. Bake at 375°F 10 to 12 minutes or until brown. Makes 5 dozen.

Chocolate Refrigerator Cookies

Baking Secrets with Miss Minneapolis Flour, Minneapolis Milling Company, 1916
- 1/2 cup soft shortening (such as Crisco)
- 1 cup sugar
- 1 egg
- 1/4 cup milk
- 2 squares unsweetened baking chocolate, melted and cooled
- 1 cup sifted all-purpose flour
- 2 teaspoons baking powder
- 1/4 teaspoon salt
- 1 cup chopped walnuts

Mix shortening, sugar, egg, and milk thoroughly in large bowl. Stir in melted chocolate. In separate bowl, mix flour, baking powder, and salt. Stir flour mixture into chocolate mixture. Add nuts. Mix dough thoroughly with hands. Press and mold into a long, smooth roll about 2 inches in diameter. Wrap in waxed paper; chill several hours or overnight in electric refrigerator. Preheat oven to 375°F. Cut dough in thin slices (1/8-inch thick). Place slices a little apart on lightly greased baking sheet. Bake 8 to 10 minutes. Makes about 2 dozen.

Fun for kids to make

CHAPTER SIX

A Place of Our Own

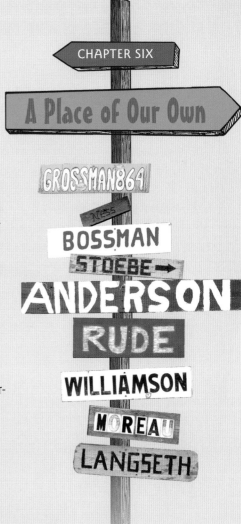

GROSSMAN864
Ness
BOSSMAN
STOEBE →
ANDERSON
RUDE
WILLIAMSON
MOREAU
LANGSETH

OWNING A SUMMER COTTAGE OR CABIN was a uniquely upper midwestern dream due to the availability of thousands of miles of shoreline that surrounded Minnesota's thousands of lakes. By the 1920s, affordable automobiles were plentiful, roads were improving, and a migration of would-be cabin owners headed out to survey lakeshore lots. In addition to the joy of having a cabin of their own, escape from stifling city heat and fear of illnesses such as polio and tuberculosis were further compelling reasons to pack up the family and find a place on a lake.

Idyllic shoreline lots awaited the arrival of cozy cottages and rustic cabins. Sandy beaches attracted swimmers, protected bays lured fishermen, expanses of open water provided boating space, and high rocky perches afforded spectacular views. Which to choose?

Families could easily build vacation lodgings with space to raise active kids in wholesome environments and to entertain friends on weekends. For people who needed a break from their workaday world, cabins nestled in birch and pine provided back-to-nature relaxation.

Early cottages and cabins were built for a summer stay. Although some were winterized, most cabins were not insulated, water pumps and picnic tables sat outside the kitchen door, and an outhouse hid in the woods out back.

Do-it-yourself design was the heart and charm of early lake cottages. Furnishings of family odds and ends sat in every corner, linoleum and rag rugs covered the floors, Betty Crocker giveaways filled kitchen drawers, and Gold Bond Stamp redemptions furnished the bedrooms. Antlers and wasp nests picked up in nearby woods provided cabin-kitsch decoration.

The sounds of summer included the unmistakable crunch of tires on gravel roads, screen doors slamming, dogs barking in the woods, and a cranky outboard motor next door. At night, tired sleepers on breezy porches welcomed the soothing songs of loons along with the whisper of waves rolling into shore—and the buzz of mosquitoes and flies.

Cabins became part of Minnesota culture. The pleasant task of opening up in the spring, airing out musty-smelling rooms, raking up soggy leaves, and putting in a weather-beaten dock never seemed a chore. Cabins held memories of long rainy days with chili simmering on the stove, or sunny days picking blueberries for the pie that would soon bubble over in the oven. Then came the inevitable sad, last look around and closing up for the winter.

Eventually, a short summer season wasn't enough. With the growing popularity of winter sports, summer cabins became winter escapes and potbellied stoves warmed up frosty skiers, snowshoers, and snowmobilers. The summer cottage would become a year-round hideaway.

◀ *Cabin on Moose Lake, Deer River*

Building a place of our own

Twin City manufacturers built cottages in packages, then shipped them off to be assembled on lakeshore lots. They were simple rectangles of compact efficiency—four rooms and a porch—that were ready for furnishing in a matter of weeks. The cottages were cute, sturdy, and inexpensive; their ample porches and cross-ventilation made life at the lake cool and comfortable.

Paul LaPlante Cabin, North Shore, *watercolor by Josephine Lutz Rollins, 1948*

Artists had a wealth of vacation subjects in Minnesota, and cabin owners who wanted artful summer memories for a wall in their winter home commissioned many oil and watercolor paintings.

The Book of Cabins, *1941*

MuniSaver Cottages & Garages

90

Cutting logs, 1936

Constructing a log cabin, 1890

Cabins made of hand-hewn logs took time to build. A summer's worth of chopping, peeling, planing, scribing, fitting, and chinking produced a woodsy retreat second to none. True log cabins were worth the effort—they lasted nearly forever and personified the quintessential Minnesota cabin.

Building the Powers' cabin, Orr, 1918

Setting the logs, 1941

Cabin among the northern pines

Clapboard cottages nestled comfortably on their plots, but log cabins looked as if they had branched out from deep in the forest.

Boathouses and outhouses

Once the cabin was up, attention turned outside to putting in docks and building boathouses, pergolas, and gazebos—all of which could be set up right on the water or at the water's edge.

Hazlett's cottage, Verndale

Building a boathouse, 1950

Boathouse and picnic pavilion in winter, 1909

Peg's Resort, Nevis

Putting in the dock, Whitefish Lake, 1967

Medayto Lagoon boathouse, Green Lake, Spicer

Relaxing on a dock bench or in a fanciful little pavilion
by the shore was reward enough at the end of the day.

Fountain Lake, Albert Lea, 1915

Lake Sylvia, South Haven, 1915

Lake Darling, Alexandria, 1913

Gull Lake pavilion, Camp Comfort, 1930s

Picnic dock, Tower

> *Buy land.*
> *They've stopped making it.*
> MARK TWAIN

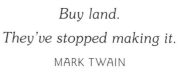

Outhouses were a necessity at early cabins and they sat far back
in the woods to protect the quality of lake water. Decades later
efficient septic systems allowed plumbing to move indoors.

Goofing off in the old outhouse, 1960

Outhouse in the winter—brr!

Watch out for wood ticks!

93

Clapboard cottages and rustic cabins

Early Minnesota lake cottages and woodsy cabins came in all sizes, shapes, and levels of splendor. They were inevitably expressions of both the family budget and personal taste and all had in common the charm and personality of their owners. Many were family-owned and family-loved, and passed down as cherished treasures from one generation to the next.

Cottage, Clearwater Lake

Cottage style prevailed in the early twentieth century. Neat and tidy white-washed cottages huddled on the ground, making little attempt to blend in with their environment, and everything hangable hung from nails hammered in exposed stud walls. In later years, lean-to additions held corner wall sinks and claw-footed tubs, maybe even a toilet. No frills here, just pieced quilts, rag rugs, and rocking chairs.

Cottage, White Bear Lake

Porch Picnic, Cedar Lake, Faribault, 1890s

Summer cottages were popular on Minnesota's southern lakes before railroads and cars took tourists west and north. Cottages shared shorelines with sheep and dairy cow pastures and rich cropland. Ample porches provided shade for picnics, gables kept out the rain, and clapboard siding was easy to paint. But farming and other industries soon took over southern Minnesota's fertile lands and many vacationers set out for other parts of the state.

Cabin exterior and interiors,
Whitefish Lake, 1960s

Real log and log-sided cabins became popular in the 1930s. Hiding in the pines, these structures mingled with the trees and forests around them. Made of natural materials gathered nearby, getaways of log and stone were the dream for many cabin owners and soon became a Minnesota icon. Warm knotty pine finished the walls, linoleum protected the floors, fieldstone fireplaces reached to the rafters, and furnishings were often "early attic, nicely refinished."

Camps and hideaways

Cabin camps and clubs attracted members with common interests: preserving and restoring natural habitat, climbing rocky cliffs along the North Shore, or maintaining lakes and woodlands for fishing and hunting. Friends and acquaintances joined together to buy property and build individual cabins along with a lodge or community center. Cabin communities were popular at the turn of the twentieth century and many survived in one form or another for future generations to enjoy.

Chinese pagoda on Star Island, Cass Lake

Star Island was a summer community dating from the early 1900s. This pagoda-style cabin stood out from a clearing in the forest.

Vermillion Trail Lodge, McComber, 1912

Lobby

Music room

Inspecting an iron ore outcrop

"Our happy band of pirates simply landed here in 1893 and took possession." A single cabin had been rented to a fishing group who later leased the land, then purchased it for the Vermillion Trail Lodge Club. Others joined the group and their interest soon focused on nature activities and social get-togethers, while fishing became a sideline.

Summer cabin at Lake Adney, Crow Wing County, 1964

As early as the 1930s, African American families from the Twin Cities formed a vacation community on the south shore of Lake Adney near Brainerd. Fishing occupied summer days on this bountiful lake and friends gathered on shore to visit alongside inviting clusters of painted cottages.

Beaver Bay, oil painting by artist Elof Wedin, 1935

Fifteen men paid $1,000 each in the 1920s for a sweeping point of land on Lake Superior. Beaver Bay Club members with names like Pillsbury, McMillan, and Loring found the abandoned lumber camp a perfect hideaway. Art and antiques were abundant as old lumberjack snuff bottles and ancient Indian artifacts were waiting to be unearthed from the ruins, and artists of the era painted scenes of the rugged terrain.

Encampment Forest entrance gate, North Shore

Encampment Forest started as a remote summer colony along a meandering Lake Superior shoreline. Families stayed for the summer season and husbands commuted on weekends, often by train to Duluth, where they kept automobiles or were collected by family members at the station. Encampment Forest owners embraced architectural diversity to pay tribute to the beautiful lakeshore that they occupied even during the snowy winter.

Tettegouche Camp, Mic Mac Lake,
near Lake Superior, Silver Bay

A Minnesota logging company sold its cleared land along with rustic buildings to a group of Duluth businessmen. They named their new retreat the Tettegouche Club and moved into sturdy cabins that took advantage of wide-ranging hiking and fishing grounds. Pine forests slowly returned to the spectacular landscape and today the land remains rich in lakes and waterfalls, scenic overlooks and rocky trails. Tettegouche is now a state park.

Edwin Lundie's cabin nearing completion, North Shore, 1940s

Architect Edwin Lundie first experimented with cabin design on his own cabin on the North Shore. Four huge corner posts that he named Mathew, Mark, Luke, and John anchored the efficient one-room log structure. Lundie carved Mathew and Mark himself. Decades later, a respectful new owner commissioned carvings for Luke and John in the same style as their fellow disciples. Minnesotans loved Lundie's Scandinavian-inspired designs and he was long admired on the North Shore for his many interesting cabins and his famed lodge at Lutsen Resort.

Sigurd Olson standing outside his log cabin, 1960
Open Horizons, by Sigurd Olson, cover illustration by Les Kouba.

Sigurd Olson, author, educator, and wilderness advocate, sought out an authentic Finnish log building for his cabin. Once he found it, Olson took the precisely fitted logs apart one by one and rebuilt the cabin on a rocky point by Burntside Lake near Ely. While at Listening Point, the name he gave the cabin and surrounding rugged lakeshore, Olson wrote many books on nature and conservation and became widely known and admired.

Jun Fujita Cabin, Rainy Lake

Noted Chicago photographer Jun Fujita built his cabin retreat on an island in Rainy Lake. Rocks and stones formed a foundation that integrated with the environment. The peaceful cabin with a Japanese shrine provided Fujita with a seriously remote getaway from his demanding career in the Windy City.

Minnesota's famous gangsters also needed their vacation getaways. Daniel "Dapper Dan" Hogan (left), St. Paul's underworld czar, relaxes at his Big Bass Lake cabin west of Bemidji with his wife, Leila, and father-in-law, Fremont Hardy.

*Chores around the cabin
came first, then play
and relaxation took up
the rest of the day.*

Finally, heat for the winter!

Did you remember the clothespins?

Did we catch any minnows?

Do I have to mow the whole yard?

Bandanna parade

A bite in a hammock

Panoramic view

Picking bittersweet

Rainy-day recreation

Rainy days could be interesting even for families cooped up in a cabin. A surprisingly large number of toy and game companies developed their amusements in Minnesota and they really knew how to keep kids entertained. Names like Tonka, Gopher, and Lakeside reflected their northern origins and were recognized worldwide for clever fun. National magazines created by local writers amused readers of all ages for hours while adults settled in with a good novel by local authors Sinclair Lewis or F. Scott Fitzgerald.

3M made intriguing games for only a few years, then they went back to sticking with what they did best.

In 1916, John Lloyd Wright, the son of architect Frank Lloyd Wright, invented a line of sturdy interlocking logs for building toy cabins. The avant-garde sets were an instant success with children who loved the creativity, and with educators who encouraged the constructive learning. Building a cabin of Lincoln Logs, inside a real cabin of logs, made a rainy day short.

William Schaper was a postal carrier—and an avid Minnesota angler—who carved little wooden cootie bugs and gave them to children along his mail route. Based on that early whittling, he invented the game of Cootie. It was introduced in 1949 at Dayton's Department Store and became an overnight success that lasted for decades. Schaper invented other children's games, many of which included bug and insect themes. The W. H. Schaper Manufacturing Company eventually sold more than twenty-five different popular games nationwide.

Hormel offered SPAM can radios—perfect for listening to the Beatles on a local AM radio station.

Breezy Point Resort's owner Billy Fawcett published a variety of national magazines in the twenties and thirties and they were perfect for passing the time on a rainy day. *Willie the Worm* was good clean fun for kids, but adults hid the risqué *Capt. Billy's Whiz Bang.*

Towle's Log Cabin Syrup, made in Minnesota, came in tins showing a variety of cabin activities. Once emptied, the containers became toys.

Laughter is an instant vacation.

MILTON BERLE

Humor lifted the mood in cottages and cabins. Goofy souvenirs found their way into bedrooms and bathrooms alike—and everyone smiled at the joke year after year!

Cabin kitsch

Cabin furnishings were the original "cabin kitsch" and local products often illustrated the style. Talented cottage owners with time on their hands sewed, embroidered, weaved, or made playful lamps and whimsical furniture from found objects. All were ready to survive the rough-and-tumble lake crowd.

Lake O'Brien, Cross Lake

Carpenters found their vacation imaginations in high gear and made furnishings out of just about anything lying around.

Minnesota companies gave cabin-bound sewers creative projects to keep hands busy. Flour sacks were printed with doll patterns to cut and sew or the sacks themselves became linens for the cabin. Free needle kits were all a seamstress needed to finish the job.

Printed satin pillows were glitzy souvenirs even in the 1940s.

National stamp companies and stamp redemption centers abounded in Minnesota and cabins benefitted with furnishings, sportswear, and appliances purchased with savings stamps.

Minnesotan Curt Carlson founded the Gold Bond Stamp Company in 1938. Customers purchased merchandise and received stamps that they saved to redeem products in catalogs. Carlson turned his highly successful stamp business into the even more successful Carlson Companies.

Wild Wings cabin, Leech Lake, Walker

Minnesota Stoneware Company and Red Wing Pottery provided cabin cooks with cheerful tableware and robust kitchenware that have been American favorites for decades. Company artists designed artful hand-painted tableware and cabin-perfect crockery.

Cabin furnishings were the perfect use for product give-a-ways. Linens, china, and tableware were often packed inside food packages. The Queen Bess pattern was so popular that General Mills became the largest silverwear distributor in the world during the 1950s.

Winter wonderland

Cabins that had heat, wood-burning stoves, or fireplaces warmed up fast when owners arrived to play in the snow. Naturally, Minnesota manufacturers produced some of the country's best equipment for an exhilarating season of skiing, snowshoeing, snowmobiling—and rosy cheeks.

Young women at a winter cabin, 1927

Vigorous Health *and a* Million Thrills

J. G. SCHMIDT

Manufacturer of

Toboggans *and* Skis

TERMS   CASH

Established 1886

Corner Minnehaha Street and Virginia Ave.
TAKE Como-Hopkins Como-Harriet CAR FROM St. Paul or Minneapolis to cor. Como and Virginia Avenue.
Tri-state or Twin City Phone 4692

J. G. Schmidt, Toboggans and Skis, St. Paul

Northland Skis

TOBOGGANS
SNOW SHOES
HOCKEY STICKS

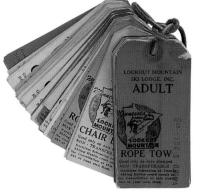

Northland Imported Skiing Boot

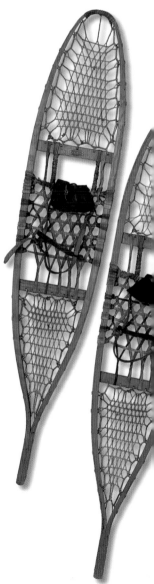

Norwegian C. W. Lund started the Northland Ski Company in 1911 in St. Paul. It quickly became one of the largest winter sports equipment makers in the world. Lund was an avid advocate of winter activity as a tonic for good health and championed his products for maintaining vigor and vitality, as a cure for ills, and as the cheapest insurance against early old age. He also made some of the most graceful and durable sports equipment of its time.

Popular interest in snowshoeing began with America's first club formed at the St. Paul Winter Carnival in 1886. Northland's snowshoes were designed by Walter F. Tubbs—"the world's most famous snow shoe maker."

Since the days of Henry Ford's Model T, cold weather enthusiasts have tried to motorize snow sleds. Most machines were amusing to look at, clumsy to maneuver, but thrilling to drive. Several snowmobile manufacturers began in Minnesota. They grew to dominate the winter pastime across the northern tier, and Minnesota's more than 20,000 miles of snowmobile trails are a tribute to their popularity. Born in Waverly, Hubert H. Humphrey claimed central Minnesota was "the snowmobiling capitol of the world."

Snowmobile on the Mississippi River to Hastings, 1910

Handmade with surplus engines, airplane propellers, and scrap wood, early snowmobiles scrambled over snow for wintry adventures.

1968 Polaris Mustang with sled

Northern Minnesota's winters are legendary, so it isn't too surprising that three Roseau men introduced the first commercial snowmobiles to the awaiting public. Polaris Industries unveiled their first model in 1955 and have thrived in the outdoor recreation business through innovation and leadership.

The Thief River Falls company Arctic Cat began in 1961 and is one of the country's premier recreational vehicle manufacturers.

Propeller-driven air sleds were made by Trail-A-Sled for Polaris in Crosby beginning in 1959. This 1963 model featured a two-seat sled capable of speeds up to a hundred miles per hour.

When Trail-A-Sled patented a continuous rubber track for their Scorpion, they revolutionized the snowmobile industry. Eileen Harrison, wife of Trail-A-Sled cofounder Richard Harrison, posed on a 1967 Scorpion for a company brochure.

Cabin cooking

Cooking at the cabin was a lot more fun than cooking at home. Comfort food was the rule because it was easy to prepare and really did taste the best, be it a summer salad, cool and fresh, or crispy chicken turning on a grill, or maybe a hearty Minnesota hot dish. Everyone gathered merrily around a sturdy kitchen table or down by the lake at a weather-worn picnic table—and it was a lot more fun than eating at home.

Shucking corn at Whitefish Lake

Kitchen at Wild Wings, Leech Lake, Walker

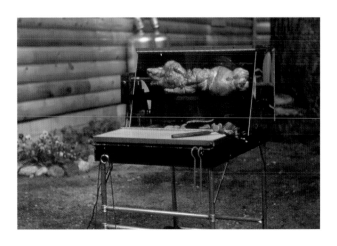

Dining room, Manhattan Beach

My idea of a seven-course dinner is a hot dog and a six-pack.

HENNY YOUNGMAN

Good times, Cross Lake

106

Cabin cooking

Easy one-pot meals were a goal for cooking at the cabin. But green bean hot dish alongside crispy chicken could bring raves from the troops as well. Here are the cabin classics.

The following recipes have been adapted for easy preparation, modern cooking methods, and ingredients that are readily available.

Chicken Noodle Soup

Tried & True Money-Saving Meals,
Creamette & Borden's, 1980s

- 1 cup chopped celery
- 1 cup chopped onion
- 1/4 cup margarine or butter
- 3 to 4 cups diced cooked chicken or turkey
- 9 cups chicken broth
- 1 cup diced carrots
- 1/2 teaspoon dried marjoram leaves
- 1/2 teaspoon pepper
- 1 bay leaf
- 8 ounces Creamette Egg Noodles
- 1 tablespoon chopped parsley, optional

In large Dutch oven, cook celery and onion in margarine until tender. Add chicken or turkey, broth, carrots, marjoram, pepper, and bay leaf. Bring to a boil. Reduce heat; simmer covered 30 minutes. Remove bay leaf. Add noodles and cook 10 minutes longer, until noodles are tender, stirring occasionally. Serve hot topped with minced parsley. Makes 12 to 15 servings. Refrigerate leftovers immediately.

Strawberry "Moose" ◼◣

With Old Home Creameries and Nordic Ware, 1950s

- 1 cup boiling water
- 1 (3-ounce) package strawberry-flavored gelatin
- 1 cup cold orange juice
- 1 banana, chopped
- 8 strawberries, chopped
- Old Home cottage cheese or whipped cream

Stir boiling water into gelatin in medium bowl for 2 minutes, until completely dissolved. Stir in orange juice. Stir in bananas and strawberries. Pour into 4-cup serving container or individual Nordic Ware molds coated with cooking spray. Refrigerate 4 hours or until firm. Serve as salad with a side of cottage cheese, or as dessert with whipped cream.

Babe's Green Bean Hot Dish ◼◣

Green Giant, 1960s

- 2 cans Green Giant French-style green beans, drained
- 1 can cream of mushroom soup
- 1/4 cup milk
- 1 teaspoon soy sauce or Worcestershire sauce
- 3/4 cup canned or sliced fresh mushrooms
- 1 can French-fried onions

Combine all ingredients except onions in 1-1/2 quart casserole or glass baking dish. Bake at 350°F for 30 minutes or until bubbly. Top with onions during last 5 minutes of baking. Makes 8 servings.

Crispy Chicken ◼◣

Festive Food Favorites from Minnegasco, Minneapolis Gas Company, 1930s

- 2 cups finely crushed cheese crackers, corn chips, or potato chips
- 1/2 teaspoon garlic or onion salt
- 3-pound broiler-fryer chicken, cut up (or 4 chicken breast halves)
- 1/2 cup butter or margarine, melted

Combine crushed crumbs and garlic or onion salt. Dip chicken pieces in melted butter and roll in chips. Place skin side up in shallow pan spacing chicken so pieces do not touch. Bake in a gas oven at 425°F for 30 minutes, or until juices run clear. Makes 4 servings.

Paul Bunyan's Hot Dish ◼◣

Tried & True Ideas from Creamette and Borden's, 1980s. Creamette called a similar dish "Manhattan Casserole," but midwestern cooks know it as the quintessential "Minnesota hot dish" and a Paul Bunyan favorite at that!

- 1 pound ground beef
- 2 tablespoons butter or margarine
- 3/4 cup chopped onions
- 2 cloves garlic, finely chopped (add only if made in Manhattan)
- 1/2 cup finely chopped red pepper or pimiento
- 1/2 cup finely chopped green pepper
- 1-1/2 cups sliced mushrooms
- 1 15-ounce can diced tomatoes
- 1 8-ounce can tomato sauce
- Salt and pepper to taste
- 2 cups, or 7-ounce package uncooked Creamette Elbow Macaroni
- 1 cup cottage cheese
- 1-1/2 cups shredded cheddar cheese

Brown the ground beef in butter in a heavy skillet. Add onions, garlic, red and green pepper, and mushrooms. Cook and stir until tender. Combine tomatoes, tomato sauce, salt, and pepper with ground beef mixture. Simmer covered 15 minutes. Cook macaroni in salted water until done, drain. In a buttered 3-quart casserole or 13x9-inch dish, layer cooked macaroni, meat mixture, cottage cheese, and cheddar cheese. Bake uncovered in 350°F oven 30 minutes or until hot. Makes 6 generous servings.

Beef Birds with Vegetables

Home Packing and Preserving the Red Wing Way, Red Wing Union Stoneware Company, Red Wing, 1940s

- 1-1/2 pounds flank steak
- 1 cup dry bread crumbs
- 1 small onion, chopped fine
- 1 tablespoon chopped parsley
- 1 teaspoon salt
- 1/2 teaspoon rubbed sage
- 4 tablespoons melted bacon drippings or oil, divided
- 1 egg, beaten
- String for tying birds
- Salt, pepper, and flour to coat birds
- 1/3 cup boiling water or beef bouillon
- Small whole onions
- Diced carrots
- Green beans

Cut steak into 5 portions; sprinkle lightly with salt and pepper. In large bowl, mix crumbs, onion, parsley, salt, sage, 2 tablespoons of melted drippings, and egg; if mixture is dry, stir in a little hot tap water to moisten. Spread 1/5 of this dressing in center of each piece of steak and roll up, fasting securely with string. Melt remaining drippings in heavy skillet. Sprinkle beef birds with salt, pepper, and flour. Brown birds in hot drippings. Place in a stoneware casserole. Add the boiling water; cover casserole closely and cook in a 350°F oven about 30 minutes. Meanwhile, parboil onions, carrots, and beans 10 minutes. Surround beef birds with vegetables. Cover casserole and cook 30 more minutes, or until meat is tender. Makes 5 servings.

Cottage Pudding ◼◣

Gold Medal Flour, 1904

- 1-3/4 cups Gold Medal Flour
- 3/4 cup sugar
- 2 teaspoons baking powder
- 1/2 teaspoon salt
- 1/4 cup soft shortening (such as Crisco)
- 1 egg
- 3/4 cup milk
- 1 teaspoon vanilla
- Sweetened blueberries or sliced strawberries
- Lemon sauce or whipped cream

Stir flour, sugar, baking powder, and salt together in mixing bowl. Cut in shortening until mixture looks like fine crumbs. Stir in egg, milk, and vanilla; beat until smooth. Bake in greased and floured 8-inch square pan at 350°F for 25 to 30 minutes. Cut into 9 squares. Serve warm topped with fruit and lemon sauce or whipped cream.

Fun for kids to make ◼◣

107

CHAPTER SEVEN

Fish Stories

A T THE TURN OF THE TWENTIETH CENTURY, fishermen boarded city streetcars toting fishing poles, buckets, bait, and a sandwich. They headed for Lakes Calhoun or Como and on longer summer days they rode the rails out to Lake Minnetonka or White Bear Lake. On the trip home, other passengers on the streetcar had no doubt as to the success of the fishing trip and the fisherman's family enjoyed a fresh fish dinner that night.

As roadways improved, anglers in search of big catches traveled farther out from the cities. At farmhouses located by lakes they rented rooms and a boat or pitched a tent and camped with friends. Fishing camps and fishing resorts quickly grew to meet the demand of an increasingly popular pastime and rapidly growing sport.

There were a lot of fish in Minnesota rivers and lakes in those early days. The daily catch might be a packed stringer of fish as wide as a cabin. Some fish were as tall as a young boy and there seemed to be no end of good fishing spots. There are more photographs of people proudly holding "the big catch" than nearly any other Minnesota vacation snapshot.

With more fishing licenses per capita than any other state, Minnesota rewarded its anglers with their choice of more than 150 species of fish, almost 6,000 well-stocked lakes, and 15,000 miles of fishable streams.

All those fish needed to be lured by something eye-catching. Minnesota companies grew like tadpoles to accommodate clamoring fishermen looking for new ways to trick a fish. Flies, plugs, spinners, and spoons, tackle boxes and creels, boats and motors all emerged from the warehouses of local manufacturers.

Fishermen shoved off for the day, alone in a boat or with a group of friends along with bag lunches and freshly stocked tackle boxes. Oars squeaked and lures hit the water with a splash—and the bass were hungry! It was easy listening to the drone of a trolling motor and the sound of water slapping against a wood boat or the whiz of a well-placed cast. Whiffs of gas and oil in the outboard, smells of fresh lake water, and the anticipation of the big fish tickled the senses.

Fishing and hunting resorts made recreation effortless by providing meals and accommodations, boats and expert guides. Fishing parties set out to find the best spots and enjoy a day of sunshine, camaraderie, cold beer, and a fish-fry shore lunch. Bringing in the catch and packing it under sawdust at the icehouse completed the day and Minnesota "fish stories" became legends around the evening campfire.

◀ *Preparing fishing equipment, Sherwood Forest Lodge, Lake Margaret, Nisswa, 1945*

All those fish!

Fishing comes in many forms, from casting for trout on a lazy river to setting the jiggle stick over an ice hole and waiting for the bobber to bob. Anglers go where they like it best—walking down a path with a cane pole and a can of worms or arriving by seaplane for a first-class fishing experience.

Trout fishing, Straight River, Park Rapids, 1955

Fishing from a seaplane, 1945

Smelt fishing, Lake Superior

Catch at Long Lake

Fishing pier, Lake Pepin, Lake City, 1980

Family Fishing Guide, Northwestern Banks, 1969

A big fish is a true trophy and these lunkers were Minnesota's finest in 1969. Twin Citians heading for outdoor activities watched the famous "Weatherball" signs atop Northwestern Bank buildings. From 1949 to 1982, colors on the flashing ball indicated the U.S. Weather Bureau forecast and everyone knew the famous jingle:

When the weatherball is red, warmer weather is ahead.
When the weatherball is white, colder weather is in sight.
When the weatherball is green, no change in weather is foreseen.
If colors blink by night or day, precipitation's on the way.

Boys returning with their catch, 1940

Catch of northerns and walleyes, Basswood Lake, Ely

Minnesota sporting goods stores published catalogs full of fishing equipment in the 1930s that provided hours of armchair fishing fun.

Walleye is the official state fish, and rightly so due to the abundant quantity and popular mild flavor. For sheer numbers (and the amounts are in the millions), the most-caught fish in the state are panfish, walleye, and northern pike.

The earliest setup for luring and spearing fish in the winter was a hole in the ice with a blanket tucked tightly over a fisherman's head, making it dark enough to see the fish. Then came tar-paper fishhouses that darkened the area and provided a modicum of warmth, but these primitive shacks soon grew into sanctuaries of creativity and comfort that included spaces for the latest in ice fishing technology. Playful amateur architects began a lively competition for fishhouse design and together they gathered into colorful shantytowns of fanciful shapes and sizes.

Fifty-one pound muskie, Smokey Point Lodge, Walker, 1940s

Ice fishing from an automobile, 1935

Winter anglers simply dropped a line through a hole chopped in the ice, sat comfortably on the running board, and waited for a tug on the line.

Fishhouses, oil painting by Cameron Booth, 1923

Ice fishing contest, St. Paul Winter Carnival, 1955

Fishing camps

"Live where the fish are biting" was the message from Pete's Cabin Boats at Ely where, in fact, you lived right on top of the fish. Many resorts and private lodges were camps dedicated solely to fishing— no water slides or shuffleboard allowed.

Izaak Walton Lodge, Mora, 1930

Sir Izaak Walton was a seventeenth-century English sportsman and author of a popular book *The Compleat Angler.* Izaak Walton Lodges were formed in 1922 by a group of anglers to combat water pollution. The Lodge fishing clubs attracted thousands of "defenders of the soil, air, woods, water, and wildlife" and concentrated on promoting clean water and angling ethics nationwide. In 1923 the Lodge helped stop plans to build a road to every lake in the Boundary Waters in order to preserve the vast, remote fishing wilderness.

Basswood Fishing Lodge, Ely, 1931

Johnson Resort fish house, Lake Kabetogama, Ray

Cline's, Lake Kabetogama

Bunkbeds in Pete's Cabin Boats

Guides who knew the best spots out on the big lakes ran fishing party boats. They took care of everyone's needs on board, kept out of the way of other boats, and still made sure that their anglers could brag at the end of the day.

Denny's Resort, Bena

Twin Pines Resort, Mille Lacs, Garrison

Fishing launch, Oak Island Resort, Warroad, 1955

Heading for pike grounds, Mille Lacs, 1925

Anglers enjoyed the whole fishing experience: selecting companions and resort outfitters, shopping for gear, getting there, swapping yarns with fellow anglers—even actually fishing! Groups of men, or "fishing parties" as they were called by guides, concentrated on angling techniques and wagered on who would catch the first, the biggest, and the most fish. It was simply about being there.

What did the fish say when he hit a concrete wall? Dam.
GARRISON KEILLOR

Men fishing, Sherwood Forest Lodge, Lake Margaret

..GREETINGS.. FROM

EVEN A FISH WOULDN'T GET INTO TROUBLE IF HE KEPT HIS MOUTH SHUT

Fishing party at Sherwood Forest Lodge, Lake Margaret, 1944

Well taken care of, this group enjoyed comfortable lodging, modern boats, excellent guide service, and very fresh fish dinners prepared by cooks who knew big outdoor appetites.

Cline's Minnows, Hackensack, 1970s

Kirk's Resort, Lake Winnibigoshish, Cass Lake

New Lakeside Inn, Mille Lacs, Onamia

Huddle's, Leech Lake

"The big catch"

At the height of the big fish catches, there were no fishing licenses, no fishing limits, and the catch of the day could feed an army. Anglers thought the fish supply was endless—but times changed, limits were established, and although the catch was downsized, the pride of the fisherman was not.

Roseau Lake, 1915

String of bass, Osakis

Studio portrait with muskie and bass, Stillwater, 1910

Fishermen proud of their efforts often hauled their fish straight into a photography studio to record the daily catch. John Runk's photo studio received these men still in their fishing clothes—suits and neckties.

Return train trip, Leech Lake, 1896

Round Lake, 1934

Kamberling's Resort, Crow Wing County, 1929

Stringer of fish, Okabeno Lake, Worthington, 1905

Hunters display prairie chickens on their car, 1920

Larson's Hunters Resort, Lake Valley Township

Fishing and hunting seasons overlapped in the spring and fall. Originally the limits on game were the same as for fish—no limit at all. Sportsmen posed proudly with their booty in an era of wildlife plenty unmindful of any reaction other than envy.

At the turn of the twentieth century railroads sponsored hunting trips to western Minnesota. The area was abundant in prairie chickens, ducks, geese, grouse, and other game birds. Farmers hired out their houses and land, provided boats, and served as guides. Larson's Hunters Resort opened with fourteen rooms that included eight bedrooms, lounges, and a dining room, as well as an additional five cabins. The family also lived in the house and provided breakfast, bag lunches, and dinner for up to sixty hunters at a time. Larson's was a typical farmer-resort business at the time that operated for hunters and fishermen from around the state.

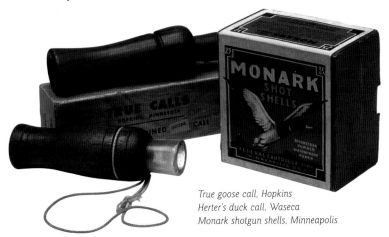

True goose call, Hopkins
Herter's duck call, Waseca
Monark shotgun shells, Minneapolis

Drake merganser with moose hair, Swede Larson, Bloomington
Drake mallard, Don Branscom, Bloomington
Hen mallard, Don Branscom, Bloomington
Drake mallard, K. D. Drake Manufacturing, St. Paul
Hen mallard, K. D. Drake Manufacturing, St. Paul

Duck decoys have bobbed alluringly in the water for thousands of years. Native Americans across North America made bird decoys from reeds, grasses, feathers, and rushes that fooled even the most sharp-eyed birds flying overhead. When carved wooden decoys became popular in the nineteenth century, they unwittingly became more than just an appealing lure from hunters—they are considered a quintessential American art form and are highly collectible as folk art sculptures.

Guide and duck hunter, Huron Lake, 1900

Comic vacation postcards

Postcards have tempted tourists at attention-getting racks in resort lobbies, corner drugstores, and sightseeing locations for more than a hundred years. Picture-perfect scenery and flawless vacation scenes validated vacation messages sent back home. Wish you were here? You bet they did!

Struggles with the big fish was one of the most common subjects on comic postcards. Brightly colored cartoons humored anglers with drawings of exaggerated fish—or the big ones that got away!

Fishing strictly Minnesotan

Even before the 1900s, Minnesota companies made it their business to tackle the interests of anglers. The extent of products made to attract fishermen—and fish—grew to muskie proportions. From tiny trout flies, sinkers, and shear pins, to minnow buckets, tackle boxes, and landing nets—products made for the sport of fishing became a sizeable and illustrious industry in Minnesota.

*Gift box,
Paul Bunyon Bait Co., Minneapolis*

Leader Spinner, Strike Master, Inc., Minneapolis
Little Joe Pike Spinner, Mille Lacs Mfg. Co., Isle
Prescott Spinner, Mankato

Bobbers

*Horsefly,
Natural Fly Co.*

*Horseflies,
Brainerd Bait
Co., Brainerd*

*Fish Trap,
Larsen Bait Co.,
Aitkin*

*Spoon,
Larsen Bait Co., Aitkin*

*Ruby Spoon,
Paul Bunyan Bait Co.,
Minneapolis*

*Doctor Spoon,
10,000 Lakes, St. Paul*

*Gold Cap Dodger,
Brainerd Bait Co., Brainerd*

*W. R. Burkhard reel,
St. Paul*

*Swimmin' Pippin,
DeCoursey Mfg., Minneapolis*

*Bass Charmer,
Taylor Mfg.,
Minneapolis*

*Underwater Minnow,
Marshall Wells
Hardware, Duluth*

*Fisheretto,
Brown Bros.,
Osakis*

*Baby Bird,
handmade*

Handmades

*Dubl-Pop,
Lucky Day
Bait Co.,
Long Lake*

*Blooy Looy,
Hep Bait Co.,
Minneapolis*

Pike Minnow, Herter's, Waseca

Water Gremlin dipsey
swivel sinker box,
White Bear Lake

The "Cedar" Minnow,
Powers Merc. Co.,
Minneapolis

The Viking Frog,
Oscar Christiansen,
St. Paul

Mice

Halik Jr. Frog,
Moose Lake

Scandinavian Sockaroo,
Scandinavian
Bait Co., Stillwater

Folding landing net,
Herter's, Waseca

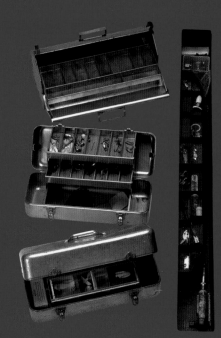

The Fold-a-Tray tackle box by Upper Midwest
Manufacturing Company of Minneapolis featured trays that popped up, while the Roll-a-Tray
box had a revolving cylinder for easy access to
its contents. Mankato's TAC-ALL created the
nearly five-foot-long tackle box that fit neatly
on the side of a rowboat.

Warren Manufacturing of Minneapolis produced
the Torpedo minnow bucket that resembled a
Buck Rogers spaceship. George N. Thomas of
Mankato made his bucket in a submarine style
to glide sleekly through the water. The Falls
City minnow bucket was short on style, but
was "The Angler's Choice."

The catch of the day

Heaven for some was freshly caught, golden brown, pan-fried fish, served with an icy cold beer, and finished off with a mellow cigar!

"World's largest fish fry," Crane Lake, 1970

Steaking a pike, 1920

Cooking the catch, 1935

Fish must be brain food,
because they travel in schools.
MILTON BERLE

Shore lunch

120

Fish Fry

Fishing lodges often prepared just-caught fish that were carried to the kitchen by the anglers themselves. Chefs had many great fish recipes, but beer-battered was usually the favorite, and potato pancakes and corn oysters completed the popular menu.

The following recipes have been adapted for easy preparation, modern cooking methods, and ingredients that are readily available.

Cabbage Peanut Salad

Watkins Almanac, 1917

- 1 cup chopped peanuts
- Salt and pepper to taste
- 6 cups shredded cabbage
- 1 cup salad dressing (half mayonnaise and half sour cream)

Brown peanuts in dry, heavy skillet over medium heat stirring constantly. Add 2/3 cup peanuts, salt, and pepper to shredded cabbage. Mix with 1 cup dressing and top with 1/3 cup chopped peanuts. Makes 6 to 8 servings.

Wilted Lettuce Salad

Rita Martin Test Kitchen at International Milling Company, Minneapolis, 1950s

- 1 medium-sized head lettuce
- 5 slices bacon, diced
- 1/4 cup Karo Red Label Light Corn Syrup
- 1/4 cup vinegar
- 1 teaspoon salt
- Dash pepper
- Dash paprika

Cut lettuce into small pieces into salad bowl. Fry bacon until crisp, stirring often. Drain. Add syrup, vinegar, salt, pepper, and paprika. Bring to a boil. Add hot sauce to lettuce and toss lightly. Serve at once. Makes 4 to 6 servings.

Fish & Beer Batter

Fifty Great Recipes for Camp Cooking, Better Homes & Gardens, 1950s

- Oil for frying
- 1-1/4 cups packaged biscuit mix (such as Bisquick)
- 3/4 cup beer
- 1 egg
- 1/4 teaspoon salt
- 4 pan-dressed fresh fish fillets

Start heating oil in skillet. In wide bowl, beat together biscuit mix, beer, egg, and salt. Pat fish dry. Dip in batter to coat both sides. Fry fish in hot oil in skillet for 4 to 5 minutes on each side or until fish flakes. Makes 4 servings.

Fish and Capers

Skipper Sam's Fisheries, Duluth, 1960s

- 2 pounds fish fillets, cut into 2-inch lengths
- 4 large onions, thinly sliced
- 1 tablespoon olive oil
- 1 tablespoon butter or margarine
- Salt and pepper to taste
- 6 tablespoons sour cream
- Juice and grated rind of 1 lemon
- 3 tablespoons capers
- Paprika

Catch or buy fish large enough to fillet. You may use bass, bluefish, flounder, haddock, halibut, pike, or pickerel. In large skillet, brown onions in oil and butter, stirring with wooden spoon. Reduce heat; sprinkle onions with salt and pepper. Add sour cream, lemon juice and rind, and capers. Add fish; cook over low heat about 10 minutes, stirring sauce and basting fish with it. When fish is tender and easily flaked with fork, remove from skillet and serve on hot plates. At the last minute, redden each morsel with a touch of paprika. Makes 6 to 8 servings.

Potato Pancakes

Bull Cook and Authentic Historical Recipes and Practice, by George Leonard Herter and Berthe E. Herter, Waseca, 1969

Herter's recipes always came with a well-intentioned lecture: "Here is the basic Indian recipe with cracker crumbs substituted for coarse ground seeds, onion substituted for wild leeks, chicken eggs substituted for wild bird eggs, and a little pepper and salt added. Take 3 or 4 large potatoes and peel them. There is a theory that if you soak them in cold water overnight that it will remove some of the starch from the potatoes making them better. Soaking potatoes in cold water does nothing for them as any chemist will tell you. Now grate the potatoes. For every pint (2 cups) of grated potatoes, proceed as follows: Take 2 eggs and place them in a bowl and beat them well. Then mix them with the grated potatoes. Add 4 level tablespoons cracker crumbs, 1/2 teaspoon salt, 1/8 teaspoon pepper, and half a 2-inch-diameter onion, well grated. Melt some butter in your frying pan. Drop large spoonfuls of the potato mixture into the frying pan. Flatten them out so that they make pancakes not more than 1/4 of an inch thick. If potato pancakes are made thick they are not good at all. Turn and brown them slightly on both sides. Serve hot with applesauce. Pancakes made with 2 cups grated potatoes makes 6 servings."

Corn Oysters

Aunt Jane's Cook Book, McConnon & Co., Winona, 1930s

- 2 cups grated fresh sweet corn
- 2 eggs, well beaten
- 1 teaspoon baking powder
- 1/8 teaspoon black pepper
- 1 or 2 tablespoons cream
- 1/4 teaspoon salt
- 4 tablespoons flour
- Butter for griddle
- Maple syrup

Stir together corn, egg, baking powder, pepper, cream, salt, and flour. Drop dough by spoonfuls onto a hot buttered griddle and fry until brown on both sides. The finished fritters look something like oysters when done. Maple syrup is delicious poured on the fritters. Makes 4 servings.

Devil's Food Cake

Occident Flour, 1940s

- 1-1/2 cups all-purpose Occident Flour, sifted
- 1-1/2 teaspoons baking powder
- 1/2 teaspoon soda
- 1/2 teaspoon salt
- 2 squares (2 ounces) unsweetened baking chocolate
- 1 cup sugar
- 1 cup thick sour cream
- 2 eggs
- 1 teaspoon vanilla
- Chocolate Cream Cheese Icing (recipe follows)

Grease and flour one 9-inch loaf pan or two 8-inch round layer cake pans. Sift flour, baking powder, soda, and salt together. Melt chocolate. In separate bowl, beat sugar, cream, eggs, and vanilla with rotary egg beater until sugar is dissolved. Add melted chocolate. Add sifted dry ingredients, folding in slowly. Pour batter into loaf or layer pans. Bake in a 350°F oven 40 minutes for loaf or 25 minutes for layers. Cool cake; frost with Chocolate Cream Cheese Icing. Makes 8 servings.

Chocolate Cream Cheese Icing

Recipes from the Land O' Lakes, Land O'Lakes Creameries, 1930s

- 6 ounces cream cheese, room temperature
- 1/4 cup canned evaporated milk or fresh milk
- 4 cups (1 pound) powdered sugar
- 4 squares (1 ounce each) unsweetened baking chocolate, melted

Beat together cream cheese and milk. Add sugar, sifting in 1/2 cup at a time and beating until smooth after each addition. Add melted chocolate; beat until smooth. Makes enough for a two-layer cake. Delicious on both devil's food and yellow cake.

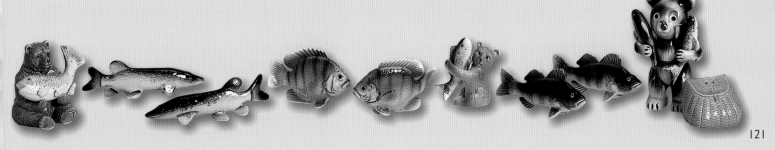

CHAPTER EIGHT

Full-Service Resorts

MINNESOTA'S FIRST LAKE RESORTS were basic hotels that provided rooms and meals and little else. But when vacation crowds began arriving by train in the late 1800s, beautiful stretches of lakeshore were developed into fashionable resorts. Hotelkeepers put up unique turn-of-the-century buildings in striking styles, offered appealing outdoor activities, and arranged for entertainment that engaged guests in the best Victorian style.

These large resorts, as opposed to small "Mom and Pop" resorts, have always provided a different vacation experience. Spacious lakeside buildings that resembled hotels or large lodges held dining rooms, lounges, porches, and wide-ranging outdoor attractions. They often required investments that small resort owners did not have or want to make.

By the 1920s, automobiles brought multitudes of vacationers to resorts in all corners of the state, and the Minnesota getaway changed dramatically. Customers were attracted to lodges with imaginative architecture, garages for automobiles, dancing pavilions, fine dining, and no end of outdoor activity. Employment was provided for hundreds of students during the summer who enabled sizeable resorts to run efficiently.

Eventually clapboard siding gave way to the rustic aesthetic in northern Minnesota and vacation preferences turned to rugged log cabins and active outdoor pursuits. Walks along groomed garden paths gave way to adventurous hikes in the woods. The painted beadboard walls and chintz curtains of smaller resorts lost out to the grander scale of craggy stone fireplaces, pine-paneled dining rooms, and peeled log porches. Parents dropped off their kids at an energetic summer camp and headed to a nearby lodge for a relaxing vacation of their own. A log cabin by a lake or deep in the woods came to represent the quintessential Minnesota vacation.

But Minnesota's large-scale resorts with handsome lodges, rustic dining rooms, and dozens of cabins, faced changing economies. Higher operating costs, accelerating land prices, and fickle vacation weather caused dramatic adjustments and hard decisions in the economics of running a traditional resort in the state.

After serving loyal customers for generations, expansion became one way to stay in business. Many resort properties added sprawling golf courses, water parks, tennis camps, and winter activities. Other resorts, small and large, took a hard look at their soaring costs and offers to buy the resort's individual lakeside cabins. Many owners chose to sell, and their lodges and cottages became private summer homes and permanent residences.

For a century and more, Minnesotans have supported countless resorts whose modest beginnings have evolved into vast entertainment centers on our resort landscape. Many resilient survivors have earned recognition from the National Park Service and are now listed on the National Register of Historic Places.

◄ *Sherwood Forest Lodge employees, 1943*

The first resort hotels

Early sightseers, called coaching parties, toured the country-side by horse and carriage, then stayed the night at small-town hotels. They explored local lakes and rural scenery, enjoyed town attractions, and returned home after a pleasant getaway with friends.

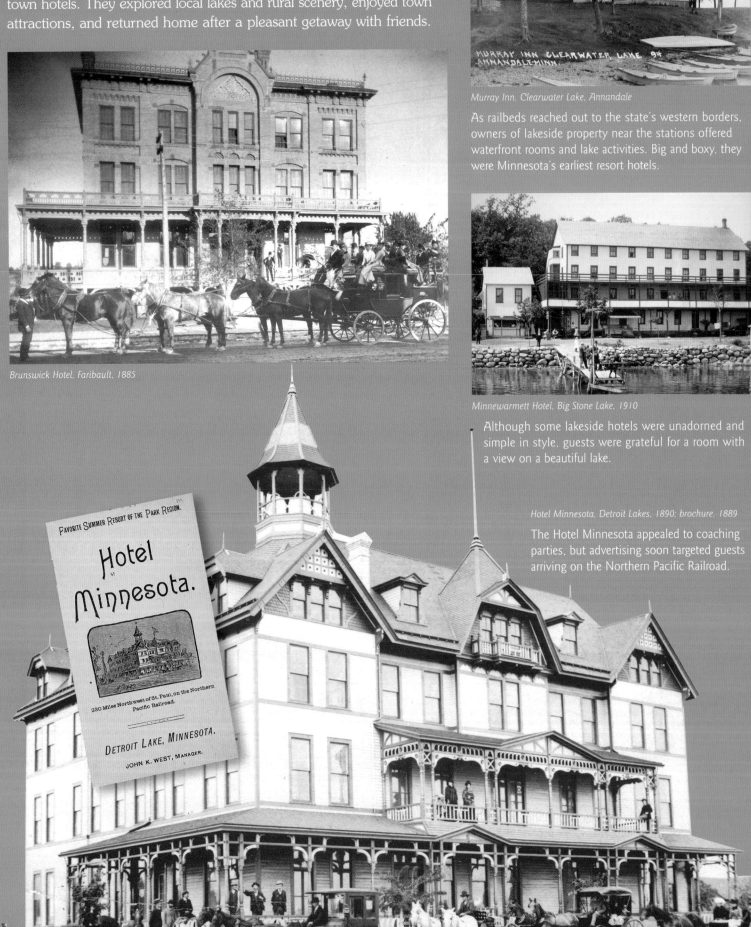

Murray Inn. Clearwater Lake, Annandale

As railbeds reached out to the state's western borders, owners of lakeside property near the stations offered waterfront rooms and lake activities. Big and boxy, they were Minnesota's earliest resort hotels.

Brunswick Hotel, Faribault, 1885

Minnewarmett Hotel, Big Stone Lake, 1910

Although some lakeside hotels were unadorned and simple in style, guests were grateful for a room with a view on a beautiful lake.

Hotel Minnesota, Detroit Lakes. 1890; brochure, 1889

The Hotel Minnesota appealed to coaching parties, but advertising soon targeted guests arriving on the Northern Pacific Railroad.

FAVORITE SUMMER RESORT OF THE PARK REGION.

Hotel Minnesota.

230 Miles Northwest of St. Paul, on the Northern Pacific Railroad.

DETROIT LAKE, MINNESOTA.

JOHN K. WEST, MANAGER.

Brightwood Beach Resort, Lake Ripley, Litchfield

Brightwood Beach cottage

When it opened in 1889, Brightwood Beach Resort offered cultural activities such as classes in fine arts, music concerts, and popular live entertainment. Trainloads of guests arrived for other summer festivities that included dancing, ball games, canoeing, and steamboat excursions on Lake Ripley. A single octagon-shaped cottage survives as an early example of an unusual Minnesota cottage style from the 1890s.

Holtgren's Lodge, Spicer

Hotel Tepeetonka, Green Lake

Dating from 1895, the Tepeetonka was one of several large resort hotels in the western part of the state that drew railroad travelers as well as vacationers from the surrounding area. The large lake appealed to boaters and fishermen, while others relaxed in the shade under sprawling elm trees.

Hotel Blake, Alexandria
Souvenir plate from Hotel Blake

The Hotel Blake borrowed its look from East Coast Shingle-style architecture that included broad verandas and a rustic gazebo. Dining rooms, lounges, porches, bridges, water canals, and rowboats kept everyone entertained. A gift shop offered souvenirs that made sure guests remembered their vacation days all year long.

It wasn't long before resort owners became aware of the advantages of stylish architecture and added attention-getting features to their buildings. Roomy porches and verandas, lookout towers, and pavilions attracted increasingly sophisticated guests.

Geneva Beach, Alexandria

Queen Anne–style towers and open porches with sweeping views of the lake provided lodgers with breezy—if not mosquito-free—sanctuaries.

The automobile era

By the 1920s, the automobile age brought an ever-increasing procession of tourists to all corners of Minnesota. Cars and buses filled with vacationers came in droves, they parked everywhere, and hotels and resorts scrambled to accommodate them.

Hotel Lyon, Lake City

Dunn's Lodge, Pelican Rapids

Architecture became an increasingly important element for twentieth-century resorts and Dunn's sported an unusual Spanish Mission Revival style. The lodge offered everything an automobile vacationer could desire—garages, gas pumps, lounges, dining rooms, a dance hall, up-to-date cottages, and a water wheel that actually provided electricity. All stood ready at the whim of discriminating guests.

Arrowhead Hotel, Grand Marais

As waves of auto travelers arrived, resorts modified their services by installing new conveniences for guests and their cars. Automobile stables, car garages, and gas pumps along with water supplies for thirsty radiators stood ready to serve.

Garage at Kamberling's Resort, Whitefish Lake, Crow Wing County, 1920s; waitresses at Kamberling's Resort, 1930

As travelers parked their cars they found Kamberling's cheerful summer waitresses waiting to welcome them.

Automobile stables, Idlewilde, Osakis

When road travel became popular, resorts looked for new ways to draw in customers and many became virtual villages of their own. New amenities and conveniences attracted more lodgers and fond memories of summer relaxation kept guests coming back year after year.

Pettibone Lodge, Shoreham

With comfortable lobbies and dining rooms, a popular dance pavilion, and cabins waiting for a party, Pettibone Lodge provided a complete vacation—and guests never left the property.

Pettibone Entertainment Pavilion, Shoreham

Dining porch, Minnewawa Lodge, Nisswa, 1925
Staff at Minnewawa, 1903 ▶

A Shakespearean actor from New York built Minnewawa Lodge to serve as a retreat for fellow actors who came to memorize lines and rehearse plays. Lodgers arrived by train in the 1890s at the Lake Hubert railroad station, then traveled by boat to the lodge on the lake. In addition to guest rooms, cottages, and recreation areas, the two-story main building held a large kitchen to serve a sprawling dining porch that awaited theatrical recitations from eloquent guests.

Cottages, Pettibone Lodge, Shoreham

Fair Hills Resort, Pelican Lake, Detroit Lakes, 1915
Truckload of happy kids, 1930s

In 1906, three brothers rented out vacation rooms in their Pelican Lake farmhouse. Soon they expanded the house, then built a new lodge, and later more lodging. Vacationers in their summer whites relaxed on the lawn and filled up the rooms every summer. Fair Hills Resort provides family activities and plenty of space for adults and kids alike.

Classic northern getaways

Northern resorts often depended on steamboat service to bring in their customers. In wilderness areas, steamers were the only way to visit sought-after remote locations that were attractive to early admirers of woods and fauna.

Steamer Northland *and passengers, Walker, 1915*

The *Northland* steamboat left the busy Walker dock filled with passengers heading to resorts around Leech Lake.

Marybelle steamer, Pehrson Lodge, 1910

Early in the twentieth century, the *Marybelle* brought guests to the dock at Pehrson Lodge, but roads eventually arrived and the resort became a desirable fishing and vacation destination.

Chase Hotel, Walker

The 1892 Chase Hotel first catered to tourists who arrived by rail. In later years automobiles brought guests to the huge wood-framed hotel constructed in classic Eastern-style resort architecture. Located in the heart of town on Leech Lake, the hotel had easy access to sailing and excursion boating as well as other exhilarating water amusements.

Pehrson Lodge, Lake Vermilion, 1947

Located on an island in Minnesota's only national park, the Kettle Falls Hotel has welcomed visitors since 1913. The wood-frame building originally catered to lumberjacks and fishermen. If the saloon's sloping wood floor, called the "Tiltin' Hilton," could talk, it would tell of the building's history of gambling, bootlegging, and rumored financing by Madame Nellie Bly. Cleaned up and restored in 1988 by the National Park Service, Minnesota's most remote hotel can be reached by boat or seaplane from a base station on land in Voyageurs National Park.

Kettle Falls Hotel, Rainy and Namakan Lakes, Voyageurs National Park

Cascade Lodge, Lake Superior, Grand Marais 1935; 1950

An architecturally sensitive addition added more rooms to the original lodge building.

Popular northern resorts were often faced with the need to expand. Adding space in the style of the original building enhanced the design and size of the structure in the best possible way, and refurbished interiors gave the resort a new lease on life.

Cascade Lodge room, 1935; 1950s

When television sets became a requirement for attracting customers, rooms were reoriented and the furniture was placed to capture both outdoor and indoor views.

The favorite part of a resort was often the porch. Rocking chairs were always ready for a quiet moment or for lively social debates.

Spring Park Villa, Bald Eagle Lake

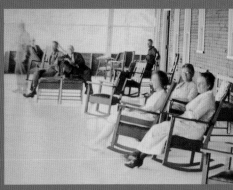

Interlachen Lodge, Hackensack

Rustic or refined? Open-air porches held chairs made of twigs and branches straight out of the woods, while wicker and upholstered seating furnished an all-season porch with a cocktail bar at the end.

Inn, Lake Vermilion, Tower

Big Leech Resort, Walker

129

Sticks and . . .

It took exceptional skill and a love of woodworking to erect buildings that were fashioned completely from logs. Posts, beams, stairways, and rafters echoed the forest outside while twig carpentry and dovetail joinery provided both rustic and stylish furnishings for woodsy indoor settings.

Isles O'Dreams Lodge, Bad Axe and Mantrap Lakes, Park Rapids, 1950

Gateway-Hungry Jack Lodge dining room, Gunflint Trail

Gateway-Hungry Jack Lodge recreation room, Grand Marais

Many resorts filled their log lodges with twig furniture that created an appealing and woodsy environment.

Fair Hills, Detroit Lakes, 1940

The result of time and patience, tree limbs tied together for a footbridge became a memorable stroll.

Whimsical folk-art walkways blended into their watery surroundings.

Spirit Lake

Hotel Blake, Alexandria

Lake Itasca

Dunn's Resort, Pelican Rapids

. . . Stones

Stonework—one rock upon another with scarce evidence of mortar—
became walls and stairs, chimneys and entrances. Hefty boulders and rocks
collected from nearby farm fields or gathered from lake shores lent subtle
color and dramatic texture to resort grounds and interiors.

Lutsen Resort, Lutsen

Sherwood Forest Lodge, Gull Lake, Brainerd

Douglas Lodge, Lake Itasca State Park, Bemidji

Vermilion Beach Resort, Tower, 1940

Fireplaces were the heart of many lodges and stone was the most popular building
material. Fieldstones could be split in half and installed with the flat face out or left
whole for a gently rounded surface.

Forestview, Leech Lake, Walker

Hamilton Lodge, Park Rapids

Cyrana Lodge, Beltrami Lake, Bemidji

Sawbill Lodge, Tofte

131

Rustic old timers

Sturdy north woods resorts have withstood the havoc from exuberant crowds of fun-seeking vacationers. Their beautiful rustic interiors survive in whole, or in part, and many have become legends in the panorama of uniquely Minnesota vacation settings.

Clearwater Lodge, Gunflint Trail, 1950s

Located midway along the Gunflint Trail, Clearwater Lodge provides a home base and outfitting for canoeists embarking on adventures in the Boundary Waters. The historic log lodge was built in 1926.

Mr. and Mrs. Charles Boostrom invite you to the Grand Opening Clearwater Lake Lodge Saturday Night July thirty-first Road now open to lodge. Celebrate the event by being there. Dancing

Loon Lake Lodge, Gunflint Trail

Constructed of logs from the surrounding area, a getaway at Loon Lake Lodge included the company of deer and loons—inside and out.

Rockwood Lodge, Grand Marais

Rockwood's rustic log lodge was hand built of native Norway red pine in the 1920s. Located on the original Gunflint Trail, it is surrounded by the Boundary Waters Canoe Area and Minnesota's wilderness at its best.

Edgewater Beach Hotel cottage, Detroit Lakes, 1940

An unusual method of log assembly was the unique feature of this Edgewater Beach Hotel cottage. Stovewood, or logs sawn into short lengths and stacked with the cut ends facing out, was reminiscent of cabins in Scandinavia and northern Europe and rarely seen in Minnesota. The resort's original rustic-style lodge and cottages date to the 1930s.

Gingerbread House, Izatys Resort, Mille Lacs, Onamia, 1940s

Named after a seventeenth-century Indian village on the shores of Mille Lacs, Izatys opened in 1922. The resort has grown and evolved from its early days to become a modern golf and yacht club with a championship 18-hole golf course and 120-slip marina. The "Gingerbread House" provided a fairy tale retreat.

Buffet and waitresses, Slone's Pine Cone Lodge, Park Rapids

Kare-Phree Pines, McGregor

Northern Pine Lodge, Park Rapids

Birchdale Villas, Lake Bertha, Pequot Lakes

Dinner in the pines was the reward for a busy day in the north woods. Comfort food at its best came on plates and platters served under wagon-wheel chandeliers. Showshoes and antlers decorated honey-colored pine paneling and views of the forest were only a window away.

Cookout, Lost Lake Lodge, Brainerd

Come and get it! Anderson's Resort, Ely

Island View Lodge, Gull Lake, Brainerd

133

Horseshoes at Grand View Lodge

Breezy Point tee time

We need a fourth for doubles

Croquet at Long Beach

Lawn games, golf, and tennis were the hottest activities in vacation sports. Swings and lawnchairs pro-vided cool and restful alternatives.

Pinecone shuffle

Swinging at Train Bell

Lakeside with a four-footed friend

Fair Hills bridge fun

Pull up a chair

Enduring resorts and their favorite recipes

Resort vacations become traditions for a variety of reasons. Success may come with proximity to beautiful lakes and forests or popular ski hills. Others survive due to dogged determination during ever-changing times and economic conditions. Many owners have stood watch over beloved rustic buildings that have endured intact for a hundred years or more. Great food is one good reason people return year after year and resort dining is a delectable Minnesota tradition that survives today—and the following resorts have shared their favorite recipes.

Grand View Lodge

Gull Lake, Nisswa

Minnesota's lakes weren't always lined with cabins and resorts. In the early 1900s, Brainerd Lakes real estate developer Marvin Baker was selling land around Gull Lake when he came up with a grand idea. To accommodate prospective buyers, he built Grand View Lodge. The 1918 three-story building survives as one of the classic examples of rustic log architecture in northern Minnesota. In 1937 the resort was bought by "Brownie" Cote, owner of two nearby camps, as a place for parents to come for their own fun after dropping off their kids at summer camp. The vast resort and recreation area remains in the Cote family.

Lounge, 1940s

Grand View Lodge, 1928

Sherwood Forest, 1950s

Now a historically designated lodge, Sherwood Forest is part of the Grand View family. The spectacular dining hall was built in 1929 from giant logs abandoned at the Nisswa depot on their way to becoming pilings for Duluth's harbor. One of the now privately owned cabins was a summer writing retreat for Sinclair Lewis and rumor had it that Ma Barker and her gang once hid out at Sherwood Forest.

Lutsen Resort

Lake Superior, Lutsen

Well before roads were established along the North Shore, Swedish immigrant and tugboat captain Charles Axel Nelson planned to live on Lake Superior. In 1885 he built a home overlooking the lake and named it Lutsen, after a town in Germany where a former King of Sweden was killed in battle. Before roads led to the area, early lake voyagers were invited to spend the night at Nelson's house, and as his reputation for hospitality grew, so did the accommodations. The homestead buildings were replaced in 1952 by a Scandinavian-style lodge designed by Minnesota's honored architect Edwin Lundie. Perched on Lake Superior's rugged shoreline, Lutsen is the state's oldest resort.

Lutsen Lodge, 1960s

As picturesque in the winter as it is in the summer, Lutsen provides year-round entertainment.

Dining room, 1950s

Tasty Scandinavian meals charm both summer vacationers and winter skiers.

The lobby's view overlooking Gunflint Lake, 1940s

Gunflint Lodge

Gunflint Lake,
Grand Marais

Gunflint Lodge opened in 1925 at the end of a former Indian path that became the legendary Gunflint Trail. A few years after the resort was established, it was sold to Mae Spunner. Even without indoor plumbing, electricity, or telephones, Mae and her daughter Justine turned the resort into a sought-after destination for hunters and fishermen. Over the years the resort has grown in size and amenities, and has become legendary in its own right as a fourth-generation lodge in the Boundary Waters Canoe Area.

Breezy Point

Big Pelican Lake, Pequot

Built in 1925 from the proceeds of owner Billy Fawcett's successful magazine publishing career, Breezy Point was known as the "Riviera of the North." In its grand heyday of the 1930s, its rooms hosted dozens of celebrities including John Wayne, Joan Crawford, Lionel Barrymore, and Clark Gable. Architects Magney and Tusler designed the vast log complex a few years before they designed the famous Foshay Tower. The lodge burned to the ground in 1959, but one original structure survived—owner Billy Fawcett's ten-bedroom log home, now listed on the National Register of Historic Places.

Wilford "Captain Billy" Fawcett House, 1950

Lobby reception desk and cigar counter, 1925

A special five-day rate was offered for the Fourth of July holiday in 1955. $80 per person included all meals, dancing, and entertainment.

Breezy Point Lodge trapshoot, 1940s

Ludlow's

Lake Vermilion, Cook

A ring of log cabins circle Ludlow's Island which in turn is surrounded by the sapphire waters of Lake Vermilion. A luxury resort with wilderness overtones, the buildings are designed with architectural integrity and creative diversity. Generations of Ludlows have greeted guests since 1939.

Cabin with loft, Ludlow's Island Lodge, Lake Vermilion

Cragun's

Pine Beach, Brainerd

Started in the 1940s, Cragun's sprawling resort is run by the family's second generation. Irma's oatmeal rolls are legendary and "Dutch" has been overseeing resort functions since his first job at the age of nine as "manager of worms and minnows!" Scandinavian-style influences are found on the main lodge and on many surrounding buildings that comprise this successful year-round holiday destination.

Ruttger's

The Ruttger's resort empire grew from the humble roots of a berry farm. Joseph and Josephine Ruttger homesteaded property on Bay Lake near Deerwood in 1898. In addition to farming their land, they let fishermen camp on the shore and stay in their barn. Soon Josephine was cooking dinners, cottages were built, and a resort was born. Their four sons were raised in the business and today several resorts bear the Ruttger name and are operated by fourth generation descendants of Joseph and Josephine.

Rustic cabin No. 25, Bay Lake Lodge

In the 1920s, guests at Ruttger's Bay Lake Lodge paid $3 a day for food, lodging, and a boat.

Relaxing by the cut-stone fireplace, Bay Lake Lodge, 1950s

Bay Lake Lodge, the first Ruttger's resort, is the oldest family-owned resort in Minnesota. The Ruttger family was a pioneer in early tourism publicity. Innovative brochures attracted newcomers and handwritten notes were mailed to guests encouraging them to come back—and many did year after year.

Birchmont Hotel, Lake Bemidji, 1927

The picturesque lakeside hotel opened in 1913 and was acquired by the Ruttgers in 1936. Many of the early visitors arrived by train from Grand Forks, North Dakota.

Burntside Lodge

Burntside Lake, Ely

Established in 1911 as a hunting lodge, Burntside originally catered to the influx of tourists arriving on the Duluth & Iron Range Railroad. Automobile travelers soon discovered the rustic lodge and the resort became popular for all vacation styles. Many of the log and stone buildings are listed on the National Register and together they form a recognized historic district.

Gift shop, Burntside Lodge, 1940s

Hunting at Burntside Lodge included hunting for souvenirs in the gift shop during the 1940s. Beautiful Indian crafts from the area were some of the most popular items featured in the shop for many decades.

Burntside Lodge, 1940

Tall pines surround a collection of log buildings at the edge of the Boundary Waters Canoe Area.

Madden's

Gull Lake, Brainerd

The Pine Beach Peninsula on Gull Lake is a perfect resort location. It was home to Roberts Pine Beach hotel, Ruttger's Pine Beach Lodge, and Madden's Lodge. Over the years, the Madden brothers, Jack and Jim, bought them all and combined them into one gigantic extravaganza of vacation fun. Golf courses and marina activities dominate leisure time today, along with children's activities, art shows, and live entertainment.

Madden's Lodge, 1940s

Cook Aunt Nora put Madden's Lodge on the pie lovers' circuit for decades.

Peters' dining room, 1940s

Peters' Sunset Beach Resort

Lake Minnewaska, Glenwood

In the early 1900s, Henry Peters was a Soo Line conductor living in North Dakota. His route traveled through the bustling Minnesota town of Glenwood where the depot oversaw more than fifteen trains a day. In 1908 Peters bought a cottage on the shore of Lake Minnewaska with a dream to build a summer hotel. In 1915 a two-story wood-frame building with twelve guest rooms opened as "the best hotel in all the land." Sinclair Lewis signed the register a year later. Peters soon bought out his original investors and the resort has stayed in the family for four generations.

Peters' historic dining room features beautiful murals painted by Gustav Krollmann illustrating the legend of Indian maiden Minnewaska.

Conductor H. P. Peters, early 1900s

Naniboujou Resort

Lake Superior, Grand Marais

Planned as an exclusive hunting lodge, Naniboujou opened in 1929 on a rocky Lake Superior shore. The handsome lodge was on its way to becoming a national club—until the 1929 stock market crash. Within months after opening, members, including baseball player Babe Ruth and boxer Jack Dempsey, stood by as Naniboujou closed. Named after the Cree Indian god of wilderness, the resort was eventually reborn and the grand lodge, with the largest stone fireplace in Minnesota, survives as a historic treasure for future generations to enjoy. Brightly colored Cree Indian motifs cover the walls and ceiling of the magnificent dining room—a fitting background for the inspired cuisine served there today.

Naniboujou dining room, 1950s

Nelson's Resort

Crane Lake, Orr

With access to more than a thousand miles of hiking trails and picturesque waters for canoeing, Nelson's Resort has been home to adventurers since 1931. Nestled on the shoreline, cabins built of logs provide remarkable comfort at the edge of a vast wilderness.

Cabin, 1950s

Big resorts

Minnesota resort guests have enjoyed flavorsome cuisine in beautiful lodge environments for decades. An extraordinary group of creative and often well-known chefs work the busy summer season in resort kitchens, then spend winter months in culinary adventures honing their skills. Graciously, these popular resorts have shared their favorite recipes!

Ludlow's Campfire Corn and Eggs

The Ludlow recipe for Campfire Corn was originally prepared over a campfire by Hod Ludlow. It became a Ludlow's staple for a "special breakfast" and Ludlow children and grandchildren prepare it for themselves as well.

- 1/2 pound lean bacon
- 1 red pepper, diced
- 1 green pepper, diced
- 1 medium onion, diced
- 2 cups fresh corn cut off the cob or frozen whole kernel corn
- 1 dozen eggs

Cut bacon into small pieces and fry in a pan. When bacon is crisp, place the bacon aside and remove excess grease. Sauté the red and green peppers and onion until soft. Add corn. Add eggs and bacon, and cook thoroughly. Makes 6 servings.

Peters' Sunset Beach Celery Seed Dressing

This dressing was served on a citrus section and lettuce salad in Peters' dining room for many years. It is equally good on plain lettuce, cabbage, or fruit of any kind.

- 1 small onion, quartered
- 3/4 cup sugar
- 1 teaspoon dry mustard
- 1 teaspoon salt
- 1 cup oil
- 1/2 cup vinegar
- 1 teaspoon celery seed

Place onion, sugar, dry mustard, salt, and oil in blender container. Cover and blend thoroughly. With blender on low, slowly add the vinegar and celery seed. Pour into jar, cover, and refrigerate before using to meld flavors. Shake before using. Makes 1 pint.

Ruttger's Boiled Salad Dressing

Sisters Amy and Bertha ran the kitchen at Ruttger's for decades and developed many of the famous recipes that kept lodgers coming back year after year.

- 1/2 cup sugar
- 2 teaspoons flour
- 1 teaspoon salt
- 1 teaspoon dry mustard
- 1/2 cup vinegar
- 1/2 cup cold water
- 2 whole eggs

Mix sugar, flour, salt, and mustard in saucepan. Add vinegar and water and heat. When hot, pour over beaten eggs and cook until thick in top of double boiler. Chill. When ready to use, thin with sweet, sour, or whipped cream. Serve on spinach or salad greens.

Cragun's Oatmeal Rolls

Irma Cragun wrote: "In the late 1960s, I began researching new bread recipes to feature nightly on our salad bar. It was a challenge to get guests to move from white bread to healthier grain. This recipe was accepted and a good transition—still popular today."

- 4 cups all-purpose flour, divided
- 1 tablespoon active dry yeast
- 2 cups quick oats
- 2 eggs
- 1/3 cup molasses
- 2 tablespoons soft margarine
- 2 cups warm water
- 2 teaspoons salt
- Egg wash: 1 egg beaten with 1 tablespoon cream

Combine 2 cups of the flour, yeast, and oats in a bowl; set aside. In large mixing bowl, beat eggs. Add molasses, margarine, warm water, and salt. Then mix in flour mixture. Beat at medium speed for 3 minutes. Let covered dough rise until double in volume, 30 to 45 minutes. Add the remaining 2 cups flour until you have a soft dough. Place dough on lightly floured surface. Keep kneading dough until elastic in texture. Turn dough into a well-greased bowl. Let dough rise again until double, another 30 to 45 minutes. Form round rolls. Place in greased muffin tins—cups should be 2/3 full—or arrange on a baking sheet. Brush with egg wash. Let dough rise again until double. Bake at 350°F for about 20 to 30 minutes. Makes about 3 dozen rolls.

Gunflint Lodge Grilled Elk Loin with Cherry Confit

Chef Kate Randy Roberts offered this favorite elk recipe and the observation that Gunflint dining goes hand in hand with moose watching.

- Whole elk loin
- Unsalted butter
- Kosher salt
- Fresh cracked pepper
- Cherry Confit (recipe follows)

Buy whole elk loins. Clean and portion them into 4-ounce medallions. Brush both sides with melted butter. Sprinkle with kosher salt and fresh cracked pepper. Grill meat to desired doneness— medium rare is suggested. Allow meat to rest 5 to 10 minutes before serving. Brush the grilled elk with additional melted butter, slice and serve with Cherry Confit, potato pancakes, and grilled asparagus. One serving is two 4-ounce medallions. Note: If elk is not available, use pork loin instead.

CHERRY CONFIT:
- 2 tablespoons unsalted butter
- 1 large shallot, minced
- 1 cup dried tart cherries
- 1/4 cup brandy
- 1/3 cup port
- 2 tablespoons red wine vinegar

In a sauté pan, melt the butter. Add the shallots, sauté, but do not brown. Add the cherries and the brandy and carefully flame with a match. Add the port and red wine vinegar. Serve warm.

Grand View Lodge English Beef Chuck Roast

Chef Jamie's beef roast is tender and flavorful with this method of cooking, and the gravy becomes a burst of rich flavor from the unusual vegetable mixture. Be sure to serve it with mashed potatoes.

- 2-pound chuck roast
- 1/2 cup chopped carrots
- 1/2 cup chopped onions
- 1/2 cup chopped parsnips
- 1/2 cup chopped turnips
- 12 cloves garlic, peeled
- 2 sprigs parsley
- 2 tablespoons salt
- 1 tablespoon black pepper
- 4 cups water, divided
- 1/4 cup cornstarch

Preheat oven to 400°F. Place roast, vegetables, garlic, parsley, salt, and pepper in a roasting pan. Add 3 cups of water. Cook in the oven 30 minutes uncovered. Turn down the oven to 325°F, cover the pan, and roast another 2 hours. When the meat is fork-tender, remove to a platter and keep warm. Bring the liquid in the roasting pan to a boil; thicken with a mixture of 1/4 cup cornstarch stirred into 1 cup water. Cook and stir until gravy is desired consistency. Slice roast and serve with gravy and mashed potatoes. Makes 4 to 6 servings.

Naniboujou French Glazed Carrots

The name Naniboujou is synonymous with fine cuisine. Neighbors, travelers, and lodgers fill the extraordinary dining room year after year.

- 4 cups sliced carrots, cut in 1-inch diagonal slices
- 4 tablespoons butter
- 5 tablespoons brown sugar
- 1/2 cup orange juice
- 1 teaspoon ground ginger

Fill a medium saucepan with salted water. Bring to a boil over high heat, add carrots, and cook 10 to 15 minutes, until almost fork-tender. Drain. In a medium-sized skillet, melt the butter and add the brown sugar and orange juice. Bring to a boil and add the ginger, boiling 5 minutes. Add the carrots; simmer until sauce somewhat thickens and carrots are fully cooked and nicely glazed. Makes 6 to 8 servings.

Burntside Lodge Wild Rice Casserole

Lonnie LaMontagne writes: "This is one of my favorite recipes from my mother-in-law, Nancy LaMontagne. Wild rice that was originally sold in the gift shop years ago required the method for repeated boiling before being able to proceed. Today, the rice we purchase allows an easier preparation with just one quick boiling."

- 1 cup hand-parched wild rice
- 2 cups water or chicken or beef broth
- 6 tablespoons butter or margarine, divided
- 3/4 cup finely chopped celery
- 3/4 cup finely chopped onion
- 1/2 cup mushrooms, sliced
- 2 to 3 tablespoons butter or margarine
- 1 cup cubed bread
- 1 cup chicken, turkey, or beef broth

Rinse rice under cold water. Bring to boil in water or broth and cook approximately 20 minutes. Melt 3 tablespoons butter or margarine in saucepan. Add celery and onion. Do not brown; cook until tender. Remove to casserole. In the same pan, melt 3 tablespoons butter and sauté mushrooms. Remove to casserole. Sauté bread cubes in pan, adding more butter if necessary. Add to casserole with celery, onion, and mushroom mixture; add the drained rice. Season to taste with salt and pepper. Stir in broth and bake at 350°F for 45 minutes. Makes 6 servings.

Breezy Point Antlers Chicken on Wild Rice

Breezy Point has been known for fine food for decades. This all-time favorite is yet another culinary success and a hit with guests all year.

- 4 boneless 8-ounce chicken breast halves
- Flour
- Olive oil
- 1 cup slivered almonds
- 1/8 cup butter
- 1 ounce amaretto
- 1/2 cup butter-sautéed sliced mushrooms
- Hollandaise sauce (your favorite recipe or from packaged mix)
- Fresh parsley
- Favorite wild rice casserole

Flour both sides of chicken breasts. Sauté in heated olive oil until golden brown, about 10 minutes, turning once; cook until juices come out clear. At the same time, in separate pan, toast almonds in hot butter. Stir until almonds are light brown, then add the amaretto. As you stir, there may be a brief flame from the liqueur. This step candies the almonds. For each serving, place a cup of wild rice casserole on a serving plate, top with hot chicken breast. Garnish with sautéed mushrooms, hollandaise sauce, candied almonds, and parsley. Makes 4 servings.

Madden's Aunt Nora's Almond Macaroon Torte

Aunt Nora was known as one of the best cooks in vacationland and served appreciative guests of Madden's for many years.

- 1/2 cup sifted flour
- 1 cup sugar, divided
- 3/4 cup blanched or unblanched almonds, chopped fine
- 5 egg whites (save yolks for Cream, below)
- 1/4 teaspoon salt
- 1 teaspoon vanilla
- Mocha Butter Cream (recipe follows)
- Toasted slivered blanched almonds, finely chopped

Grease two 8-inch round cake pans with vegetable shortening. Line bottom of pans with parchment paper. Grease the paper well. Sift flour and 1/2 cup of the sugar into mixing bowl. Add finely chopped almonds and set aside. Beat egg whites with salt until soft mounds are formed. Gradually add vanilla and remaining 1/2 cup sugar, beating constantly until very stiff, glossy peaks are formed. Fold in flour-sugar-almond mixture a few tablespoons at a time, folding gently but thoroughly. Spread in prepared pans. Bake in 350°F oven 35 to 40 minutes, or until dried to the touch but not colored. Carefully remove torte rounds from pans. On a large plate place the first round smooth side down. Spread with Mocha Butter Cream.

Add second crust, smooth side up and cover with Cream. Finish by frosting sides with the Cream. Sprinkle with toasted almonds. Chill at least four hours before serving. Makes 8 to 10 servings.

MOCHA BUTTER CREAM:
- 5 egg yolks
- 1/2 cup sugar
- 3 tablespoons flour
- 1/4 teaspoon salt
- 1/2 cup heavy cream
- 1/2 cup strong black coffee
- 1 tablespoon baking cocoa
- 1/2 cup butter
- 1 teaspoon vanilla

In saucepan, beat together egg yolks, sugar, flour, and salt until light and fluffy. Blend in cream and coffee. Cook over medium heat, stirring constantly, until thick. Remove from heat; add cocoa and blend thoroughly. Cool to lukewarm. Beat in butter and vanilla until soft and smooth. Use to fill and frost torte layers.

Lutsen's Swedish Crème with Lingonberries

Diane E. Loh wrote "This dessert is light, flavorful, and a nice way to end an excellent meal."

- 1/2 tablespoon unflavored gelatin
- 2-1/2 tablespoons cold water
- 2 cups heavy whipping cream
- 1 cup sugar
- 2 cups sour cream
- 1 teaspoon vanilla
- 1 teaspoon almond extract
- Lingonberries

In a small bowl, sprinkle gelatin on top of cold water. Do not stir. Combine heavy cream and sugar in a small saucepan. Using a rubber spatula, blend gelatin mixture in cream mixture. On medium heat, bring cream mixture to a low simmer. Remove from heat and allow to cool slightly. Add sour cream, vanilla, and almond extract. Blend until smooth. Pour into dessert dishes immediately. Chill until set, about 4 hours. Serve topped with lingonberries. Can also be served with strawberries, raspberries, or blueberries. Makes 8 servings.

Nelson's Swedish Tea Ring

Jerry Pohlman wrote: "This traditional sweet bread is served each Thursday that we have Smorgasbord at Crane Lake."

FOR SWEET DOUGH:
- 2 envelopes active dry yeast
- 1/2 cup warm water
- 1/2 cup lukewarm milk (scalded and cooled)
- 1/2 cup sugar
- 1 teaspoon salt
- 2 eggs
- 1/2 cup shortening
- 4-1/2 to 5 cups all-purpose flour

FOR FILLING:
- 1/2 cup sugar
- 1/4 cup shortening
- 1 egg
- 1 teaspoon salt
- 1 teaspoon vanilla
- 2 cups semisweet chocolate chips
- 1/2 cup chopped walnuts
- 1 cup chopped maraschino cherries, well drained

Dissolve yeast in warm water. Stir in milk, sugar, salt, eggs, shortening, and 2-1/2 cups of flour. Beat until smooth. Mix in enough of the remaining flour to make dough easy to handle. Turn dough out on lightly floured board and knead until smooth and elastic. Place in greased bowl, cover and let rise in warm place until double, about 1-1/2 hours. Meanwhile, stir together 1/2 cup sugar, 1/4 cup shortening, 1 egg, 1 teaspoon salt, and vanilla for filling. Punch down dough. Divide in half. Roll out half of dough into a rectangle 15 inches by 9 inches. Spread half of filling mixture on dough, sprinkle with half the chocolate chips, half the nuts, and half the cherries. Roll up tightly beginning at wide side. Seal by pinching edges together. Form rolled-up dough into a ring on lightly greased baking sheet, pinching ends together. Use scissors to cut deep slashes 1/2 inch apart. Turn each slice partly on its side. Repeat for second ring. Let rings rise 1/2 hour. Bake at 350°F for 20 to 25 minutes, until golden. Frost with powdered sugar frosting and sprinkle with more chopped nuts. Makes 2 rings.

CHAPTER NINE

Boat Show

TWO OF MINNESOTA'S NATURAL RESOURCES, wood and water, came together to launch the state's passion for boating. Water was a given, with countless miles of navigational waterways and lakes, while native wood was the material that kept passengers afloat.

Many vacationers in Minnesota experienced their first water adventures aboard handsome wood steamboats and launches. For people who had little time for long vacations, day excursions provided a happy choice. Would-be sailors found their seats and steamers chugged off from docks on sightseeing tours, day trips, and nighttime pleasure cruises. Excursions became so popular in the late 1800s that even hard-hitting river steamers once used for pushing rafts of logs downstream were converted to fun and fanciful pleasure boats.

With miles of water in all directions, the passion of vacationers for the pure joy of boating blossomed like water lilies in protected bays. Watercraft was bound to become big business and Minnesota boatbuilders began to make some of the best boats in America.

Using ready stocks of cedar, maple, oak, and pine, boatmakers incorporated native wood in canoes, rowboats, launches, and steamers from stem to stern. Plank-on-frame construction was applied on boats from eight to eighty feet. Steam power, once developed for industry, became the driving force for paddle wheelers, excursion launches, and enormous side-wheelers.

By the turn of the century, water devotees wanted their own boats. Fishing boats, rowboats, sailboats, and canoes—all manner of floating vessels were slipping into waters from lakeside marinas and landings. Outboard motors powered pontoons and houseboats, inboard engines propelled speedboats and cruisers; they trolled along lazily or powered up to dizzying speeds.

Buyers in later years had their pick of material from elegantly handcrafted wood to maintenance-free fiberglass or lightweight aluminum. Outboard motors, inboard motors, running lights, oars, and fittings for every make and model completed the offerings from our own local factories.

Minnesotans who built boats and the people who used them—riverboat captains, resort owners, fishing guides and adventurers—became local heroes. Some even became legendary figures known worldwide and made an enduring mark on the country's boating history: a boatbuilder from Minnesota produced speedboats that won international races year after year; the pontoon boat was invented in St. Cloud; and a scale model of a Minnesota sailboat found permanent harbor in the collections of the Smithsonian Institution. And Minnesota's distinguished boating heritage had only just begun.

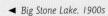

◄ *Big Stone Lake, 1900s*

St. Croix and Mississippi riverboats

Wood-fired steam engines, hissing and puffing, drove the paddle wheels of flat-bottomed steamboats. Because they drew very little water, the boats were perfectly suited for shallow rivers filled with sandbars and floating debris. From Taylors Falls to as far south as Winona, elaborate vessels steamed around river bends on day or evening excursions. Resplendent in jigsaw carpentry known as "steamboat gothic," they drew huge crowds along the shoreline. Rivertown residents and carriage trade excursionists packed the decks to experience a sophisticated outing on the river.

Steamer J. S., steamer W. W., and barge

Steamboat excursion landing, Hastings

Steamer Red Wing *and barge* Manitou, *1920*

Excursion companies looked for ways to accommodate the overflowing crowds—barges could double the number of passengers normally carried by steamers. Barges were built to match their decorative steamboats and were carefully attached to avoid the paddle wheels on the side of stern-wheelers or aft on side-wheelers.

Interior of steamer Red Wing, *1875*

Man on steamer Red Wing, Mississippi River, *1904*

"Piloting a steamboat was a genuine science, especially on the St. Croix and upper Mississippi. Not only did the pilot have to know every channel on the river, but he also had to know every bend in the river. The pilot was absolute master when in the pilot house, and his word was law. . . ." 1912

Verne Swain pilot house

Most of the steamboats plying the waters of the Mississippi and St. Croix were built in states other than Minnesota. But one unusual Stillwater boatbuilder made sturdy steamboats for the big rivers, and along the way he designed a better stern-wheeler. David M. Swain opened the Stillwater Marine Engine Works in 1867 to repair engines used in the logging and lumber industry. In 1881, his first sternwheeler, the *Percy Swain,* made use of his design of cross-mounted engines—it provided steamboat captains much better navigational control. Other Swain steamboats in many sizes and barge conversions soon followed.

Steamer Verne Swain, *Stillwater, 1913*

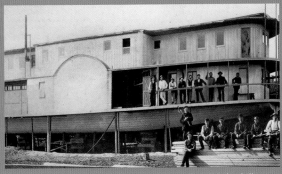

Steamer Kabekona *under construction at Swain Boat Works, Stillwater levee, 1907*

Swain named the steamer *Kabekona,* the Indian name for "Stillwater."

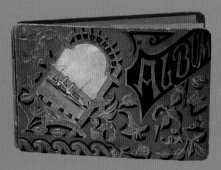

Steamer Ben Hur, *Stillwater, 1911*

Steamer Sidney, *Winona*

Steamer Purchase, *St. Croix River, Stillwater, 1914*

When push came to shove, barges once used for freight were hastily retrofitted and pressed into service to hold the crowds. The fanciful steamer *Purchase* towed the unadorned barge *Twin Cities* but passengers on both vessels enjoyed equal dance and refreshment privileges.

The Streckfus Lines

Bubbling fountains, chic restaurants, gourmet buffets—and soda fountains decorated with pink elephants, purple snakes, and green monkeys—were all offered on the Streckfus Line of excursion steamers. The beautifully designed and well-appointed boats boasted luxury ocean liner service on local Mississippi River tours and it cost only a few cents more than a movie house ticket.

Cover of the Streckfus Line monthly magazine

Lounge on steamer J. S. De Luxe, The Streckfus Line Magazine

Passengers on one of the luxurious steamers in the Streckfus fleet

Captain John Streckfus on the S.S. President

Cool alfresco dining room on the steamer J. S. DeLuxe

The engine room on the steamer St. Paul

Capitol daylight excursions

Sightseeing trips and evening dinner-dance excursions filled Streckfus steamers with passengers on day-long holidays. The colorful Riviera Roof Garden of the steamer *President* was ideal for breezy views of the passing river. Its six powerful, smokeless, oil-burning boilers allayed fears of a sudden shower of soot and cinders that were common on other vessels. After dinner, evening passengers sauntered to the ballroom for a night of dancing to the music of the Louisiana Swing Master orchestra.

Steamer President *at Winona, 1940*

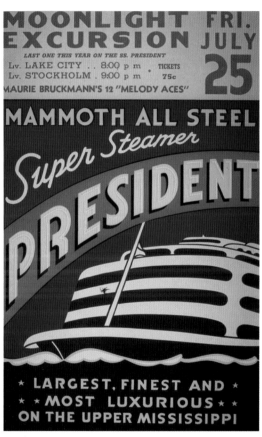
President *excursion poster*

Riviera roof garden

Coloramic Rainbow Ballroom on the President

147

Leisurely lake excursions

Boat rides were extremely popular on lakes all over the state. Most people did not own personal boats during the early half of the twentieth century, but they enjoyed the luxury of commercially run outings.

The prime motivation for gliding over the waves was the adventure and fun, but being on cool water was also a great way to escape the heat of a humid summer.

Keenora landing, Lake of the Woods, Baudette, 1916

Steamship Keenora, *Lake of the Woods, 1914*

Interior of an excursion boat, 1920
▼ *Group of people in a small steam launch, 1910*

Native pilot on steamship Keenora, *1914*

Launch, Lake of the Woods, 1922

The 1920s gave us flappers, bootleg gin, and party boats as elegantly appointed as the summer homes where they docked.

Passengers on a small launch, 1916

Steamboat Minnie Corliss at dock, Detroit Lake, 1889

Passenger steamer on Battle Lake, Otter Tail County, 1912

Boats with steam engines needed a licensed engineer on board to reduce the chance of the boilers blowing up. Later, less hazardous compact naphtha engines were used, and they in turn were replaced with a safe single-cylinder gasoline marine engine.

Passengers aboard the steamer Irene, 1908

Wind in our sails

Sailboats have gathered the wind and sailed for centuries. Though there are many different designs of sailboats, pleasure crafts essentially fall into just two categories: cruising and racing. Large cruising yachts had classic V-shaped hulls with a solid keel beneath for stability. Small cruising sailers had centerboards that could be raised to navigate shallow waters and for ease of storage and transport. Racing sailboats were built for speed, not comfort. The flat-bottomed scow was the inland racing craft that revolutionized the sport and won countless races. Minnesotans enjoyed both kinds!

After the Races, White Bear Lake, 1940, watercolor by Edna G. M. Kahlert

Regatta day, Lake Minnetonka, 1909

Lake Minnewaska, Glenwood, 1910

Sailing on Okabeno, Worthington, 1915

Lake scene, Lake Elmo, 1910

Lake Hazel, Benson

Sailboat Annette, Minneapolis, 1895

Yacht clubs made the sport of sailing as much a social experience as it was a racing challenge. Lake Superior wind gusts usually found the sails fast, while capturing winds at Lake Minnetonka and White Bear Lake could take a little patience.

Minnetonka Yacht Club, Deephaven, 1903

The Minnetonka Yacht Club opened in 1882 as the first inland sailing club in the United States.

Duluth Yacht Club, 1910

White Bear Yacht Club, Dellwood, 1920

Johnson X boat

Johnson C boat, White Bear Lake

J. O. Johnson with models he made of the Minnezitka *and an A boat.*

In the 1900s, White Bear Lake boatbuilder John O. Johnson, a twenty-five-year-old immigrant from Norway, set about to build a new style of sailboat for C. Milton Griggs. Johnson designed the hull to skim across the water, and when it heeled up, it would glide like a canoe. Griggs had the drawings checked with a naval architect, who after examining the plans said, "Johnson might well have invented the fastest sailboat in the world!" It would be a scow design hull 38 feet in length with a flat, square-shaped bow. When finished, it looked fast and it was. In its inaugural race it beat the second place finisher by a mile! Griggs named the boat *Minnezitka*, the Indian name for "water bird." Johnson went on to revolutionize sailboating with crafts ranging from the 15-foot X boat for junior sailors to the awe-inspiring 38-foot A boat racing scow for advanced competition. The Smithsonian Institution now has a model of Johnson's A boat.

Canoe with sail, Lake Minnetonka 1907

"June, 1907—Two of our Boats. Bert is in the canoe, it holds two, but not for me—it tips too easy. Lill."

Watching sailboat races, 1900s

Racing became a popular spectator sport and regattas drew crowds of fans.

There is nothing —absolutely nothing— half so much worth doing as simply messing about in boats.

KENNETH GRAHAM

Iceboats kept many sailors sailing right through the winter. Like sailboats, they came in all sizes. In the 1920s, the Johnson Boat Works made A class ice boats. They were 36 feet long with runners 24 feet apart and huge mainsails and jibs. They weighed 1,300 pounds and set speed records of over one hundred miles per hour!

Ice boating on White Bear Lake, 1930

Lake City Ice Yacht Club, 1898

Early Minnesota boat manufacturers

Boatbuilding flourished in Minnesota at the start of the twentieth century. Small rowboats to fifty-foot launches were built in several locations around the state. Pride in craftsmanship, a hallmark of Minnesota boatbuilding, produced high-quality boats of great utility and beauty. The 1908 Moore Boat Works of Wayzata catalog said it best: "On account of our location we have been brought in close contact with the lake dweller and have learned from them to know the requirements necessary to be embodied in a pleasure craft in order to obtain the most satisfactory results!"

Ramaley Boat Works, White Bear Lake, 30-foot Standard Runabout

White Bear Lake was a major center for boatbuilding in Minnesota. Several boat companies designed small rowboats or sailboats, others specialized in large yachts. When Ramaley Boat Works bought Moore of Wayzata, the combined factories offered a complete line of personal watercraft.

Ramaley Boats

Sailboat Marion Jean

Marion Jean was the winner of the Inland Lakes and Minnesota State Regatta in 1910.

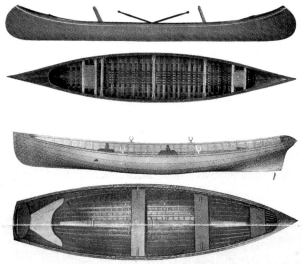

Minnetonka Indian model canoe, and Minnetonka stock rowboat

Costs in 1900 for canvas-covered canoes were $85 for a 17-foot canoe and $95 for an 18-foot canoe. The cost of one paddle? $1.75.

Moore Boats

Moore Boat Works, Wayzata, 35-foot Raised Deck Cruiser

Wayzata's Moore Boat Works built several sizes of large boats for more than twenty years. They were designed for passenger service and day cruising. Moore often used a reliable and easy-to-operate motor made by Campbell Motor Company, a neighboring firm also located in Wayzata.

Interior of 48-foot Glass Cabin Cruiser

48-foot Glass Cabin Cruiser

50-foot Excursion Boat

30-foot Family Auto Boat

Red Wing Boat Mfg. Co.

The Red Wing Boat Manufacturing Company built a line of motor launches and passenger boats up to fifty feet in length. The boats were powered with 14- to 40-horsepower motors also manufactured by the Red Wing Boat Company.

Red Wing Boat Manufacturing Company, Red Wing, 31-foot Cabin Cruising Motor Boat

Auto Boat with canvas top

38-foot Cabin Cruising Motor Boat

Small boatbuilders had few motorized machines. Most did the sawing and shaping by hand and rigged their own steam boxes to bend the wood into the graceful curves needed for a handsome quality boat.

The Spicer Boat Works, Wilmar, 1930s

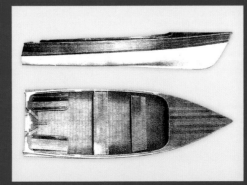

Ole Lind Boat Works, Detroit Lakes, 1920s

Wayzata Boat Building Company, Wayzata, 1925

Beautiful wooden boats

Glamorous, graceful, and proudly bearing the engraved nameplates of their makers, these could only be the classic wooden powerboats—the "woodies," complete with polished brass, varnished mahogany, and a shine that reflected the world on a sunny day. Inboard engines burbled and bubbled as they sat along the dock patiently waiting for passengers to board.

Chris-Craft powerboat, Duluth Harbor, 1945

The Robert C, St. Croix River, 1950s
Cruiser Jerilu, 1947 ▼

70-mile mailboat trip, Leech Lake, Walker

When the mailboat was in sight, dockhands reached out for special speed-by mail delivery.

Powerboat at Grand View Lodge, Gull Lake, 1950

Woodie on Whitefish Lake, 1956

Dock at Deauville Landing, Gull Lake

Chicago Queen, *Duluth, 1957*

Yacht North Star *with the steamer* Capitol. *Wabasha, 1933*

The yacht *North Star* was one of three large river boats owned by the Mayo brothers of Rochester. The 120-foot-long *North Star*, built by Dingle Boat Works, St. Paul, held sleeping accommodations for twenty passengers and cruised downstream on the Mississippi all the way to the Gulf of Mexico.

Motorboating, Minnesota Arrowhead country

The Commodore, *designed by Norman Bel Geddes, 1941*

Gar Wood had a passion for boat racing that began when he was a boy on Lake Osakis. His father Walter operated a ferryboat in the early 1900s and won races against the lake's rival ferry, much to his son's delight. As an adult, Wood invented a hydraulic hoist for trucks in St. Paul. His fortunes grew rapidly and his interest in racing boats resurfaced. Gar Wood Boat Company began in Michigan in 1927 with fast and popular lines of personal speedboats that for decades to come proudly bore the name Gar Wood.

Gar Wood and mechanic Orlin Johnson in Miss America X, *1932*

Thirty-eight-foot *Miss America* X, a Gar Wood racer, was powered by four supercharged Packard V-12 engines with total output of 7,600 horsepower. The lightning-fast boat won a speed record of 124.9 miles per hour. A multiple Gold Cup winner, Gar Wood became an international racing celebrity.

Baby Gar 40 speedboat, 1929

Modern Minnesota boat companies

Larson, Lund, Crestliner, Pipestone, and Aluma Craft were the major players in the development of modern Minnesota boat-building. They made boats of wood, marine plywood, aluminum, and fiberglass. The material, plus the time to produce the boat, made a big difference in the cost. In addition to the price, the buyer's decision was affected by the weight, handling, noise quality, maintenance, and durability. Minnesota companies offered the most trustworthy boats made to satisfy their customer's needs and enjoyment.

In 1939, a distinctive new designer boat came to market called the Falls Flyer. Paul Larson, of Larson Boat Works in Little Falls, was a schoolmate of Charles Lindbergh and was inspired by Lindbergh's first airplane, a Curtis Jenny. Paul designed a 14-foot boat with a twin cockpit and round hull, painted black and white, with the forward deck rounding off to the water line. Produced in a variety of sizes from sleek outboards to 21-foot inboards, Falls Flyers drew fans whenever they appeared. Production of the beautiful boat ended in 1960.

Larson

Larson Boats ran full-page color advertisements in national magazines and credited Paul Larson as "master builder" of Larson Boats for forty-five years.

Alumacraft

Located in Minneapolis, Alumacraft offered a full line of aluminum boats. Boats like the Merrie Lady were made with aluminum and fiberglass and were marketed under the Aluma Glass brand name.

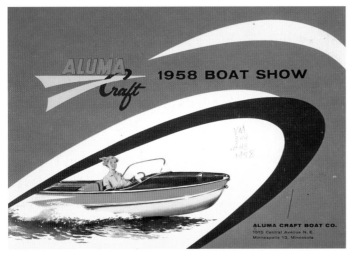

Alumacraft Boat Show brochure, 1958

17-foot Merrie Lady

14-foot runabout

The Ducker, duck boat

Alumacraft Boat Company, Minneapolis, 1957

During the 1950s, shorter workweeks and higher salaries brought about dramatic changes for people—especially boaters who now had more leisure time and the resources to own a boat of their own. Minnesota boatbuilders grew right along with one of the fastest growing recreational pursuits in the state and they soon offered more sizes, new materials, greater power, and faster styles.

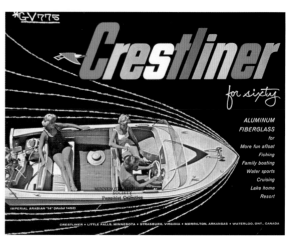

Crestliner brochure

Crestliner offered both aluminum and fiberglass boats perfect for loading atop the car or trailering off to favorite Minnesota lakes. The company began in Little Falls and opened plants in other states as their popularity grew.

Lund

Howard Lund made a boat for himself in New York Mills at his family home. A boat salesman passing through town saw the double-pointed hunting boat, liked it, and placed an order for fifty of them. The rest is history. In 1948, the Lund Boat Company began to build a quality line of aluminum boats, from the small John Boat, a shallow draft, square-bow hunting boat, to 25-foot boats for fishing, cruising, or skiing.

Crestliner

17-foot Flying Crest

Lund Fisherman
All new Fish 'N Ski ▼

Canoe

12-foot Sportsman

Crestliner in its lift, Leech Lake, 1960s

Luger Boat Kits catalog cover, Minneapolis, 1950s

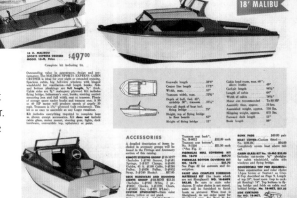

Luger catalog pages

Do it yourself! Luger offered boat kits in a range of styles from a basic 12-foot fishing boat to an 18-foot express cruiser. Even a speedy little hydroplane called the Aqua Skipper could be put together in the garage!

Pipestone Fiber Glass Boats catalog cover, Pipestone, 1959; 18-foot Apache Overnighter; 18-foot Siouxliner; 16-foot Chieftain

Designers at the Pipestone Boat Company were pioneers in molded fiberglass boats. The hulls were manufactured in a true mold process that eliminated any deviation in bottoms or centerlines—no one could complain of discomfort and rough rides.

Hiawatha outboard motors, 1948

Snappy action and an auto rewind starter.

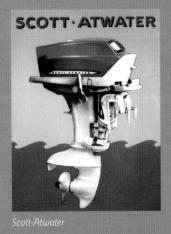

Scott-Atwater

Super quiet and bails your boat.

Champion outboard, 1950s

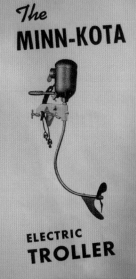

Minn-kota brochure

Minnesota-made outboard motors offered two desirable qualities for buyers: economy and range of power. The lightweight Minn Kota electrics were ideal for quiet trolling, while Hiawatha, Champion, and Scott-Atwater motors gave choices in power at reasonable prices.

159

Houseboats and pontoons

On and around Rainy Lake, the rental of house-boats equaled the number of resort cabins rented in the area—a remarkable indication of their popularity. Houseboats were the best of both worlds—a summer cabin plus the ability to tour, fish, and enjoy the water as on any other boat. They offered vacation getaways, whether puttering around a bay or anchored in secluded island coves.

Fisher's House Boat Rentals, Leech Lake, Walker

Houseboats in Winona, 1950s

Voyaguaire House Boats, Crane Lake

Fishers "boatels," Leech Lake, Walker

Pontoon on Lake O'Brien, 1970

Pontoon party, 1960s

Pontoon on Whitefish Lake, 1977

Hello from Walker

Boat harbor and gas dock, Winona

Weeres Richmond, marine pontoon boat

In 1951, Ambrose Weeres of Richmond, Minnesota, created the very first pontoon boat. The unusual contraption featured fifty-gallon oil drums welded together and topped with plywood, carpet, wood railings, and an outboard motor. The Weeres Pontoon Boat Company sold just three boats the first year, but in time the ugly duckling emerged a swan—and became a $200 million company.

Pontoon parades

Pontoon parades challenged the imaginations of shoreline neighbors. Owners decorated their boats for a colorful parade around the lake, then threw out their anchors for a buoyant party.

Lake Minnetonka, 1958

*A lot of people ask me
if I were shipwrecked,
and could only have one book,
what would it be?
I always say
'How to Build a Boat.'*
STEPHEN WRIGHT

Pontoon parade, Lake O'Brien, Cross Lake

Pontoon party snacks

When it was pontoon party time, a big cooler by a folding table held the sustenance for a long ride around the lake. Some days, the appetizers were so good, there was no need for dinner.

The following recipes have been adapted for easy preparation, modern cooking methods, and ingredients that are readily available.

Shrimp in Wine
Wild in the Kitchen by Will Jones, 1961
- 1 bottle Rhine or sharp red wine
- 2 tablespoons dry mustard
- 2 tablespoons salt
- Black pepper to taste
- 4 pounds fresh or frozen peeled and deveined large uncooked shrimp
- Drawn butter or cocktail sauce

Place the wine in a kettle. Add mustard, salt, and pepper and bring to a fast boil. Add shrimp. Reduce heat and cook covered about 5 minutes, or until shrimp turn pink. Serve warm with individual cups of drawn butter or cold with shrimp cocktail sauce. FOR SALAD: Place shrimp on finely shredded lettuce and shredded cucumber. Top with Thousand Island dressing. Serves 12 or more.

Cheese Puffs and Olives
Adapted from Food of My Friends by Virginia Safford, 1944
- 2 (5-ounce) jars bacon cheese or Old English spread
- 1/2 cup butter or margarine (1 stick), room temperature
- 2 dashes hot pepper sauce
- 2 dashes Worcestershire sauce
- 1-1/2 cups all-purpose flour
- 1 jar small green salad olives stuffed with pimiento

Mix cheese and butter together until light and fluffy. Add pepper sauce and Worcestershire sauce; mix well. Stir in flour and mix to form dough. Roll dough into small balls about the size of a large marble or shape dough around pimiento-stuffed salad olives,

drained and dried. Place on ungreased cookie sheets and bake at 400°F for 15 to 20 minutes. Serve piping hot. Or freeze before baking for future parties.

Applesassy Sausage Links
The Little Meat Cookbook, Schweigert Meat Company, 1960s
- 1 package of tiny pork sausages
- 2 cups applesauce
- 1/4 cup red cinnamon candies

Cut each sausage link into bite-size pieces and brown in skillet. Heat applesauce in chafing dish; add candies. Heat until candies are dissolved, stirring occasionally. Place cooked sausages in chafing dish. Serve warm; use wooden picks for spearing 50 bite-size appetizers.

Gluek's Avocado Dip
Have Fun . . . Have a Gluek's Beer-B-Cue, Gluek Brewing Company, Minneapolis, 1960s
- 1/4 cup Gluek's Beer or other favorite beer
- 2 ripe avocados, mashed
- 4 tablespoons mayonnaise
- 2 tablespoons minced capers
- 2 teaspoons lemon juice
- 2 teaspoons grated onion
- Seasoned salt to taste
- Vegetable dippers or potato chips

Blend ingredients thoroughly to make a smooth, calorie-light dip. Serve with your choice of crisp, chilled, raw vegetables, such as sliced cauliflower, carrots, celery hearts, radishes, scallions, cherry tomatoes. Also delightfully tasty with the traditional potato chip.

Peanut and Raisin Snack
Summer Fun: A Pillsbury Classic Cookbook, 1980s
- 2 cups cocktail peanuts
- 1 tablespoon oil (vegetable or olive)
- 1 teaspoon curry powder or five-spice powder
- 15-ounce package (2 cups) golden raisins

Preheat oven to 350°F. In ungreased 15x10-inch pan, spread peanuts in single layer. Drizzle evenly with oil; sprinkle with curry powder or five-spice powder. Bake 5 to 8 minutes, stirring frequently. Cool; stir in raisins. Store in tightly covered container. Makes 4 cups.

CRACKER SPREADS

Curried Crab or Shrimp
Minnesota's Greatest and Best Recipes: A University of Minnesota Cookbook, 1980s
- 8 ounces cream cheese, room temperature
- 3 tablespoons mayonnaise
- 1 teaspoon curry powder
- 7 ounces thawed small shrimp or crabmeat
- 1/4 cup chopped green onion
- 1 hard-cooked egg, chopped
- Water crackers

Blend cream cheese, mayonnaise, and curry powder until smooth. Spread onto serving plate. Cover the spread with shrimp or crabmeat. Top with chopped onion, then hard-cooked egg. Serve with water crackers.

Bummers Blue Cheese Spread — a la Treasure Cave
Cedric Adams for Duluth Universal Flour, 1940s
- 4 ounces Treasure Cave blue cheese
- 1 tablespoon brandy
- 1/2 tablespoon olive oil
- 1 teaspoon Worcestershire sauce
- 1/4 cup cottage cheese

Remove wax coating from blue cheese. In small bowl, crumble

blue cheese with fork. Mix in brandy, oil, and Worcestershire sauce. Mix in cottage cheese. If a thinner spread is desired, add brandy, 1 teaspoon at a time.

Nut and Olive Spread
Duluth Universal Flour and Midland Cooperative Wholesale, 1940s
- Chopped English walnuts
- Chopped green olives with pimientos
- Mayonnaise
- Flat bread or rye rounds

Mix equal quantities of chopped walnuts and olives with mayonnaise and a little olive juice to moisten. Serve with flat bread or rye rounds.

French Ham and Peanut Spread
Cedric Adams for Duluth Universal Flour, 1940s
- 1 cup finely chopped ham
- 1/2 cup finely chopped peanuts
- 2 tablespoons sweet pickle relish
- 1/4 cup finely minced celery
- 3 tablespoons salad dressing
- Thin sliced white bread, lightly buttered

Combine ham, peanuts, relish, and celery. Mix to a paste with salad dressing. Spread on bread. Cut into quarters or triangles or serve ham mixture as a cracker spread.

Fruit Canapés
Zinsmaster Baking Company, 1950s
- 1/2 cup cream cheese at room temperature
- 2 tablespoons finely chopped crystallized ginger
- 1/4 cup chopped dates
- 1/4 cup chopped nuts (pecans or walnuts)
- Thin sliced whole wheat bread

Beat cheese until creamy. Add the ginger, dates, and nuts. Blend thoroughly. Serve with squares of thinly sliced whole wheat bread.

CHAPTER TEN

Camping & Parks

CAMPING, CANOEING, AND APPRECIATING the great Minnesota outdoors have been passions since the early days of explorers and voyageurs. The state's varied landscape is due to its geologic history including four glaciers that scraped and gouged the earth, leaving many lakes and rocky terrains. Outdoor enthusiasts embraced the more than 10,000 lakes, paddling and portaging their canoes and setting up campsites on tranquil beaches. The shores and forests became weekend homes with sleeping and cooking facilities right at hand.

Minnesota companies jumped at the opportunity to manufacture goods for the growing number of vacationing naturalists. Tents were engineered in a variety of innovative designs from cottagelike, canvas-sided buildings to contraptions rigged with branches and trapezoidal tents tied directly to owners' Model Ts. All the equipment necessary for camping followed suit. Folding camp stools, cots, and sleeping bags, waterproof clothing, and even bug spray were made within the state's border. A pack invented in Duluth in the late 1900s revolutionized backpacking. Canoes made of materials ranging from hand-stripped birch bark to aluminum have made Minnesota known throughout the country for excellent craftsmanship. By gearing up for the North Woods, not only were Minnesotans prepared for outdoor adventures, they also supported local industries.

The earliest campers pitched tents in farmer's fields and along roadsides pretty much wherever they desired. Communities then opened free municipal parks to encourage tourism in the area and to keep the growing activity safe and comfortable. Privately run campgrounds offered amenities such as running water, shared common areas, and snack bars—but for a fee.

Minnesota was the second state in the country to enact a state park system. Beginning with the designation of Itasca State Park in 1891, state parks offered escapes for pleasant day trips or overnight camping experiences. From prairie grasslands in the southwest to the North Shore's rugged coast, our park system protected the natural and cultural environments of the state. Within the state, nearly six hundred buildings are on the National Register of Historic Places, including many historic log and stone structures built in the 1930s.

In addition to many state parks, Minnesota has one of the country's premier wilderness areas stretching across the northern border. This vast region encompasses a national park, two national forests, and the Boundary Waters Canoe Area Wilderness. Federally protected land and waters ensure tranquil experiences for those who want to venture away from humanity. And thanks to many conservationists and naturalists who've called the state home, our thirteen million acres of water continue to provide recreation and inspiration.

The Complete Camper's Manual, *1903*

◄ *Early Minnesota campers, 1915*

Early tenting

Even before mosquito spray and inflatable mattresses were invented, Minnesotans loved to camp. Conditions were rustic, amenities minimal, and windowless tents stuffy and warm. But campers hitched up their horses or cranked up their Model Ts and headed off to a Minnesota paradise.

Straw bed, 1905

Comfort in camping sometimes meant gathering moss for a pillow or sharing a straw mattress. But the air was fresh and lapping waves lulled everyone to sleep.

Looking for moss, 1925

Campsite, 1905

Family in tent, 1900

Civilized camping for this group included bedspreads and a tidy clothes rack.

Camping along the Mississippi River, Little Falls, 1899

Entrance sign, Cass Lake

A welcoming sign announced arrival for travelers on this rutted sandy road to Cass Lake.

Lake Lida, 1915

Hopefully, corsets were left at home, but floor-length dresses were still the fashion for these camping women.

Camping near the North Shore, 1912

Whether on the shore, in the woods, or at organized tourist campgrounds, Minnesotans lugged their cooking equipment, fishing poles, and sleeping bags and took full advantage of the state's great outdoors.

Minnesota campground

Idyllic campsites included benches and picnic tables for hungry campers.

Tent, 1920

Semipermanent tents were built on wood platforms and had real swinging screen doors.

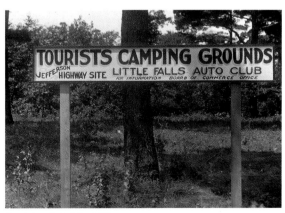

Road sign, Little Falls, 1920

The Little Falls Board of Commerce and Auto Club established campgrounds for cross-country travelers. National routes such as the Jefferson Highway ran through Little Falls on its way from Winnipeg to New Orleans.

Early camping equipment manufacturers

To accommodate the growing number of camping enthusiasts, Minnesota companies manufactured a variety of products. Tents of all sizes and shapes were raised by a system of poles and cables. Some enterprising inventors made tents that anchored directly to campers' automobiles. Furniture, sleeping bags, and cooking equipment completed the ensembles of early camping gear and provided nearly all the comforts of home.

St. Paul Tent & Awning Company

Square hip-roofed tents

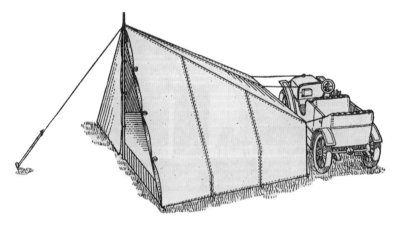

Only one pole was needed to raise this auto tent—provided the emergency brake was set.

Reclining chair, Gold Medal folding camp chair, comfort swing chair

The top-of-the-line chair in a 1914 catalog was the comfort swing. A "fancy striped canvas" seat and back were suspended from a steel frame allowing the user to swing back and forth. A bargain at $6.60.

Open Air Cottage Company

"Camport" cottage, Open Air Cottage Company, St. Paul, 1910

A hardwood floor and fluttering curtains made this tent a sophisticated escape. The Open Air Cottage Company set up models in front of their headquarters in the heart of St. Paul's Cathedral Hill. The lure of a tamed wilderness captured the hearts of urban dwellers.

Mosquitoes ran into several Minnesota companies that made repellent—B-V Mosquito Chaser, by the makers of Burma Shave; Zizz; Watkins; and Fly-ola.

Gokey's

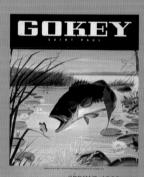

Making boots at Gokey's, St. Paul, 1936; spring 1963 catalog

Since 1850, Gokey's sporting goods store was chockfull of camping equipment, including its own line of world-famous, hand-sewn boots: the Gokey Botte Sauvage.

Duluth Tent & Awning Company

1910 Duluth Pack; Patent illustration, 1882

Duluth Tent & Awning began manufacturing camping equipment in 1911, but the company's origins go back even further. In 1882 Camille Poirer, a Duluth shoemaker, filed a patent for a new type of packsack. His design featured improved shoulder straps, a revolutionary sternum strap, and three buckled closures that adjusted to fit the pack's contents. He sold the idea to Duluth Tent & Awning and it's been called a Duluth Pack ever since. It revolutionized backpacking and eventually companies throughout the country made their own versions. The packs are still for sale today in Duluth's Canal Park.

Duluth Tent & Awning touring tent

Carrying bulky gear in early touring cars created a packing problem. The AutoPack, a canvas bag with steel clamps, attached to the car's running board. Except for a few stakes in the ground, the "mosquito proof" Touring Tent attached directly to a car and cost $6.50; $30 dollars bought a 7' x 7' touring tent in the early 1930s.

Hoigaard's

C. J. Hoigaard's Gopher Flex-Frame Umbrella Tent

An early Hoigaard's patented umbrella tent was rigged with a series of chains and springs that could be set up within five minutes. Four generations of Minneapolis Hoigaards have tended the company, from its founding in 1895 to the greatly expanded outdoor equipment and active apparel business today.

Tenting in the woods still had the accoutrements of modern living.

Herter's

Herter's catalog, 1973; Plastaug water repellent; wilderness cook set; station wagon double sleeping bag

Founded in 1893, Herter's carried a full line of everything a camper or sportsman needed: fishing lures, rifles, boats, long underwear, tents, sleeping bags, cooking utensils, and freeze-dried chop suey! Waterproof clothing was essential for outdoor adventure and Herter's claimed their Swiss Plastaug waterproofing was so easy on fabrics that "your wife can use it on her finest party dress with safety." The mail-order catalog company was located in Waseca and customers around the country anxiously awaited the bulky catalog complete with often outrageous captions.

Canoeing

The earliest canoes to ply Minnesota waters were covered with a fragile layer of birch bark that needed constant care and upkeep. Native Americans and French Canadian voyageurs traveled the rivers and lakes as a way of life and commerce. Canoes gained popularity as pleasure boats and while they maintained the beauty of their centuries-old design, lighter and more durable materials cut swiftly through waters and made portaging easier.

Canoe trip in Ely, 1930s

Lake Minnetonka, 1936

Canoe portage, 1920

Karl and Betty Ketter

Karl Neil, Ken, and Karl Ketter, 1950s

An energetic eighteen-year-old in the 1930s, Karl Ketter nearly paddled the length of the Mississippi River before being stopped by a hurricane in Arkansas. When he married Betty several years later she knew canoeing would be their life's pursuit. Together they founded Ketter Canoeing in 1967 and helped launch canoe racing as a competitive sport. They were also instrumental in forming the Minnesota Canoe Association that promotes racing and canoe building. Ketter Canoeing is run by the family's second generation.

More than just a store filled with camping and canoeing equipment, outfitters provide expert camping advice and arrange guides for simple weekend trips or extended fly-in excursions.

Border Lakes Outfitting Company, Winton, 1950s

Canoe Country Outfitters, Ely, 1958

Belands Outfitters, Ely

Marie Sarkapate, 1950s

The first woman guide in the Boundary Waters and daughter of Ely resort owners, Marie Sarkapate was known for her clever ability to roll out pie dough on the bottom of a canoe with a Scotch bottle.

170

Canoe manufacturers have been plentiful in the state. From finely crafted, one-of-a-kind wooden canoes to factory-assembled molded forms, Minnesota builders design canoes in a variety of shapes, sizes, and materials.

Joe and Nora Seliga, Ely

Handcrafted in a small Ely garage, Seliga canoes have been made one at a time since 1938. Individually signed and dated, Joe and Nora Seliga's cedar-and-canvas canoes are considered by many to be works of art. Adventurers at the nearby YMCA Camp Widjiwagan have paddled Seliga canoes since 1946.

Earl Nyholm, birchbark canoe maker

Considered America's premier birchbark canoe maker, Earl Nyholm was the subject of a Smithsonian documentary in the late 1990s. Nyholm grew up in Michigan, but lived for many years in the Bemidji area. In addition to making more than fifty canoes, he taught in Bemidji State University's Indian Studies program and coauthored *A Concise Dictionary of Minnesota Ojibwe*. Nyholm's canoes are made with freshly peeled birch bark, seams are sewn with jack pine, and the vessel is sealed with spruce pitch.

We-no-nah Canoe

Established in 1968 in the Mississippi River town of Winona, We-no-nah Canoe is among the state's oldest canoe manufacturers. Combining modern technology with historic ideals make these canoes popular for leisure paddling as well as competitive sport.

Bill Hafeman, Big Fork

A practical man, Bill Hafeman built his first canoe in the 1920s so he could get to town quicker than by car. Soon other people admired his craftsmanship. Lady Bird Johnson and Charles Kuralt number among those who've owned a Hafeman Boat Works original. Granddaughter Christy and husband Ray Boessel continue the tradition, producing a dozen handcrafted birchbark canoes per year.

Alumacraft canoes

Alumacraft started in Minneapolis in 1893 as an iron works company. After fabricating aluminum aircraft parts during World War II, the company's owner put the excess material to use by building boats. The revolutionary techniques launched the company into fame.

Minnesota husband-and-wife team Florence and Francis Lee Jaques collaborated on several books about the wild outdoors. Her popular writings and his scratchboard illustrations became legendary. Francis also designed the 1940 federal duck stamp and many dioramas and murals for museums, including the James Ford Bell Museum and New York's American Museum of Natural History.

Camps for kids

Minnesota lakes were perfect settings for kids' camps. They were in all corners of the state and beckoned to those wanting physical activities or intellectual stimulation alike. There were private camps, scout camps, YMCA and YWCA camps, church camps, Scandinavian and Jewish camps, language camps, and camps for children with special needs. Many were formed to introduce young boys and girls to the rigors of outdoor life and shape their skills on water and in the woods. Other activities focused on building confidence and character through lake activities and social, cultural, and craft skills. And then there was mess hall duty!

Camps for kids and Grand View Lodge for the folks

Sunshine and smiley faces

Time to say good-bye

An adventure in the woods

Staff and campers become friends

Is it clean enough?

Ready, set, go!

Chow time

Camp chores included doing dishes

Don't swamp the boat

Arts and crafts are fun

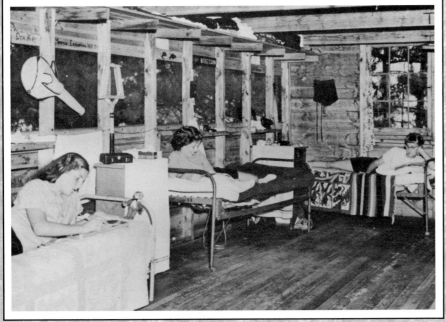

Dear Mom and Dad . . .

Sing along everybody

Minnesota state parks

Itasca, Minnesota's first state park, was a treasured destination even before its designation in 1891. Many explorers tried to find the Mississippi River's headwaters, but it wasn't until 1832, when Henry Schoolcraft consulted Native American guide Ozawindib, that it was found. The lake was named Itasca from the Latin words for "true source."

Old-growth red and white pines surrounded Lake Itasca, and in the late nineteenth century the towering trees were a majestic sight for early tourists. But encroaching loggers saw them differently. Fortunately the loggers were stopped and today Itasca represents the best of our state parks.

Logging devastation, photo by Mary Gibbs, 1903

In the early years, Itasca's grounds were home to park employees and homesteaders as well as loggers. Greedy timber interests would have endangered the entire area if it weren't for Mary Gibbs. Daughter of the park's second commissioner, Mary was twenty-four when she assumed her father's job, and as acting commissioner saved Itasca and the headwaters from potentially devastating floods caused by a logging dam.

Douglas Lodge exterior

Minnesota's most historic lodge was built in 1905. Mary Gibbs chose the logs herself, and true to her conservation spirit, all logs were cut from trees already down. The building was named after Attorney General Wallace B. Douglas who, from his office in St. Paul, was also instrumental in preserving our first state park.

Log cabin, mansard-roofed clubhouse ▼

Most of Itasca's buildings were constructed in the early twentieth century in a rustic style typical of national park archtecture. Over fifty structures in the park, including those on this page, are on the National Register of Historic Places.

Lunch counter at the Forest Inn, Itasca, 1942

Franklin Delano Roosevelt created the Civilian Conservation Corps (CCC) in 1932. Unemployed men joined "camps" for paid work on forestry projects. The CCC was responsible for numerous park projects around the state including seventy log and stone buildings at Itasca alone. The Forest Inn is one of Minnesota's most impressive buildings of the era with massive log trusses and walls of split stonework.

Spanning the headwaters, 1930s

Campgrounds, Itasca, 1945

> *The mosquitoes, my wife and I had a most enjoyable time.*
> ITASCA STATE PARK GUEST BOOK
> MAY 31, 1937

A sampling of Minnesota state parks

Thanks to the diversity of Minnesota's geologic history, the state has a wide variety of landscapes. Our state park system protects and interprets this natural history as well as provides opportunities for daylong and extended recreation. Numerous structures throughout the park system are on the National Register of Historic Places.

Gooseberry Falls, park established 1937

Eight state parks cling to the edge of Lake Superior along the North Shore. Nearly every stream entering the lake tumbles over rocky landscapes into cascading waterfalls. Gooseberry State Park has five beautiful falls.

Dalles of the St. Croix, Interstate Park, established 1895

Majestic cliffs surround the St. Croix River as it cuts its way through a basalt gorge. Above the river ancient flows of lava hardened then eroded into cylindrical depressions to become the park's distinctive kettle-holes.

Soudan Underground Mine, park established 1962

Once the oldest, deepest, and richest of Minnesota's iron ore mines, this unusual state park is a half-mile underground. Listed on the National Register of Historic Places, the Soudan mine is the country's only underground iron ore mine open to the public.

Blue Mounds, park established 1937

The great plains begin in southwestern Minnesota where bison roamed native grasslands. A large outcropping of Sioux quartzite is covered with a blue-green lichen that gives the park its name. Novelist Frederick Manfred's former home is now the park's interpretive center.

Northern Minnesota's natural wonders

Lake of
the Woods

Warroad

Rainy River

Rain
Lake

More than three quarters of Minnesota's northern state line shares a water border with Canada. This interconnected series of lakes and rivers is an internationally known wilderness area. Tourists have been coming here for years. Before roads were built, visitors, homesteaders, and loggers reached the area by train. Many individuals, politicians, and environmental groups, such as the Isaak Walton fishing camp, eventually saved the area from logging and invasive building of roads.

Voyageurs National Park, 1970s

Minnesota's only national park is named for the French-Canadian fur traders, the first Europeans to travel the state. The rugged terrain, vast number of lakes, and some of the oldest exposed rock formations in the world make this park an escape to the time of the voyageurs.

Lake of the Woods, photo by Carl G. Linde, 1922

Lake of the Woods is as far north as you can go in the continental United States. These international waters have 65,000 miles of shoreline, 14,582 islands, and an abundance of walleye considered second to none.

Famed Ontario photographer Carl G. Linde documented the Ojibwe people and vacation culture of the early-nineteenth-century Lake of the Woods region.

Rainy Lake, Ernest Oberholtzer and longtime traveling companion Billy Magee, 1910s

A leader in the conservation movement and one of the founders of the Wilderness Society, Ernest Oberholtzer is credited for saving Voyageurs National Park and the Boundary Waters from logging. His home on Rainy Lake hosted Theodore Roosevelt, Aldo Leopold, and many other renowned conservationists in the quest to save the environment.

Chippewa National Forest, portaging a canoe, 1940

Designated by Theodore Roosevelt in 1908, the Chippewa National Forest was the first national forest east of the Mississippi River. Within the park is the Lost Forty, a section of 350-year-old virgin pine that escaped nineteenth-century loggers due to a surveying error. But it's not all trees here—there are more than 1,000 lakes within the park's 1.6 million acres.

Southern Minnesota's cultural and scenic landscapes

Leaping Rock, Pipestone National Monument, 1949

Pipestone National Monument was designated in 1937 to preserve the soft red sacred stone Native Americans have carved into ceremonial pipe calumets for centuries. The American Indian cultural center helps continue the art of carving as well as generate income through souvenir sales.

Jeffers Petroglyphs

More than 2,000 symbols were chiseled in rock up to 5,000 years ago. The Jeffers Petroglyphs are the largest collection of these in the Upper Midwest.

Canoeing on Rainy Lake, 1930

In this tranquil watershed, popular with canoeists, as many people rent houseboats as they do lakeshore cabins.

International Falls

Voyageurs National Park

Chippewa National Forest

Superior National Forest, nature's beauty

More of Minnesota's wilderness was protected in 1909 by Theodore Roosevelt in the Superior National Forest. Five thousand lakes dot the landscape of what was considered the country's largest national forest. Prehistoric painted rocks survive along the shores of several lakes.

Lac La Croix, 1964

The Boundary Waters Canoe Area Wilderness stretches nearly 150 miles along the Canadian border between International Falls and Grand Portage. The landscape was carved and gouged into lakes and streams, islands and rock formations by ancient glaciers. Today it's a canoeist's paradise. With 1,200 miles of canoe routes, the Boundary Waters was protected by acts of Congress in 1964 and 1978. The National Geographic Society recommends the area as one of the fifty greatest places to visit in a lifetime.

Boundary Waters Canoe Area Wilderness

Superior National Forest

Pink Cove at Beaver Bay, oil painting by Robert Conant, 1940

Entrance to the Gunflint Trail, Grand Marais, 1950s

Starting near the shores of Lake Superior in Grand Marais and ending in the Boundary Waters, the Gunflint Trail is a legendary road. Dotted with idyllic campsites, historic and contemporary resorts, and helpful outfitters, the trail provides the "entrance to the greatest canoe and resort country in America!"

Gunflint Trail

Grand Portage National Monument

Grand Marais

The North Shore

The legendary North Shore is the scenic route where waves of Lake Superior crash against Minnesota's rocky cliffs and bold headlands. Along the 150-mile drive between Duluth and Grand Portage there are nine state parks filled with waterfalls, hiking trails, and camping facilities.

St. Croix River National Waterway

A former fur trade and logging route, the St. Croix River has seen human activity for 10,000 years. Nature lovers now enjoy its federally protected waters.

Lake Pepin from Wabasha, oil painting by Clement Haupers, 1949

Towering bluffs, rolling farmlands, and quaint river towns make this extra-wide spot along the Mississippi a scenic treasure.

Curtis Trailer Co. catalog, Minneapolis, 1922

As automobiles gained popularity, entrepreneurs were attempting to create mobile habitats on wheels.

The Camp Trailer cost $250 in 1922. It was furnished with tent, ropes and stakes, hinged raised beds, collapsible table and stove, and an ice box that rode on the running board.

The Curtis Home on a Car opened up to 12' x 14' and held two good beds, icebox, stove, table, and large drawers for clothes and provisions. It cost $625 in 1922—owner must have the car body and Fords were best.

Trailer camping

As Minnesotans discovered their bountiful parks, they looked for new and creative ways to visit them. Trailers and campers had advantages over tents and Minnesota manufacturers created some of the most interesting trailers around. There was no worry over rain, mosquitoes, or wild animals. The beds were a lot better than air mattresses and cooking started with a flick of a burner.

Curtis Trailer Co.

Camp trailer closed

Camp trailer opened

Home on a Car closed

Home on a Car opened

Ecklund Brothers

Ecklund Brothers trailers were completely outfitted for the road 1930s style. While not quite an Airstream, the exterior shape was mindful of wind currents and interiors were comfortable and space efficient.

Trailers at Kamp Dels Campsite, Lake Sakatah, Waterville

Those planning a trip on the road had decisions to make—would they choose pop-up-trailers, camping trailers, truck campers, or motor homes?

Tent mounted on top of a station wagon, 1958

Tent mounted at the back of a station wagon, 1958

They never caught on with the public, but these tent inventions turned campers' heads at the 1958 Sportsmen's Show.

Superior Motor Home

Motor homes were first made from converted school buses, but they evolved quickly into luxurious dwellings on the move.

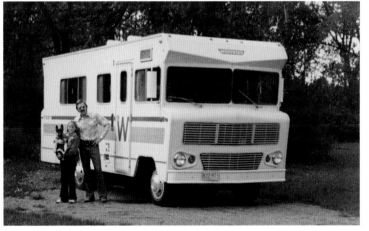

Winnebago camping, 1970s

Even the family pet could join in on the fun of vacation adventures in a recreational vehicle.

Outdoor cooking

The canoe turned upside-down for a table, a rock made do for a chair, fish sizzled on the campfire; it was the lap of luxury lakeside— and only the pot and a plate needed to be portaged in. Evening campfires became the heart of the daily trek and tired muscles soon disappeared at the aroma of wood-fired meals and hot coffee. In the morning, a pan of trout with crisp potatoes and eggs warming started the day in the best possible way.

Mary Welsh Hemingway, Ernest Hemingway's fourth wife who grew up on Leech Lake, said it best: "No two aromas compliment each other better than those of freshly-crushed balsam and frying bacon."

Breakfast on a canoe, 1960s

Cooking on an outdoor fireplace, 1935

Camp cooking, 1925

Campfire at Burntside Lake, 1960s

KampKook by American Gas Machine Co., Albert Lea

Kampkookery hints on motor camping advised that even the most timid tenderfoot can load his car and go out with the assurance of many happy hours with the KampKook stove.

Campfire breakfast

Bacon and eggs frying and blueberry muffins warming could rouse the sleepiest little trekker. Breakfast aromas made a camper's morning and healthy snacks tucked in the aluminum cooler kept everyone hiking for the rest of the day.

The following recipes have been adapted for easy preparation, modern cooking methods, and ingredients that are readily available.

Maple Grapefruit

Towle's Log Cabin Syrup, 1940s

Cut grapefruit in half, score the sections, and take out the core. Pour a generous amount of Towle's Log Cabin Syrup on each half and let it soak in well before serving.

FOR GRILLED GRAPEFRUIT: *Wrap foil securely around fruit. Cook on grill 15 to 18 minutes, turning once. Serve one-half grapefruit per person.*

Eggs on a Raft

A classic from the 1940s
- 6 thick slices bacon
- 2 slices white bread
- Soft butter
- Salt and pepper
- 2 eggs

Fry bacon until crisp, remove from pan and keep warm. Drain bacon fat from pan. Cut or pull out a 2-inch circle of bread from the center of each bread slice. Butter and lightly salt and pepper both sides of bread. Place bread in the hot frying pan; break 1 egg into the center of each slice. Cook until the egg is half done; turn and cook the other side until egg is done to taste. Serve with bacon. Makes 2 servings.

Daybreak Omelet

The Cure/81 Hambook, Hormel, 1970s
- 1/3 cup butter or bacon drippings
- 3 cups peeled and cubed raw potatoes (3 medium)
- 1/3 cup minced onion
- 9 eggs
- 1 teaspoon salt
- Dash of pepper
- 1/4 cup cream

- 1-1/3 cups cubed Cure 81 Ham or SPAM
- 3/4 cup shredded Monterey Jack or Swiss cheese

Melt butter in 10-inch square fry pan or 12-inch round skillet. Add potatoes and onion. Cook, covered, stirring occasionally, about 20 minutes, until potatoes are tender. While potatoes cook, beat eggs, seasonings, and cream together. (Or, at home, break eggs into quart jar, add seasonings and cream, close with lid and take along in a cooler; shake to mix.) Add ham to skillet and fry briefly. Pour egg mixture over potatoes and ham. Cover and cook until eggs are almost set, about 10 minutes, occasionally lifting egg mixture gently with spatula for even cooking. Remove from heat. Sprinkle with cheese; cover again until cheese melts. Makes 6 servings.

Scotch Scones

Ceresota Cook Book, The Northwestern Consolidated Milling Co., 1940s
- 2 cups all-purpose flour
- 2-1/2 teaspoons baking powder
- 1 teaspoon salt
- 4 tablespoons butter or soft shortening
- 1 egg
- 1/2 cup milk

Stir together flour, baking powder, and salt. Using two knives, cut in butter until mixture looks like fine crumbs. Mix in egg and milk. Gather dough into a ball and knead 4 to 5 times. Divide dough in half. Pat each half into a 6-inch round. Mark each round into 4 wedges.

Place wedges on a greased griddle and bake over hot coals until golden brown, turning once (or bake at 375°F for 15 minutes). Serve with butter and jam. Makes 8 scones.

Fruit with Apple Jelly Sauce

Kitchen Kapers, Dairy Council of the Twin Cities, 1959
- 3 to 4 cups fresh fruit chunks (bananas, apples, grapes, oranges, strawberries, etc.)
FOR SAUCE:
- 1/3 cup apple jelly
- 1/2 cup orange juice
- 2 tablespoons lemon juice
- 2 tablespoons vinegar
- 2 tablespoons honey

Beat apple jelly with rotary beater. Add remaining ingredients. Add fruit chunks to sauce and mix gently.

SPAM and Bisquick Cakes

Let's Eat Outdoors, a tie-in cookbooklet with Hormel and General Mills, 1950s
FOR PANCAKE BATTER:
- 2 cups Bisquick biscuit mix
- 1 egg
- 1-1/3 cups milk
FOR SPAM CAKES:
- 12-ounce can SPAM
- Oil for frying
- Syrup

FOR BATTER: *Beat Bisquick, egg, and milk with rotary beater until smooth. Grease griddle if necessary. Cut SPAM into six lengthwise slices. Cut each slice in half. Fry SPAM pieces in hot skillet 3 to 4 inches apart. With 1/3-cup measuring cup, pour batter over each slice. Turn cakes when bubbles appear. Serve with syrup. Makes 12 SPAM cakes.*

Roasted Potatoes with Onion

The Ford Times Traveler's Cookbook, Ford Motor Company, 1965
- Potatoes
- Onion
- Salt and pepper
- Butter

Place thick slices of potatoes and onion on double-thick squares of heavy-duty aluminum foil. Salt and pepper and dab generously with butter. Wrap tightly and roast over hot coals for 45 minutes, until package is soft to gloved thumb.

Yum-Chow Cheesy Toast

Kampkook direction book, 1920
- 4 slices bacon, diced
- 1 onion, sliced
- 1 small can (1 cup) tomatoes
- 1/4 pound American cheese, diced
- Toasted bread

Fry bacon and onion together. Add tomatoes and cook 10 to 15 minutes. Stir in cheese and let it melt. Serve on toast.

Blueberry Muffins

Favorite Recipes, by Rita Martin, International Milling Company, 1950s
- 2 cups sifted all-purpose flour
- 1/3 cup sugar
- 3 teaspoons baking powder
- 1 teaspoon salt
- 2 tablespoons soft shortening or Crisco
- 1 egg
- 1 cup milk
- 1 cup fresh or well-drained canned blueberries

Sift dry ingredients together into a bowl. Cut in shortening with a pastry blender. Add egg and milk, stirring just until all flour is moistened. Fold in blueberries. Fill greased muffin pans 2/3 full. Bake at 400°F 20 to 25 minutes, or until golden brown. Makes 1 dozen.

Apple Snack Stacks

Summer Fun: A Pillsbury Classic Cookbook, 1980s
- 4 medium apples
- Peanut butter

Wash and core apples. Fill center with peanut butter, packing gently. Wrap tightly in plastic wrap; refrigerate 30 minutes to set filling. Slice each apple crosswise into 1/2-inch slices. Rewrap each slice tightly and refrigerate until hiking time.

CHAPTER ELEVEN

Vacation Entertainment

EARLY VACATIONERS knew how to have fun in Minnesota! Taking advantage of the state's geological wonders, they climbed treacherous rock formations, descended into clammy caves, and hiked near rushing waterfalls. But not all of the state's attractions were natural. Giant animal sculptures and greater-than-life statues of folk heroes became community icons and were visual reminders of the state's ever-present humor.

When tourists first headed out across the state in their Model Ts, many destinations were outcroppings of rock. Catchy names like "Devil's Chair" and "Sea Lion Rock" were enough to inspire a long drive. Barn Bluff in Red Wing and Sugar Loaf in Winona lured climbers to their lofty summits while fire towers and high bridges provided breathtaking views.

Soon, rocks alone weren't enough. Enterprising gardeners trucked, piled, and rearranged the landscape to create gardens of splendor that tourists visited in droves. Stone arches, grottos, and picnic benches looked like they had sprung from the earth and surrounded sparkling ponds with lily pads and Japanese-style bridges.

Minnesota wildlife also became the focus of tourist destinations. Tame deer ate corn from children's hands in the state's many deer parks. Black bears in cages or at the town dump provided hours of entertainment for gawkers. Wilder life was experienced in Minnesota resort towns in the form of dining and entertainment. Swing bands played in lakeshore pavilions as dance partners twirled on smooth maple floors.

For many, the landscape and nature were enough. Others sought out the state's wacky attractions. A giant fiberglass pelican, a thirteen-foot-tall prairie chicken, and the world's largest ball of twine have seen their share of tourists. The legendary Paul Bunyan is honored in statues as well as theme parks. A talking Paul resided over a lakes-area park that shared another Minnesota cultural treasure—the Tilt-A-Whirl.

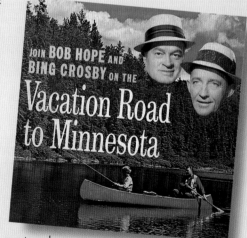

But along with all this fun and sightseeing, tourists needed proof they had been there. Souvenir makers stamped the names of towns on nearly every saleable tourist item, including the popular leather-clad photo albums to fill with vacation photos. Souvenir shops and merchants of Indian arts catered to the influx of mid-twentieth-century tourists. Masquerading as log lodges and voyageur fur trading posts, these packed stores were meccas for trinket seekers as well as outlets for selling authentic Native American products.

Vacation area cafés attracted travelers with a locally inspired bite-to-eat and nightspots featured music and dancing into the early morning hours. Whether enjoying natural or artfully crafted landscapes or supporting local tourist stores and amusements, Minnesota vacationers were sure to be entertained.

◄ *Morell's Chippewa Indian Trading Post, Bemidji, 1956*

Rocky places and tumbling waters

As soon as better roadways and faster automobiles carried travelers farther afield, tourists clamored for more places to visit and sites to see. Natural wonders, the long-time favorite attraction of nineteenth-century travelers, provided new destinations for motor touring and geological formations, underground caves, waterfalls, and rock gardens became popular wayside stops.

The Old Man of the Dalles, Taylors Falls

Devil's Chair, Lake City

Mystery Cave, Spring Valley

Mystery Cave, a twelve-mile series of interconnected limestone caves, holds two brilliant turquoise lakes and plenty of stalagmites and stalactites for spelunkers.

Entrance Lodge, Niagara Cave, Harmony

With the slogan, "where nature smiles for most two miles," the caves of Niagara were bound to be awesome. Discovered in 1924, the caverns had been carved by water that swirled through solid rock for millions of years. Walkways lead visitors through a colossal wonderland of underground canyons and tunnels rich in crystal formations as the rushing river cascades past ocean fossils embedded in the ancient walls. Sounds from a sixty-foot waterfall reminiscent of Niagara Falls prompted the name.

Showboat Inn, Taylors Falls

Hundreds of beautiful waterfalls throughout the state were among Minnesota's most popular natural attractions. Groups of admirers assembled below splashing waters or viewed rushing rivers from fanciful bridges above.

Minneopa Falls, Lake Crystal

Rustic Bridge, Lester Park, Duluth

Noonan "Little Bit O' Heaven"

Creative Minnesota gardeners piled their rocks in artistic, architectural arrangements. Miniature castles guarded rambling waterfalls and moats flowed into reflecting pools. The greenery of flowers, shrubs, trees, and ivy-covered wishing wells appealed to garden fans ready for a relaxing stop along their journey.

Noonan Rock Garden, Alexandria

Ak Sar Ben Gardens, Deerwood

Ak Sar Ben is Nebraska spelled backwards, a nod to the owners' original home state. The sprawling gardens with castles, wishing wells, water wheels, and goldfish ponds became a north woods Garden of Eden for adults and children alike.

Christensen's Rock Garden, Albert Lea

185

High places

Vacationers in northern Minnesota looking for a change of pace headed to Duluth and the North Shore where majestic views and aerial rides provided breathless entertainment.

Duluth Aerial Lift Bridge

The original 1905 Aerial Bridge over the Duluth–Superior Canal held a huge suspended gondola that shuttled pedestrians and horse-drawn wagons between Duluth's waterfront and the long stretch of land called Minnesota Point. The bridge was modified as a vertical lift bridge for cars in 1929. When the bridge went up, autos lined up to wait for Great Lakes ships to pass through the canal.

Coaching party on Boulevard Drive, Duluth, 1900

Long-distance views from Boulevard Drive enthralled riders as early as horse-and-carriage days. Early excursions were called "coaching parties" or "tally-ho tours"; they later became "sightseeing tours."

Sightseeing car on Boulevard Drive, Duluth, 1920s

Incline Railroad Station, Duluth

The Incline Railway was essential transportation for residents of Duluth during snowy winters, but for summer visitors it provided an exciting ride to the top for a spectacular view.

Boys at the edge of the cliff at Split Rock, 1949

Early tourists plotted a course on precarious gravel roads carved into cliffs along the North Shore. Split Rock Lighthouse was built in 1909 to warn ships away from the rocky coast. Tourists have stopped at the lighthouse for years and peered over the towering cliff at the world's largest inland lake.

Climbing high rocks and sky-scraping towers attracted thrill-seekers, and the sheer danger of the height challenged a climber's derring-do. Not only did the ascent result in fabulous views of the surrounding area, vacation photos taken from the top provided stunning proof for dubious friends.

Castle Rock, near Winona, 1930s

Barn Bluff, Red Wing, 1950s

Red Wing's towering Barn Bluff provided an important navigational landmark for nineteenth-century steamboat captains traveling on the Mississippi River. Even pioneering tourists, such as writer Henry David Thoreau, made it to the top to enjoy the spectacular view. Decades later, Barn Bluff attracted more hill-hikers when wooden stairways were cut into the rocky face making it easier for high-altitude fans to enjoy the expansive view.

Forestry lookout tower, Itasca State Park, 1930s

Fire watchtowers were the best places for spotting forest fires early in the century. They quickly became attractions for sightseers, and accommodating forest rangers allowed climbers to share their panoramic views.

Itasca State Park lookout tower, 1935

Forestry tower, Brainerd, 1930s

Fun on a day out

From wildlife to wild rides, Minnesota amusement seekers have had abundant choices for entertainment. On days away from the cabin, children looked for a little four-footed entertainment and always managed to find a few animals to visit—tame or wild.

Green Valley Park, Garrison

Wading with the world's largest pelican, Pelican Rapids, 1950s

Riding one of Minnesota's big fish, 1970s

Feeding a bear, 1940s

Bears on the roadway, 1950s

The Minnesota black bear has captivated hunters as well as curiosity seekers. Early tourist attractions featured caged bears where people could stare the "savage" beast right in the eye. Trained bears drank out of soda bottles for entertainment and town dumps provided an unlimited source of bear sightings. In early days, people did not realize the danger of feeding wild bears or the inhumanity of caging them.

Everyone on family outings enjoyed powwows, parades, and county fairs, and the town schedule was sure to be checked for upcoming events.

Brainerd parade and Paul Bunyan's caterpillar, Brainerd, 1930s

Local parades were among the most popular happenings on warm summer days. Sitting on a curb listening to high-spirited marching bands and watching goofy floats promenade down the street made great vacation memories.

Huddle's Resort parade car, Walker, 1950s

Ojibwe Powwow
Shakopee Powwow ▶

Powwows are an important part of Native American life and dancers and drummers traveled across the state for competitions. Tourists looked forward to these celebrations and admired the grass and jingle dances to the beat of lively drum songs. Fans also appreciated traditional Native flavors and brought home one-of-a-kind, handcrafted products.

County and state fairs were often eagerly anticipated all year and many times attending them was a family's only vacation. Some fairgoers hoped for a blue ribbon for their entries in canned goods, others perused the latest tractors, and many were certain to visit the Midway for a ride on a Tilt-A-Whirl.

Tilt-A-Whirl, 1960s

Herbert Sellner of Faribault knew how to have a good ride and, since he was an inventor, thought Minnesotans could share in the fun. His first invention in 1923 was the Farie-Bow water-toboggan slide that shot thrill-seekers down a steep incline and out across a hundred feet of water. His next invention, the Tilt-A-Whirl, came three years later. An early breathtaking ride at carnivals and amusement parks, its passenger cars dipped and whirled and spun around to the gleeful shouts of riders.

Morrison County fair poster
State Fair poster, 1920s

Paul Bunyanlands

Legend has it that Minnesota's 10,000 lakes were created by Paul and Babe's footsteps as they tromped through the new territory! Fable or not, the land of big logs has more big tales of the big logger than any other state. Minnesota statuary celebrate Paul's life from cradle to grave and local folklore reminds us of his playful inventions, from the reversible dog to trained ants.

Folklore by Ray Bang, 1939

Minnesota's animated Paul Bunyan

America's largest mechanical Paul held court in Brainerd's Paul Bunyanland where he moved, sang, told stories, answered questions, and astonished little kids by calling out their names as they entered his log fortress.

Paul's cradle, "located at his birthplace in Akeley"

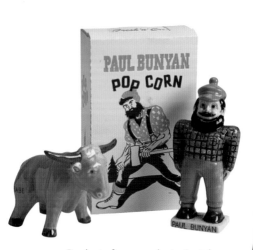

Products from snacks to Scotch were packaged in Paul Bunyan look-alikes.

Paul Bunyan's sweetheart, Lucette Diana Kensack, Hackensack, 1960s

Paul's reversible dog, Brainerd

Paul's squirrel, Brainerd

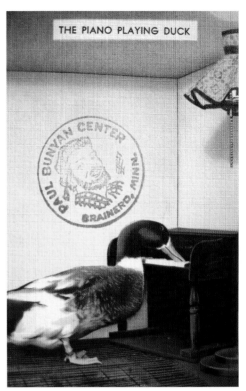

The piano-playing duck, Brainerd

In a cage decorated like his own little living room, this trained live duck played the piano for visitors who put food through a slot in the door.

Up in the air, Brainerd

Paul Bunyan Amusement Park, Bemidji, 1960s

Paul Bunyan and Babe the Blue Ox, Bemidji, 1950s

Bemidji's Paul Bunyan and Babe, originally unveiled at Bemidji's Winter Carnival in 1937, became famous Minnesota celebrities even before finding their way to a position on the National Register of Historic Places in 1988.

Gifts to go

Gift shops and food stores offered Minnesota-made products that enticed locals and travelers alike. Food products were a way to taste local flavors while on vacation or when brought back home. Artisans and craft makers captured the spirit of the state in objects that became a pleasant reminder of a past vacation.

Pine Island Cheese Store

North of Rochester, this highway shop was famous for Pine Island Cheddar. Motorists who stopped for cheese also filled up their automobiles on standard gasoline.

Lakeview Berry Farm Jelly Shop, Park Rapids

Andy's Pottery Shop, Red Wing
▼ *Walt's Craft Shop and Museum of Natural History, Winona*

Chippewa Indian Co-op Marketing Association, Cass Lake, 1930

Minnesota's native wild rice is actually a grain that grows in shallow lakes. For centuries it was harvested by hand by Native Americans who tapped ripe grain off the stalks into canoes. Ever present in Minnesota gift shops, bags of the state grain have been popular souvenirs for decades.

The Morey Fish Company, Motley

In a state abundant with fish, Morey's made a business out of packaging "the ones that got away."

Agate Shop, Beaver Bay

Minnesota's state stone, the Lake Superior Agate, was a free souvenir for those who found them, but it was much easier to get one at a local rock shop. "Lakers" are the oldest agates in the world. They formed over a billion years ago in air pockets of hardened lava flows. Each band represents a different mineral deposit.

The Whittle Shop, Walker, 1955

Collectors headed to this Leech Lake destination for realistic bird and wildlife carvings that became north woods mementos.

All vacationers have fond memories of their trips, but souvenir collectors can't resist material proof of their escapes in the form of trinkets from tourist shops. Town or park names silk-screened, stamped, or burned onto keepsakes are forever associated with the destination. Leather photo albums, lapel pins, billfolds, silk pillows, and novelty mailers were a few of the thousands of products made by Minnesota souvenir companies.

Bloom Bros. of Minneapolis began making souvenir postcards in 1906 and within fifty years became one of the oldest and largest souvenir manufacturers in the country.

Souvenirs are still a big business in Minnesota. G & G Souvenir Mfg. Company started in the 1950s in the warehouse district of Minneapolis. They make and distribute souvenirs for towns and festivals throughout the Midwest as well as nationally. The company is run by a second-generation family member.

Souvenir shops and trading posts

For many Minnesotans, nothing goes better with a vacation than shopping. Souvenir stores, trading posts, and roadside stands cropped up in resort communities throughout the state. Selling everything from suntan lotion to fine crafts, these jam-packed stores aimed to have something irresistible for everyone.

The glory days of souvenirs peaked in the mid-twentieth century. As more and more vacationers hit the road, the art of souvenir-makers thrived. Cedar boxes, leather photo albums, Minnesota-themed trinkets, and printed porcelain plates jammed crowded store shelves.

Trading posts regularly featured Indian crafts and products, but often perpetuated negative stereotypes with mass-produced imported souvenirs. Fortunately, the work of true Native American artisans was proudly displayed and honored Minnesota's Indian heritage.

Wigwam, Lake George, 1966

Nisswa Indian Trading Mart

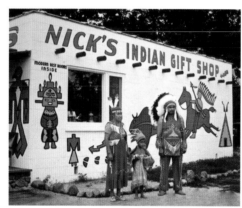

Nick's Indian Gift Shop, Onamia, 1956

Voyageur Trading Post, Grand Marais, 1960s

Treasure City, Royalton, 1969

Free Museum and Souvenir Shop, Garrison

Roe's Trading Post, Pipestone

In 1937 Ethel and Jack Roe opened a trading post on Pipestone's main street. The shop sold carvings made from local stone as well as Native American handicrafts from across the country. In addition to selling items, the Roes exhibited their own vast, personal collection. When the trading post closed in 1965, their collection was sold to a museum in Calgary, Canada.

Chippewa Trading Post, Grand Rapids

Morell's Chippewa Trading Post, Bemidji

Minnetonka Moccasin

Long a staple of souvenir shops from Grand Rapids to the Grand Canyon, Minnetonka Moccasin began making soft-sided shoes in 1946. From the hippie and flower-child days in the 1960s to the cowboy craze in the 1970s, Minnetonka Moccasins never go out of style. Today the successful Minnesota company is run by a third-generation family member.

THUNDERBIRD STYLES

No. 156 — WOMEN'S SOFTIE MOC
With foam insole. Made of glove cowhide.
Attractive Thunderbird beading design.
COLORS: Palomino, White, Turquoise, Black.
SIZES: 4 to 10 (½ sizes).

No. 256 — WOMEN'S WEDGIE MOC
Made of glove cowhide with neolite type sole. Thunderbird beading design.
COLORS: Palomino, White, Turquoise, Black.
SIZES: 4 to 10 (½ sizes) Medium
5 to 10 (½ sizes) Narrow

Trading Post, 1930s

On the west shore of Mille Lacs, Harry and Jeanette Ayer operated a legendary trading post. The store opened in 1919 and featured craftwork by local as well as national tribes. Elsewhere on the grounds the Ayers ran a museum and small resort. Many employees lived on the nearby Ojibwe reservation and used the trading post for community gatherings. When the Ayers retired in 1959 they donated the trading post, its contents, and their personal collections to the Minnesota Historical Society.

Mille Lacs Indian Trading Post
Indian Souvenirs and Rugs
H. D. AYER, TRADER

195

Native American crafts

Minnesota's Native Americans traded with French Canadian voyageurs as far back as the seventeenth century. Some of the most popular trade items were glass beads from Italy. First sewn onto ceremonial dress, the colorful beads were later used on items made for the souvenir market. Small "seed" beads were sewn by hand in Woodland floral designs or woven in geometric patterns on looms.

Other sources for native products came from the land. Birch bark was a renewable resource; when carefully removed from the tree, the bark grew back. Birch was the material of choice for canoes and sap buckets and miniature versions became souvenirs. From out of the earth in southwestern Minnesota, sacred pipestone was quarried then carved into pipe calumets and figurines for admiring tourists.

Families sold their products to trading posts as well as directly to tourists at roadside stands. Between the 1920s and '50s, the state's growing tourism industry was a viable economic venture for many local Native American artisans.

Pincushion exhibited at the Chicago World's Columbian Exposition, 1893

Index

Northern Pine Lodge, Potato Lake, Park Rapids

Van Villa Cottage, Pine River

Cass Lake

Room service?
Send up a larger room!

GROUCHO MARX

Old Mill Inn, Spicer

Pleasure Boat Minnewaska, Glenwood